SPARTA

SPARTA

τὸ κρυπτὸν τῆς πολιτείας τῶν
Λακεδαιμονίων

BY

H. MICHELL, M.A.

Professor Emeritus of Political Economy
in McMaster University,
Hamilton, Ontario

CAMBRIDGE
AT THE UNIVERSITY PRESS
1964

PUBLISHED BY
THE SYNDICS OF THE CAMBRIDGE UNIVERSITY PRESS

Bentley House, 200 Euston Road, London, N.W. 1
American Branch: 32 East 57th Street, New York 22, N.Y.
West African Office: P.O. Box 33, Ibadan, Nigeria

First edition　　　1952
First paperback edition　1964

First printed in Great Britain at the University Press, Cambridge
Reprinted by offset-litho by John Dickens & Co., Ltd, Northampton

FILIAE·ET·FILIO·CARISSIMIS

PREFACE

To solve all the 'mysteries of the Lacedaemonians' is an impossible task for anyone to essay. In the following pages I have tried to suggest what would appear to be likely solutions of the most difficult of the problems which confront the scholar in his study of the way of life of that extraordinary people. In some cases I have been forced to acknowledge myself completely baffled, since the meagre evidence at our command admits of no certain solution. Throughout I have cited many forerunners in the field, giving their opinions, as well as my own, for what they are worth.

That many of the solutions I have tentatively arrived at will be accepted by all critics I have no hope. All that I can say is that I have not consciously shirked any difficulties, and that I have tried to follow the rule laid down by the famous Sherlock Holmes: 'When you have eliminated the impossible, whatever remains, however improbable, must be the truth.' I am grateful for the help and encouragement I have constantly received from my colleague Dr E. T. Salmon and from Mr Wade-Gery, who made some important and illuminating suggestions.

The literature on Sparta is very extensive, and I have thought it best to append only a select bibliography, in which I have included only those books and articles in learned publications available to students in the larger libraries. Much excellent material can be found in German doctoral dissertations, and these have been cited in footnotes in the text.

H. MICHELL

ABBREVIATIONS

A.B.S.A.	*Annual of British School at Athens.*
C.A.H.	*Cambridge Ancient History.*
C.I.A.	*Corpus Inscriptionum Atticarum.*
C.I.G.	*Corpus Inscriptionum Graecarum.*
D.S.	Daremberg-Saglio, *Dictionnaire des Antiquités Grecques et Romaines.*
F.H.G.	*Fragmenta Historicorum Graecorum.*
I.G.	*Inscriptiones Graecae.*
I.G.²	*Inscriptiones Graecae.* Editio Minor.
J.H.S.	*Journal of Hellenic Studies.*
Klio.	*Klio, Beiträge zur alten Geschichte.*
Phil. Woch.	*Philologische Wochenschrift.*
P.W.	Pauly-Wissowa-Kroll, *Real-Encyclopädie der klassischen Altertumswissenschaft.*
Rev. ét. grecq.	*Revue des études grecques.*
Rhein. Mus.	*Rheinisches Museum für Philologie.*

All dates are B.C. unless specifically marked A.D.

CONTENTS

Asterisks in the text refer to
the Additional Notes, pp. 337, 338.

CHAPTER I

INTRODUCTION

The Spartans were a strange people who always have excited, and always will excite, the curiosity of those who would essay the difficult and, at times, baffling task of studying them and their political and social institutions. Their contemporaries in the ancient world were intrigued by the 'mystery' that surrounded them, by their secretiveness, their peculiar manner of life and the impenetrable seclusion into which they had withdrawn. In their own way they were a great people; but their greatness sprang from qualities violently and astonishingly different from those that the world regards as typically Greek. The debt that the world owes to the Greeks is a very great one. In art and letters, in science and philosophy, in all those things of the spirit that elevate and ennoble the soul and lift mankind above the brute creation, the Greeks have left us an imperishable heritage. And yet among them, exercising a decisive influence upon their destiny, was a people who had deliberately turned away from all cultural pursuits; who devoted itself with a singular intensity to a way of life utterly different from that of the other Greeks; and who prided itself in an asceticism and a discipline that excited the astonishment of its contemporaries.

The Spartan way of life, the discipline to which its adherents were subjected, was a strange one, unequalled in severity in any other time or place. The Spartan child was toughened by athletic exercises, a meagre fare and scanty clothing. He was probably taught to read and write—but even of that we are not perfectly sure—and trained to self-reliance by throwing him on his own resources to supplement his monotonous diet. He lived in barracks and not until he was thirty could he set up his own establishment and live openly with his wife and family, though still under the discipline of his military superiors and the watchful eyes of the magistrates. Not until he had reached the age of sixty, when declining physical powers made him of no use in the army, did he escape from this ceaseless vigilance over his daily life. He was trained to be 'tough', taciturn—our word 'laconic' bears witness to that[1]—unquestioningly obedient and with a notably slow-moving, but actually far from dull, intelligence. To compare him with the volatile, quick-witted and voluble Athenian provides a contrast so startling as to excite bewilderment and dismay.

The general 'queerness' of the Spartans, if we may use such a term, has always been intriguing to those who have observed their peculiar way of life. Strabo[2] is quite certain that it was deliberately assumed.

As regards the various arts and faculties and institutions of mankind, most of them, when once men have made a beginning, flourish in any latitude whatsoever, and in certain instances even in spite of the latitude; so that some local characteristics of a people come by nature, others by training and habit. For instance, the Athenians did not devote themselves to literature by nature, but rather by habit and discipline; whereas the Lacedaemonians (also the Thebans, who are still closer to the Athenians) lacked any interest in this art, again as a result of habit and not by nature.

He goes on to argue that the fact that the Spartans lived in Laconia and the Athenians in Attica had not made them different. The peculiarities of each had arisen because the Athenians deliberately chose one way of life, the Spartans another. Both peoples were Greeks, or Hellenes, as they chose to call themselves, sprung from the same origins and inhabiting lands markedly similar in geographical environment. Therefore they should have been similar in their way of life; but amazingly they were not so. Given these assumptions, Strabo was correct when he put down their differences to 'habit' and not to 'nature'.

But were the assumptions correct? The answer is very emphatically 'No'! Although all Greeks thought they were of

---

[1] Plut. *De garr.* 510 F, 511 A, has some amusing examples of their brevity of speech. Cf. also Plato, *Protag.* 342 E.

[2] II, 3, 7 (C. 103).

the same race, the contrary was true.[1] The Spartans were
Dorians, the Athenians were Ionians; as different as chalk
from cheese, a difference that was at the bottom of the un-
appeasable animosities that continually distracted the Greek
world and culminated in the disastrous Peloponnesian war,
in which Athenian and Spartan, Ionian and Dorian, fought out
the hegemony of Greece to a bitter and ruinous end.

And yet there was a time when Sparta seemed to be advancing
along the same road of culture as the Athenians, when the arts
flourished and poets and musicians found a welcome in
Laconia. Then this seemed to die away, as if the effort had
been too much for them, and the Spartans relapsed into
a narrow formalism and a rigorous discipline under which the
cultural arts withered. This was really the 'mystery' of Sparta,
and reflection will reveal that actually it was not so very
mysterious after all. After a period of prosperity and advances
in the arts, the Spartans relapsed into the outward forms of
their more primitive culture. The preoccupation of holding
down a sullen and resentful peasantry in the Helots, both in
Laconia and Messenia, was too much for their pretensions to
vie with other Greeks in the arts. The Spartans had their own
particular contribution to make to the chronicle of Greek
achievement. Whatever their shortcomings, and they were
many, they did at least leave to the world an imperishable
memory of constancy in the face of danger, of ordered discipline
and devotion to their way. There are few nobler epitaphs than
that upon the grave of those who died at Thermopylae:
'Stranger, tell the Lacedaemonians that we lie here in obedience
to their laws.'

LACONIA

The land of Laconia[2] in the Peloponnese is about 1600 sq.
miles in area, of which the greater part is mountainous. Three

---

[1] The Dorians were 'probably Alpine', the Athenians were 'Caspians':
vide R. B. Dixon, *Racial History of Man*, pp. 35, 94, 515.

[2] Art. 'Sparta, Geographie', by Bölte in P.W.

zones may be distinguished. The first is the Eurotas valley, under 50 sq. miles in area, fertile and well watered, and to-day, as in ancient times, thickly populated. This valley is bounded on the west by the Taÿgetus mountains, which run from the Arcadian range in the north to the promontory of Taenarum in the south. The second zone on the east, with broken, hilly country, and Mount Parnon the highest elevation, runs southwards to Cape Maleia.

The plain of Sparta is not continuous, since a rocky barrier, cut by a gorge through which flows the river Eurotas, divides the northern portion from the third or southern, which is a swampy and unhealthy, but highly fertile, coastal plain. Access to the sea by the Eurotas river is impeded by this rocky barrier and the only route is by a difficult road across the Taÿgetus hills to the port of Pharae, the modern Kalamata. The only other port is Gythium in the south; for the eastern coast on the Aegean is rocky and without any harbours. In the fertile valley of the Eurotas lay the home estates of the Spartan peers, the nucleus of the land system which presents so many puzzles; but the land of Messenia provided them with the greater part of their wealth. How disastrous the loss of Messenia was to the Spartan State will be seen hereafter.

Leake,[1] in his old, but still invaluable, book of travels in the Morea, remarks:

On quitting Laconia, and especially on quitting it by one of the northern passes, one cannot help reflecting how much the former destiny of this province of Greece, like that of most other countries, depends upon its geographical structure and position. Those natural barriers which marked the limits of the several states of ancient Greece, and which were the real origin of the division of that country into many small independent states, from whence arose all the good and bad effects resulting from the consequent spirit of jealousy and rivalship, are nowhere more remarkable than in the Laconice. The rugged sea-coast, which forms three-fourths

[1] *Travels in the Morea*, III, pp. 24 ff. Cf. also Frazer's enthusiastic description of the valley in his edition of Pausanias, III, p. 322.

of its outline, combined with the steepness, height and continuity of the mountains on the land side, give it security from invasion. ...It is to the strength of the frontiers and the comparatively large extent of country inclosed within them, that we must trace the primary cause of the Lacedaemonian power....It is remarkable that all the principal passes into Laconia lead to one point. This point is Sparta, a fact which shows at once how well the position of that city was chosen for the defence of the province, and how well it was adapted, especially as long as it continued to be unrivalled, to maintain a perpetual vigilance and readiness for defence, which are the surest means of offensive success.

MESSENIA

Messenia[1] is 'a softened, more open repetition of Laconia with a westward outlook', with a milder and moister climate and of great fertility. Through it runs the river Psamios, the ancient Pamisus, and, as in Laconia, there is a northern and southern section, although the division is less marked. The districts on which the traditional reputation of the country rests for fertility and richness are the two plains between the Taÿgetus hills and the coastal range. These plains are divided into upper and lower sections by a line of low hills which extend from Ithome to the foothills of the Taÿgetus mountains. The scantiness of ancient remains in these plains may probably be ascribed to the desire to utilise as much land as possible for cultivation, which is well watered by drainage from the coastal range, the Phigalian mountains and Taÿgetus. The city of Messene on the western slopes was the central point of the whole country, from which roads ran north, linking sites on the upper plain and leading to Arcadia and the west coast.

The western coastal range is lower than the eastern and less continuous, thus providing a less formidable barrier between sea and land in the interior. On the west coast are well watered terraces and valleys and a fertile coastal plain. Pylos, the modern Navarino, an excellent port, Methone and Cyparissia

[1] Leake, *ibid.* I, pp. 340 ff.; C. A. Roebuck, *History of Messenia from 369 to 146 B.C.*; M. N. Valmin, *Études topographiques sur la Messénie ancienne.*

provided harbours on the west coast. Roebuck[1] gives good reason to suppose that the Spartans used only the upper plain, the lower west of the river Pamisus, and probably the Soulima plain for their estates or *cleroi*, while the coastal region was occupied by tributary or perioecic[2] towns, except for the district of Pylos situated in the central part of the west coast.

THE DORIANS

It is notable that Homer's single mention of the Dorians is in Crete 'where there is confusion of tongues; there dwell Achaeans and there too Cretans of Crete, high of heart, and Cydonians and the three tribes of the Dorians[3] and goodly Pelasgians'.[4] Evidently at that period the Dorians were not masters of the whole island; they had only recently arrived and were but another of the various tribes who inhabited the land and were yet to struggle for mastery. The ancient tradition[5] that the Dorians were Heraclids, claiming descent from Heracles, who were led by Temenos and his brothers into the south and east of the Peloponnese, may well have a substratum of truth in it. Another chieftain, Oxylus, who came with them, led the tribe of the Aetolians into Elis, while others overran Thessaly, from whence they drove the inhabitants southwards into Boeotia. The former conquerors of the Peloponnese, the Achaeans, were driven from the valley of

[1] *Class. Phil.* XL (1945), p. 151.

[2] For explanation of this word *vide infra*, p. 64.

[3] *Od.* XIX, 175.

[4] τριχάικες. Very uncertain, may mean 'with three waving plumes', cf. Hesiod, fr. 8; or refer to the three kingdoms of Pelops; cf. Wade-Gery, *C.A.H.* II, p. 525, n. 12.

[5] Paus. II, 28; Strabo, VIII, 8, 5 (C. 389); Thuc. I, 12; Beloch, *Griechische Geschichte*, I, pt. 2, pp. 76 f., rejects the whole tradition. But cf. also Nilsson, *Homer and Mycenae*, p. 70, who accepts it, and Pareti, *Storia di Sparta arcaica*, pp. 66 ff. The claim of Cleomenes I that he was an Achaean and not a Dorian (Herod. v. 72) need not be taken seriously. It probably refers to the mythical relationship of the Heraclids with the ancient rulers of Mycenae. It is even possible that Cleomenes, when denied entrance to the temple of Athena at Athens, invented the claim on the spot.

the Eurotas to the extreme north of the peninsula, besides which only Arcadia and Attica were left to them. Dorians who could find nowhere to settle in the Peloponnese went overseas to Crete, Rhodes and the south-west coast of Asia Minor.[1]

When did the Dorian conquest of the Peloponnese take place? It is impossible to speak with certainty; but probably we should not be too far out if we surmised some time between 1200 and 1100 B.C. Whenever it was, it certainly shattered the last remnants of the Mycenaean civilisation, already reduced by the Achaeans to a shadow of its former glory, as the scenes in Homer so vividly portray. The Dorians were a backward race, first-class fighting men, but evidently far different from and inferior to the Achaeans in culture. Certainly upon their irruption into the Peloponnese a 'dark age' followed, when art was stagnant, and all that the archaeologist can find is the 'geometric' style of ornamentation of pottery, which is characteristic and common to all primitive peoples.[2]

If we assume that the Dorian invasion took place some time in the twelfth century,[3] we certainly know nothing of them for the next hundred years. Archaeologists who have excavated the site of the city of Sparta place its foundation some time during the tenth century, so we are left with the conclusion that between their irruption and that date they had

[1] Very doubtful, but on the whole the most likely reconstruction of the Dorian movements. The suggestion of Wilamowitz-Moellendorf, *Staat und Gesellschaft der Griechen*, II, p. 19, that the movement was the other way, from Crete to the Peloponnese, seems improbable. For detailed discussion cf. Beloch, *Griech. Gesch.* I, 2, pp. 76 ff. Another reconstruction of the early movements of the various tribes would have the Achaeans of Achaea come from north of the gulf, pushed thither by 'Epirotes'. According to this view the Arcadians were the former conquerors of the Peloponnese; but they had few ethnic connections with the inhabitants of Attica, who, if Homer is to be believed, were outside the 'Achaean' world.

[2] Cf. J. D. Beazley in *C.A.H.* IV, pp. 579 ff.

[3] The traditional date of the 'return of the Heraclidae' is 1104. The suggestion of Peake and Fleure, *The Law and the Prophets*, p. 31, that the Achaeans were so exhausted by the Trojan campaign and impoverished of leaders and resources that, after two generations of ineffectual rule, their power gave way before the incoming Dorians, may be right.

settled down. We know that there were three tribes or families, the Hylleis, Dymanes and Pamphyloi, presumably with their own chieftains. These were the ancient tribes of the Dorians, who traced their lineage, quite fancifully, back to Pamphylus and Dymas (the sons of Aegimius), and Hyllus, who was a Heraclid. It is to be noted that all three did not claim the same descent, a very good piece of evidence of the mixed character of the Dorian tribes.[1] The analogy between them and the twelve tribes of Israel is not without interest. Probably, although the evidence is obscure, they were ruled by two kings of the royal houses of Agiads and Eurypontids. But why there were not three 'kings' or chieftains of the three tribes, and what exactly was the relation of the two kings to the three tribes, it is impossible to say. Perhaps the third 'royal' house had died out. But we do know that these two were of very ancient origin and may well go back to their nomad days.[2]

THE EMERGENCE OF SPARTA

To reconstruct the sequence of events that led to the emergence of the Spartan State, as known in historical times, is difficult and indeed impossible of exact verification. The two royal houses were at enmity with each other and dissensions within the narrow confines of the Eurotas valley were intolerable. This period of troubles (κακονομία) was settled conjecturally about 800, by an alliance on a permanent basis and a drawing together or synoecism of the divisions of the people.[3] It was agreed, we must suppose, that the two kings should reign together with equal powers. This was the first step in the evolution of the Spartan constitution. With this synoecism the power of the Spartans began to increase and their numbers to multiply. The Eurotas valley could no longer contain them

---

[1] Ephorus, in *F.H.G.* I, p. 235, 10, 11; Pindar, *Pyth.* I, 63 ff.

[2] The point is discussed more fully hereafter, p. 97.

[3] Busolt-Swoboda, *Griechische Staatskunde*, II, p. 643; Schömann-Lipsius, *Griechische Altertümer*, I, p. 214; Niccolini, 'Per la Storia di Sparta. Il Sinecismo', *Rivista di Storia Antica*, IX (1904), p. 94; K. J. Neumann, *Hist. Ztschr.* XCVI (1900), p. 40.

and it became necessary to look for further territory. Obviously the rich land of Messenia offered the best chance for expansion, and the first Messenian war followed, which may be tentatively dated 743–724.[1] The long struggle of nineteen years ended in the triumph of the Spartans and the division of the land among the conquerors.

But although they had achieved unity through synoecism and room to expand through conquest, serious problems still confronted them. At about this time a constitutional crisis arose which was the second step in the evolution of the Spartan constitution. We are able to assign this to the period of the first Messenian war with something like reasonable certainty, since we are told that King Theopompus, the hero of the war on the Spartan side, was involved in it. A study of sections 5 and 6 of Plutarch's *Life of Lycurgus* will reveal that he has telescoped two totally different steps in the evolution of Spartan government which were chronologically widely separated from each other and both of which he erroneously attributes to Lycurgus. The first was the wringing from Theopompus of the consent to found the Senate or *Gerousia*. The next was the granting to the General Assembly or *Ecclesia*[2] of the final power of approval or veto in matters brought before it by the Senate. This was embodied in the great *rhetra* or 'act of parliament' quoted in section 6.[3] Still

[1] Or, according to Dickins, *J.H.S.* XXXII, p. 15, at latest 735–716. It is impossible to fix the date with certainty. For detailed discussion cf. Beloch, *op. cit.* I, pt. 2, pp. 262f.

[2] The so-called *Apella*. For reasons for rejecting the use of this word *vide infra*, p. 140.

[3] Wade-Gery in *Class. Quart.* XXXVII (1943), p. 62, demonstrates that the *rhetra* was an act of the Spartan 'parliament' which was attributed to a Delphic oracle, and not vice versa, thus controverting the view in Busolt-Swoboda, *op. cit.* I, p. 43, n. 1, which holds that it was an oracle turned into an act of parliament. Of the two theories that of Busolt seems to be the more likely. When the people are in doubt they send to Delphi for a divine pronouncement, and if it appears suitable to their case they embody the principle in an enactment. We know that the oracle could be obliging in its decisions, and at a time of crisis the people may well have desired divine approval of their wishes.

another step, the final one, had to be taken—the seizure of power by the ephors, the five elected representatives of the Spartan people. That certainly took place after the *Ecclesia* had restrained the unlimited power of the Senate and completed the 'democratic' revolution, if such a term may suitably be used of so distinctively an oligarchic form of constitution as the Spartan.

THE FRUITS OF VICTORY

With the conquest of Messenia and the settlement, for the time being, of the constitutional question, the Spartans emerged from the status of a federation of imperfectly civilised tribes, under petty chieftains or 'kings', into a closely knit race, dominating a rich area and enjoying to the full the fruits of their conquests. The aborigines—the helots—had been long since reduced to the status of serfs who tilled the land for their Spartan lords. Outside the Eurotas valley and their estates in Messenia, lay the lands of the *perioeci*, allies who, though free, nevertheless did not enjoy all the privileges of full citizenship.

The dark age of Spartan history ended with the eighth century, when a new civilisation began to permeate Greece. Population increased with mounting prosperity and this led to emigration. At the end of the eighth century Tarentum was colonised by the Partheniai, a band of younger Spartans who left their native land to seek their fortunes abroad.[1]

[1] Or at the latest 650 B.C., *vide* R. M. Cook, 'Ionia and Greece 800–600 B.C.' *J.H.S.* LXVI (1946), p. 77. It is not easy to distinguish with certainty more than a few Dorian colonies. Thera undoubtedly was Dorian (Herod. IV, 147; Paus. III, 1, 7; VII, 2, 2), and was the mother-city of Cyrene (Herod. IV, 150ff.); Melos was also certainly a colony (Herod. VIII, 48; Thuc. V, 84). Gortyna may have been, and probably if not certainly Cnidus, colonised by Triopas (Paus. X, 11, 1). Orestes was supposed to have founded colonies in Aeolis, Lesbos and Tenedos, but this is mythical. Cf. Müller, *Doric Race* (E.T.), I, p. 136; Pareti, 'Ricerche sulla potenza maritima d. Spartani', *Memorie d. R. Accad. d. scienze di Torino*, LIX, p. 74.

THE AGE OF ALCMAN

For the Spartan 'peers' this period was one of great material prosperity. The conquest of Messenia had provided them with estates and serfs. While the Athenians and Corinthians turned to overseas commerce, Sparta remained a land-locked region of territorial lords, who enjoyed a peaceful existence and cultivated the arts of peace as pictured in the poems of Alcman.[1] From the fragments that have survived it is not hard to form a picture of a care-free life of country squires, who delighted in hunting and pampered their womenfolk. The maidens' songs are charming.[2] The singers are decked in purple with girdles fashioned like 'speckled snakes of pure gold'.[3] We read of a great vase 'all of gold' and 'flagons of wrought gold'. Drinking, dancing and feasting, with a good deal of love-making—Alcman had the reputation of being licentious[4]—give us a picture of a happy life of a prosperous landed aristocracy. Hunting, which is always the chosen recreation of a rich upper class, was a passion with them. We read of 'the well-knit steed of ringing hoof that overcometh in the race'. 'O Castor and noble Polydeuces—ye tamers of swift steeds, ye skilful horsemen.'[5] Spartan hunting dogs were famous, the great 'Castor hounds'* and the little dogs which we may fancifully identify with a kind

[1] C. M. Bowra, *Greek Lyric Poetry*, pp. 16ff. A notably good treatment of the poems of Alcman. Herac. Pont. says he was a slave bought by Agasidas, *F.H.G.* II, 210, 2.

[2] J. A. Davison, 'Alcman's Partheneion', *Hermes*, LXXIII (1938), p. 440, an examination of the evidence from the structure of the poem.

[3] Blakeway, *Class. Rev.* XLIX (1935), p. 185, appositely remarks that the gold necklace illustrated in *The Sanctuary of Artemis Orthia at Sparta*, (by R. M. Dawkins et al.), Plate 203, no. 14, might well serve as an example.

[4] There is a scandalous story of Alcman in Athen. XIII, 600 F.

[5] Perhaps in these references to horses there is a connection with the cult of Demeter and later of Helen, both of whom were connected with horses. But this is very uncertain. Cf. C. M. Bowra, *op. cit.* pp. 54ff., and *Artemis Orthia* (Dawkins et al.), p. 241, and Plate 172, no. 1.

of fox terrier.[1] A love of beasts, birds and flowers is evident throughout.

The excavations of the British School at Athens at the site of the city of Sparta[2] reveal a flourishing state of the arts and manufactures in Laconia carried on, if not wholly by Laconian workmen themselves, at least by foreign artists who were welcomed and encouraged to ply their crafts without any of that dark suspicion of strangers which was so marked in later times. Particularly notable is a high degree of artistic attainment in ceramics. The vases hitherto attributed to Cyrene are now supposed to have come from the studios of Laconian artists.[3] Figurines in lead and terra-cotta, the latter in the 'Daedalic' style, statuettes and plaques of ivory, jewellery, articles of toilet and masks made of clay, all betoken a flourishing state of the arts. The most famous example is the so-called Arcesilas vase, which was probably, if not certainly, fashioned by a Cyrenean potter in Sparta.[4]

[1] Xen. *Cyneg.* III; Claudian, *Laud. Stil.* III, 300; Plut. *Apoph. Lac.* 215 B, says that it was forbidden to export dogs from Sparta. It is not impossible that a religious significance attached to this, if Plutarch is correct, in that dogs were sacred to Heracles. Cf. Robertson Smith, *Religion of Semites*, p. 292, n. 2. Boys sacrificed puppies to Enyalius before the fight on the Plane Tree ground. Paus. III, 14, 8. *Vide infra* p. 191. O. Keller, 'Hunderassen im Altertum', *Jahreshefte d. österreichischen archäologischen Instituts in Wien* (1905), VIII, pp. 251.

[2] Ollier, *Le Mirage spartiate*, pp. 13 ff.; *A.B.S.A.* XII–XVI, XXVI–XXX; *Artemis Orthia* (Dawkins *et al.*) (1929); Tod and Wace, *Catalogue of the Spartan Museum* (1906); art. 'Sparta als Kunststadt' by Lippold in art. 'Sparta' in P.W.

[3] E. A. Lane in *A.B.S.A.* XXXIV (1933–4), pp. 161, 182 f., *ibid.* XXIII, pp. 60 ff.; R. J. H. Jenkins, *Dedalica.* Cf. Dugas, 'Les vases "cyrénéens" du Musée de Tarente', in *Revue archéologique*, XX (1912), p. 88; 'Les vases lacono-cyrénéens', *ibid.* XXVII (1928), p. 50; O. Waldhauer, 'Zur lakonischen Keramik', *Jahrbuch des deutschen archäologischen Instituts*, XXXVIII (1923), p. 28.

[4] Lane, *ut supra.* Generally thought to be a representation of King Arcesilas of Cyrene superintending the stowing of a cargo of silphium on shipboard. Another interpretation of the scene suggests that Arcesilas is sitting under an awning watching the stowing of bales of wool in a cellar. The argument that

Architecture reached a high state of accomplishment in the shrine of Artemis Orthia, originally built in the ninth but rebuilt and embellished in the sixth century. Gitiadas, a Spartan artist, covered the walls of the temple of Athena Chalcicoecos with bas-reliefs in bronze.[1] Theodorus of Samos built and decorated the Skias, a building with a roof in the form of a tent.[2] Bathycles of Magnesia executed at Amyclae a statue and throne of Apollo.[3]

A remarkable list of artists in the 'archaic style' may easily be compiled.[4] Dorycleidas, 'a Lacedaemonian', was the sculptor of a gold and ivory figure of Themis at Olympia. His brother Medon was the maker of a statue of Athena,[5] and in the treasury of the Megarians were figures of cedar wood inlaid with gold by the same artist.[6] Also at Olympia there was a great statue of Zeus by Ariston and Telestas.[7] Syadras and Chartas, 'men of Sparta', kept a school of sculptors.[8] The statue of Philles of Elis, 'who won the boys' wrestling match', was made by the Spartan Cratinus.[9] At Olympia there were figures of the five Hesperides by Theocles.[10] Laconian drinking cups seem to have been highly prized. We hear of Callicrates of Laconia as a famous worker in relief on these goblets.[11]

Music and poetry were cultivated. There was a sanctuary of

silphium, or asafoetida, was not shipped in bales but rather in jars is a very pertinent one. But the scene so strongly suggests the deck of a ship that we can hardly think of it otherwise.

[1] Paus. III, 17, 2; 18, 5. Cf. Frazer's ed. of Pausanias, III, p. 350; *A.B.S.A.* XIII, pp. 137 ff.

[2] Paus. III, 12, 10; or a dome, *Etym. Mag. s.v.* Σκίας.

[3] *Id.* III, 18, 6. Cf. Frazer, III, p. 351.

[4] Art. 'Sparta als Kunststadt', by Lippold in P.W.

[5] Paus. V, 17, 2.

[6] *Id.* VI, 19, 14. Dontas, a corruption for Medon. Cf. art. Medon (12), by Lippold in P.W.

[7] Paus. V, 23, 7. *I.G.* V, 2, 85, 102.

[8] Paus. VI, 4, 4.   [9] *Id.* VI, 9, 4.

[10] *Id.* V, 17, 2. G. Dickins, 'Art of Sparta', *Burlington Magazine*, XIV (1908), p. 66.

[11] Athen. XI, 782 B.

the Muses at Sparta.[1] Plutarch, in his treatise on music,[2] has the following to say of it in Sparta:

> The first establishment of Music at Sparta was due to Terpander. The second is best ascribed to Thaletas of Gortyn, Xenodamus of Cythera, Xenocritus of Locri, Polymnastus of Colophon and Sacadas of Argos. For we are told that the institution of the Feast of Naked Youths at Sparta...was due to these musicians.

The place of Terpander in the development of Greek music is treated hereafter.[3]

Poets flourished and were given a welcome. We have but to remember Terpander, Alcman and Theognis.[4] Tyrtaeus, of whom we speak elsewhere, Cinaethon,[5] Thaletas[6] and Nymphaeus of Cydonia,[7] all of whom spent some time there and make up an imposing list of poets who, at one time or another, lived during the golden age of Sparta and found a ready appreciation of their muse in that city.[8]

Two other aspects of the earlier Spartan social life are significant. Theognis[9] speaks of Sparta 'the glorious town of reedy Eurotas', which 'made me welcome in right friendly fashion'. Hospitality was evidently practised as freely as in the Homeric Age, a very different thing from the niggardly

---

[1] Paus. III, 17, 5.

[2] *De mus.* IX. Plutarch's reference in *Moral.* 779 A to Thales, a lyre-maker, having put an end to faction in Sparta can only be understood, if at all, in the sense that the lyres made by him provided the music to which the songs of the poets were sung. The idea seems far-fetched and probably Plutarch is mistaking this Thales for Thaletas the poet.

[3] *Vide infra*, p. 183.   [4] Herod. I, 23.

[5] Paus. III, 17, 5.

[6] Plut. *Lyc.* IV; Paus. I. 14, 4; Plut. *De mus.* XLII. Thaletas was so successful that his muse quelled a raging pestilence in Sparta.

[7] Aelian, *V.H.* XII, 50.

[8] It is quite superfluous to believe the legend recorded by Suidas that Arion of Methymna, inventor of the dithyramb, was a pupil of Alcman. There is no evidence of his having been in Sparta before he met with his astonishing adventure with a dolphin, and certainly he was never there afterwards. Cf. Rohde, *Rhein. Mus.* XXXIII, p. 200. Art. 'Arion' (5) in P.W. by Crusius.

[9] *Elegy and Iambus*, I (Loeb ed.), p. 323.

and grudging entertainment in historic times of any who had
to go to Sparta on business or diplomatic errands. The
sufferings of Alcibiades when an exile in Sparta are amusing.
But he outdid them all in his enthusiasm for the simple life.[1]
Secondly, the references in the poems of Alcman to the sea are
remarkable. Evidently the rich men of Sparta owned ships.
The maidens sing of 'the steersman on shipboard with a loud
voice', the 'bloom of the wave', 'spring's own bird that is
purple as the sea', 'the depths of the purple brine', 'the sea-
queen Ino', 'dipt in the sea', all of which show that their
vision was not wholly confined to the mountain-girt valley
of their home, but that from their menfolk they had heard of
the sea and its marvels—Herodotus speaks of a Spartan ship
of fifty oars.[2] Perhaps these early Spartan seafarers were
merchants, or more probably they were pirates. There is
reason to suppose that Orthia was a protectress of sailors.[3]
Certainly what has been called 'the largest and finest of all
the ivories' discovered at the shrine represents a ship and was
dedicated to Orthia.[4] There seems little doubt that in earlier
times there was a close connection between Sparta and the sea.
In any case there was undoubtedly a coming and going with
foreign parts, more particularly with Ionia, whence customs,
fashions in clothing, ornaments and furniture were imported
into Sparta.[5] We can also trace connections with north Africa
through the famous Arcesilas vase,[6] with northern Europe
through finds of amber objects[7] and with Egypt through paste
figurines and scarabs.[8]

Perhaps the earliest contact of Sparta with the East was with
Ephesus, conjecturally about 700 B.C.[9] Recent excavations in

---

[1] Plut. *Alc.* XXIII.

[2] I, 152. Cf. also III, 54; *Il.* II, 587, the Spartan contingent.

[3] *I.G.* II², 1623, 76.

[4] *Artemis Orthia* (Dawkins *et al.*), p. 214 and Plates 109 and 110.

[5] Tod-Wace, *Cat. of Spart. Mus.* p. 99. Hogarth, *Ionia and the East*,
pp 34ff.

[6] *A.B.S.A.* XIV, p. 45.

[7] *Ibid.* XIII, pp. 73f.

[8] *Ibid.* XIII, p. 75; XIV, p. 141.

[9] *Ibid.* XIII, p. 84.

Sardes have found Laconian pottery, and Herodotus[1] tells us that in 560 Sparta made a firm alliance with Croesus, sending a gift to him on his accession to the throne. This gift consisted of a brazen bowl covered outside with figures, supposedly in repoussé work, holding 300 amphoras. Since the amphora was a liquid measure of approximately 1 cu. ft. of water—the Greek foot measuring about 0·97 of the English—this bowl must have been colossal, and we may suppose the account is exaggerated.

TYRTAEUS

The Messenians revolted. If we accept the chronology of the first war as already laid down and note that Tyrtaeus says that the grandsons of the conquerors of Messenia fought in the second war[2] we are forced to the conclusion that the very latest date of this event must be 650; an interval of from sixty to seventy years between grandfather and grandson being of military age would be reasonable. It is said that the struggle lasted for seventeen years and taxed the strength and courage of the Spartans to the utmost. To inspire them a poet Tyrtaeus[3] was brought to Sparta at the bidding of the Delphic Oracle.[4] Who or what Tyrtaeus was is very difficult to say. That he was a lame schoolmaster of Athens, of no repute in his own city, who suddenly was inspired by the Heavenly Muse to save the day for Sparta by his warlike poems seems hard to believe. But whoever he was, the tradition that the encouragement he gave to the flagging energies of the Spartans in their struggle with the Messenian rebels was the turning-point of the war seems so sure that we may accept it without too much hesitation.

[1] 1, 70.   [2] ap. Strabo, VI, 3, 3 (C. 279).
[3] Poems in *Elegy and Iambus* (Loeb ed.). The authenticity of Tyrtaeus has been the source of much controversy. Various views are conveniently summarised by Ollier, *op. cit.* pp. 188 ff.
[4] Suidas, *s.v.* τυρταῖος; Schol. ad Plato, *Legg.* 629 A; Paus. IV, 15, 6; Arist. *Pol.* 1307 A.

Tyrtaeus sounds a new note, 'dulce et decorum est pro patria mori'.[1] Throughout his poems runs an insistent refrain:

Ye are of the lineage of the invincible Heracles; so be ye of good cheer; not yet is the head of Zeus turned away. Fear ye not a multitude of men, nor flinch, but let every man hold his shield straight towards the van, making Life his enemy and the black spirits of Death dear as the rays of the sun.

Prowess in athletics, victories in the Olympic games, were of little worth if men were not victors on the field of battle.

I would neither call a man to mind nor put him in my tale of prowess in the race or the wrestling, not even if he had the stature and strength of a Cyclops and surpassed the Thracian north wind, nor were he a comelier man than Tithonus and a richer than Midas or Cinyras, nor though he were a greater king than Pelops son of Tantalus, and had Adrastus' suasiveness of tongue, nor yet though all fame were his save of warlike strength.

It was something new to bid a man die cheerfully for his fatherland; such an appeal was unknown in the Homeric epics. For the first time the virtue of the citizen, who looked upon obedience to the dictates of the State as his highest duty, was put before a people who were in peril.[2]

The revolt of the Messenians was put down at last, but another task awaited Tyrtaeus. Grave constitutional troubles had to be settled and he was constrained to remind the Spartan people of their ancient mode of government—kings, senate and people which had been given to them from Heaven itself.

The passage in the *Eunomia* of Tyrtaeus that evidently refers to a constitutional settlement is as follows:

They heard the voice of Phoebus and brought hence from Pytho oracles of the God and words of sure fulfilment; for thus the Lord

---

[1] Unless we accept Callinus of Ephesus (who voices the same sentiment) as pre-dating Tyrtaeus. Cf. art. 'Kallinos' by Kroll in P.W.

[2] Werner Jaeger, *Paideia*, pp. 74ff.; 'Tyrtaios über die wahre Arete', *Sitzungsberichte der preussischen Akademie der Wissenschaften, Philos.-hist. Klasse* (1932), p. 537. Wilamowitz-Moellendorff, *Textgeschichte der griechischen Lyriker*, pp. 97ff.; 'Tyrtaios', in *Abhandlungen der kgl. Gesellschaft der Wissenschaften zu Göttingen*, N.F. IV (1900), 3.

of the Silver Bow, Far-shooting Apollo of the Golden Hair, gave answer from out his rich sanctuary. The beginnings of counsel shall belong to the god-honoured kings whose care is the delightsome city of Sparta and to the men of elder birth; after them shall the commons answering them back with forthright ordinances, both say things honourable and do all that is right, nor give the city any given counsel; so shall the common people have victory and might; for this hath Phoebus declared unto their city in these matters.[1]

It is quite clear what the poet is referring to. Kings and *Gerousia* are the initiators of all action both executive and legislative, but they cannot act without the approval of the people, who have the power of approval or veto but not of initiative. This is exactly the form of constitution which we see in the *rhetra* attributed by Plutarch to Lycurgus. It is to be carefully noted that the ephorate either does not exist, or its powers are so small that they are not even mentioned.

It is not necessary to accuse Tyrtaeus of being a reactionary in pleading for the retention in office of the 'god-honoured' kings and the senators. He is a conservative, who fears to see the ancient forms swept away, as they might well have been in the popular clamour for constitutional reform. He is willing enough to see the ultimate power rest with the people, but he pleads for a place in the constitution for the other two component parts of government. He is appealing to age-long tradition not to depose their kings nor sweep away the council of elders. It is impossible to say how far the influence of Tyrtaeus went in effecting a settlement. It is a favourite theme of history to find peace brought by a single agency, a poet, a lawgiver, a pacifier. We cannot deny the possibility that the poems of Tyrtaeus may have done something to soothe the angrier passions that had been aroused. Perhaps the music of Terpander was also helpful. We know from Suidas[2] that Terpander was credited with composing the strife of factions, and we are in no position to deny the possibility.

---

[1] Trans. by Edmonds in *Elegy and Iambus* (Loeb ed.), p. 63.
[2] *S.v.* μετὰ Λέσβιον ᾠδόν.

Why is the ephorate not mentioned? It is remarkable that neither in Tyrtaeus, nor in the life of Lycurgus by Plutarch, is there a single mention of the ephors. As we shall see later[1] the ephorate was certainly in existence at that time; it was either an ancient college of priests, or more likely was composed of the headmen of the five tribes, into which, in place of the ancient three, the people of Sparta were then divided. But, equally certainly, the ephors had not advanced to the position of authority that they occupied in later times. Their assumption of supreme power must have come some time after the second Messenian war.

And lastly, what of Lycurgus? Where does he fit in? Was there ever such a lawgiver and, if there was, when did he flourish and exactly what was his contribution to the evolution of Spartan constitutional forms?

LYCURGUS[2]

As Grote remarks, Plutarch commences his life of the lawgiver Lycurgus with the ominous words:

There is so much uncertainty in the accounts which historians have left us of Lycurgus, the lawgiver of Sparta, that scarcely anything is asserted by one of them which is not called into question or contradicted by the rest. Their sentiments are quite different as to the family he came of, the voyages he undertook, the place and manner of his death, but most of all when they speak of the laws he made and the commonwealth which he founded. They cannot by any means be brought to an agreement as to the very age in which he lived.

Undeterred by these difficulties, however, Plutarch gives us an account of his life and the constitution and system of education

---

[1] *Vide infra*, p. 118.

[2] Art. 'Lykourgos' in P.W., by Kahrstedt; *Ehrenberg, Neug. d. Staates*, pp. 7ff.; K. J. Neumann, 'Die Entstehung des spartiatischen Staats in der lykurgischen Verfassung', *Hist. Ztschr.* XCVI (1906), p. 1; E. Meyer, *Forschungen zur alten Geschichte*, I, pp. 213ff.; Beloch, *Griech. Gesch.* I, pt. 2, p. 253; Niese, *Hermes*, XLII (1907), pp. 446ff.

that he was supposed to have bestowed upon Sparta. It is safe to say that not a single statement in this narrative can be accepted with certainty, and that even the very existence of Lycurgus is strongly open to doubt. There is a good deal to suggest that he was regarded as a god. Herodotus[1] says that when he went to Delphi the priestess greeted him as divine. We hear of several gods or heroes of divine origin named Lycurgus in various countries.[2] Lycurgus was one-eyed through the assault of an enemy,[3] so perhaps he was a sun-god. Or perhaps he can be identified with Arcadian Zeus Lycaeus, who was god of the wolf-mountain and conqueror of wolves.[4] Certainly in Laconia he was honoured with a shrine or *heroum*,[5] so perhaps he had been taken over by the Dorians from the former inhabitants, presumably Arcadians.

By no means all writers identify the constitution with him. Pindar[6] says the Spartans got their laws from King Aegimius. Hellanicus[7] says they got them from Eurysthenes and Procles. The name Eunomus in the list of the kings of Sparta suggests that he was the author of the Eunomia.[8] Tyrtaeus[9] says that the

[1] I, 65.

[2] In Arcadia, *Il.* VII, 142; in Triphylia, Paus. V, 5, 5; in Nemea, Paus. II, 15, 3; in Thrace, *Il.* VI, 130; Paus. I, 20, 3.

[3] Plut. *Lyc.* II; Paus. III, 18, 2; Aelian, *V.H.* XIII, 23. Cf. Beloch, *op. cit.* I, 2, p. 254. There was a one-eyed Zeus at Argos: Paus. II, 24, 3. Cf. also W. R. Halliday, *Greek Questions of Plutarch*, p. 193, referring to *Quest.* XLVIII.

[4] Meyer, *op. cit.* p. 281; P. Foucart, *Le culte des héros chez les Grecs*, pp. 12 ff.

[5] Herod. I, 66; S. Wide, *Lakonische Külte*, pp. 281 f., remarks that the only certain thing about Lycurgus is that he was honoured by a cult in Sparta. The narrative in Herod. I, 65–6 is very confused. In the first part the reforms of Lycurgus are placed in the reigns of Leon and Hegesicles; later on Lycurgus is said to have lived at the time of Leobotas some centuries earlier. Herodotus must have been misinformed by the Spartans who thought that any troubles that had arisen in the past must have been put right by Lycurgus, without considering the chronological impossibilities involved.

[6] Pyth. I, 120.

[7] Frag. 91, *F.H.G.* I, p. 57; Strabo, VIII, 5, 5 (C. 366).

[8] Beloch, *op. cit.* I, 2, p. 255.

[9] Frag. 4, *Elegy and Iambus* (Loeb ed.), p. 63. Cf. Plato, *Legg.* I, 624 A.

constitution came straight from Apollo, which suggests the
story of the visit of Lycurgus to Delphi. Nor is his place in
the genealogy of the Spartan royal houses any more certain,
although all are agreed that he was of royal lineage. Herodotus[1]
makes him uncle of Leobotas and a son of Agis I. Later he
was thought to be guardian of Charilaus, son of Eunomus of
the line of the Eurypontids.[2] But Plutarch gives it up and says
that perhaps he was a son of King Prytanis and a brother of
Eunomus,[3] the latter name being under suspicion as a somewhat obvious aetiological fiction.

If his genealogy is uncertain, so equally is the time when he
was supposed to have lived. Xenophon[4] says he lived at the
time of the Heraclids, i.e. in the first half of the eighth century.
Ephorus[5] says he lived six generations after the founding of
the royal houses. Aristotle, according to Plutarch,[6] agrees with
various chronicles that identified Lycurgus with the name
inscribed upon a quoit preserved at Olympia, dating from the
time of Iphitus, the founder of the Olympic Games in 776,
and the sacred truce that accompanied them. That such a quoit
existed and may have actually been seen by Aristotle is quite
likely; but that the name Lycurgus can be identified with the
lawgiver is much less certain. Eratosthenes and Apollodorus
put the age of Lycurgus much earlier than the founding of the
Olympic Games, and Timaeus supposes that there were two
men of the same name living at different periods, the elder at
the time of Homer and the younger considerably later.[7]

To discover any common measure of agreement among
these accounts, other than that Lycurgus had lived a long

[1] *Ut supra.*

[2] Plut. *Lyc.* I; Ephorus ap. Strabo, x, 4, 19 (C. 482); Arist. *Pol.* 1271 B;
Aelian, *V.H.* XIII, 23.

[3] *Lyc.* I.

[4] *Resp. Lac.* x, 8. Cf. Plato, *Minos*, 318 C.

[5] ap. Strabo, x, 4, 18 (C. 482).

[6] Plut. *Lyc.* I. Beloch, *op. cit.* I, 2, p. 256, sweeps the whole story away
contemptuously. Cf. Paus. v, 20, 1; art. 'Iphitos' (2) in P.W. by Kroll and
'Olympia, c. 2525', by Ziehen.

[7] Plut. *Lyc.* I.

time ago, is obviously impossible. We must, therefore, do the best we can through the medium of conjecture to arrive at some tentative conclusion with regard to the whole confused problem. In the first place, to brush the whole jumble of stories aside and content oneself by saying that they represent myths, and that no person that can be identified with Lycurgus the lawgiver ever existed, is far too drastic and too easy a way of getting out of the difficulties. Evidently Lycurgus belongs to the array of lawgivers met with elsewhere, such as Moses, Draco and Solon. They were pacifiers, who at a time of serious dissension, brought about a settlement. That one man should be chosen to do so is altogether likely; things are generally done in this way—they are one-man jobs. It is hard to believe that the Spartan system was the production of an evolutionary process, 'a broadening down from precedent to precedent'. As Nilsson remarks:[1]

> The methodical and purposeful way in which everything has been made to lead towards one single goal, forces us to see here the intervention of a consciously shaping hand.... The existence of one man, or of several men, working in the same direction, who have remodelled the primitive institutions into the *Agoge* and the *Kosmos*, is a necessary hypothesis.

It is by no means impossible, indeed we may say it is quite probable, that there was a pacifier of the name Lycurgus, who did effect a settlement of internal discords. We cannot definitely affirm his existence; but equally we cannot deny it, and the balance of probability is on the side of Lycurgus having actually lived and done his work for the benefit of Sparta.

Secondly, if such a pacifier did exist, it must have been at a time of crisis in the affairs of Sparta. That there were two critical periods in the early history of Sparta we know. The first and second Messenian wars were both followed by constitutional crises. The first settlement was a victory of the

---

[1] *Klio*, XII (1912), p. 340.

Spartan peers over the kings and a curbing of the royal prerogatives and powers. It was an aristocratic revolution and has no resemblance whatever to anything corresponding with the so-called Lycurgan settlement. The crisis after the second Messenian war was, at least within the ranks of the Spartans themselves, a 'democratic' one, if that very dubious word can be used. It is certain that Lycurgus did not consider it so. 'In answer to a man who was insistent that he create a democracy in the State, Lycurgus replied, "First create a democracy in your own home."'[1]

The 'Lycurgan' constitution was not, in fact, a pure democracy. It constituted the *Ecclesia* on a legal footing, defined its procedure and made it the final arbiter in legislation. It was a return to the ancient practice when the tribesmen met together to listen to the proposals of their chiefs and decide what they should do. This had fallen into abeyance and the kings and their wise men no longer consulted the people. The fact that it was a revival of an early custom probably, if not certainly, accounts for the legends that have gathered around the name of Lycurgus. They confused two facts—the ancient usage of the Dorian tribes and their revival—and put them down to the invention of a divinely inspired lawgiver, who must have lived centuries before he did. When did Lycurgus live and effect his reforms? The balance of probability identifies him with the second rather than with the first constitutional crisis, and his date at some time in the second half of the seventh century.[2]

Into the details of his life it is unnecessary to go. That he went off on his travels, visited Crete where he studied the constitution and adopted some points for his projected reforms in Sparta, is not impossible, although suspicious as an easy explanation of the striking resemblance between the customs

---

[1] Plut. *Apoph. Lac.* 228 c.
[2] This is Wade-Gery's view, *C.A.H.* III, p. 558. Ehrenberg, *Epitymbion für Swoboda*, p. 19, proposes the middle of the sixth century for a lawgiver who may, or may not, be identified with Lycurgus.

of both countries. But the rest of his travels may be regarded as totally mythical. An itinerary that reached from Spain to India need not occupy our attention. These details are evidently late accretions of imaginative writers. A journey to various countries to observe their constitutions would be entirely correct, the kind of thing that a great lawgiver ought to do. If Solon went off on his travels, so must Lycurgus, to keep strictly in character. And so with all or most of the incidents recorded. For instance, the loss of an eye at the hands of an opponent, followed by his magnanimous forgiveness is quite in keeping with the imaginative chronicle.[1] He must suffer at the hands of his enemies and by his forgiveness win them to a better understanding.

Having finished his work he departed this life by the expedient of starving himself to death. But where he died and where he was buried are as unknown as everything else in his life. Half a dozen places claimed the honour of his tomb. Again this is strictly in character; the great lawgiver like Moses disappears to add to the mysterious circumstances of his existence.

That the constitution and way of life attributed to him were the fruits of his wisdom need not be taken seriously. Most, if not all, of the peculiar features of the Spartan discipline may be traced to primitive customs of the Dorian tribes. That is not to deny, however, that a pacifier and lawgiver such as Lycurgus did recommend, and conceivably impose, upon his fellow-countrymen a return to, or perhaps an intensification of, an austere way of life, which increasing wealth and love of ease had caused to fall into desuetude.

But precisely at that point we arrive at the greatest difficulty of all. Assuming that we are correct in identifying Lycurgus with the settlement after the second Messenian war, where does he fit in with Tyrtaeus? Is it possible that the reference in the

---

[1] Plut. *Lyc.* 11. As usual Plutarch is doubtful about the story. Dioscorides says he did not lose the eye, but was cured and built a temple to Athena Optiletis in gratitude for his recovery.

poet's *Eunomia* to the voice of Phoebus and the oracles of Pytho has to do with the supposed visit of Lycurgus to Delphi? That is not an impossible supposition; but it does suffer from one fairly formidable objection, why if this refers to the incident of Lycurgus at Delphi did not Tyrtaeus mention his name? It might quite plausibly be argued that at a particularly critical time of constitutional crisis the poet wanted to emphasise the divine origin of the *rhetra* and not the human vehicle by which it was taken back to Sparta. Obviously the passage in Tyrtaeus and the great *rhetra* of Plutarch's *Life of Lycurgus* refer to the same thing. Tyrtaeus says nothing of Lycurgus; but equally obviously Plutarch says nothing of Tyrtaeus. It would introduce a very human touch to find a natural jealousy between the poet and the lawgiver.

Grote's view that the division of the land into equal lots attributed to Lycurgus was an invention of the reformers of the third century cannot be accepted. There must have been some division of the lands they had conquered among the victorious Spartans. It is also certain that, in order to endow the Spartan warrior with land sufficient to keep him, a system of lots or *cleroi* was instituted. It is not impossible that a redivision of the land and a regrouping of the tribes was the work of a single reformer.

In conclusion we may safely say that out of all the confusion and contradictory accounts there does emerge the figure of a lawgiver who, at a time of internal crisis and disorder, was able to persuade his people to adopt certain expedients that were useful and curative of ills within the body politic. While we cannot with certainty affirm the historicity of Lycurgus, neither can we deny it. To say, as does Mr Andrewes,[1] that the perpetuation of his name was 'one of the most successful frauds in history' is much too sweeping a statement.

[1] A. Andrewes, 'Eunomia', *Class. Quart.* XXXII (1938), pp. 88 ff.

THE CHANGE IN SPARTAN LIFE

It is certain that a change began in the life and manners of the Spartans that was to modify profoundly their history. That this was due to the 'reforms' of Lycurgus and that it was quickly and designedly carried out as a settled policy of state-craft cannot be true. Under the force of circumstance after the stamping out of a formidable revolt there was a change which altered everything and produced the typical Spartan, with that austerity of life and devotion to duty which so markedly distinguished him in historical times. That the Spartans themselves were aware of this decline in the arts and tried, characteristically, to account for it through the action of Lycurgus, is shown clearly by a passage in Plutarch's *Life*.[1] The divinely inspired lawgiver 'declared an outlawry of all needless and superfluous arts'. But he might have spared himself the trouble since by outlawing the precious metals he took away all incentive for artificers to practise their crafts or merchants to bring foreign goods.

So there was now no more means of purchasing foreign goods and small wares; merchants sent no shiploads into Laconian ports; no rhetoric master, no itinerant fortune-teller, no harlot-monger, or gold- or silversmith, engraver or jeweller, set foot in a country which had no money; so that luxury, deprived little by little of that which fed and fomented it, wasted to nothing and died away of itself.

This highly desirable consummation led to Spartan crafts-men turning their energies to making useful, if unornamental, articles, bedsteads, chairs and tables. Laconian cups, Critias says, were much admired for the somewhat remarkable reason that their colour concealed the disagreeable appearance of impure water and their shape made the mud cling to the sides. 'For this also they had to thank their lawgiver, who, relieving the artisans of the trouble of making useless things, set them

[1] *Lyc.* IX.

to show their skill in giving beauty to those of daily and indispensable use.'

It is to the labours of the archaeologist in his excavations in Laconia to which we owe the more correct view of this momentous change. The late Mr Blakeway[1] has set forth what we may accept as the facts of the case. He has demonstrated from archaeological evidence that between *c.* 600 and *c.* 550 foreign imports into Sparta practically ceased. Corinthian pottery, which had been common in Sparta in the early or 'proto-Corinthian' period, is exceedingly rare after *c.* 600. Ivory, amber, Egyptian scarabs and Phoenician goods likewise cease before *c.* 550, and the same is true of gold and silver jewellery.

On the other hand, Spartan art does not degenerate in this period. Laconian vase painting is at its best in the second quarter of the sixth century, and the carving of bone, which takes the place of ivory between *c.* 600 and *c.* 550, is in no way a decadence of the art of the seventh century. It is not till the second half of the sixth century that there are any signs of decay in Laconian art, and then only in the furniture of everyday life.

Meier,[2] in confirmation of this view, points out that the change had not gone very far in the second half of the sixth century. Foreign artists were at work in Sparta and Amyclae as late as 520 according to Pausanias.[3] Theodorus of Samos, who flourished *c.* 540, was certainly at work in Laconia at that period. Only at the very end of the sixth century was deterioration rapid.

So far we may accept this reconstruction, but we must disagree with Mr Blakeway when he attributes this falling-off in imports to 'an economic rather than to a political or social cause' in the retention of an iron currency which by *c.* 600 was obsolescent, if not obsolete, throughout the Greek world.

[1] Review of Ollier's *Le Mirage Spartiate* in *Class. Rev.* XLIX (1935), p. 184.
[2] 'Das Wesen der spartanischen Staatsordnung', *Klio*, Beiheft XLII (1939).
[3] Paus. III, 12, 10; 18, 8.

It is probable enough that this retention of an obsolete currency was deliberate policy rather than stupid conservatism. But such policy is very different from the series of disciplinary and moral measures instituted in the interests of military efficiency so often deduced from the archaeological evidence.[1]

It is difficult, or rather impossible, to adopt the view that a retention of the so-called iron currency had much, or indeed anything, to do with this change. As will be seen later, the Spartans used money, although not of their own minting, as freely as did other Greeks. There is no evidence to show that the retention of the iron money was a deliberate policy, for the reason that no motive for this policy can be discovered. To what then may this change be attributed? We are on safe ground when we say that it was due to the peculiar internal conditions within the Spartan State. A dominant caste of alien conquerors had imposed itself upon a subject race. This caste, never numerous and indeed slowly diminishing in numbers, was forced to maintain its position in the face of a sullen opposition on the part of its subjects—the Messenian and Laconian helots. That this opposition was full of explosive elements the second Messenian war had amply demonstrated, and successive helot uprisings and never-ending sedition were to show quite as forcibly in the future. The Spartans lived on top of a volcano which might erupt at any time and safety was only to be bought at the price of unrelenting vigilance. That the 'reforms' of Lycurgus were instigated, more or less on general principles, to heal internal strife among the Spartans themselves is certainly not true.

GROWTH OF SPARTAN POWER

The conquest of Messenia, with the enslavement of the population and parcelling out of the land into *cleroi*, was the last territorial gain to Sparta wherein these means towards complete assimilation were used. It is noteworthy that the

---

[1] *Loc. cit.* Cf. also Leake, *op. cit.* I, pp. 158 f.

subsequent conquests of the small territory of Sciritis and the larger and more important Tegea were settled on the basis of alliance; the inhabitants were given the status of allies and not of helots, which was a very important difference.[1] Why was this? We can only conjecture that it was a deliberate policy, entered upon with the purpose of limiting the actual territory over which the Spartans held their estates.

If Tegea and Sciritis had been treated like Messenia, more *cleroi* or lots would have been available for Spartans to share, and they already had land enough and to spare to provide lots for everyone. They were not going to swell the ranks of Spartan peers by admitting newcomers to citizenship; consequently it was easier to turn the conquered Tegeans into allies than into slaves. They had too many helots on their hands as it was to want to add to that distinctly embarrassing possession. Already there was visible that deliberate closing up of their ranks among the Spartan *homoioi* that was to make them the most exclusive economical and political caste in all Greece. It was also, as they could not have foreseen at the time, to spell their own doom through the gradual dwindling of their numbers and the engendering of economic difficulties of the greatest severity. But that was still hidden, and for another two centuries the Spartan nobility was to enjoy the fruits of its superior position. Not that the *homoioi* enjoyed them in idleness and luxury; being a Spartan was a serious thing, entailing heavy responsibilities and submission to a galling discipline.

In spite of domestic troubles the power of Sparta was continually growing. With the successful close of the war with Tegea, which can conjecturally be placed *c.* 550, there emerged the so-called Peloponnesian Confederacy, which included all states within the Peloponnese except Argos and Achaea.[2] We are ill informed with regard to its exact nature, but it must have been a loose federation of 'the Lacedaemonians and their

[1] Dickins, *J.H.S.* XXXII (1912), p. 22; Busolt, *Die Lakedaimonier*, p. 261.
[2] Larsen, *Class. Phil.* XXVIII (1933); XXIX (1934).

allies', οἱ Λακεδαιμόνιοι καὶ οἱ σύμμαχοι, under the leadership of Sparta as the predominant partner. By this time a new factor in the Spartan constitution had emerged—the college of five annually elected magistrates or ephors whose functions are examined at length hereafter. The power of the ephors had become supreme and had already come to be directed towards three main objectives: first, the maintenance of home defence and the limiting of the Spartan dominion to Messenia and Laconia; second, the fostering of a steady hostility towards any tyranny set up in other Greek states, a policy which led to intervention in the struggle at Athens with the Pisistratids and the expulsion of the family;[1] third, an unrelenting hostility to the pretensions of royal power within the State. How far this policy could take them can be realised when we see how they thwarted the ambitions of Cleomenes I at every turn, procured the ruin of Pausanias and, we may strongly suspect, deliberately abandoned Leonidas at Thermopylae.[2] This was a significant evolution in Spartan statecraft. The ephorate was a profoundly democratic institution that feared and fought against tyranny both within and without the borders of Lacedaemon.

CLEOMENES I AND THE EPHORS

Complete as was the 'democratic' victory, it was nevertheless open to attack from able and ambitious kings and generals. The first struggle between ephors and would-be 'tyrants' was engendered by Cleomenes I of the Agiad house, who began to reign conjecturally c. 520. This very able Spartan, perhaps the ablest that ever reigned with the possible exception of the somewhat shadowy Theopompus, had great ambitions and

---

[1] Cf. Herod. v, 92; Thuc. I, 18; Isocrates, IV, 125; Arist. *Pol.* 1312B. According to the *Catalogue of Greek Papyri in John Rylands Library*, p. 29, no. 18, Chilon after his ephorate in concert with King Anaxandridas put down tyrannies in several Greek cities. The papyrus is late second century B.C. and the attribution to Chilon may be fanciful. Cf. Ehrenberg, *Neug. d. Staates*, p. 47.

[2] Cf. Dickins, *Class. Quart.* v, pp. 240 ff.

a restless, perhaps an unbalanced, energy. That he was mad is not impossible; but we are hampered in our final judgement of him by the grossly one-sided character of the evidence of his actions remaining to us. That he was in active opposition to the ephors is certain. It is also quite evident that we hear only the worst of him, and the accounts of his final relapse into madness and his suicide may, or may not, be true. There is more than a suspicion that the ephors deliberately falsified the records and represented him as an unbalanced enemy of the constitution, afflicted by a *folie de grandeur* that imperilled not only the Spartan State but all Greece as well and culminated in his final downfall.[1] Mr Dickins has given evidence to suggest that the 'imperialist' schemes of Cleomenes and his instrumentality in forming the Peloponnesian Confederacy led him to plot an insurrection of the helots in 480 to aid him in his struggle with the ephors. The evidence for this, as Mr Dickins admits, is slender and has been strongly controverted by Mr Grundy.[2] Whether or not Cleomenes was responsible, there does seem to be ground to suppose that in 490, at the time of Greece's greatest peril from the Persian invasion, a rising, or an attempted rising, of the helots took place.[3] It is not without significance that only 2000 Spartans were sent to the support of the Athenians at Marathon, suggesting that affairs at home were in such a critical state that more could not be spared. This is admittedly conjectural and it must be acknowledged that, if it had been the case, it is remarkable that we hear nothing about it. Whatever may be the true facts, it is quite sure that in Cleomenes the democratic Spartan State did find a danger, and it is more than likely that the ephors made away with a king whose ambitions were dangerous both at home and abroad.

[1] S. Luria, 'Der Selbstmord des Königs Kleomenes I', *Phil. Woch.* XLVIII (1929), p. 27. J. Wells 'Some points as to the chronology of the reign of Cleomenes I', *J.H.S.* XXV (1905), p. 193. G. Dickins, *J.H.S.* XXXII (1912), pp. 27 ff.

[2] *J.H.S.* XXXII, pp. 261 ff. Reply to criticisms, *ibid.* XXXIII (1913), p. 111.

[3] Plato, *Legg.* III, 692 E, 698 E.

The next danger came from Pausanias, the victor of Plataea and would-be leader of Greece after the end of the Persian war. Undoubtedly he was in conflict with the ephors[1] and tried to raise the helots against them. But the ephors were too strong for him and he perished as had Cleomenes. Not again, until the time of the decadence of Sparta, did any Spartan king or successful general attempt to end the domination of the ephors. The revolutionary efforts of Agis IV, Cleomenes III and the tyranny of Nabis will be related hereafter.

THE GREAT EARTHQUAKE

The next crucial event in Spartan history was the great earthquake of 464. Diodorus[2] says that 20,000 were killed in Laconia, which is not impossible but probably an exaggeration. Plutarch says it was the greatest catastrophe in human memory and that only five houses were left standing in the city of Sparta.[3] Apart from the destruction of life and property, the catastrophe had immediate repercussions in an attempted revolt of the helots, who were joined by the Thurians and the Aithaians among the *perioeci*.[4] The immediate danger of an attack upon the stricken city of Sparta and those who had survived was met by the prompt measures of King Archidamus, who rallied the survivors and met the advancing helots in battle array. Foiled in their attempt on Sparta, the revolutionaries retired to Mount Ithome, where they held out for some time until subdued.[5]

[1] Arist. *Pol.* 1301 B, 1307 A, 1333 B; Thuc. I, 128f. Meyer, *Rhein. Mus.* XLI, p. 578, suggests that this Pausanias was the king exiled after the battle of Haliartus, Xen. *Hell.* III, 5, 25. This seems unlikely except on the assumption that Aristotle is totally mistaken. Cf. Gilbert, *The Constitutional Antiquities of Sparta and Athens* (Eng. trans.), p. 22, n. 2.

[2] XI, 63.

[3] *Cimon*, 16; cf. also Polyaenus, I, 41, 3; Aelian, *V.H.* VI, 7; Polybius, IV, 24, 6; only five houses left standing, i.e. one house for each of the five phyles or tribes, a picturesque exaggeration.

[4] Thuc. I, 101. Thuria, a perioecic town in Messenia on the river Pamisus. Aithaia unidentified; *s.v.* Steph. Byz.

[5] Thuc. I, 103, says for ten years. This may be correct, but is open to doubt.

But, although the helot rising had been put down, it is certain that the disaffection among them, which had been fostered by the intrigues of Cleomenes and Pausanias, had become increasingly serious and that the Spartans were forced to intensify their mode of life in order to preserve their domination. Eternal watchfulness was the price they had to pay. As we shall see later, there is reason to doubt that the secret police—the *crypteia*—were quite as ruthless in their methods as we are led to suppose by Plutarch. But even at that, we must suppose that from that time forward the suppression of the least sign of disaffection among the helots became a major preoccupation with their Spartan lords, and the appalling slaughter of 2000 of them in 424, as recounted by Thucydides,[1] is intelligible. The Spartan lords were living on a volcano, which might bring them to destruction at any moment if their vigilance relaxed. In no other way can the extraordinary discipline they imposed upon themselves be explained.

THE SPARTAN HEGEMONY

With the accession of Archidamus II to the throne in 469 the opposition of the ephors to the royal power was continued, but the direction changed. By his firmness in the danger of a helot revolt after the great earthquake, Archidamus had gained great prestige and, had he chosen, he could have been a very formidable opponent to the ephors. But he was of a pacific nature and no imperialist; his speech in the debate on the declaration of war against Athens is proof of that. The ephors had been thwarted at their own game, and they had to revise their policy and become imperialists. The Peloponnesian war was undertaken on their responsibility, not the kings', a startling change of tactics for the hitherto anti-imperialist ephors.

The triumph of the Spartans in the long-drawn-out Peloponnesian war left them in a unique and extraordinary

[1] IV, 80; Diod. Sic. XII, 76.

position, for which they were ill-fitted. Their hegemony in the Grecian world was undisputed and the spoils of victory were poured upon them. The effects were unsettling and indeed disastrous. The old system of an austere life devoted to the service of the state broke down and wealth multiplied. It seemed as if all virtue had gone out of them, and this hitherto brave and simple people were debauched with riches and power with which they were utterly unfitted to cope. It is curious to realise that the hegemony of Sparta over the rest of Greece lasted only for twenty-three years and then collapsed when their army, hitherto supposed invincible, was put to rout by the Thebans. From their defeat at the battle of Leuctra in 371 the Spartans never recovered; they were defeated again and again. They were distracted by internal quarrels, a prey to party strife, to that sickness of the body politic that the Greeks called *stasis*. The proud Spartan peers had wrought their own downfall; they had attempted to buttress their domination on a prestige in battle which an enemy of genius very easily destroyed. They had built their economy on unsound foundations which must, sooner or later, collapse and bring them all down in common ruin. When Epaminondas broke the Spartan phalanx at Leuctra he broke the spell of Spartan prestige and no Greek was ever afraid of them again.

CHAPTER II

THE SPARTANS

The rulers of the Lacedaemonian State were the Spartans, οἱ Σπαρτιᾶται, who represented, actually or theoretically, the original 'Dorian' conquerors of Laconia.[1] They formed a privileged social caste, in which was vested all the political power of the State. In return for their possession of the *cleroi*, or lots into which the Eurotas valley and a large part of Messenia were divided, they owed obedience to the State and submitted to the discipline imposed upon them. Their status was sharply differentiated from that of the 'dwellers on the outskirts', the *perioeci*, of whom we shall speak at length hereafter, and still more sharply from that of the helots, the serfs who tilled the land and supported their Spartan lords.

In the eyes of the law the Spartans were ὅμοιοι, they were equals or 'peers'. This equality never at any time extended to their economic status. There always were rich and poor Spartans and, as we shall see, this economic inequality was at the root of the troubles that in the end led to the decay and fall of the State. An interesting and, in some particulars, a curiously exact comparison between the Spartans and the Samurai of Japan can be drawn.[2] Both were warrior castes which devoted themselves to the profession of arms and imposed upon themselves a high code of honour, with a corresponding distaste for the vulgar pursuits of trade or industry, in which they were forbidden to engage. They were like the knights of the Feudal System, supported by their serfs and vowed to austerity and deeds of chivalry. Such a caste

[1] The word Λάκων seems never to have been used by the Spartans themselves, but only by foreigners. Thuc. III, 5, 2; VIII, 55, 2. Λακεδαιμόνιοι was an all-inclusive term comprising Spartans and *perioeci*.

[2] Takao Tsuchiya, *An Economic History of Japan*, chaps. 5 and 6. *Trans. Asiatic Society of Japan*, 2nd ser., vol. XV (1937). Toynbee, *Study of History*, III, pp. 22 ff., compares the Spartans with the Osmanlis.

invariably develops in any age or country, where a landed aristocracy is successful in imposing itself upon a conquered or economically depressed peasantry. The maintenance of their political domination is not too difficult a task; it is their economic decay that invariably brings them down in the end. Spartan peer, feudal knight, Japanese Samurai, all fell on evil days because they were beaten by changing economic conditions to which they were incapable of adapting themselves.

QUALIFICATIONS FOR CITIZENSHIP

Every city-state of the ancient world hedged about its citizenship with safeguards that made it next to impossible for an alien to become enfranchised therein. That the Spartan peers formed a privileged body, a 'close corporation' was, therefore, no strange thing; the same was true of the citizens of Athens, who just as jealously guarded their rights and preserved their exclusiveness. It is probably true to say that it was as difficult for an alien, a 'metic', in Athens to gain the franchise as it was in Sparta.

There were three qualifications necessary for a dweller in Laconia to claim inclusion among the Spartan *homoioi*: birth, membership in a mess or *syssition*, and submission to the education and discipline imposed by the Spartan system. At first sight these may appear straightforward and simple; closer examination will reveal that all three bristle with formidable difficulties.

1. *Birth*. The fully enfranchised Spartan peer must be a descendant of the original conquerors of Laconia. How direct the descent and how pure the stock may have been is naturally open to doubt. But at least he must be able to establish his descent to the satisfaction of the elders of his tribe who, we may be reasonably sure, demanded some fairly convincing proofs of his lineage. We know from many instances in Athens that a claim of citizenship was not easy to establish. Illegitimacy certainly was an insurmountable barrier. That seems clear enough, but one more problem remains. Could a foreigner achieve citizenship by adhering to the

Spartan way of life and possession of land? Kahrstedt[1] seeks to
establish the conclusion that he could, by citing three passages.
Teles in Stobaeus[2] says, 'whoever submits himself to the way
of life is as good as the best, even if he is a stranger or born
of helots'. Plutarch[3] is more cautious and says, 'Some used to
say that whoever from foreign peoples will take upon himself
the discipline of the state according to the wish of Lycurgus,
may partake of the share of the land according to the ancient
rule.' A third passage from Heracleitus[4] goes even further and
says that if a Scythian or one of the Triballi or some one from
a nameless land comes to Sparta and makes himself amenable to
the severe Lycurgan discipline, he becomes *ipso facto* a Laconian.

It is evident that we here are faced with a conflict of evidence
that presents great difficulties. Was birth of pure Spartan stock
not a necessity for full citizenship? If so, and if submission to
the Spartan discipline was the only prerequisite, what becomes
of the supposed aversion of the Spartans to strangers and their
expulsion or *xenelasia*? We know that the Spartans were very
unwilling to grant citizenship to outsiders. The first known
instance was that of Tisamenos of Elis, a diviner of renown
whose help was greatly desired,[5] and his brother Hegias, who,
Herodotus states, were 'the only persons of all mankind ever
to be made Spartan citizens'. He seems to have been in error
here since, if we accept the story told by Plutarch,[6] the poet
Tyrtaeus who came from Athens was made a citizen 'so that
a stranger shall never appear as our leader'. The only other
known instance, at a much later date, was Dion of Syracuse
who, Plutarch says, was made a citizen of Sparta.[7] It is to be

[1] 'Die spartanische Agrarwirtschaft', *Hermes*, LVI (1919), p. 279.
[2] *Flor.* XL, 8 (233).   [3] *Inst. Lac.* XXII (238E).
[4] *Litt.* IX, 2; Schömann-Lipsius, *Griechische Altertümer*, I, 4, p. 216.
[5] Herod. IX, 35.   [6] *Apoph. Lac.* 230D.
[7] *Dion.* XVII. Hecateus was received into one of the *syssitia*, under protest
we are told. Apparently this did not carry citizenship with it. Plut. *Apoph. Lac.*
218B. The incident related by Herodotus (IV, 145f.) of the Minyans' being
received into Sparta clearly shows that they were given the status of *perioeci*.
When later they demanded full citizenship they were drastically dealt with.

noted that Plutarch in the passage cited above is careful to qualify his statement by 'some used to say', which clearly indicates that he is uncertain about it in his own mind. Both the spurious letters of Heracleitus and the evidence of Teles, quoted by Stobaeus, are very late, and it is altogether probable that this willingness to include foreigners in the ranks of the Spartans was characteristic of the state in its degenerate and helpless condition after the Roman occupation. That it was willing to grant citizenship to all and sundry, even on its own terms, when at the height of its power and prestige, is so unlikely that we may dismiss it as even a possibility, much less a probability.[1]

A point on which we are not fully informed is the law on miscegenation. Could a Spartan peer legally marry a foreigner or even a woman of the *perioeci*? And if so, what was the status of the children? From the accusation brought against Leonidas II[2] that he had married a 'foreigner', it would seem that these marriages were either illegal or severely frowned upon. If they were illegal, then the children must have been illegitimate and fell to the status of 'inferior'. We are probably on safe ground in supposing that marriages with helots were always illegal. Although comparisons are dangerous, yet it is permissible to compare the laws of Sparta with those of the Roman Republic, where a long struggle between plebeians and patricians raged over the *jus connubii*, the right of intermarriage between members of the two social orders. In Rome also, the son of a freedman, a *libertinus*, became *ingenuus*, a sort of half-citizen not enjoying full gentile rights, that is to say he belonged to no gens or family, nor could he advance to the ranks of the higher magistracy, although his grandson could do so.

2. *Membership in a syssition.* We are probably, if not certainly, on safe ground in asserting that membership of a *syssition* and ability to pay the dues necessary to keep the

---

[1] This is the conclusion at which Meier arrives: *Klio*, Beiheft LXII, p. 22.
[2] Plut. *Agis*, XI.

mess going were necessary to the political status of the *homoios*. Unfortunately, however, we are confronted with a severe conflict of evidence which is hard to resolve in this case. Aristotle's[1] assertion that failure to pay the dues entailed political disenfranchisement is very clear and unequivocal, and gains in emphasis by being repeated in a subsequent passage. What then are we to say of Xenophon's[2] equally emphatic statement that Lycurgus 'made the privileges of citizenship equally available to all who observed what was enjoined by the laws, without taking any account of weakness of body or scantiness of means'? The only interpretation that can be put on this is that, if a Spartan was too poor to pay his dues to the mess, he suffered no political disability.

It might plausibly be argued that Xenophon here is speaking of the ideal 'Lycurgan' system and Aristotle of the hard and realistic facts of a later age. But it is a little difficult to believe that Xenophon, who is giving a picture of Sparta as he saw it from actual observations as a resident, should not have mentioned that 'scantiness of means' was a barrier to political privileges in his day, whatever may have been the good intentions of the lawgiver. On the other hand, it is obviously impossible to reject Aristotle's statement. It is incredible that he should have been mistaken on so vital a feature of the Spartan political system.

There seems only one possible explanation that can provide a way out of this deadlock. Xenophon was writing at a period before the loss of Messenia; Aristotle at a time of political and economic decline. Many, if not most, of the Spartans must have been impoverished by the loss of their estates. The circle of *homoioi* had always been small, now it became even more constricted. Heedless of diminishing numbers, the remaining Spartans sought to buttress their defences by denying membership in the Assembly, or eligibility to office, to those who could not pay dues to the *syssitia*. The easy days of opulence and enough for all were over and, with character-

[1] *Pol.* 1271A, 1272A.   [2] *Resp. Lac.* X, 7.

istic selfishness and lack of foresight of the ultimate consequences, they closed their ranks. It may have been necessary
in the straits in which they found themselves. We may even
say that it was successful, for a long time elapsed between
Leuctra and the final break-up of the Spartan state.

3. *Submission to discipline.* The third requirement for full
citizenship—education in the rigorous discipline prescribed
for the youth—presents fewer difficulties than the other two.
It is quite plain that if a Spartan male child did not advance
through the various stages of training laid down for him and
thus qualify for election to a *syssition*, he could not claim full
citizenship.[1] Stobaeus[2] says that even a king's son, if he did
not undergo the training of a Spartan youth, could not qualify
as a full citizen. So much is sure, and need detain us no longer.
But we are on very uncertain ground when we come to
another class, the *mothaces** or *mothones*. These, Phylarchus[3]
tells, us, were the sons of helots who had been brought up as
foster-brothers of young Spartans and so had been made pets
of. 'For all the sons of the citizens, according as their private
means suffice, choose their own foster-brothers, some one,
some two or even more. Hence the *mothaces* are free to be
sure, yet not altogether, though they share the training of the
boys throughout.' Evidently the expenses were paid by the
fathers of the young Spartans. At first sight it appears a
curious system, but reflection will show that it had its advantages. Selected helot boys were given the same training
as Spartans in order to turn them into good soldiers. It is not
unlikely, although there is no evidence to support it, that the
helots who were enrolled in the army, for instance the
Brasideioi that Brasidas used successfully in his campaign in
Chalcidice, were *mothaces*. Could they qualify for full citizen-

[1] Plut. *Inst. Lac.* 238 E.

[2] *Flor.* XL, 8 (233). This is in direct opposition to the statement in Plutarch,
Agesilaus, 1, that the heir-apparent to the throne was not subjected to the
discipline. It might be that this exemption did not apply to younger sons of
the kings.

[3] ap. Athen. VI, 271 B. *Vide infra*, p. 89 for further discussion on *mothaces.*

ship? Phylarchus[1] seems to indicate that a *mothax* could be enrolled among the peers, provided he were elected to membership of a *syssition*, and this is borne out by similar statements by Plutarch[2] and Aelian.[3]

Lysander was a *mothax* according to Phylarchus[4] and Aelian.[5] But according to Plutarch[6] he was the son of Aristocleitus 'not indeed of the royal family, but of the stock of the Heraclids'. So again we are left in doubt.

There seems only one rational conclusion to which we may arrive. These *mothaces*, sons of helots, the favourites and playmates of the Spartan boys, shared the discipline of their young masters, living in barracks with them, messing in what we may call the junior *syssitia* and enjoying all privileges, if such a word can be appropriately used of so severe a regimen. But they were never *homoioi*. They received no *cleros*, they were not members of the *Ecclesia*. It might be thought that their position was far from enviable. They were subject to all the hardships of the Spartan discipline, which their helot relations were not, without the social standing and prestige that went with it. No doubt at times their position was galling. They emphatically were 'not gentlemen' and could be terribly snubbed by haughty Spartans. That was what Cinadon felt to be so unbearable. While they did not work on the land like their more lowly relations, they were always under suspicion as being potentially dangerous. A concerted and well-led rising of these *mothaces* would have been a formidable affair which might well have overturned the Spartan regime.[7]

The Spartan who refused to submit to the discipline was disgraced. He was cut by everyone, and became ἀδόκιμος or 'of no repute'.

---

[1] *Ut supra.*
[2] *Inst. Lac.* 22, 238 F.
[3] *V.H.* XII, 43.
[4] ap. Athen. VI, 271 F.
[5] *V.H.* XII, 43.
[6] *Lys.* 2.
[7] *Vide* art. 'Mothax' in P.W. by Ehrenberg, and Kahrstedt, *Griech. Staatsr.* p. 43. The latter is emphatic on the eligibility of anyone for citizenship who had gone through the routine of Spartan training.

The penalty for shirking the duties was exclusion from all future honours. He [Lycurgus] thus caused not only the public authorities, but their relations also, to take pains that the lads did not incur the contempt of their fellow citizens by flinching from their tasks.[1]

It is not apparent from this that these shirkers actually lost their civic rights. Certainly they could not hope for preferment or aspire to be senators or ephors. But there must always have been boys whose physique was not up to the strain of the toughening process and for no fault of their own could not go through the training.

The story in Plutarch[2] of the demonstration by Agesilaus of the military superiority of the Spartans over their allies may be apocryphal but it is at least interesting.

Agesilaus ordered all the allies, of whatever country, to sit down promiscuously on one side and all the Lacedaemonians on the other. Which being done, he ordered a herald to proclaim that all the potters of both divisions should stand out; then all the blacksmiths; then all the masons; next the carpenters, and so he went through all the handicrafts. By this time almost all the allies had risen, but of the Lacedaemonians not a man, they being by law forbidden to learn any mechanical art. Then Agesilaus laughed and said, 'You see, my friends, how many more soldiers we send out than you do.'

Uncertain and obscure as are many of the details, yet there does emerge a tolerably clear idea of the status and prerogatives of the Spartan *homoios* or peer. He claimed descent from the original Dorian conquerors of the country and as such clung, with all the tenacity characteristic of a landed aristocracy, to his privileged status. Entrance to the class of peers was jealously guarded and the number of inferiors who did attain to that charmed circle was microscopically small. Beneath them and bitterly jealous of their social prestige, was a mixed class of inferiors, free but not possessed of the full franchise. We must admit that we are not fully informed as to the question who some of these inferiors were. Nevertheless,

---

[1] Xen. *Resp. Lac.* III, 3.   [2] *Ages.* XXVI.

obscure as some of the details may be, it is quite clear what their status was. Beneath them again were the state-owned serfs, the helots, who had no freedom whatever. Quite apart from all the above mentioned were the *perioeci* whose origin and status will be dealt with hereafter.

NO HEREDITARY NOBILITY

That there existed among the Spartans an hereditary nobility, as distinguished from the common throng of equals, rests upon very scant evidence. Aristotle[1] says that the senators or *gerontes* were elected from οἱ καλοὶ κἀγαθοί. This is a very well-known phrase and may be translated 'best families'. But that these best families constituted a recognised class of nobles, who alone had the right of election to the *Gerousia* or Senate, as argued by some commentators,[2] does not follow at all. No doubt membership of the *Gerousia* was a highly honourable and much sought-after office, and we may well imagine that only those of wealth and renown would have a chance of election. But the very use of the term 'equals' (or 'peers') shows that every Spartan citizen was as good as his neighbour, and there could not have been an exclusive nobility within the ranks of the peers. Nor does it seem likely that the ephors were the representatives of the peers who did not belong to this nobility. Any comparison between the ephors and the Roman tribunes is a very unsafe one to make. However, it

[1] *Pol.* 1270 B.
[2] Gilbert, *op. cit.* pp. 12, n. 2, and 48, n. 2. Wade-Gery in *C.A.H.* III, p. 560. The latter suggests that at the Lycurgan settlement new citizens were admitted and the older ones reserved certain privileges and rights to themselves, e.g. religious precedence at the festival of the Carneia and the sole right to be elected Senators. This is merely a conjecture that cannot be substantiated. Busolt-Swoboda, *Griech. Staatsk.* p. 662, n. 4, discusses the problem at length and concludes that there must have been an aristocracy by birth among the peers. These did not, however, enjoy any political privileges or advantages over the others. Kahrstedt, *op. cit.* p. 144, rejects the idea of an aristocracy within the *homoioi*, as also does Meyer, *Forschungen*, I, p. 255, n. 2. The references in Aeschines, *in Timarch.* 173, and Polybius (VI, 10, 9; 24, 1), with the use of the term ἀριστίνδην, seems clearly to show that there was an 'aristocracy' of wisdom, not of birth.

must be candidly admitted that, if there was no hereditary nobility, Sparta was unique in the ancient world. To which it might pertinently be retorted that Sparta was unique in more ways than this.

LOSS OF CIVIL RIGHTS

For a Spartan peer to lose his civil rights a special decree of disgrace or ἀτιμία had to be directed against him. This, while it was in force, deprived him of his honourable standing in the community and, until removed, he could not hold any office, nor vote, nor take part in the proceedings of the *Ecclesia*. Such disgrace might arise from some crime, but principally from cowardice in battle. The lot of those who ran away or surrendered was highly disagreeable. We are told that life was not worth living, they became a mockery to all. Unshaved and clad in special dress they went about shunned by everyone. No one would eat or practise exercises with them. At the festivals they must sit alone and rise from their seats before the youngest. If they had daughters no one would marry them, and if they wished to marry themselves no one would give his daughter to them.[1]

So intolerable a state of affairs bore so heavily on the cowards, or *tresantes* as they were called, that, after those who had surrendered at Sphacteria were condemned to *atimia* and disfranchised, even while some were holding office, 'with a disfranchisement of such a kind that they could neither take office nor have power to buy or sell anything', the State evidently became afraid they might be goaded into rebellion, and subsequently, having reversed the decree, enfranchised them again.[2] A similar fear of the consequence of wholesale disgrace was seen after Leuctra, when it was realised that 'to execute so rigid a law when the offenders were so numerous and some of them of such distinction, and that in a time when

---

[1] Xen. *Resp. Lac.* IX, 4. Art. 'Tresantes' by Ehrenberg in P.W.
[2] Thuc. V. 34. Cf. Köhler in *Sitzungsberichte der preussischen Akademie der Wissenschaften zu Berlin* (1896), p. 362, n. 1.

the commonwealth was in so great need of soldiers, would be too dangerous'. Agesilaus was therefore made a kind of intermediary to deal with the problem and he proclaimed that the law should be enforced on the morrow, a very ingenious device for getting out of a difficult situation.[1] Subsequently he took off the unfortunates on an expedition when some plunder was taken and a small town of the Mantinaeans captured.[2] Honour was thus satisfied. There were evidently limits beyond which the stern rules of the Spartans could not be taken.

SPARTAN WOMEN

Of all the attributes of this remarkable community there is none more difficult to make out clearly than the condition and character of the Spartan women.

Thus Grote begins his excellent survey of the subject. It is true, and hardly to be wondered at, that the prim and early-Victorian historian should have been slightly bewildered. Writing at a time when the emancipation of women was still far off, he found it almost as difficult as did Aristotle to appraise fairly the contribution made by the women to the Spartan way of life. And yet it must be acknowledged that his treatment of a difficult subject is eminently judicious and fair.

As is invariably the case in anything to do with the Spartans, the difficulty arises almost wholly from the difference of opinion and viewpoint of the various writers who have dealt with the subject. The Spartan system astonished and puzzled the rest of the Greeks, who did not understand it and who interpreted it in various ways according to their own idiosyncrasies, either with enthusiastic commendation or severe disapproval. The Spartans were most notably different from other Greeks, and Spartan women by their training and demeanour were unique. The contrast between a Spartan and an Athenian woman was

---

[1] It recalls the equally ingenious rule in *Alice Through the Looking-glass* where jam was served yesterday and to-morrow but never to-day.

[2] Plut. *Ages.* xxx; *Reg. et Imp. Apoph.* 191 c; Polyaenus, II, 1, 13.

startling; quite as much as any comparison between a modern emancipated woman of the occidental nations to-day with the secluded women of Asia. Lampito in the *Lysistrata* of Aristophanes is, of course, a caricature; but it is easy to imagine how they were regarded in Athens, and with what gross exaggeration the character was played on the stage.

Their beauty and grace were famous everywhere and ever since Homer they had been accounted the most beautiful women in Greece.[1] Heraclides[2] of Lembos said that the handsomest men and the most beautiful women in the world were born in Sparta.

It seems to have been a case of beauty unadorned, since, at least in the best Spartan period, they were forbidden to adorn themselves or wear jewellery.[3] Nor were they allowed to use cosmetics or perfumery. The manufacture of ointment was forbidden because the perfumer corrupted the natural goodness of the oil.[4] Nor was their clothing attractive, since the art of the dyer was also forbidden, except for the crimson cloaks which formed the soldier's uniform. Lucian[5] seems hardly to have admired them when he speaks of 'a woman with her hair close clipped in the Spartan style, boyish-looking and quite masculine'.

Plutarch[6] is full of enthusiasm for them. By their upbringing they were trained to be fit companions to the Spartan men, mingling freely with them, sharing their sports. Lycurgus, he tells us, had ordered the young women to play and walk in the processions naked, 'to the end that he might take away overgreat tenderness and fear of exposure to the air and all acquired womanishness'. To excuse this somewhat startling custom he hastily adds 'nor was there anything shameful in this nakedness of the young women; modesty attended them and all wantonness was excluded. It taught them simplicity

---

[1] *Od.* XIII, 412; Strabo, X, 13 (C. 449).
[2] Athen. XIII, 566A.
[3] Herac. Pont. in Müller, *F.H.G.* II, p. 211.
[4] Athen. XV, 686F. [5] *Fugitivi*, 27 (379).
[6] *Lyc.* XIV, XV; *Apoph. Lac.* 227E.

and a care for good health and gave them some taste for higher feelings, admitted as they were to the field of noble action and glory.'[1]

It is more than doubtful, as Grote very justly says, whether the Spartan maidens exercised and walked naked in the processions. They wore a 'slit skirt', σχιστὸς χιτών, to give freedom to their limbs,[2] and we may well believe that their garments were not voluminous. It has been appositely pointed out[3] that such a garment was once common to all the Greeks. Herodotus,[4] in telling the story of the fate of the sole survivor of the Athenian expedition against Aegina at the hands of the women, says that to punish them they were forced to adopt the 'Ionian' chiton which was a more encumbering garment than the 'Dorian'. 'For all Grecian women in ancient times wore the dress which we call Dorian.' Plutarch[5] says that the maidens were allowed to appear in public unveiled, but the married women must be veiled; for the excellent reason that the girls wanted to find husbands and the married women should keep the husbands they already had. In any case, as with the men, luxury in dress was strictly forbidden.[6] How far this was observed may be only surmised. Clement of Alexandria,[7] who may or may not be right, says that flowered dresses were only permitted in Sparta to courtesans.

---

[1] Toynbee, *Study of History*, III, p. 59, n. 1, says, 'This spectacle...was really, of course, a demonstration of the remarkable degree of sexual self-control to which under the Lycurgan system it was possible for the Spartan society to attain'. *Vide* also art. by Italo Lana, 'Sull elegia III, 14 di Properzio', in *Rivista di Filologia Classica*, XXVI (new series), 1948, p. 37; also Paus. v, 16, 3; Pollux, II, 187; VII, 55; Plut. *Lyc. et Num. Comp.* 77A; Seneca, *de Beneficiis*, V, 3.

[2] Pollux, v, 77.   [3] Meier, *Klio*, Beih. XLII, p. 51.

[4] v. 88. Cf. Abrahams, *Greek Dress*, pp. 39 ff.; art. 'Vestis' by Boulanger in D.S. Euripides, *Androm.* 598, is rather shocked at the women with bare thighs. It is safe to say that if they had been completely nude he would have said so.

[5] Plut. *Apoph. Lac.* 227F; a custom found among modern savage tribes. Cf. Westermarck, *History of Human Marriage*, p. 197.

[6] Herac. Pont. Fr. 8, *F.H.G.* II, p. 211.

[7] Clem. Alex. *Paed.* II, 10, 105. Art. 'Anthina' by Man in P.W.

Nurtured in this freedom the Spartan girls grew into womanhood and marriage to be the mothers of heroes and warriors,
worthy helpmeets of their noble husbands, chaste and steadfast. Adultery,[1] Plutarch tells us, was unknown, at least in
the Spartan sense. The Spartan mother who bade her son to
return from battle either with or upon his shield has become
proverbial. When some foreign lady told Górgo the wife of
Leonidas that the women of Lacedaemon were the only women
in the world who could rule men, 'With good reason,' she
replied, 'for we are the only women who bring forth men.'[2]

In this time of trial and danger they stood by their men.
When Sparta was attacked by Pyrrhus[3] it was proposed to
send the women and children away to Crete. 'But the women
unanimously refused and Archidamis came into the Senate
with a sword in her hand, in the name of them all asking if the
men expected the women to survive the ruins of Sparta.' They
all, young and old, girding their garments about them, went
to the aid of the old men digging trenches round the city.
The young men who were to resist the onslaught on the
morrow they bade rest, and at break of day they brought their
arms and, giving them charge of the trench, exhorted them to
defend it bravely, 'happy to conquer in the view of their
country and glorious to die in the arms of their mothers and
wives, falling as became Spartans'. We are told that after the
battle of Leuctra the womenfolk of the survivors were put to
shame, while those of the fallen were joyful.[4]

Plato,[5] with certain reservations, approved of the training
given to the Spartan women, which he contrasts favourably
with the Athenian. 'We huddle all our goods together, as the

---

[1] *Lyc.* 15. Unfortunately Plutarch rather spoils the picture of Spartan
chastity by the anecdote in *Apoph. Lac.* 240 C. We even know the name of
two notorious courtesans at Sparta—Cottina and Olympia; Athen. XIII,
574 C, D, 591 F. [2] *Apoph. Lac.* 240 E.

[3] Plut. *Pyrrhus*, XXVII; Justin, XXV, 41. The story told by Lactantius,
Div. Inst. I, 20, 29, of the routing of an attack of the Messenians by the
Spartan women need not be taken seriously.

[4] Xen. *Hell.* VI, 4, 16. [5] *Legg.* 805 D, E.

saying goes, within four walls, and then hand the dispensing of them to the women, together with control of the shuttles and all kinds of wool-work.' In Sparta 'the girls share in gymnastics and music and the women abstain from wool-work, but weave themselves instead a life that is not trivial at all nor useless, but arduous, advancing as it were half-way on the path of domestic tendance and management and child nurture, but taking no share in military service'.

THE OTHER SIDE OF THE PICTURE

As may well be expected, another and far less favourable view of Spartan womanhood can very easily be drawn. There may be little significance in Xenophon's silence on the subject, but it is a trifle remarkable that, when he tells us he is going to describe the educational system of both sexes, he does nothing of the sort and ignores the training of the girls entirely, except that, purely on eugenic grounds, he commends athleticism.[1]

Aristotle[2] disapproves profoundly of Spartan women. As an offset to their own hard and ascetic lives, the Spartan men spoiled their womenfolk, who in consequence 'live without restraint in every improper indulgence and luxury'. Unruly and undisciplined, at the time of the Theban invasion 'they were of no use at all, as they are in other cities, but made more disturbance than even the enemy'.[3] All the efforts of Lycurgus to bring them into line with his system had utterly failed in face of their obstinate resistance. Two-fifths of the land and wealth had come into their hands, simply because lack of men

---

[1] *Resp. Lac.* I, 3, 4.   [2] *Pol.* 1269 B, 1270 A.

[3] This is confirmed by Plut. *Ages.* XXXI and Xen. *Hell.* VI, 5, 28. Grote, II, p. 383, n. 3, gallantly tries to excuse their conduct on the ground that it arose from indignation, not fear. But Xenophon's words, αἱ μὲν γυναῖκες οὐδὲ τὸν καπνὸν ὁρῶσαι ἠνείχοντο, οὐδέποτε ἰδοῦσαι πολεμίους, are unmistakable. They could not endure the sight of the burning houses and flew into a panic because they had never seen such a sight before. The fortitude with which they had borne the loss of their menfolk broke down when confronted with danger to themselves.

left them heiresses,[1] and this wealth they used extravagantly, maintaining race-horses which ,they exhibited at the Olympic Games,[2] costly equipages and fine clothes. They meddled in the affairs of state and brought undue influence upon the conduct of the government.

Although Plato theoretically approved of their system of education, he was, like Aristotle, aware that their conduct left much to be desired. It seems to have been generally accepted outside Sparta, or at least in Athens, that the Spartan women were of loose morals,[3] and he severely condemned the lawgivers for 'letting the female sex indulge in luxury and expense and disorderly ways of life'.[4] In common fairness to them we must suppose that many, or most, of the tales told about them were either utterly false or gross exaggerations and misunderstandings. For instance, Cornelius Nepos[5] makes a most outrageous statement in saying that at Lacedaemon no woman without a husband, however noble she may be, refuses to go as a hired entertainer to a dinner-party. This seems inexplicable on any ground and may be disregarded. Again in Athenaeus[6] 'the Spartan custom of stripping young girls before their guests is much praised' must be wilful misunderstanding of the alleged practice of the girls' exercising naked and not a deliberate act of 'exhibitionism'. Another extraordinary allegation is credited to Hagnon, the academic philosopher,[7] who says that among the Spartans it was customary for girls before their marriage to be treated like favourite boys. But whether the Spartan women were actually disorderly and immoral, or whether it was merely their emancipated way of life that shocked the other Greeks is hard to say.

That the phenomenon of dwindling numbers could be attributed to a large extent to the unwillingness of the Spartan women to bear children was the opinion of Cicero,[8] who

[1] Plut. *Agis*. IV.   [2] Plut. *Apoph. Lac.* 212 B.
[3] *Legg.* 637 C.   [4] *Ibid.* 806 C.
[5] *Praefatio* 4 'ad cenam' is probably corrupt. O. Wagner suggests 'obscena'.
[6] XIII, 566, 2.   [7] ap. Athen. XLII, 602 E.
[8] *Tusc. Disp.* II, 15, 36. Cf. Xen. *Ages.* IX, 6.

shrewdly remarks that the emancipated woman refused to forgo her freedom and was disinclined to relinquish the pleasures she was entitled to in favour of 'barbaric fertility'.

apud Lacaenas virgines,
Quibus magis palaestra, Eurota, sol, pulvis, labor,
Militia studio est quam fertilitas barbara.

It may be remarked that so far as medical science has been able to trace it, there is no evidence whatever of any connection between athleticism in women and a loss of fertility. A recent investigation into this gives clear proof that the athletic woman is, on the whole, more fertile than the more sedentary.[1]

A perusal of the sayings of Spartan women, collected by Plutarch, gives an impression of 'toughness' and ferocity more suitable to wives and mothers in a state of savagery than to civilised women. One is left in doubt whether Plutarch approved, or whether he collected them as extraordinary instances of callousness.

One woman, observing her son coming towards her, inquired, 'How fares our country?' And when he said 'All have perished', she took up a tile and hurling it at him, killed him, saying, 'And so they sent you to bear the bad news to us!'[2]

The old saying, 'He who fights and runs away, lives to fight another day', evidently was not current in Sparta. We can well understand that the works of Archilochus were banned from Sparta when he advised the soldier to throw away his shield rather than be killed in battle.[3]

Mr Toynbee[4] has something to say on their behalf which is worthy of attention.

[1] Düntzer and Hellendall, in *Münchener medizinische Wochenschrift*, 1835 (Nov. 1929), p. 76. Cf. also Busolt-Swoboda, *op. cit.* II, p. 702 and nn. 4, 5.
[2] *Apoph. Lac.* 241 B.
[3] *Ibid.* 239 B. Cf. Val. Max. VI, 3, 1. (Ext.) Possibly Archilochus was banished not for cowardice but for licentiousness. In any case he seems to have been an undesirable person to the Spartans, who got rid of him.
[4] *Study of History*, III, p. 75, and n. 4.

If we are right in our belief that the moral breakdown of Spartan manhood was the penalty of a moral rigidity which had been produced by the excessive severity of the Lycurgan temper, then we may conjecture that it was the relative immunity of the women from this unnatural strain that left them with the moral elasticity to bend and rebound in reaction to an ordeal which broke the spirit of the Spartan men outright.

The great Hellenic disaster of the Peloponnesian war, he says, was accompanied by a rise in the prestige of women not only in Sparta but at Athens, as evidenced by such plays as the *Ecclesiazusae* of Aristophanes, in which the women are supposed to take over the conduct of public affairs from the men, who had so mismanaged them.

But it is not easy to accept this view of Mr Toynbee. Had the emancipation of the Athenian women been used to spur the lagging spirits of their men to greater and more heroic efforts, then there would have been found a reserve of strength, hitherto unsuspected, that would have abundantly justified it. But there is no evidence whatever to lead us to suppose that this was so. With the Spartan women the very contrary is the case. They evidently got completely out of hand. The attempt of Agis IV to reform the polity of Sparta and return to the severity of the Lycurgan model broke on the hostility of the women who, Plutarch tells us,[1] were not at all ready to surrender their money and lands and thereby deprive themselves of the ease and luxury which wealth gave them. It might equally well be urged that 'the ordeal which broke the spirit of the Spartan men outright' did the same to the women, in whom no longer was found that semi-barbarous toughness that characterised them in the heroic days of their people.

The 'Lycurgan' system, however much we may condemn it, was at least a calculated and, so far as it went, a highly successful way of life aimed at one object—the maintenance of a discipline that made the Spartan soldier the best in the world. While this was practised, the women played a not

[1] *Agis*, VII.

unworthy part in maintaining it. When it broke down, the women did nothing to stem the decay that followed, but rather contributed by their conduct still further to degrade Spartan ideals. At the crisis in their people's history the women failed; of that there is no doubt whatever. To say that they possessed 'the moral elasticity to bend and rebound' is to distort the whole picture.

MARRIAGE CUSTOMS

The marriage customs described by Plutarch[1] and Xenophon[2] are by no means unique and can be matched with similar ones in every time and place. Marriage was supposed to be by capture, and when the bridegroom had taken the bride to her new home, the bridesmaid cut her hair short and dressed her in a man's cloak and sandals. It may be remarked that cutting the bride's hair is found everywhere among primitive tribes. Whether this ceremonial cutting denotes chastity or subjection of the woman to her husband, or perhaps both, is uncertain.[3] Almost certainly dressing her in male clothes, a custom also widespread, is with the idea of cheating or fooling evil spirits who are deceived by the outward appearance.[4] The custom of the bridegroom's visiting the bride by stealth was quite common among early Germanic tribes and indeed is still found all over the world. There is more than a suggestion, indeed almost a certainty, that in this clandestine intercourse there was the custom of 'trial marriage'. If the bride was subsequently found to be pregnant the marriage was lasting; if not, then the secrecy of the relations between them preserved the good name of both.[5]

[1] *Lyc.* xv. Cf. Nicol. Damas. *F.H.G.* III, p. 458.
[2] *Resp. Lac.* I.
[3] The custom is discussed at length by Westermarck, *op. cit.* pp. 175 ff.
[4] Frazer, *The Golden Bough* ('Adonis, Attis, Osiris'), II, p. 260; Nilsson, *Griech. Feste*, pp. 371 f.
[5] Trial marriage is widespread to the present day in all parts of the world. Cf. Nilsson, *Klio*, XII, p. 331.

Plutarch's statement that Lycurgus forbade the giving of dowries is open to doubt. If a Spartan *homoios* could not engage in trade, then the only way to restore a depleted fortune was to marry an heiress; certainly in later times dowry-hunting became a serious scandal.[1] The statement that legal marriage was postponed until forty is without foundation.[2] An astonishing custom, which, if true, must have been unique, is recounted by Hermippus in his *Lawgivers*.[3] All the young girls used to be shut up in a dark room along with the unmarried young men, and each man led home as his bride, without dower, whichever girl he laid hold of. Hence they punished Lysander with a fine, because he abandoned the first girl and plotted to marry one who was much prettier. We are also told by Clearchus of Soli in his book *On Proverbs*[4] that in Lacedaemon at a certain festival the married women pull the bachelors round the altar and thrash them, the object being that the young men, in trying to avoid the humiliation of this treatment, may yield to the natural affections and enter upon their marriage in good season.

A somewhat obscure passage in Athenaeus[5] seems to refer to marriage feasts at which cakes called *kribanai* were eaten. These were mentioned in Alcman according to Apollodorus.

To the same effect Sosibius, in the third book of his work *On Alcman*, says that in shape they resemble breasts, and the Lacedaemonians use them at dinners given for women, carrying them round whenever the girls who follow in the choir are ready to sing the hymn of praise prepared for the girl-bride.

Evidently before marriage a feast was given for the bride and her women friends in which these cakes were eaten and one of

---

[1] *Apoph. Lac.* 227 F. Art. 'Dos' by Caillemer in D.S.
[2] J. L. Myres, *Who were the Greeks?*, p. 304.
[3] ap. Athen. XIII, 555 C.   [4] *Ibid.*
[5] XIV, 646 A. Cf. note by C. B. Gulick in Loeb ed. of Athenaeus, vol. VI, p. 487. The above seems to be the best explanation of an obscure passage.

Alcman's songs, *Partheneion*, was sung by a choir of young girls in praise of the bride. We do not know if a similar feast was held for the bridegroom and his men friends.

WIFE-SHARING

Both Xenophon and Plutarch[1] pay particular attention to a custom among the Spartans which, if their account is correct, was unique and to be found in no other people in any time or place. Plutarch, after recounting the rules laid down by Lycurgus for the husband visiting his wife by stealth, goes on to say:

After guarding marriage with this modesty and reserve, he [Lycurgus] was equally careful to banish empty womanish jealousy. He therefore, while excluding all licentious disorders, made it honourable for men to give the use of their wives to those whom they should think fit, so that they might have children by them, ridiculing those who thought such favours objects to fight over and shed blood and go to war about.... On the other side, an honest man who had love for a married woman because of her modesty and the beauty of her children, might without formality beg her company of her husband, that he might raise, as it were from this plot of good ground, worthy and well begotten children for himself.

Xenophon, while agreeing with Plutarch, adds two important points, which must be examined closely, namely that the man who asked for a 'share' in another man's wife should be one who did not want to cohabit with his wife and 'nevertheless desired children of whom he could be proud'; and secondly, that the sons born of such irregular unions had no claim on the inheritance of their foster-fathers.

As has already been remarked, this custom was unique, and Westermarck[2] finds no counterpart of it in any people, ancient

---

[1] *Resp. Lac.* II, 7f.; *Lyc.* 15; Nicol. Damas. *F.H.G.* IV, p. 45.

[2] *Op. cit.* p. 130. But Strabo, XI, 9, 1 (C. 515) says it was the custom of the Tapyri to give their wives in marriage to other husbands, as soon as they had two or three children, 'just as in our time in accord with the ancient custom of the Romans, Cato gave Marcia in marriage to Hortensius by request of the latter'. Cf. H. L. Gordon, *Class. Jour.* XXVIII (1933), p. 574.

or modern, savage or civilised. It may be noted, however, that at least to one contemporary it did not appear extraordinary, and we may suppose that Plato[1] had this custom in mind in framing his eugenic laws for the ideal state. The easiest assumption in explaining this extraordinary custom is that it must have arisen from the ever-pressing necessity of keeping up the numbers of the Spartan *homoioi*, so that at any cost they should not diminish so far as to endanger their dominance in the political and economic order. As the Spartan women became more emancipated, they evinced, as Cicero observed, a strong disinclination to bear children. The accumulation of wealth in the form of large estates, increasing luxury and the abandonment of the simple way of life of their forefathers, all produced the familiar phenomenon of a rapidly decreasing birth rate. Of this the Spartans were acutely aware and any means that could keep their numbers from falling to a dangerously low level must be employed, however extraordinary they might be. If any woman capable and willing to bear children was found, she was eagerly sought after.

This explanation, plausible though it may appear at first sight, encounters a difficulty in a statement by Xenophon[2] in speaking of this practice. He says that the children of such irregular unions, although they are members of the family and share in its influence, do not have any legal claim on the possessions of their fathers (οἱ τοῦ μὲν γένους καὶ τῆς δυνάμεως κοινωνοῦσι, τῶν δὲ χρημάτων οὐκ ἀντιποιοῦνται).

If we are to assume that Plutarch and Xenophon are correct in their account of this singular practice, and that it actually was legally recognised, the only explanation can be that, although the children so born could not claim a part of the paternal inheritance, they could claim endowment with a *cleros*. They were *homoioi* and so the purpose of the custom, with the one qualification, was accomplished. Whether or not these sons could claim a share in the maternal inheritance is another matter. Suppose the mother of one or more sons thus

[1] *Rep.* 457–61.   [2] *Resp. Lac.* I, 9.

irregularly begotten was the sole heiress of her father, did they legally participate at her death in the estate of their maternal grandfather? We have no information on this point and conjecture is of little avail. It might be hazarded, however, that these sons could claim a share of the maternal estate and thus, in addition to the *cleros* they received, be provided for. It is not hard to imagine that such considerations entered into the calculations of those who sought these irregular unions. A shrewd appraisal of the situation might very well be a strong incentive.

Xenophon's phrase of the husband 'who did not want to cohabit with his wife' but desired children is significant, as it seems plain that the wife in these cases must have been barren or refused to bear children. We have no information with regard to divorce in Sparta, but it would be reasonable to suppose that either cause would have given good reason for it. Why then did the aggrieved husband not divorce the wife and remarry? Probably because he did not want to lose the dowry that had come with his first wife, which he would have had to restore on her leaving his house. Admittedly this is the merest supposition and can only tentatively be advanced as a more or less satisfactory explanation of a curious state of affairs.

A further statement of Xenophon adds to, rather than detracts from, the puzzle. 'For the wives want to take charge of two households': αἵ τε γὰρ γυναῖκες διττοὺς οἴκους βούλονται κατέχειν. It is practically incredible that the new 'wife' should rule the household both of her legitimate husband and her new one, if the latter is already married and his wife is in possession of his home. This would argue a submissiveness on the part of Spartan wives which, in view of their well-known independence of spirit and self-assertiveness, is beyond belief. Wives had their marital rights as well as husbands, and the spectacle of a new wife coming to 'rule the household' would assuredly lead forthwith to an action for divorce; unless, of course, the first wife connived at the new arrangement. It is not without interest to recall a similar state of affairs in the history of the patriarch Abraham, whose wife Sarah was barren. It was at Sarah's instigation that Abraham had connection with the Egyptian slave-girl Hagar, who thereupon gave herself airs and was turned out of the house by the jealous Sarah.

It is not impossible that in this case we have a reference to the law of legal relationship known as ἀγχιστεία.[1] Greek law did not recognise that daughters could inherit and carry on the inheritance themselves. If left an orphan, then a close relative (ὁ ἐν ἀγχιστείᾳ) must either marry her himself or provide a dowry for her. Such an orphan girl was called an ἐπίκληρος or ἐπιπάματις. In Attic law, if there were no paternal male relative, the maternal undertook the same duties. It is true that we do not know if the same rule applied in Sparta, but it is reasonable to suppose it did. In this light, the strange custom may be explained. Where an elderly male relative (ἀγχιστεύς) had, according to law, married an orphan heiress, the marriage had been of a *pro forma* character, and the duty of begetting children and so carry on the family might be properly deputed to a young man, who then stood in the relation of adopted son, or son-in-law, to the older man. It may be pointed out that the laws against late marriages would make it impossible, or at least unlikely, that an elderly man should marry a young wife, except under legal sanction as in the case above mentioned.

It is quite possible that in the story of Cleonymus and Chelidonis (or Chilonis) as recounted by Plutarch[2] we have a reference to this custom. Cleonymus in his old age had married a young and beautiful wife named Chelidonis. As is not unknown in such cases, Chelidonis fell in love with Acrotatus, the grand-nephew of her husband.[3] This intrigue

---

[1] Aristoph. *Aves*, 1661 f.; Demosth. *in Macart.* LIV.

[2] *Pyrrhus*, XXVI.

[3] Plut. *Agis*, III; Paus. III, 6, 3; VIII, 27, 8; 30, 3. Pausanias is wrong in calling Acrotatus the son of Cleonymus.

so angered Cleonymus, who had been excluded from the
throne because of his ungovernable temper, that in 272 he
invited Pyrrhus to invade Sparta. The invasion was defeated,
mainly through the valour of Acrotatus, and we hear no more
of Cleonymus. So far the story follows the familiar lines of
the young wife being unfaithful to an elderly husband. But
it is quite likely that Cleonymus had condoned, or even
legally sanctioned the relations between Chelidonis and
Acrotatus, and later repented of it.

The story, which we may accept as historically correct, is
of added interest in that it shows that the two royal houses
did intermarry, which is somewhat surprising in view of the
well-known rivalry between them. Cleonymus was an Agiad
and Chelidonis a Eurypontid. The accusation of Phylarchus[1]
that Acrotatus and his father Areus corrupted the simplicity
of Spartan manners need not be accepted. The corruption of
ancient simplicity of life had gone far long before their time.

There is no evidence whatever that polygamy, except in
extraordinary cases, was ever practised in Sparta, in the legal
sense of one man having several wives.[2] It is doubtful if at
any time there was a generally accepted system of polyandry,
in which one woman had several husbands, although a curious
statement by Polybius[3] seems to suggest there was. Quoting
from Timaeus, he says that sometimes several brothers would
marry the same wife and all live together on the family estate.
As Westermarck has shown, although polyandry is found in
widely scattered parts of the world, it is not an outcome of
primitive promiscuity, which he denies ever existed in any
considerable degree. It arises, as might be expected, from
a superfluity of men and a dearth of women in a particular
tribe or people. But did this state of affairs exist in Sparta?

---

[1] ap. Athen. IV, 142 B.

[2] The case of Anaxandrides being forced by the ephors to take a second
wife would appear to be exceptional and, as Herodotus (v, 41) says, 'not at
all in accordance with Spartan usage'.

[3] XII, 6, B, 8; art. 'Polyandry' in Encyclop. Brit.; Westermarck, op. cit.
pp. 115, 450 ff.

Ziehen[1] argues that it did, pointing to this passage in Polybius, the alleged custom of exchanging wives, the high esteem in which women were held, and the large number of illegitimates born of Spartan fathers and helot mothers which all point, in his opinion, to a lack of marriageable women among the *homoioi*.

This argument is, however, not easy to accept. It is quite possible, and frequently seen, that at any one period of a people's history there may be fewer women than men. It happens most frequently under pioneer conditions of settlement, notably on the American continent in the immediate past and even to the present day. But such conditions are transitory and the opposite is almost invariably found in old countries, where the women outnumber the men, as is seen very strikingly in Europe at the present time. Ziehen's suggestion might, no doubt, be true for early times in Laconia, when the Dorian invaders were predominantly male, and to take a large number of women on the march was impossible. At that time, if ever, this reference in Polybius might be true, and no doubt was. But that polyandry in any form existed in later times, when the balance between the sexes was adjusted and probably, if not certainly, inclined to the side of there being fewer males than females, is very hard to accept, and indeed may be rejected. The only possible explanation, and it must be accepted with extreme reserve, of this remarkable assertion of Polybius is that the marriage of several brothers to one woman was of the nature of a legal fiction, in order that the dowry of the wife should be shared by the brothers in common. In 'fraternal polyandry', as Westermarck shows, usually the eldest brother is the true husband and this may have been the rule in Sparta.[2]

And lastly, it is not by any means impossible that we have

[1] 'Das spartanische Bevölkerungs Problem', *Hermes*, LXVIII, pp. 218 ff.

[2] With regard to the possibility of polyandry in Sparta, *vide* Ridgeway, *Early Age of Greece*, II, pp. 135, 339. Nilsson, *Klio*, XII, p. 326, denies it ever existed. The custom of levirate marriages among the Israelites (Deut. xxv) may possibly, but far from certainly, be traced to polyandry.

in these strange customs, if we accept them as actual facts, traces of the survival of primitive matriarchy, whereby descent is traced through the mother and not the father. Paternity was of little or no importance, a child need never know his father, all that mattered was he should know his mother. As Hartland has pointed out,[1] there are faint traces of matriarchy even in Attic law, and among the much more conservative Spartans these traces might well be more pronounced. The point is, however, incapable of proof.

A tantalising and mysterious assertion by Philo Judaeus[2] provides another, apparently insoluble, puzzle. According to this, "the lawgiver of the Lacedaemonians', by whom is obviously meant Lycurgus, allowed marriages between half-brothers and sisters by the same mother but different fathers, but forbade those between half-brothers and sisters of the same father but different mothers, adding that this was exactly opposite to what Solon allowed to the Athenians. In his assertion that Athenian law allowed the marriage of half-brothers and sisters by the same father but different mothers Philo is correct, as the evidence in the case argued by Demosthenes againt Eubulides[3] and the instance in the *Life of Themistocles*[4] show quite clearly. If Philo is right with regard to Spartan law, the only explanation must be that by allowing a half-brother and sister by different fathers to marry, the estates of both fathers might be combined on their deaths; while if a half-brother and sister of the same father married, only the estate of the single father would be left; unless the sister was the sole heiress of her maternal grandfather, which might not be the case.

[1] E. S. Hartland, *Primitive Paternity*, I, p. 322; II, p. 18.
[2] *De spec. leg.* III, 23 (303), Loeb ed. Hruza, *Beiträge zur Geschichte d. griech. u. röm. Familienrechts*, II, p. 165, n. 20, has no explanation to offer. *Vide* also W. Erdmann, 'Die Ehe im alten Griechenland', *Münchener Beiträge zur Papyrusforschung u. antiken Rechtsgeschichte* XX (1934), p. 182.
[3] *In Eubul.* XX.　　　　　　　　　[4] Plut. *Themist.* XXXII.

BURIAL CUSTOMS

The excellent and all-wise 'Lycurgus' laid down the wisest possible regulations for the conduct of his Spartans from the cradle to the grave. We are told[1] that 'he did away with all superstitious terror by allowing them to bury their dead within the city and to have memorials of them near the sacred places, thus making the youth familiar with such sights and have no horror of death as polluting those who touched a corpse or walked among graves'. This is, of course, a not very successful attempt at rationalising a burial custom that is as widespread as it is ancient. Many people have buried their dead, not only within the town or settlement, but even within their own houses, to the extreme discomfort of the living, with the idea of keeping the spirits of the dead as members of the family and household.[2] It is to be observed that the kings were buried outside the city in their specially reserved cemeteries.[3] Perhaps it was thought safer that their tombs should not be in the city, in order that the influence of an evilly disposed spirit of a dead king might be removed from too close association with the living. The elaborate funeral ceremonies with lavish praise bestowed upon the dead king were held in order to propitiate his spirit.[4]

Lycurgus permitted nothing to be buried with the dead, only allowing the body to be covered with a scarlet robe and olive leaves. The scarlet robe was the uniform of the Spartan soldier. We are not told in what fashion women and children were buried. Scattering olive leaves upon the body was a *catharsis*, a cleansing of earthly pollution so that the dead might not enter the spirit world unclean.[5]

---

[1] Plut. *Lyc.* XXVII.

[2] Hastings, *Encyclopaedia of Religion and Ethics*, art. 'Death and disposal of dead' (Greek), IV, p. 472; art. 'Funus' in D.S. Plato, *Minos*, 315 D, refers to this practice as an ancient one no longer current in Athens.

[3] Herod. VI, 58.   [4] *Vide infra*, p. 115.

[5] Erwin Rohde, *Psyche*, p. 209, n. 3; p. 360, n. 1.

It was not allowed to inscribe the name of the dead on the tomb, except that of a man who had fallen in war, or of a women who had died in sacred office. It is not impossible that in this we have evidence of the primitive belief that the gravestone, stele, or funerary monument became the home of the spirit of the dead, or a place to which it might return. If there was no name on the grave, the spirit might not be able to find it; but those who fell in battle were heroes whose spirits might return to encourage the living to valour and the women to virtue. The time of mourning was made a short one of eleven days; on the twelfth a sacrifice was made to Demeter and the ceremonies ended. The extreme simplicity of these funeral observances[1] is in striking contrast with the highly elaborate rites practised in every other country. If 'Lycurgus' was successful in curbing extravagance in funerals and monuments he did more than Solon, who had tried to do the same and signally failed.[2] In Athens these expenses were not put down finally until the time of Demetrius of Phalerum.

[1] Herac. Pont. *F.H.G.* II, p. 210, frs. 2, 8.
[2] Plut. *Solon*, XXI, 4.

CHAPTER III

PERIOECI, HELOTS, INFERIORS

1. THE *PERIOECI*

The second main division of the Lacedaemonian state comprised the *perioeci*, 'the dwellers in the outskirts'. That these formed an integral part of the State, that they were free and, to some imperfectly defined degree, self-ruling but without the same political status as the Spartans, are all fairly clear facts. Who they originally were, whether 'Dorians' or 'Achaeans', and what exactly their relations were with the dominant Spartans, are not so clear and have given rise to considerable controversy.

Larsen[1] has given perhaps the best definition of the *perioeci* in saying that they were subjects of a Greek state, living in the outlying districts, who possessed their own communities, local self-government, and local rights of citizenship, but were always under the domination of a greater state, to which they were obliged to render various services. In Sparta the generic name 'Lacedaemonian' covered both Spartans and *perioeci*, but the latter had no part in the government of the State as a whole, nor voice in the formulation of foreign policy. On the contrary, they were more or less under the strict control of the dominant Spartans. It is to be carefully noted that the word *perioeci* had not always the connotation of 'underlings', but sometimes meant neighbouring peoples and allies. For instance, Herodotus speaks of the Carthaginians and Tyrrhenians as *perioeci*, or 'neighbours', of the Phocaeans at Cyrnus, and he also talks of 'neighbours' of the Pedasians near Halicarnassus.[2] It is also to be noted that *perioeci* were

[1] Art. 'Perioikoi' in P.W.
[2] Herod. 1, 166, 175. Evidently the Pedasians and their *perioeci* were identical or at least on friendly terms. The same somewhat startling warning of impending danger applied to them both.

found in several other countries, for instance Argos, Elis, Crete, Thessaly and Cyrene.[1]

Hasebroek[2] very appositely points out that there are distinct traces of early *perioeci* in Homer. For instance, Menelaus offers a city to Telemachus 'from those that lie around and are in my domain': αἳ περιναιετάουσιν, ἀνάσσονται δ' ἐμοὶ αὐτῷ.[3] Phoenix, when he fled to Phthia, was given land among the Dolopians on the outskirts of Phthia, by King Peleus. ναῖον δ' ἐσχατιὴν Φθίης, Δολόπεσσιν ἀνάσσων.[4] Agamemnon promises Achilles 'seven goodly towns... which all lie beside the sea,... whose inhabitants are rich in bullocks and sheep, and they will do homage to him, with gifts fit for a god and render him the sceptre's usual due'.[5] It is evident that these surrounding lands were, in some imperfectly defined manner, an appanage of the crown, or were at the disposal of the king. Although comparisons with the Feudal System are unsafe, yet it is pertinent to compare this custom with the granting by the king of fiefs to his chief barons. There is no evidence to show that the same right belonged to the early kings of Sparta, although they did receive in the 'Lycurgan' settlement 'choice portions of land in the territory of the neighbouring towns, large enough that they might neither be in want of moderate means nor be possessed of extravagant wealth'.[6] Caution must be exercised in any comparison between Homeric and later times.

The greatest single problem with regard to the *perioeci* is that of their origin. Who were they? If they were Dorians, why did they not enjoy exactly similar privileges as the Spartans? If they were not Dorians, why had they not shared the fate of the conquered inhabitants and been reduced to

---

[1] Argos, Arist. *Pol.* 1303 A; Plut. *Moral.* 245 F; Paus. VIII, 27, 1; Elis, Thuc. II, 25; Crete, probably but not certainly. Larsen, 'Perioeci in Crete', *Class. Phil.* XXXI (1936), p. 11. Thessaly, Xen. *Hell.* VI, 1, 19, or ὑπήκοοι; Thuc. II, 101, IV, 78; Cyrene, Herod. IV, 161.

[2] *Griech. Wirtschafts- u. Gesellschaftsgeschichte*, pp. 63 f.

[3] *Od.* IV, 177. [4] *Il.* IX, 484.

[5] *Il.* IX. 149. [6] Xen. *Resp. Lac.* XV, 3.

serfdom as helots? The evidence on this point is vague and confused and a completely satisfactory solution is impossible.

Isocrates, in his *Panathenaicus*,[1] gives one account of the origin of the *perioeci* which must be examined with some care. Apart from some obvious exaggerations which can safely be dismissed, this evidence cannot be lightly set aside, in spite of the destructive criticism of Grote.[2] According to Isocrates, when the Peloponnesus had been conquered by the Heraclids the whole land was divided among the three tribes—Hylleis, Dymanes and Pamphyloi. But internal dissensions arose among the conquerors, between the nobles and the people, which ended in the victory of the nobles or oligarchs. The victors retained for themselves the richest lands of the Eurotas valley and drove the mass of the people to the outlying and less fertile tracts. The oligarchs, who dwelt about the city of Sparta, arrogated to themselves all the privileges of a ruling caste. In order that their domination might be strengthened and perpetuated, they instituted their own system of equality among themselves, they were all equals. Those who had been driven out, while not reduced to serfdom, yet lost all their rights with respect to the central government, and were harshly treated by those who had seized the ruling power. Up to that point the narrative of Isocrates does at least give a rational explanation of the origin of the *perioeci*. Unfortunately, however, he rather spoils it by some exaggerations, saying that the Spartans always used the *perioeci* in dangerous situations when they wanted to save their own skins. This last is certainly untrue: whatever else they were, the Spartans were not cowards.

With this account of the origin of the *perioeci* may be compared that of Ephorus,[3] who says that, on the conquest of Laconia, the two kings Eurysthenes and Procles granted equal rights to the original inhabitants of the land along with their Dorian conquerors; but Agis son of Eurysthenes reversed this and degraded the *perioeci* to an inferior position. It must

---

[1] *Orat.* XII, 177 (270).   [2] II, pp. 367 ff. (2nd ed.).
[3] ap. Strabo, VIII, 5, 5 (C. 365).

be carefully noted that according to the account of Isocrates the *perioeci* were Dorians of the conquering tribes, but according to Ephorus they were the conquered. The difficulty in accepting the latter account arises from one unanswered question—why were these conquered people not reduced to the status of helots, and conversely who were the helots who did not receive the more favoured status of *perioeci*? Of the two accounts that of Isocrates contains fewer difficulties than that of Ephorus.

As Grote[1] has pointed out, the version given by Isocrates 'is nothing better than a conjecture; nor is it even a probable conjecture since it is based on the historical truth of the old Heraclid legend, and transports the disputes of his own time, between the oligarchy and the demos, into an early period to which such disputes do not belong'. To this it may be answered that, as already remarked, there is nothing to prompt us to reject the Heraclid legend, and also there is no foundation for Grote's assertion that disputes between the oligarchy and the demos were unknown in the early period. On the contrary, such disputes had occurred from the earliest times. Grote's further criticism that the conquest of Laconia by the Dorians was a long-drawn-out one, a gradual and persistent encroachment on the former inhabitants, is certainly well chosen. But it does not invalidate the account of Isocrates; it is not necessary to suppose that the *coup d'état* of the oligarchs followed immediately upon the complete conquest of the land by a sudden victory over the original inhabitants. It may have been a protracted process, a gradual 'freezing out' of the poorer members of the Dorian bands; or, it is equally likely, an offer of larger lots further out, in place of their original apportionments in the Eurotas valley. If we accept this explanation, and it is a perfectly rational one, it disposes very satisfactorily of the problem of who the *perioeci* were. They were Dorians, a conclusion to which Grote had previously arrived and in which Pareti agrees.[2]

[1] II, chap. 5.   [2] Pareti, *Storia di Sparta arcaica*, I, p. 206.

That the *perioeci* were not remnants of the conquered peoples but Dorians, may be argued on various grounds in addition to what has already been said. In the first place, we must remember that the city of Sparta was a πόλις in the narrow Greek sense of city-state. To be a citizen of the State with full legal rights and part in the government, the individual must be a 'citizen' of Sparta, although actually his place of residence might not be within the city limits. But at least he must not live too far off to prevent his taking part in public affairs, through his attendance at the sessions of the *Ecclesia*. If, as there is good reason to suppose, the perioecic towns were also πόλεις in their own right,[1] then a *perioecus* could not be a citizen of his own town and of the city of Sparta at the same time. Although no distances in Laconia or Messenia are very great, yet many of the *perioeci* must have lived too far from the centre to allow of more than infrequent visits. It is not hard to imagine, although admittedly there is no evidence whatever to support it, that when the Dorian conquerors apportioned the land among themselves, an agreement was reached whereby those who took up lands on the outer borders were accorded the right of self-government. At first the Lacedaemonian State was an alliance of free and equal tribesmen, with Sparta the dominant partner. It is also not unlikely that in the course of centuries this domination of Sparta increased and the perioecic cities, while always retaining municipal government, lost their status of being free and equal allies and all voice in the conduct of foreign policy. To say, therefore, that the *perioeci* did not enjoy equal political status with the Spartans, is by no means to prove that they were not Dorians.

Secondly, it is unfounded conjecture to explain why, if they were Achaeans, they had not been 'helotised' by saying that they were too strong and the Spartan conquerors found

---

[1] K. J. Neumann, 'Die Entstehung d. spart. Staates' in *Hist. Ztschr.* LXXXXVI (1906), p. 52, seeks to differentiate between the industrial *poleis* and the agricultural *komai*, a sharp distinction already in existence in the pre-Doric-Mycenaean epoch, which was simply taken over by the Doric conquerors. Cf. Busolt-Swoboda, *Griech. Staatsk.* I, p. 140, n. 2.

it easier to make allies of them than to reduce them to serfdom. Admittedly the *argumentum ex silentio* is seldom satisfactory; yet it is admissible to point out that no ancient author says anything of any such treaty with inconvenient, unsubdued foes.

Thirdly, no difference between *perioeci* and Spartans can be found on philological grounds, as some have sought. Undoubtedly they spoke good Doric, but Doric contained a good many Achaean forms. Such inscriptions as have been found have been in Doric.[1] The Dorians were not a pure race, but mixed with other tribes. When they conquered Laconia they certainly did not drive out or exterminate all the Achaeans, and with these they intermingled, and from them they acquired certain Achaean forms of words, some of which have appeared in inscriptions which are otherwise pure Doric.

Fourthly, as Ehrenberg has pointed out,[2] absence of common action between *perioeci* and helots shows fairly conclusively they were not of the same race. If they had been a subject people, suffering from a sense of inferiority and oppression, it is hard to believe they would not have made common cause with the helots in their uprisings. Not until after the disaster of Leuctra was there any disaffection among them.[3]

Fifthly, in the so-called 'Lycurgan' division of the land into *cleroi* the *perioeci* shared. As will be shown later, the figures for the number of lots are totally untrustworthy; but nevertheless the conclusion that some division was made is inescapable. It seems most unlikely that, if the *perioeci* were not Dorians, they should have been treated in the same way as their conquerors.

Sixthly, we know that *perioeci* competed at Olympia. We even know the name of one, Nicocles, who came from the

---

[1] Cf. Niese, *Nachrichten von der Gesellschaft der Wissenschaft zu Göttingen* (1906), pp. 101 ff.; Hoffman's review of Meister's *Dorer u. Achäer*, in *Phil. Woch.* (1906), p. 1392.

[2] *Hermes*, LIX, pp. 49–57.

[3] Xen. *Hell.* VI, 5, 25, VII, 2, 2; Plut. *Moral.* 346 B.

perioecic town of Akreai.[1] They competed as 'Lacedae-monians', evidently on an equal footing with the Spartans. It is impossible to believe that they would have been admitted as contestants if they had occupied a servile position.

While none of these reasons for the supposition that the *perioeci* were Dorians of like standing with the Spartans is absolutely conclusive, yet collectively they do afford very strong evidence favouring that conclusion. As Meier[2] has remarked, modern scholarship is coming more and more to the view that the *perioeci* were Dorians; or perhaps it would be more correct to say that it is returning to the earlier con-clusion of Grote.[3] Gilbert[4] says that they were of mixed origin; in the north, Arcadian; in Messenia, at any rate in part, Dorian; in Cynuria, Ionian; in the remaining districts, Achaean. This is conjecture; but it is true to say that it is highly unlikely they were pure Dorians. As is ever the case when a conquering people settle down in a land where the conquered are not wholly exterminated, they merge with the former inhabitants by marriage; just as the Normans merged with the Anglo-Saxons to become 'English'.

Niese's argument that they were outpost garrison cities of the Spartans, colonised originally by Dorians of the same stock as the Spartans, very probably is true at least for Laconia, but perhaps a little more doubtfully for Messenia.[5] The conclusion to which we may reasonably come is that the *perioeci* were not a vanquished people whom the conquering Spartans found it politic not to reduce to serfdom. They were 'Dorians', however mixed they may have become in course of time, and so allies of the dominant Spartan aristocracy that centred round the city of Sparta and the Eurotas valley. They were 'Lacedaemonians', and served in the army as hoplites, which the helots normally did not.

[1] Paus. III, 22, 5. [2] *Klio*, Beih. LXII, p. 24.

[3] II, chap. 5. It must, however, be admitted that the weight of authority on the side of their being Achaeans is impressive. E.g. Beloch, *Griech. Gesch.* I, 1, p. 205; Busolt-Swoboda, *op. cit.* II, p. 638, n. 8.

[4] *Grk. Const. Ant.* p. 35. [5] *Loc. cit.* pp. 101 ff.

The account given by Herodotus[1] of the mustering of the
army that fought at Plataea contains some significant points.
Pausanians marched out first with 5000 Spartans secretly to
the Isthmus. When the Athenian ambassadors arrived they
did not know that this force had already set out and reproached
the ephors with dilatoriness. On being told that the Spartan
army was already at Oresteum 'they were much surprised and
followed after them in all haste and with them 5000 picked
heavy-armed troops of the neighbouring Lacedaemonians'.[2]
It is evident that at Plataea at least the Spartans and *perioeci*
were brigaded separately. Being constantly ready for action,
the Spartans were first in the field. Being scattered and therefore more slowly mobilised, the neighbouring Lacedaemonians, namely the *perioeci*, were later on the march. The
word 'picked' is significant and is open to two interpretations.
It either means that only the best of the *perioeci* were chosen
to take the field, or that a contingent having been demanded
of them the *perioeci* were left to draft those of their own choice.
In this case, the number being so large, it is probable that the
second explanation is more correct. So long as the *perioeci*
provided the required number of men, they were left to select
them themselves. The entire male population of the *perioeci*
was liable for military service; that is certain. But they were
not, as were the Spartans, devoted exclusively to preparing
themselves for war and, when the summons came for action,
only those suitable for a campaign were called up. We need
not make too much of the figure 5000 for each contingent,
such round numbers are always misleading. It is not, however,
without significance to note that the two contingents were of
equal size, thereby suggesting that the *perioeci* were required,
at the time of the Persian wars at least, to match the number
of the Spartans put into the field. Later when dwindling
numbers reduced the available Spartan manpower, there were
many more *perioeci* than there were Spartans.

[1] IX, 10, 11.
[2] τῶν περιοίκων Λακεδαιμονίων λογάδες. *Vide infra*, p. 249.

Whether or not the Sciritai, a picked regiment of men from Sciritus on the borders of Arcadia, were *perioeci* is not easy to determine. They were not Spartans, and evidently were separated from the *perioeci* in battle. There is no evidence as to what their political status was. If, as Pareti suggests, they were Arcadians and not technically *perioeci*, they must have enjoyed all the rights of *perioeci* and therefore politically were indistinguishable from them.[1]

It is in the relationship of the *perioeci* to the Spartan kings that another problem arises which is very hard to elucidate. Kahrstedt[2] thinks that it was in the form of a personal alliance between them. The *perioeci* were 'kings' men' and looked to the kings as their protectors.[3] In this he is followed by Schaefer,[4] who suggests that a regular oath, of allegiance on the one side and of protection on the other, was taken. It is not unlikely that this may have been so; but all that can be said is that there is no evidence whatever of it. It may be urged on the other hand that the ephors supervised control over the *perioeci* and could inflict punishment upon them.[5] It is not impossible that this power was assumed by the Ephorate in the course of its gradual encroachment upon the king's prerogatives. If the *perioeci* had the right of appeal straight to the crown, we should probably have heard of it. It is unlikely that Aristotle would have overlooked so important an item of constitutional law.

There is no evidence that the Spartans treated the *perioeci* harshly, or that there was any bitterness of feeling between the two. Grote's[6] statement on this is worth quoting:

As Harmosts out of their native city and in relations with inferiors, the Spartans seem to have been more unpopular than other Greeks,

[1] Pareti, *op. cit.* p. 205. Cf. Leake, *op. cit.* III, p. 28; art. 'Skiritis' by Geyer in P.W.   [2] *Griech. Staatsr.* pp. 75 ff.

[3] A somewhat tenuous analogy may be drawn between them and the *kongelinge bonder* or king's yeomen of Denmark.

[4] *Staatsform u. Politik*, p. 231.

[5] The problem as to whether Isocrates is correct in saying the ephors could punish them without trial is discussed elsewhere, *vide* p. 158.

[6] II, p. 367 (2nd ed.).

and we may presume that a similar haughty roughness pervaded their dealings with their own Perioeki; who were bound to them certainly by no tie of affection, and who for the most part revolted after the battle of Leuktra, as soon as the invasion of Laconia by Epameinondas enabled them to do so with safety.

This is probably true, at least with regard to the Spartan attitude to the *perioeci*. The peculiar characteristics of the Spartans certainly did not endear them to other peoples; but there is nothing to show that they treated the *perioeci* with more than 'haughty roughness'. Probably the *perioeci* were used to that and took no notice of it, so long as the Spartans did them no harm. Certainly it would not have done the Spartans any good to antagonise the *perioeci*; they depended too much upon them for that. The statement of Isocrates[1] that the Spartans enslaved the souls of their *perioeci*, no less than they enslaved the bodies of their helots, need not be taken too seriously.

Unlike the Spartans, they engaged in commerce and manufacture, probably enriching themselves thereby at the expense of the aristocratic *homoioi*. No doubt this increased the scorn with which the Spartans treated them; disdain for utilitarian occupations has always been characteristic of aristocracies. As tradesmen they must have been useful; in fact the Spartans could not get on without either the *perioeci* or the helots. We hear of them making shoes, 'purple' garments (by which is obviously meant the red or purple cloaks which made up the uniform of the Spartan soldier), and objects of wood and iron.[2] When Cinadon walked round the market place and pointed out the iron instruments that would come in useful for his insurrectionaries, no doubt he was looking at the wares of the perioecic craftsmen who brought them into Sparta for sale. We know that these tradesmen were organised into hereditary guilds with epony-

---

[1] *Panath.* 178.
[2] Critias ap. Athen. XI, 76; Aristoph. *Eccles.* 542; Pliny, *Hist. Nat.* IX, 60, 3.

mous heroes as their patrons and customs of their own. 'Their heralds, musicians and cooks succeed to their fathers' professions, so that a musician is son of a musician, a cook of a cook and a herald of a herald.'[1] Those who lived on the sea-coast were doubtless fishermen, and were the best sailors in the Spartan navy; some of them rose to be admirals. We may also safely infer that the shipwrights in the navy yard at Gythium were *perioeci*.

Herodotus[2] speaks of 'many towns of the Lacedaemonians', and Strabo[3] says that formerly there were one hundred towns that sacrificed every year, but only thirty in his own day. Under Roman rule there were twenty-four towns of the 'Free Laconians'.[4] The number of one hundred may perhaps be disregarded as a rhetorical expression, just as Homer speaks of 'hundred-citied Crete'.[5] But all the same the estimate may not be so far wrong after all. We can pick out eighty of them from the classical gazetteer, the *Ethnika* of Stephanus of Byzantium. In any case the use of the word 'city' is a misnomer in the modern sense; they were at best no more than villages.

Sosibius,[6] in speaking of the *perioeci*, says that they were 'cruelly depleted by being forced to send their men into the army, and reduced to a semi-independence in a Greece where democratic ideas were always gaining ground'. They were not harshly treated, and any idea that they suffered from the supposed police methods of the central government may be dismissed. In any case it is safe to say that their existence was far more tolerable than that of the Spartans; for at least they did escape the extraordinary discipline that made of life so strange a thing for the latter.

---

[1] Herod. VI, 60.

[2] VII, 234.   [3] VIII, 4, 11 (C. 362).

[4] Paus. III, 21, 61. Aymard, *Les premiers rapports de Rome et de la confédération achaienne*, p. 250f. and map.

[5] *Il.* II, 649; cf. *Od.* XIX, 174, one hundred cities in Lacedaemon, Strabo, *ibid.* Niese, *loc. cit.* (1906), p. 101, a careful review of the evidence as to the perioecic cities.   [6] ap. Athen. XV, 674B.

THE FREE LACONIANS[1]

When, after the downfall of Nabis, Sparta was forced to join the Achaean league, perioecic towns on the coast were included. When the league was dissolved in 148, these towns did not fall again under Spartan domination, but were formed into a separate league (κοινὸν τῶν Λακεδαιμονίων).[2] Thus far the narrative of Strabo carries us, and we may suppose that these towns of the *perioeci* were made fully independent of Sparta. The point is obscured, however, by Pausanias,[3] who tells us that their liberty was finally given to them by Augustus, who formed them into the League of Free Laconians (κοινὸν τῶν Ἐλευθερολακώνων). Probably there is no conflict of evidence here and Augustus merely regulated or confirmed their liberties. The towns forming the league seem to have numbered twenty-four when first formed, but Pausanias speaks of only eighteen. Their form of government followed that of Sparta with certain minor differences and does not call for special attention.

2. The Helots

Our comprehension of the origin and status of the third class of the Lacedaemonian State, the helots, is much clearer than that of the second. They were serfs bound to the soil, *ascripti glebae*, obliged to render to their lords a certain fixed amount of the products of the land.[4] They were state serfs, the individual Spartans had no right of private possession in them and only by state action could they obtain their freedom through manumission. They possessed no political rights whatever, no freedom of movement and were constantly under suspicion of disaffection and incipient revolt. They were often harshly

[1] Gilbert, *op. cit.* p. 28. *I.G.* v, 1, p. xiv; art. 'Eleutherolakones' by Brandis in P.W.   [2] Strabo, VIII, 5, 5 (C. 366).
[3] Paus. III, 21, 6.
[4] δοῦλοι δημόσιοι, Ephorus, ap. Strabo, VIII, 5, 4 (C. 365). δοῦλοι τοῦ κοινοῦ, Paus. III, 20, 6. Cf. also Plato, *Legg.* VI, 776; Athen. VI, 263 E, 265 C.

treated, sometimes, if our information is correct, outrageously so, and were the victims of the particular attentions of the *crypteia*. But however dark a picture of their condition may be drawn, yet it is probably true to say that their condition was not entirely intolerable. Many of them prospered, some of them, because of valour in the field, were granted liberty. However harsh may have been the treatment they received at times from the State, at least they were not subject to the whims of individual lords. So long as they behaved themselves and produced their annual dues they were left alone. Certainly they never approached the wretched state that so many slaves in other countries lived in.

Practically every commentator has agreed that the helots of Laconia were the descendants of the original inhabitants of the land, non-Dorians, who had been reduced to serfdom by their conquerors.[1] In Messenia it is probable these aborigines, if we may use that term, were mixed with Dorians, which no doubt accounted for a good deal of the trouble which the Spartans had with them. This is so obvious and generally satisfying an explanation that it hardly seems necessary to seek for any other origin. But an intriguing and very interesting suggestion has been made by Kahrstedt[2] which merits careful attention. This view is that the helots were 'Dorians' and their origin had nothing whatever to do with the conquest of a non-Dorian country. They were serfs who had been reduced to that condition through debt. An exactly similar state of affairs had obtained in Attica; but there the mass of the people had been rescued from debt-slavery by the 'shaking off of burdens' or *seisachtheia* of Solon. Unfortunately no reformer such as Solon had arisen in Sparta, the richer landowners and creditors had felt no restraint upon them and the unfortunate debtors had sunk to a state of serfdom.

[1] Evidently a sharp distinction was drawn between the Laconian and Messenian helots. The former were called ἀρχαῖοι, i.e. old or of long-standing, the latter Μεσσηνιάκοι. Cf. Paus. III, 11, 8; Thuc. I, 101.

[2] *Hermes*, LIV, pp. 29 ff. Also in *Griech. Staatsr.* I, p. 57. Cf. also Niese, *loc. cit.* pp. 136 ff.

Practically all that need be said against this view is that it is extremely unlikely to be correct. All the probabilities point to the generally accepted opinion that the helots were non-Dorian aborigines who had been reduced to their condition by the conquerors. Kahrstedt's thesis can neither be proved nor disproved, and in the absence of proof by far the more satisfactory explanation is the traditional one. One argument that Kahrstedt puts forward—that helots and Spartans spoke the same language and therefore shared the same origin—is really no argument at all, or at best a very slender one. Against Kahrstedt's view it can reasonably be urged that the undoubted fact that the helots were state-owned serfs would seem to show that, on the conquest of the land, the aborigines were taken over, as captives of the State, and never lost that character. If they had been private debtors, it is far less likely that they would have belonged to the State; probably, if not certainly, they would have remained each the bondman of his creditor.

An additional argument in favour of the usual view of the origin of the helots may be derived from the probable deriva-tion of the name. All the Greek writers are notably bad etymologists, and the derivation given by Pausanias[1] that they originally were inhabitants of the town of Helos is quite fanciful and may be dismissed at once. It is most likely that helot derives from the root ἑλ- which denotes captives. It must be admitted, however, that it is not impossible that it comes from ἕλη '(dwellers in) marshy places',[2] that is, in the marshy lower courses of the river Eurotas.

The helots were bound to the land and could not move from their settlement.[3] They could neither be manumitted nor

---

[1] III, 20, 6. Cf. *Il.* II, 584.

[2] Cf. Boisacq, *Dict. Etym. de la langue grecque; s.v.* art. 'Helotae' in D.S. by Lécrivain, and 'Heloten' in P.W. by Oehler; also Hampl. 'Die laked. Periöken', *Hermes* LXXII, (1937), p. 14 n 2; Pareti, *op. cit.* p. 194.

[3] It might be plausibly suggested that the original inhabitants made their last stand in the marshes, as did Hereward the Wake in the fens of East Anglia. The helots who were freed for fighting with Brasidas were allowed to live where they liked. Thuc. V, 34.

moved from the land they occupied except by government
action.[1] So long as he paid the dues required for the upkeep
of the Spartan on his *cleros*, the helot was at liberty to make
what profit he could out of the land to which he was tied,
even to possess land himself and amass a certain amount of
wealth.[2] Plutarch[3] says that in the time of Cleomenes III
(228–219) six thousand helots were worth at least five minas
apiece. This figure should be accepted with reserve, although
there does not seem to be any particular reason for rejecting it.
Cleomenes was in need of money and to raise it he offered
freedom to those of the helots who would pay for it. In this
manner, Plutarch says, he raised 500 talents.[4] At a time when
the old political and economic system of the Spartans was in
decay, it is quite likely that many helots had enriched themselves at the expense of their impoverished masters.

Pollux[5] calls the helots 'half-slave, half-free', which describes their condition very well. Xenophon,[6] from personal
observation no doubt, says that the individual Spartan had
the right to demand the help of any helot, whether he belonged
to his *cleros* or not. Obviously this can only refer to a demand
for temporary assistance in an emergency. Whether the
Spartans employed helots in their households as domestic
servants is doubtful; although there is no reason why they

[1] Paus. III, 21, 6; Strabo, VIII, 5, 4 (C. 365); Myron, ap. Athen. XIV,
657 D; Xen. *Inst. Lac.* 239 E. Cf. Kahrstedt, *op. cit.* pp. 61 ff. The series of
inscriptions recording manumissions, *I.G.* v, 1, 1228–32, with the names of
the individuals granting freedom may refer to the ephor by whose authority
it was done. But cf. Ehrenberg, *Hermes*, LIX, p. 41, n. 3, who supposes that
the names refer to the owners of the *cleroi* whose helots were granted freedom.
The point is impossible to elucidate finally.

[2] Tyrtaeus, fr. 6, speaking of those conquered in the first Messenian war,
says they were 'like asses pressed down by heavy burdens, bearing under
grievous necessity to their masters a half of every crop that the field produces'.
This may have been a temporary exaction in the nature of a war indemnity.
We have no evidence that in later times the payment was so large.

[3] *Cleom.* XXIII.

[4] I.e. 60 minas to the talent. Both Beloch and Tarn regard this figure as
impossibly large.

[5] III, 83.   [6] *Resp. Lac.* VI, 3.

should not.[1] We do not know for certain if the Spartans possessed slaves, captured in war or purchased from abroad; but probably they did, like all other Greeks. We have no information on the point.[2] In war the helots accompanied the Spartans as batmen; but that at Plataea each of the 5000 Spartans was accompanied by seven helots is an obvious exaggeration.[3]

They were used as light-armed skirmishers (εὔζωνοι),[4] and frequently as heavy-armed hoplites. Brasidas took 700 heavy-armed helots with him to Chalcidice.[5] They were, however, untrustworthy in war,[6] which can hardly be wondered at if their bravery was rewarded by murder. In the fleet they were employed as rowers.[7] We may doubt whether helots ever attained to high office. The bitter complaints of the Thebans to the Athenians[8] on the treatment accorded other peoples by the Spartans may all have been true; but that they made helots governors or harmosts of provinces sounds like an exaggeration. The post was too eagerly sought after by Spartans to allow any rich plums to go to helots.

A difficult problem with regard to the helots is that of their treatment by their Spartan lords and their attitude towards them. Plato[9] remarks that it was the most vexed question in all Hellas, some saying that the Spartans behaved well towards them, others saying they used them ill. The probability is that, as in most cases, the truth lies between the two. When no

[1] Busolt-Swoboda, *op. cit.* p. 668, n. 5, p. 608, n. 5, and Kahrstedt, *op. cit.* I, p. 59, conclude that the helots were employed as domestic servants.

[2] The statement in Thuc. VIII, 40, that the Chians possessed more slaves than any other people except the Lacedaemonians, is inconclusive. It is most likely that Thucydides is referring to the helots. The assertion of Andreades, *History of Greek Public Finance*, p. 48, that Lysander 'introduced so much money and so many slaves that the Spartan households made one think of those in Corinth', is totally without foundation as regards the slaves.

[3] Herod. VII, 229; IX, 10. Perhaps these were the *eructeres*, but doubtful. Cf. *infra*, p. 90.

[4] Herod, IX, 28.   [5] Thuc. IV, 80; VII, 19.

[6] *Idem*, VII, 19, 58; Xen. *Hell.* III, 1; V, 2; VI, 1.

[7] Xen. *Hell.* VII, 1.   [8] *Ibid.* III, 5, 12.

[9] *Legg.* VI, 776C.

danger was apprehended from them, no doubt the Spartans treated them tolerably well; at least so far as the arrogant and overbearing manner of the overlord permitted them to do so.

In a land where the serfs vastly outnumbered the upper class it was obviously politic not to press too hardly upon them, nor to drive them to despair. But that is not to say that at the slightest sign of disaffection the most ruthless methods of suppression were not used. That we may well believe, and certainly at times these measures must have been cruel to an extreme. For instance, we have the statement of Thucydides[1] as to the murder of 2000 of the bravest in 424. This act, carried out under circumstances of the most atrocious perfidy, must have been, if true, the panic-stricken measure of a government which feared the worst, and struck ruthlessly and at whatever cost. In any case the whole affair is mysterious, as Thucydides frankly acknowledges. Probably the 700 that Brasidas took to Chalcidice came from that number, and undoubtedly they were not murdered as we hear of them engaged at the first battle of Mantinea.

Aristotle, according to Plutarch,[2] says that every year the ephors formally declared war on the helots, so that any murderous onslaughts on them might be legalized. Grote[3] very reasonably doubts this, pointing out that it is hardly likely that Aristotle would have failed to comment upon so remarkable a practice in his *Politics*. But Aristotle is not entirely to be trusted; it is quite evident that his knowledge of Spartan customs was imperfect in several respects. Xenophon says nothing of it, although it must be admitted that he says next to nothing about the helots in general. It is quite likely that, if this declaration of war upon the helots was actually made every year, it was a part of an archaic ritual, dating from the earliest perilous times of the Spartan State, which had become meaningless as national security was achieved. In any

---

[1] IV, 80. A very mysterious incident which baffled Thucydides. Probably the number is grossly exaggerated.

[2] *Lyc.* XXVIII.   [3] II, p. 378 (2nd ed.).

case the significance of the custom need not be magnified overmuch. As we shall see hereafter,[1] there are good reasons to suppose that the deeds of the 'secret police' or *crypteia* in holding down incipient rebellion through assassination have been exaggerated.

The statements of Myron of Priene[2] of the shameful treatment of the helots need not be taken too literally. If it is true that some of them were given an annual flogging, to encourage the rest of them to adopt a proper state of mind, we need only to remark that the Spartans flogged their own youths much more cruelly. The statement that they wore a distinctive dress is not particularly impressive as a sign of humiliating regulations imposed upon them. They wore a dogskin cap and a leather jerkin, we are told. But so did every country-dweller in Greece. That any helot who gave evidence of physical vigour exceeding that of a slave was put to death and their owners punished for allowing them to grow fat, may be dismissed at once. Lastly, the statement that 'after handing over to the helots land to work the Spartans required a certain share of the crops which the helots were always to render to them' is correct. If Plutarch[3] is right, and we have no grounds for doubting him, this entailed no hardship. 'The helots tilled the soil, paying a return regularly settled in advance. The Spartan lords were not allowed to let their land for a higher price, in order that the helots might make a profit and so be glad to work for their masters, and the masters might not look for a greater return.' It was an integral part of the system of serfdom.

Plutarch[4] says that sometimes the helots were made drunk

[1] *Vide infra*, p. 162.
[2] ap. Athen. XIV, 657 D. Cf. Müller, *Doric Race*, II, pp. 37f.
[3] *Inst. Lac.* 239 E.
[4] *Demetrius* I. *Lyc.* XXVIII. Cf. Plato, *Legg.* VII, 816 D. Müller rejects the whole story as being quite absurd and suggests that the grotesque dance, the *mothon*, was mistaken for drunkenness. This may be so, but little is known of this dance and it is not perfectly sure that it was performed by helots. Müller, *op. cit.* II, p. 39. For further comment on *mothon*, *vide infra*, p. 189.

to serve as a warning against insobriety to the Spartan youth, which is probably untrue. But no doubt suitable subjects for this exhibition could easily be found. Both Aelian and Pausanias[1] say that the helots were compelled to mourn the death of a king and attend the funerals of their masters. Neither of these obligations would seem to be very onerous or degrading. Every Spartan was obliged to go into mourning at the death of a king, and probably the helots regarded a funeral as a welcome break in the day's work. Busolt's statement,[2] that while in Thessaly and Athens a master could not kill a slave 'this lawful protection the helots did not enjoy', must be carefully understood. If a helot could not be moved from his place of settlement by his master without the sanction of the government, it is perfectly sure that much less could the master put him to death at discretion. But the State could, and frequently did, murder the helots without any pretence of legality.

The truth would seem to be that accounts of bad treatment are exaggerated. Myron of Priene is an author of very doubtful accuracy, and in any case on examination his statements are seen to be of little importance. In all times and places a system of serfdom has given rise to abuses which we need not suppose were lacking in Sparta. That the system existed there for centuries and persisted into Roman times[3] is sufficient evidence that it could not have been intolerable. The helots were necessary to their masters to till the soil; to have made their existence impossibly miserable would have been bad policy. A certain amount of leniency was absolutely necessary, otherwise the system would have broken down under its own weight of discontent and misery.

But that is not to say that in the helots the Spartans did not face a constant menace. Thucydides[4] says that 'at all times most

---

[1] Ael. *V.H.* VI, 1; Paus. IV, 14, 5.
[2] Busolt-Swoboda, *op. cit.* II, p. 669.
[3] Strabo, VIII, 5, 4 (C. 365).
[4] IV, 80. Cf. also I, 132; IV, 41, 55; V, 14; VII, 26.

of the Lacedaemonian institutions were framed particularly with a view to guarding against them'. Whenever the Spartan State was in danger trouble might be expected from the helots. At least twice during the Persian war attempts were made to raise the serfs against their lords, first by Cleomenes I and later by Pausanias. Apparently both insurrections were abortive, although it must be acknowledged that our information is very slender. But quite certainly the great earthquake of 464 was followed by a very serious helot rising. The disaster at Pylos in 425 gave an opportunity for what must have been large-scale desertion to the Athenians, and the alleged mass murder of 2000 of them in 424 is obviously an echo of this critical period in Spartan affairs. When peace was declared in 421, two articles of the treaty were significant. In return for Amphipolis the Athenians were to withdraw the Messenians and helots they had used in garrisoning Pylos. We are told that later these deserters were settled at Cranii in Cephallenia. The second article of significance was that, if the 'slaves' should rise, the Athenians should come to the assistance of the Spartans.[1] Evidently a serious insurrection was feared, which might tax the powers of the Spartans so much to put down that outside help would become necessary.

After Leuctra, when Messenia was lost to the Spartans, all the Messenian *perioeci* and helots became freemen of a hostile state; or at least we must suppose that the Messenian helots did not continue in a state of serfdom. But it is significant to note that we hear of no disaffection among the Laconian helots. That this loyalty was induced simply by fear of their Spartan masters cannot be true, because we are told that 6000 were drafted into the army.[2] If they had been dangerously disaffected, it is hardly likely that the Spartans would have done so risky a thing as to arm them. A force of that size might

---

[1] Thuc. IV, 41; V, 14, 23.
[2] Xen. *Ages.* II, 24, and *Hell.* VII, 2, 2, says all the helots. This does not agree with *Hell.* VI, 5, 28, where the 6000 are added to the army. The first two passages must refer to the Messenian, the last to the Laconian helots.

easily have overturned the State had it chosen to rebel. The truth is that the Messenian helots were always troublesome; not primarily because of their economic and social disabilities, but rather because they were Messenians and resented the Spartan domination. Laconian helots were certainly tolerably well treated and, as we know, were not unprosperous. They were serfs who, so long as they behaved themselves and paid their seigneurial dues to their lords, were left alone. For Aristotle[1] to say that the helots were 'perpetually revolting' is an exaggeration. The words of Grote sum up their condition very well:

The various anecdotes which are told respecting their treatment at Sparta, betoken less of cruelty than of ostentatious scorn—a sentiment which we are noway surprised to discover among the citizens of the mess-table.

As we remark elsewhere,[2] the statement of Plutarch that young Spartans were sent out into the country parts to lie in wait for innocent and unsuspecting helots and murder them in cold blood, is so monstrous as to be utterly incredible. But the last we hear of them seems to fit into the pattern. When Nabis was in desperate straits at the invasion of Sparta by the Romans he guarded against 'fifth column' dangers, and the helots he suspected he had scourged through the streets and later murdered.[3]

3. THE INFERIORS

Sparta, like every other land in the ancient world, or in the modern for the matter of that, where slavery is part of its economy, was plagued and even sometimes seriously imperilled by the various sorts of 'inferiors'—not slaves but not citizens. In the case of Sparta the various classes of 'inferiors' provide some very difficult problems to elucidate. We have already

[1] *Pol.* 1272B. [2] *Infra*, p. 162.
[3] Livy, XXXIV, 27.

spoken of the *mothaces*; it will be necessary to start again and go back very far in Spartan history and examine what was meant by the term *Partheniai*.

THE PARTHENIAI

Some time after the close of the first Messenian war there occurred the incident of the so-called 'insurrection' of the Partheniai and the colonisation by them of Tarentum.[1] The story seems to be a simple and straightforward one at first glance: further examination reveals it as decidedly queer and to be involved in serious difficulties.

When the Spartans marched out to conquer Messenia they vowed they would never return home until final victory. The war lasted for nineteen years and there were heavy casualties, so the Spartan women were left without husbands and the birth rate fell alarmingly. To remedy this it was decreed they should seek temporary unions, and from these a numerous progeny resulted. After the close of the war those who had been born from these irregular unions and who were called Partheniai, sons of unmarried or legally virgin mothers, were looked down upon, refused Spartan citizenship and denied *cleroi* in conquered Messenia. This so enraged them that a conspiracy was planned to overturn the government, the uprising to take place at the time of the festival of the Hyacinthia.[2] Their leader was Phalanthus, who was either a traitor or whose courage failed at the last moment, and the plot was revealed to the authorities. Evidently the number involved was so great that summary justice could not safely

[1] Lenschau, in *Bursian's Jahresberichte*, CCXVIII (1928), p. 17, wants to put the founding of Tarentum before the first Messenian war. The probabilities seem to favour a date after the war. Studniczka, *Kyrene*, p. 175, rejects the whole story; also Strabo, VI, 3, 2; Athen. VI, 271 C, D; Justin, III, 4, XX, 1; Arist. *Pol.* 1306 B; Paus. X, 10; Diod. Sic. VIII, 21; Xen. *Resp. Lac.* I, 7; Plut. *Lyc.* XV; Polybius, XII, 5, 6.

[2] Gilbert, *op. cit.* p. 19, suggests that the mysterious *Aegeidai*, as being sacerdotally connected with this festival, were involved in the conspiracy and in consequence were expelled from Sparta. There seems to be no evidence to substantiate this conjecture

be exercised on them and recourse was had to emigration. Phalanthus was sent to Delphi to seek advice. He wanted to take his fellow conspirators to Sicyon, but the oracle advised Tarentum, no doubt as being farther off and so safer for both the emigrants and the Spartan government. This he did and a Spartan colony was founded in Magna Graecia.

The narrative, so far, seems to be perfectly straightforward. If we are to accept at its face value the account given by Plutarch[1] of the somewhat startling 'eugenic' marriage customs, or rather extra-marriage customs of the Spartans, we need not be unduly sceptical of the story. There was always an urgent necessity to keep up the numbers of the Spartan peers, and there was also the deeply ingrained desire not to let a family die out. Something drastic must, therefore, be done and this plan was carried out in true Spartan fashion.

But when we examine the story a little more closely, very serious difficulties in accepting it as it stands appear. In the first place, who were the fathers of these Partheniai? Theopompus[2] says they were helots, who as a reward for their services were subsequently made citizens under the name of *epeunactai*. He adds that a similar class called *catonacophori* were found in Sicyon. This, it may be parenthetically remarked, perhaps explains why Phalanthus wanted to go there. But can we accept this version? It seems strange to think that the wives and daughters of the proud Spartans should have been subjected, willingly or unwillingly, to what must have been a degradation. That these helot fathers were made citizens, full Spartan peers, we may very seriously doubt. If we are to accept this story at all, we should suppose that they were given their freedom from servitude but nothing further.[3]

But, far from being helots, we are told by Aristotle[4] that these irregular fathers were Spartans who, for one reason or another, had not gone to the Messenian war but remained in

---

[1] *Lyc.* 15.   [2] ap. Athen. VI, 271 C.
[3] I.e. they entered the class of *neodamodeis*, about whom *vide infra*, p. 90.
[4] Arist. *Pol.* 1306 B. ἐκ τῶν ὁμοίων γὰρ ἦσαν.

Sparta. Perhaps they were old or disabled; we are left to wonder, however, why they were punished and their offspring denied full citizenship and a share in the spoils of Messenia if they had merely obeyed the orders of the government. Ephorus in the same passage in Strabo gives quite a different version of the affair. According to him the Spartans who had gone to Messenia had vowed never to return until victory had been won. But after ten years had passed, the women of Sparta complained that there were no husbands left and that the whole future of the Spartans was endangered as no children were being born. So the youngest and most vigorous of the men at the front, who had not taken the oath not to return because at the time, ten years before, they had been too young to do so, were sent back and bidden to cohabit with the women. When the main body of the army got back after another nine years they found the children of these unions growing up and refused to give them lots in Messenia. The plot of Phalanthus followed and, fearing it would become formidable, they sent the malcontents off to Tarentum, but promised that if they were not satisfied there they could return to Sparta and receive one-fifth of Messenia.

All three stories as they stand are unsatisfactory. We must suppose that the distribution of Messenian land took place immediately after the war, when, according to the version of Ephorus, these Partheniai must have been about eight years old; this hardly accords with the picture of a serious political situation which could only be composed by drastic means. The whole story of these youths being born while the Spartan men were away is very difficult to credit and we must fall back on another explanation. All through Spartan history there were 'inferiors', who were not full Spartan citizens and were for one reason or another excluded from the ranks of the *homoioi*. Many of them, no doubt, were illegitimate—the children of Spartan fathers and helot mothers. It is much more difficult to suppose that there were many of Spartan mothers and helot fathers. But whoever they were, these 'inferiors', insultingly dubbed Partheniai, received no part of the spoils of Messenia and were numerous enough to form a menace to the Spartan State and so were got rid of. An exact parallel is to be found in the conspiracy of Cinadon after the close of the Peloponnesian war, which was stopped before it had a chance of becoming dangerous.

The story that these Partheniai were the offspring of irregular connections during the first Messenian war must be rejected, the probabilities against its being true are far too great. It is another example of those numerous stories which on reflection are seen to be impossible as they stand.[1]

OTHER INFERIORS

Later in Spartan history, we are confronted with a number of apparently different classes who were neither slaves, helots, *perioeci* nor full Spartan peers. It is evident that some of them were descendants of former Spartan *homoioi* who had fallen in the social scale. The reason for their fall is very hard to tell; but they or their fathers must have suffered some disgrace or misfortune and could no longer claim full equality with the other Spartans. Others clearly were freedmen, helots who, for some meritorious service to the State, had been rewarded with their freedom. What these various classes were must now occupy our attention.

The term *hypomeiones*,[2] used only once, would seem to be a generic term to denote all those who, not being helots, were not on the same social footing as the peers. Cinadon, on being

---

[1] Szanto, art. 'Epeunaktoi' in P.W., regards the story as a variant of the expulsion of the Minyae in Herod. iv, 145. Eduard Meyer, *Geschichte des Altertums*, ii, p. 478, says we know no more about the Partheniai than did the ancients and that historically the whole story is worthless. Nilsson, *Klio*, xii, pp. 308 ff., while deeply suspicious of the story, thinks it is not impossible and may have some basis of historical fact. Busolt, *Griech. Gesch.* i, p. 407, with his usual thoroughness collects all the evidence, but refuses to come to any conclusion. Cf. Busolt-Swoboda, *op. cit.* ii, p. 658, n. 1. Kahrstedt, *op. cit.* p. 42, ignores the Partheniai.

[2] Xen. *Hell.* iii, 3, 6.

asked why he had plotted against the State, replied that he did not wish to be 'inferior' to anyone in Sparta. The parallel between the insurrection of the Partheniai and the abortive rising of the *hypomeiones* is very close. In both cases they were protests against the exclusiveness of the privileged class. Toynbee[1] suggests that the *hypomeiones* were those young Spartans who, by being blackballed, had failed to gain entrance into a *syssition*. This is hard to credit, since the dwindling numbers of the Spartans, even at the beginning of the fourth century, would have made for a deficiency of candidates for entrance to a *syssition* rather than an excess. Busolt more plausibly suggests they were those who could not pay their dues to the *syssitia*.

MOTHACES

The *mothaces* were undoubtedly young helots who had been the playmates and, we must assume, had shared to some degree in the training and education of the Spartan boys. As we have already seen, it is very doubtful if they ever attained citizenship except under extraordinary circumstances. The other name applied to them, *mothones*, may have been derisory in describing their impudent behaviour. In Aristophanes[2] Mothon is the god of impudence and elsewhere the word is used to denote a vulgar dance. It is not quite certain who were the *trophimoi* alluded to by Xenophon.[3] Among those who went on the expedition to Olynthus with King Agesipolis in 380

---

[1] *J.H.S.* XXXIII (1913), p. 261. Busolt-Swoboda, *op. cit.* p. 659, n. 4. Cf. also Kahrstedt, *op. cit.* pp. 50 ff.

[2] Aristoph. *Equites*, 635, 695; Schol. ad 697; and Schol. ad *Plutus*, 279; Euripides, *Bacchae*, 1060.

[3] *Hell*, v, 3, 9. Art. 'Trophimoi', by Ehrenberg in P.W. Kahrstedt, *op. cit.* p. 53. But for a totally different explanation, cf. Cantarelli, 'I Motaci Spartani', *Rivista di philologia*, XVIII (1890), pp. 465 ff, who tries, not with complete success, to demonstrate that the *mothaces* were sons of *perioeci* who had been brought up in the Spartan discipline while the *mothones* were sons of slaves. Cantarelli's interpretation was destructively criticised by von Schoeffer in *Phil. Woch.* XI (1891), 1013. Suidas, Hesychius and the *Etym. Mag.*, *s.v.* Μόθωνες, all say that they were slaves of the Spartans.

were 'many of the *perioeci*; men of honour and respectability, as well as many strangers of those called *trophimoi*, and illegitimate children of the Spartans, persons of excellent appearance and not unacquainted with the honourable discipline of the State'. This would seem to suggest that the *trophimoi* were sons of foreigners who had been sent to Sparta for their education, as for instance the two sons of Xenophon. Naturally they would not become Spartan citizens.

NEODAMODEIS

With regard to one class we can speak with greater certainty. Helots who had been given their freedom by the State for some meritorious action were called *neodamodeis*.[1] It seems certain that they never attained to the status of peer, but in return for their freedom were liable for military service. Their number must have been considerable, for Agesilaus took 2000 of them to Asia,[2] and we hear of them as engaged in all major military operations.[3] Their position in the Spartan army will be considered more fully hereafter.[4]

The conclusion at which we must arrive is that the numbers of the *homoioi* were very severely restricted and entrance to their order was either impossible or extremely difficult. Beneath them were a number of nondescripts—freemen who, for one reason or another, were excluded from the superior class and enjoyed none of the political or social privileges which pertained to the peers. More than that would be unwise to say.

Myron of Priene[5] tells us that the Spartans often freed their slaves, 'calling some *aphetai* [released], some *adespotoi* [masterless], some *eructeres* [controllers] and others *desposionautai* [master-seamen], the last being assigned to the navy'. Evidently the first two were nicknames and did not constitute distinct classes of freedmen. With regard to the *eructeres*, anybody's

---

[1] Thuc. VII, 58; Pollux, III, 83.   [2] Xen. *Hell.* III, 4, 2; Plut. *Ages.* 6.
[3] Thuc. VII, 19; VIII, 5; Xen. *Hell.* I, 3, 15; III, 1, 4; 4, 20; V, 2, 24.
[4] *Vide infra*, p. 251.   [5] ap. Athen. VI, 271 E.

guess is as good as another. Müller[1] thought they were stretcher-bearers who brought the wounded off the battlefield. Kahrstedt[2] thinks they were squires who accompanied their masters to war and had been given their freedom for having saved their lives on the battlefield. Neither of these suggestions can be substantiated. Perhaps the most likely explanation of these mysterious freedmen is that they were policemen who served under the command of the *epimeletes*.[3] We know that in Athens the policemen were slaves, the famous Scythian archers. The *desposionautai* evidently had something to do with the navy. Possibly they were helots who for gallantry in action had been given their freedom and acted as petty officers in the fleet. We know that helots were employed as rowers.

BRASIDEIOI

The 700 helots taken in Chalcidice by Brasidas and given their freedom for gallantry in the field were called Brasideioi. Evidently they were an exceptional class. We have one important piece of information about them—that they were allowed to live wherever they pleased,[4] and were no longer tied to the *cleroi* of their masters. We do not know to what occupation they betook themselves; perhaps they were some of the tradesmen and artisans of which we hear, or perhaps policemen or marines. But whatever it was, they must have left their original settlement; obviously they could not continue as tillers of the soil on the *cleroi* of their former masters. It is not without significance to note that, later in the same passage, Thucydides tells us that these same Brasideioi, and others of the *neodamodeis*, were subsequently settled at Lepreon on the borders of Laconia and Elis. It is tempting to conjecture that they attained the status of *perioeci*; but it is impossible to come to any conclusion on that point.

---

[1] *Op. cit.* II, p. 35. Cf. Xen. *Hell.* IV, 5, 14.
[2] *Op. cit.* p. 54 n. 2. [3] *Vide infra*, p. 148.
[4] Thuc. V, 34.

JEWS AND SPARTANS[1]

A passage in the first Book of Maccabees[2] merits passing mention. The High Priest Onias writes to King Areus of Sparta[3] saying that Jews and Spartans are brethren of the stock of Abraham, 'Therefore your cattle and goods are ours and ours yours'. Later in the middle of the second century B.C. Jonathan sent ambassadors to Sparta to renew the bonds of friendship and brotherhood,[4] and a few years later Simon sent another embassy, and a note in reply was sent to him by the ephors.

The incident is curious and its authenticity is not wholly beyond question. There seems certain proof that a settlement of Jews had been made in Sparta, for in 168 B.C. Jason the high priest fled there,[5] and the letter of Lucius Calpurnius Piso in 139 B.C. proves this.[6] Oesterley[7] rejects the whole thing on the ground that examination of the passage in the Book of Maccabees shows that it is an interpolation. Vailhe,[8] on the other hand, accepts the incident as genuine. Even if the literary sources are confused, there seems, in his view, no valid reason for rejecting it. No definite conclusion can be reached upon the subject. It is not unlikely that the Jews had heard of the Spartans as a people with a remarkable discipline and may have thought, quite erroneously, that it resembled their own way of life and that the Spartans were of their own stock, perhaps one of the 'lost' ten tribes. The incident occurred at a time of great peril for the Jews, and it is quite likely they were looking round for possible allies or an eventual place of refuge if things went against them.

[1] M. D. Ginsburg, 'Sparta and Judaea', *Class. Phil.* XXIX (1934), p. 117.

[2] I Macc. xii. 21–3. Cf. Joseph. *Jud. Antiq.* XII, 225.

[3] The King Areus must be Areus I who reigned from 309 to 265.

[4] Joseph. *Jud. Antiq.* 5, 8.　　[5] II Macc. v. 9.　　[6] I Macc. xv. 16–23.

[7] W. O. E. Oesterley, *History of Israel*, II, p. 256, n. 3.

[8] *Catholic Encyc.* XVI, p. 209. Cf. also art. 'Sparta' by Ehrenberg in P.W.; Renan, *Histoire du peuple d'Israel*, IV, p. 405; W. S. Ferguson, *Greek Imperialism*, p. 80. Undoubtedly some of their observances were alike, e.g. the remarkable resemblance of the feast of the Carneia to that of Tabernacles; *vide infra*, p. 99.

CHAPTER IV

THE SPARTAN CONSTITUTION (I)

TRIBES, KINGS AND EPHORS

CONSTITUTIONAL FORMS

Whatever philosophers and observers thought of other things in Sparta, they were all united in praise of its constitution. Even Aristotle, although he has some severe things to say about some of its manifestations of which he disapproves, on the whole is constrained to a general approval of its character. The Stoics were loud in its praise; the oligarchs and aristocrats of other countries even louder. It seemed to them the ideal form of government.

As was to be expected, it was thought to be the work of one man, Lycurgus, or perhaps some other king or philosopher. That was always the way in which men used to think of law and order; it must be of divine origin—like the Ten Commandments written by the finger of God. In fact, it is obviously a survival of an earlier and simpler stage of social development. We see the conquering tribesmen settling down in their new lands, and faced with the necessity of adapting their old forms of leadership to new conditions. While they were in their wandering, conquering stage, they were led by their tribal chieftains, to whom was confided the supreme leadership on the battlefield. The great questions that concerned them all, of peace or war, were settled by the muster of all the warriors of the tribes, who gathered together and shouted 'Yes' or 'No' to what was proposed to them. The chiefs had their council of wise men, elders and men of especial renown and valour, and these formed with the chiefs the executive that carried out the policy approved by the warriors as a whole.

This was a simple and, so far as it went, a highly effective form of leadership. Could it be transferred to a settled economy, when the tribes were no longer on the move and all the more complicated and harassing questions had to be met and solved somehow: questions of property in land, the domination of a subject race of aborigines, relations with other peoples beyond their borders, and all the intricate economic problems that pressed upon a settled state?

These questions were answered in Sparta slowly and painfully. It was no easy thing to resolve all their difficulties and we hear of a period of troubles, of κακονομία, of anarchy and internal strife, before they were all reduced to order.[1] The animosities were allayed, not by a new form of government, violently imposed, such as a tyranny or a democracy had forced on other distracted peoples, but by a strengthening of the ancient forms of tribal leadership—chiefs, elders and warriors —and later by the addition of a fourth, the ephorate, that was to hold the balance between the other three. In the assumption of power by the ephorate—a college of governors annually elected by popular vote—was found the final solution to the constitutional difficulties that were distracting the State. The ancient forms were preserved so that continuity was not lost; but the primitive simplicity of government was modified and made conformable with later and more complicated needs. It is not to be wondered at that the Spartan constitution excited the interest of ancient and modern observers alike.

THE SPARTAN GOVERNMENT

With regard to the form of government in Sparta we are well informed. We know that there were two kings; at first sight a strange phenomenon, on closer examination it proves to be by no means unique. We might, therefore, call Sparta a limited dyarchy; but since the constitutional powers of the kings were so severely limited as to be almost non-existent, such a term would be far from correct if applied to the government without qualification. Secondly, there were the ephors,

[1] The parallel between the time of anarchy among the Children of Israel on the breakdown of the judgeship and the creation of the monarchy is very striking.

the college of five magistrates elected annually by popular vote. Their executive powers were very extensive, so much so that we might feel justified in calling Sparta a bureaucracy. We should, however, hesitate to do so when we remember the existence of the Senate or *Gerousia*, an elected body of elders whose powers were also far from negligible. And lastly, we have the popular General Assembly or *Ecclesia* to which every Spartan *homoios* in good standing belonged by right of birth. We know that the powers of the *Ecclesia* were limited to a consultative capacity, but nevertheless it certainly functioned, and the gravest issues of state were within its jurisdiction.

Where, then, did sovereignty lie in the Spartan constitution? We are puzzled by the use of several terms, τὰ τέλη, οἱ οἴκοι, οἱ οἴκοι ἄρχοντες, τὰ οἴκοι τέλη and οἱ ἐν τέλει ὄντες[1] which clearly mean the highest authority in the Spartan system of government. Several commentators have identified these terms with the ephors alone: while others have thought them to refer to the kings, ephors, senators and the General Assembly in plenary session. The latter view would seem to be more correct. A passage in Xenophon on this point is almost conclusive. The Spartans are quarrelling with the Eleians and, being exasperated on this account, the ephors and assembly of the people, οἱ ἔφοροι καὶ ἡ ἐκκλησία, resolved to bring them to their senses. Sending ambassadors, therefore, to Elis they told what seemed fitting to the government (τὰ τέλη) of the Lacedaemonians. The point seems clear that τὰ τέλη and οἱ ἐν τέλει ὄντες are generic terms denoting the government, just as in Great Britain the term 'the Government' may be applied either to the cabinet or to the whole executive and administrative forces in existence.

How exactly to classify the constitution of Sparta puzzled the philosophers. Plato is hard put to it to call it either

---

[1] Xen. *Hell.* III, 2, 23; *Anab.* II, 6, 2–4; Plut. *Lys.* 14. Cf. Gilbert, *Grk. Const. Ant.* p. 54, n. 3, for full discussion of the difficulty. Also Kahrstedt, *Griech. Staatsr.* pp. 205, 282ff.; B. Fleischanderl, *Die spartanische Verfassung bei Xenophon*, pp. 39ff.

a democracy or a tyranny, as it partook of both.[1] But he is
happy to think that in any case the most vicious aspects of
either are wanting, and what was best in democracy and
tyranny happily blended. Aristotle,[2] as might be expected,
goes more deeply into the problem and arrives at the conclusion that it is 'a happy mixture of a democracy and an
oligarchy'. 'Many affirm that it is a democracy from the
many particulars in which it follows that form of government.'
These are the common form of education and discipline and
the lack of any distinction between rich and poor. 'Moreover
in respect to two magistracies of the highest rank, one they
have a right to fill by election and the other to fill, namely
the Senate and the ephorate.'[3] But others consider it an
oligarchy 'the principles of which it follows in many
particulars, as for instance in the choice of officials by vote
and not by lot', and that 'there are only a few who have the
right to sit in judgement on capital causes and the like'. By
the last he is referring to the fact that criminal jurisdiction
was the prerogative of the ephors and senators, as will be
seen hereafter. Isocrates[4] was sure it was a democracy and
that the Lacedaemonians were the best governed of peoples
because they were the most democratic. 'For in their selection
of magistrates, in their daily life and in their habits in general,
we may see that the principles of equity and equality have
greater influence than elsewhere in the world—principles to
which oligarchies are hostile, while well-ordered democracies
practise them continually.' Cicero[5] was much more cautious
and would not be more definite than to say that the Spartan
constitution was 'mixta'.

It is quite certain that the form of government was purely
oligarchical, the oligarchy in this case being the privileged
body of Spartan peers. That there were obviously 'democratic'
aspects within the oligarchy makes no difference whatever;

[1] *Legg.* IV, 712 D.   [2] *Pol.* 1294 B.
[3] For discussion of this difficult passage *vide infra*, p. 125.
[4] *Areopag.* LXI (152).   [5] *De rep.* II, 23.

no oligarchy could function at all without them, since all the members of the privileged caste must have equal rights.

As a matter of actual experience, the constitutional system of the Spartan State was an excellent one, and escaped many of the weaknesses and dangers of that extreme form of democracy found in Athens and in democracies of the present day. Whatever vicious aspects were to be found in it arose, not so much from its own inherent peculiarities, but rather from the weaknesses innate in the Spartans themselves; and whatever there was of strength sprang from the virtues of the people whom it ruled. A careful analysis of the Spartan system of government will reveal both of these aspects very clearly.

THE SPARTAN TRIBES

We know that there were originally among the Dorian invaders of Laconia three main tribes—the Hylleis, Dymanes and Pamphyloi.[1] These tribes evidently continued for some considerable time after the conquest, for we hear of them in the war-poems of Tyrtaeus.[2] At some time after the suppression of the Messenian revolt, and for some unknown reason, this threefold division gave place to another and smaller division into clans, 'septs' or tribes—the Latin *gentes*—variously named, as far as we know, as komes, phyles, phratries and obes. It seems fairly clear that the first three names are interchangeable and signify the same thing.[3] But what the last, the *oba*, was and what its relation to the komes or phyles, is by no means clear and provides us with a puzzle which is almost insoluble.

The first difficulty we encounter is in the number and names of these komes or phyles. Pausanias[4] mentions four,

[1] Herod. v, 68; Steph. Byz. *s.v.* Ὑλλέες, Δυμᾶνες. Müller, *Doric Race*, III, 5, 2; art. 'Dymanes', by Szanto in P.W.
[2] In *Elegy and Iambus* (Loeb ed.), p. 59.
[3] The conclusion of Busolt-Swoboda, *Griech. Staatsk.* II, p. 645.
[4] Paus. III, 16, 9. Konosoura or Konooura.

Limnai, Mesoa, Pitane and Konosoura. But to these Hesychius adds a fifth, Dyme. The last is very dubious, since it occurs nowhere else and the evidence of so late a writer as Hesychius is suspect. In Roman times there were six, Amyclae and Neapolis having been added to the four of Pausanias.[1] We are therefore left with the names of six and perhaps seven komes* which, at one time or another, made up the major divisions of the people.

The case for the four tribes of Pausanias is certainly a strong one, and we are tempted to perceive in it the explanation of the mysterious number of twenty-eight senators or *gerontes*, seven from each tribe.[2] But this is a very wild conjecture and must be disregarded. The case for five tribes is much stronger. The number five (or multiples of five) is constantly cropping up and must be significant. For instance, there were five ephors and five *agathoergi*.[3] There were fifteen commissioners to sign the peace of Nicias,[4] and to negotiate the surrender of Athens in 404.[5] In the great earthquake of 464 only five houses were left standing, one for each tribe, which is probably a picturesque exaggeration but is none the less significant in this context.[6]

But if there were five komes and not four, what was the name of the fifth? We have to choose between three—Dyme, Amyclae and Neapolis. Busolt[7] suggests that it may have been Dyme, but that with the dwindling numbers of Spartans it died out and that Cleomenes III founded a new one,

[1] Amyclae, *I.G.* v, 26. Neapolis, *I.G.* v, 677, 680. The problem of what exactly is conveyed by the term *Neopolitai* is far from easy. Tod, *A.B.S.A.* x, p. 77, asks whether it referred to those living in 'Sparta New Town' or to those citizens newly admitted to civic rights and thereby posted to a tribe made up of similar new citizens. He inclines to the latter. Cf. Diod. Sic. xiv, 7, 4; Athen. iv, 138 A. Wade-Gery, *Class. Quart.* xxxviii, p. 120.

[2] The problem is discussed more fully elsewhere. Cf. p. 137.

[3] Herod. i, 67.

[4] Thuc. v, 19. The two kings also signed to make seven in all.

[5] Xen. *Hell.* ii, 4, 38; but Aristotle says ten. *Ath. Pol.* xxxviii, 4.

[6] Plut. *Cimon*, 16; Polyaenus, i, 41, 3; Aelian, *V.H.* vi, 7.

[7] *Griech. Staatsk.* ii, p. 645.

Neapolis. This is not impossible, but is incapable of proof and it must be pointed out that the evidence for Dyme is very slender. There is little doubt that Neapolis was of late Hellenistic origin, although, as Mr Wade-Gery points out,[1] there is no certain proof on that score. We are left, therefore, with Amyclae, and for it the evidence is much stronger. The town was only three miles from the city of Sparta and, while we cannot definitely conclude that it was wholly Spartan and not a 'pocket' of *perioeci*, yet it would seem only reasonable to suppose it was. Again in the inscription,[2] admittedly of Roman times, it is described as an *oba*, while Geronthrai, a town also mentioned, is not. We may, therefore, with due caution, conclude that Amyclae was probably the fifth.[3]

A passage from Demetrius of Scepsis[4] remains to be noticed briefly. He says there were nine phyles and twenty-seven phratries. But here he is referring exclusively to arrangements for the feast of the Carneia, when tents or sunshades (σκιάδες) were erected, each to shelter nine men. Each *skias* held three brotherhoods or phratries, and the festival lasted nine days. Evidently this was a special arrangement confined solely to the feast. Thomson, in his article 'The Greek Calendar' in the *Journal of Hellenic Studies*,[5] referring to this feast, points out that nine was a sacred number in Minoan-Mycenaean religion and was clearly connected with the octennium. The whole problem is highly obscure.

If we are in some doubt as to tribes or phyles, we are in still greater in an attempt to solve the problem as to what was the

[1] *Class. Quart.* XXXVIII, p. 120, n. 7.

[2] *I.G.* v. 1, 27.

[3] Pareti in *Rendiconti della R. Accademia dei Lincei*, XIX (1910), pp. 455 ff., suggests there were always six, the original four of Pausanias with Dyme and Neapolis. This ignores Amyclae. *Vide* also Kahrstedt, *op. cit.* pp. 18 ff.

[4] ap. Athen. IV, 141 E, F. Cf. Kahrstedt, *op. cit.* p. 70 and Tod, *A.B.S.A.* x (1903), p. 75.

[5] *J.H.S.* LXIII (1943), p. 64. The resemblance to the Jewish Feast of Tabernacles is striking. Both were harvest festivals. For further on the feast in Sparta *vide* Farnell, *Greek Hero Cults*, IV, p. 259; S. Wide, *Lakonische Külte*, p. 81.

oba.[1] Beyond the fact that it was a division of the people of very ancient origin we know little. That it was not identical with the phyle or kome seems certain from the *rhetra* quoted by Plutarch.[2] The Delphic Oracle was supposed to have told Lycurgus to inaugurate the *Gerousia* in the following terms:

After having built a temple to Zeus Syllanius and Athene Syllania, and having 'phyled the phyles' (φυλὰς φυλάξαντα) and 'obed the obes' (ὠβὰς ὠβάξαντα) you shall establish a council of thirty elders, the leaders included.

Apparently the passage is corrupt. If φυλὰς φυλάξαντα mean anything they must mean 'having guarded or preserved the phyles'. This is at least intelligible. But ὠβὰς ὠβάξαντα are very strange words. Yet, however much we may hesitate in our literal interpretation of those words, it is not difficult to get the general sense. What the *rhetra* means is that, after the people had been divided according to their different tribes, phyles and obes, they shall take in hand the inauguration of a settled form of government.

Undoubtedly the *oba* was some division of the people. Gilbert[3] concludes that it was a subdivision of the phyle, and in this most likely suggestion he is followed by Neumann.[4] Pareti[5] takes the view that there were three obes corresponding with the three original Doric tribes, each subdivided into three triecades, and that the *Gerousia* originally numbered twenty-seven with three phylarchs or kings of the royal houses of the Eurypontids, Agiads and Aegeidai. The last dropped out for some unknown reason, so presumably one more senator was added to make up the number thirty with the two remaining kings. This suggestion is highly ingenious and utterly incapable of proof. Francotte[6] is cautious and abandons as

---

[1] Art. 'Obai' by Ehrenberg in P.W. For various views, Busolt-Swoboda, *op. cit.* II, p. 646 n. 2.

[2] *Lyc.* v.

[3] *Op. cit.* p. 41.

[4] *Hist. Ztschr.* XCVI, p. 42.

[5] *Ut supra.*

[6] *La polis grecque*, p. 139.

insoluble the problem of what the *oba* was. Hasebroek[1] suggests that the *oba* was the civil, the *lochos* the military division of the people, and that the two were based on the same five territorial divisions.

Mr Wade-Gery[2] holds that when the tribal army was superseded by the five regiments (*morai* or *lochoi*) these took their names from the four districts of the city of Sparta, along with the town of Amyclae. They were called obes, and the 'new model army' he calls the 'obal army'. He assumes, probably with truth, that every Spartan had his legal domicile in the city of Sparta or in Amyclae although the latter is far more doubtful. His estate or *cleros* might lie far away in the valley of the Eurotas or in Messenia; but he probably seldom visited it, unless he periodically inspected it to see that his helots were not misbehaving themselves.

This theory is perfectly rational although incapable of exact proof. One difficulty remains, however, in the use of the words φυλὰς φυλάξαντα. If the new obal system was set up superseding the tribal or phyle classification, why were the phyles apparently retained? The only answer can be that, with their innate conservatism, the Spartans were not ready to discard their old tribes. They still officially existed, although their legal significance had vanished. We may well imagine a Spartan boasting that he was a member of the renowned tribe of Dymanes, a fact which the military authorities ignored when calling on him for army service. The important question was to which *oba* did he belong.

THE KINGSHIP[3]

Sparta was a dyarchy not a monarchy. There were two royal houses and two kings, a fact which has always surprised and puzzled observers, who have been prone to suppose that it was a unique phenomenon not found in any other state,

---

[1] *Griech. Wirtschafts- u. Gesellschaftsgeschichte*, p. 205.
[2] *Class. Quart.* XXXVIII, p. 122.
[3] Kahrstedt, *op. cit.* pp. 119 ff.; Busolt-Swoboda, *op. cit.* II, pp. 671 ff.

ancient or modern. Actually that is by no means correct, and it is possible to find quite a surprising number of examples of dyarchies in ancient times. For instance, the king of the Lycians, after having tried unsuccessfully to get rid of Bellerophon, abandoned the attempt and gave him his daughter in marriage and 'half the royal honour'.[1]

Evidently two kings or chiefs were reigning in Messenia before its conquest by the Spartans. Pausanias says, 'In Messenia Antiochus and Androcles, the sons of Phinteas, were reigning.'[2] Later he speaks of a dispute between the same two which ended in the death of Androcles, leaving Antiochus sole king.[3] This ended the dyarchy, for on the death of Antiochus his son Euphaes succeeded to the crown.[4] But later, after the conquest of Messenia in the first war, the Spartans recognised the royal pretensions of the house of Androcles and gave Hyamia to his daughter, who had fled to Sparta with her children on the death of her father.[5]

At Pharae, Nicomachus and Gorgasus succeeded to the kingdom on the death of Diocles.[6] At Elis, Augeas gave a share of the government to Amarynceus.[7] We are then told, rather surprisingly, that on the death of Augeas the kingdom of Elis devolved upon his son Agasthenes along with Amphimachus and Thalpius.[8] Thucydides, in speaking of the Chaonians 'who were not under kingly government', says they were led by Photys and Nicanor 'of the family to which the chieftainship was confined, with a yearly exercise of that power'.[9] Traces of a dual or multiple kingship can be found in Cyme,[10] Mytilene, Cyzicus and in Epirus.[11] Nilsson[12] draws a comparison between Homeric and later Spartan kingship and that among the Teutonic tribes, where co-regents were not uncommon. In Albania and ancient Sweden it was usual,

---

[1] *Il.* VI, 192.   [2] Paus. IV, 4, 4.   [3] *Ibid.* 5, 6–7.
[4] *Ibid.* 5, 8.   [5] *Ibid.* 14, 3.   [6] *Ibid.* 30, 3.
[7] *Ibid.* V, 1, 11.   [8] *Ibid.* 3, 3.   [9] Thuc. II, 80.
[10] Art. 'Basileus', by Schoeffer in P.W.
[11] C. Klotsch, *Epirotische Geschichte*, p. 57.
[12] *Homer and Mycenae*, pp. 219 ff.

if a monarch died leaving two sons, that they should divide the royal honours. There are traces also of dyarchy in ancient Siam.[1] It is quite clear that dual or even multiple kingship or chieftainship was by no means uncommon, and it is a mistake to regard the dyarchy of Sparta as unique.

Consideration will suggest that such a system arose quite naturally, where the evolution of a state had passed from a federation of two or more tribes to a centralised government under a form of chieftainship or kingship. It is quite clear that this had been the case in Sparta through the coming together or synoecism of the Dorian tribes that had conquered the valley of the Eurotas.[2] Whatever may have been the number of clans—whether they were originally three, the Dymanes, Pamphyloi and Hylleis, or more[3]—it is quite clear that there

[1] *Idem*, *Klio*, XII, p. 337.

[2] Cf. Busolt-Swoboda, *op. cit.* pp. 340, 671 ff.

[3] The tantalising problem of the Aegeidai remains unsolved, and into the intricacies of this mysterious family it is unnecessary to go in detail. The simplest explanation is that they were of Theban origin, hereditary priests of Apollo Carneios. When the Spartans were hard put to it to conquer Amyclae, the oracle advised them to seek the help of the Aegeidai. Not finding them in Athens they went to Thebes. The Aegeid Timomachus accordingly went to Sparta, organised the discouraged fighters and conquered Amyclae. This is the version both of Ephorus and Aristotle, except that the latter says they were found at Athens (Ephorus, fr. 11; Arist. fr. 532. Schol. ad Pind. *Pyth.* v, 92, 101; *Isthm.* VII, 18). After this victory the Aegeidai settled in Sparta and introduced the cult of Apollo Carneios. By the time of the first Messenian war, the family had risen to great honour in Sparta and Euryleon 'now a Spartan but of Theban origin of the house of Cadmus' (Polyb. IV, 7, 8), was commander of the centre of the army.

After the conquest of Messenia, their position in Sparta evidently became difficult through the jealousy of the two kings. Gilbert's suggestion (*Grk. Const. Ant.* p. 19), that they were involved in the Partheniai conspiracy, is not impossible but incapable of proof (cf. Gelzer, *Rhein. Mus.* XXVIII, p. 13). The statement of Herodotus (IV, 149), that the Aegeidai formed 'a large tribe' in Sparta may be doubted.

Whatever happened, it seems fairly clear that the family left Sparta and established itself on the island of Thera (Herod. IV, 147), taking with it the cult of Apollo Carneios (Pind. *Pyth.* v. 75). Kaibel, *Epigrammata Graeca*, 191, 192, records the epitaph of a priest of the cult who claimed descent from Spartan 'kings', and also, strangely, from Thessaly. From Thera the cult spread to Cyrene, taken there possibly by members of the Aegeid family

were two chiefs of the houses of the Agiads and the Eurypontids,[1] and on agreeing to join politically, these two royal
houses were given equal powers in the constitution. We are
abundantly justified, therefore, in regarding at least one
'mystery' of Spartan polity as not being very mysterious after
all. The double kingship was a retention of a primitive system
of chieftainship which sought a practicable compromise
between the claims of two or more royal houses to domination,
and was by no means unique but was to be met with in a
number of other states.

The rule of succession, according to Herodotus,[2] was that
'if some children were born before their father became king
and one was born subsequently to his coming to the throne,
this last born should succeed to the crown'. If the king left
no sons at his death, then the throne went to the next male in
the strict line of succession.[3] If the new king was a minor, the
male relative next in succession performed the duties of
guardian and regent or πρόδικος.[4] The official title of the
king was ἀρχαγέτης.[5] Hesychius gives the title βαγός which
he says was a compound of βασιλεύς and στρατηγός. This
sounds a trifle too plausible and need not be taken seriously.
In any case the title is found nowhere else and may be
disregarded.

(Callimachus, *Hymn*, II, 72 f.). The supposed claim of Pindar that he was
a descendant of the Aegeidai is founded on *Pyth.* v, 76, ἐμοὶ πατέρες. But
it is more reasonable to suppose that it refers to the leader of the Cyrenean
chorus (cf. Sandys' note *ad loc.* in the Loeb edition of Pindar, p. 240;
Studniczka, *Kyrene*, pp. 73 ff.). That the Aegeidai were kings of the 'Minyans'
(Herod. IV, 147) is entirely conjectural. (Cf. Gilbert, *Studien zur altspartan-
ischen Geschichte*, pp. 191 f.; art. 'Minyas' by Fiehn in P.W.)

It is possible that the reference in Herod. IV, 149, points to the family
having died out. *Vide* also Momigliano, 'Sparta e Lacedemone e una ipotesi
sull'origine della diarchia spartana', *Atene e Roma*, XIII (1932), p. 4,
Niccolini, 'Il Sinecismo', *Rivista di Storia antica*, IX (1904), p. 98.

[1] Origin of the names explained by Ephorus ap. Strabo, VIII, 5, 5 (C. 366);
vide also Paus. III, 7, 1; cf. C. Wachsmuth, *Der historische Ursprüng des
Doppelkönigtums in Sparta*.

[2] Herod. VII, 3. [3] Xen. *Hell.* III, 3, 2; Corn. Nep. *Ages.* 1.
[4] Plut. *Lyc.* III; Xen. *Hell.* IV, 2, 9. [5] Plut. *Lyc.* VI.

The kings were bound by oath to uphold the constitution, and were in turn guaranteed by the oath of the ephors in their tenure of the throne, so long as they acted in a constitutional manner, and by inference were amenable to the will of the ephors. It is not hard to imagine that whatever went against the wishes of the ephors could easily be condemned as unconstitutional. An easy-going acquiescence in whatever the ephors·desired was the safest thing for a king. Whether these oaths were taken once and for all at the king's accession,[1] or whether, as is alleged by other authorities, they were renewed every month, is not of great importance. Perhaps the monthly oath-taking gave the ephors the chance of checking up formally on the kings and threatening that if both, or either, did not behave better the oaths would not be taken, and makes it more likely that the latter view is correct.

In tracing the evolution of the royal power in Sparta, it is illuminating to compare it with that seen in Homer. Homeric kings, such as Agamemnon, were leaders in war and intermediaries between the people and the gods. Once in the field their power was unlimited. As intercessors between gods and men they exercised priestly functions, as Moses did for the people of Israel.[2] For instance, to stay the plague, Agamemnon orders purifications and offers sacrifices.[3] Odysseus offers hecatombs to appease the wrath of Apollo.[4] The administration of justice was evidently not an essential part of the king's power. He was never represented as a judge; except, perhaps, in the doubtful instance where Odysseus speaks of the blameless king who fears the gods and 'maintains the right'.[5] The whole

---

[1] Nicol. Damas. *F.G.H.* III, p. 459, says only on accession; Xen. *Resp. Lac.* XV, 7, says every month. Of the two, the evidence of Xenophon is to be preferred.

[2] Instances of the intercessory functions of the kings of Israel are numerous, e.g. Num. xvi 44 f.; II Sam. xxiv. 15 f., etc.

[3] *Il.* I, 313.   [4] *Il.* I, 443.

[5] *Od.* XIX, 110 f. It is evident that Aristotle, in *Pol.* 1285 B, is not referring to the powers of the kings as depicted in Homer. The Homeric king certainly was not 'supreme judge'. Justice was administered in the popular assembly. Where judges are referred to they seem to be identified with the nobles

passage is an interesting one, since evidently, so long as the king is blameless and his conduct pleasing to the gods, his people will prosper under the heavenly grace; an idea which is common to many primitive peoples as innumerable instances cited by Frazer in *The Golden Bough* attest. The Homeric king enjoyed certain privileges. They have 'particular honour, of seat and mess of flesh and brimming cup' and they were looked upon as gods.[1] They received a special portion of the spoils of war.[2]

In Sparta we find almost exactly similar functions and privileges exercised by the kings. They were leaders in war, or at least one of them was. After the unfortunate division of counsel between Cleomenes and Demaratus, it was found more politic to have only one in the field.[3] They had, at least nominally, the right to declare war,[4] but actually they never did so. In the great debate at Sparta upon the decision to declare war on Athens, king Archidamus counselled prudence but his advice was overruled. In fact by that time all pretence of the power of the kings to come to so weighty a decision had been discarded, and their conduct of a campaign was under the close supervision of the ephors. If the king made a failure of the campaign he might be heavily punished.[5]

The divine origin of the double kingship was explained by contemporaries on the ground that the two royal houses were Tyndarids, descended from the Dioscuri* or great Twin Brethren, Castor and Pollux, sons of Tyndareus king of

---

(*Od.* XI, 186); cf. Nilsson, *Homer and Mycenae*, p. 223; Busolt-Swoboda, *op. cit.* p. 350; Bonner and Smith, *Administration of Justice from Homer to Aristotle*, p. 26.

[1] *Il.* XII, 310.   [2] *Il.* I, 163.

[3] Herod. v, 75; cf. Xen. *Hell.* v, 3, 10. But Pleistoanax, having raised a scratch army in Sparta, went to the support of Agis in 418. Thuc. v, 75. The rule evidently was that they were never joint commanders of the same army. On hearing of the victory at Mantinea, Pleistoanax returned to Sparta leaving Agis in supreme command of the expeditionary force.

[4] Herod. VI, 56.

[5] E.g. Agis, Thuc. v, 63; Pausanias, Xen. *Hell.* III, 5, 25; Plut. *Lys.* XXX.

Lacedaemon,[1] who after the death of their father reigned as
two kings of Sparta.[2] As Frazer has shown by numerous
examples, primitive peoples have always looked with awe
upon twins.[3] In Sparta this claim of descent from the Dioscuri
was sufficient to endow the two royal houses with a sacrosanct
character. Apparently the two kings in their priestly and
military functions were supposed to be possessed or led by
the Dioscuri. When a campaign was undertaken, one of the
Dioscuri accompanied the Spartan king in spirit, while the
other remained in Sparta with the king who had been left
behind.[4] We infer from the fact that the Spartans advanced to
the battle to the sound of 'Castor's tune' that his spirit was
active in the field, while Pollux remained inactive at home.[5]

Before setting out on a campaign, the king who was to lead
the army sacrificed to Zeus. If the omens are favourable,
'the fire-bearer, taking fire from the altar, leads the way to
the confines of the country', when the king again sacrifices
to Zeus and Athena. 'When favourable omens have been
obtained from both these deities, he then crosses the boundary
of the country and the fire from these sacrifices is carried
before him, never being extinguished, and all sorts of victims
are carried with him.' These victims were reserved for sacrifice
before battle when the king for the last time took the omens.[6]
When the king advanced into battle the sacred insignia of the
Dioscuri, the δόκανα, were carried before him.[7]

---

[1] *Od.* XI, 298. Farnell, *Greek Hero Cults*, pp. 175 ff., treats of the cult of
the Dioscuri at considerable length.   [2] Paus. III, 1, 5; Herod. VI, 52.

[3] *The Golden Bough: The Magic Art*, I, pp. 49, 262 f.

[4] Herod. V, 75. The idea of spiritual support in battle was not unique to
the Spartans. Cf. Farnell, *op. cit.* p. 196.

[5] Plut. *Lyc.* XXII. Meyer, *Forschungen*, I, p. 245, n. 2, has no doubt whatever of the close connection of the idea of the Dioscuri with the Spartan
dyarchy. A comparison with the two Roman consuls, and the legends of the
great Twin Brethren, Romulus and Remus, are interesting and suggestive.

[6] Xen. *Resp. Lac.* XIII, 2, 8; Nicol. Damas. *F.H.G.* III, pp. 458, 114, 14;
Plut. *Lyc.* XXI, XXII; Athen. XIII, 561 E; Thuc. V, 7; Polyaen. I, 10.

[7] δόκανα: Plut. *De frat. amore*, I; Suidas, *s.v.*; two upright bars joined at
each end by horizontal bars, as in the astronomical figure of the Gemini.
Nilsson, *Minoan-Mycenean Religion*, p. 470, explains this on the ground that

As intermediaries between gods and people a mystical character surrounded the kings. If things went well with the nation, the gods were pleased; if things went wrong, the intercessions of the kings had failed and the blame was placed, singularly unfairly, on them and the wrath of the people might be visited upon them.[1] They held their office so long as the gods favoured them, and a sign of heavenly approval or displeasure was looked for every ninth year. This undoubtedly springs from an octennial tenure of the throne, a custom of extreme antiquity.[2] The custom of an eight-year reign was ingeniously called into use when Lysander deposed Leonidas II. 'Every ninth year the Ephors, choosing a starlight night, when there was neither cloud nor moon, sit down together in quiet and silence and watch the sky. And if they chance to see a shooting star they presently pronounce their kings guilty of some offence against the gods, and thereupon they are at once suspended from all exercise of royal power, till they are relieved by an oracle from Delphi or Olympia.'[3]

the Dioscuri were the house gods of the Spartan kings and the symbol represented a house. Cf. also Farnell, *op. cit.* p. 189; *A.B.S.A.* XIII, p. 214; Tod-Wace, *Cat. of Spart. mus.* fig. 588, p. 193.

[1] Frazer, in *The Golden Bough*, gives numerous examples of the same attitude of primitive peoples towards their kings.

[2] To correct the excess of $11\frac{1}{4}$ days of the solar over the lunar year the Greeks adopted the octennial cycle, intercalating three lunar months in every period of eight years. Cf. Frazer, *The Golden Bough* ('Spirits of the Corn and the Wild'), 1, p. 82. Unger, 'Zeitrechnung der Griechen u. Römer' in Müller's *Handbuch*, XII, p. 732. An eight-year cycle also governed the tenure of the throne by the legendary Minos of Crete, if we take the words ἐννέωρος βασίλευε as meaning 'reigned for nine years' (*Od.* XIX, 178). Cf. Plato, *Legg.* 624 A, B; *Meno*, 81 B; Strabo, X, 4, 8 (C. 476); Frazer, *The Golden Bough* ('The Dying God'), pp. 68 f.; Nilsson, *Klio*, XII, p. 339; G. Thomson, 'The Greek Calendar', *J.H.S.* LXIII (1943), p. 63, δι' ἐνάτου ἔτους, i.e. at intervals of eight years. In reckoning intervals of time the Greeks included both the terms which separated the intervals, whereas English custom includes only one of them. Cf. the French *quinzaine* meaning a fortnight; Frazer, *op. cit.* p. 59, n. 1.

[3] Plut. *Agis*, XI. The significance of falling stars among primitive peoples is discussed by Frazer, *ut supra*.

Parke[1] has pointed out that this procedure may have been used more than once. Leonidas II was deposed in the year 243–242, and reckoning back by eight-year cycles we come to the deposition of Demaratus in 491–490 on the charge of Cleomenes that he was not the son of king Ariston. The case was referred to Delphi which pronounced against him.[2] Three other cases of deposition, that of Leotychidas in 476–475, of Pleistoanax in 446–445 and of Pausanias in 395–394, are much more doubtful. The first two do not fit into the cycle, but the last does. Kahrstedt[3] had already surmised the use of the shooting-star method of deposition in the case of Pausanias and it would seem too convenient an expedient to reject. Parke, however, doubts this because it was not a typical case, since legitimacy was not in question and the political differences between the king and ephors would hardly seem suitable for adjudication of the Oracle. The case must, therefore, be left in doubt.

It was the duty of the kings to obtain for their people the direction of the oracle at Delphi, and for that purpose they appointed two *pythioi*,[4] who were special couriers sent to consult the oracle when necessary and report back to the kings, who, as Herodotus says, had the keeping of the oracles that were pronounced, 'but the Pythioi are also privy to them'. It is amusing to remember that the ephors had their rival oracle in the inspirations accorded to them at the shrine of Ino Pasiphae. The kings were also, in their own right, priests of Zeus Lacedaemonios and Zeus Uranios,[5] the tutelary deities of their respective families.

The sacrosanct character of the kings did not preserve them from danger at the hands of the people who on at least four occasions deposed one of them, namely Demaratus, Leotychidas, Pleistoanax and Pausanias. The last was actually

[1] H. W. Parke, 'Deposing of Spartan Kings', *Class. Quart.* XXXIX (1945), p. 106.

[2] Herod. VI, 61, ff.; cf. Busolt, *Griechische Geschichte*, II, p. 573.

[3] *Op. cit.* p. 126, n. 1; Xen. *Hell.* III, 5, 25.

[4] Herod. VI, 57.   [5] *Ibid.* 56.

condemned to death, but escaped by fleeing to Tegea.[1] But the murder of Agis IV was a shocking thing and we are told that some of the soldiers protested against laying hands on the royal person.[2] The king should also be without blemish or deformity. An oracle had warned Sparta against a lame king, but this was plausibly explained away by Lysander when he sought to put the lame Agesilaus on the throne against the claim of Leotychidas, whom he alleged to be illegitimate.[3]

The judicial functions of the Spartan kings were very limited, or rather non-existent. Criminal cases were judged by the *Gerousia*, civil by the ephors.[4] To the kings was allotted the duty of betrothing orphan heiresses; the ceremony of adoption of a son was made before them, and they had under their jurisdiction the public highways.[5] Why this last should have been allotted to them is by no means clear. It has been suggested that this was a religious function connected with limiting the encroachment of the roads upon lands wherein reposed the ashes of the owner's ancestors.[6] Perhaps a simpler explanation may be found in the character of the kings as the commanders-in-chief of the army, and in the fact that the upkeep of the roads was highly important for the movement of the troops.[7] We speak to-day of the 'King's Highway'.

---

[1] Xen. *Hell.* III, 5, 25.　　　　　　　[2] Plut. *Agis*, 19.

[3] Xen. *Hell.* III, 3, 3; Plut. *Agis*, 3; Paus. III, 8, 9. A curious point arises in the case of the lame Agesilaus. Why was he not condemned at birth by the 'Triers', who inspected infants to see if they were healthy and not deformed? Kahrstedt, *op. cit.* p. 127, suggests that technically the two royal houses belonged to no tribe and therefore this practice did not apply to them. Or perhaps the lameness developed later, or the rapidly diminishing number of male Spartans deterred the strict working of the law.

[4] Arist. *Pol.* 1275 B; Plut. *Apoph. Lac.* 217 B, 221 B.　　　[5] Herod. VI, 57.

[6] Bréhier, 'La royauté homérique', *Revue Historique*, LXXXV (1904), p. 19.

[7] Schömann-Lipsius, *Griech. Altert.* I, 4, p. 234. Curtius, 'Gesch. des Wegebaues bei den Griechen' (*Abhandlungen d. Berl. Akademie*), 1854, p. 246, wants to make control by the king a kind of *octroi* for raising taxes. Naber, *Mnemosyne*, IV, p. 25 and V, p. 139, wants to read προσόδων, i.e. the public revenues. Stern, 'Zur Entstehung...des Ephorats in Sparta', *Berl. Studien für klass. Philologie*, XV, pt. 2, p. 30, n. 2, proposes ὅρων, i.e. boundaries.

No definite conclusion is possible upon the point. The reference to Agesilaus sitting as a judge is unexplainable, except on the ground that it was during a campaign and as commander-in-chief he settled all disputes.[1]

A point of some importance in our understanding of the royal prerogatives, but unfortunately one upon which it is difficult to form a conclusion, arises from the plea of Lysander and Mandrocleidas to King Agis IV to the effect that, if the two kings acted together, they could disregard the edicts of the ephors.

For that board of magistrates, they said, derived its power from dissension between the two kings, by giving their vote to the king who offered the better advice, whenever the other was at variance with the public good. But when the two kings were in accord, their power was indissoluble and it would be unlawful for the ephors to contend against them; although, when the kings were in contention with one another, it was the privilege of the ephors to act as arbiters between them, but not to interfere when they were of one mind.[2]

Dum and Kahrstedt accept this as a sound constitutional principle.[3] The individual king was merely a magistrate and could be proceeded against; but the two kings acting together represented the royal power which was, at least theoretically, absolute. It should be observed that Cleomenes III, feeling his legal position as the sole king to be anomalous, as it indeed was, summoned from Messene Archidamus, the brother of Agis, 'who was the rightful king from the other house, thinking that the power of the ephors would be diminished if the royal power were restored to its full strength so as to counter-balance it'. Later, after the murder of the unfortunate Archidamus, 'desiring to give the name of absolute power a less offensive sound, he associated with himself in royal

[1] Plut. *Apoph. Lac.* 213 D.

[2] Plut. *Agis*, XII. Lysander, not the conqueror of Athens in 404, but the supporter of Agis in his abortive schemes of reform; *vide infra*, p. 318.

[3] Dum, *Entstehung u. Entwicklung d. spartanischen Ephorats*, p. 66; Kahrstedt, *op. cit.* p. 120. For criticism of this view cf. Stern, *loc. cit.* pp. 39 ff.

power his brother Eucleidas. And this was the only time when the Spartans had two kings from the same house.'[1] In support of the view that the two kings acting together wielded absolute power may be cited the rule that if they both wanted to dine at home and not at their *syssition* their rations were sent to them;[2] but if one wished to stay away, the polemarch could refuse to allow it, as in the case of Agis on returning from a campaign.[3]

The monthly oath was an individual one (ὑπερ ἑαυτοῦ) and not taken jointly by both kings, who together were under no compulsion to swear to uphold the constitution.[4] No proceedings could be taken against both kings together, as is shown by the incident of the grievance of the Aeginetans against Cleomenes and Leotychidas who had seized hostages and handed them over to Athens for safe keeping.[5] No indictment was of any avail against these two jointly; but immediately after the death of Cleomenes the Aeginetans took proceedings against Leotychidas.[6] It is extraordinary to realise that the Spartans were quite ready to hand him over to the Aeginetans; but the latter were restrained by wiser advice which warned them that serious consequences might follow if violent hands were laid on a reigning king of Sparta. Leotychidas and the Aeginetans then went to Athens and demanded the hostages. But the Athenians refused to give them up, alleging that since two kings had delivered them they could not give them up to one only.

The evidence, however, is far from conclusive. It is to be noted that Plutarch, in his account of the star-gazing ceremony of the ephors, says that if the portent discloses the displeasure of the gods the kings are suspended from the exercise of their functions until a pronouncement is obtained from the oracle. What if the kings together denied the competency of the

---

[1] Plut. *Cleom.* V, 11.   [2] Herod. VI, 57.
[3] Plut. *Lyc.* XII. For further comment on this curious incident, *vide infra*, p. 284.
[4] Xen. *Resp. Lac.* XV, 7.
[5] Herod. VI, 73.   [6] *Ibid.* 85–6.

ephors to do this? It might be argued that in this case a superior power was functioning and that the ephors were merely following the divine commands, and their own powers to depose or suspend the kings were not in question. It is difficult, if not impossible, to come to a conclusion on the point. The only thing we can be certain of is that the royal power had become so attenuated that it was completely subordinated to that of the ephors, whatever may have been its theoretical extent.

The quarrels and jealousies of the two houses were notorious,[1] and it is not hard to imagine the crafty ephors deliberately fostering these feelings, especially if either of the kings was young and could be induced to imagine himself slighted by the other. They were strictly constitutional rulers, and would be careful not to endanger their position by absolutist methods, especially since they had the precedent of Leotychidas before them. It was not pleasant for either of them to think that, if the other died, he himself, as the survivor, might be proceeded against for the acts of both.

The kings enjoyed considerable honour. They were supported at the expense of the State,[2] and were allotted estates among the lands of the *perioeci*, from which they derived revenues.[3] Whether or not they 'lived of their own,' that is, derived all their revenues from their estates, or whether they also received a general tribute is not clear, and commentators have differed sharply on the point without coming to any conclusion. In any case they were reputed to be among the richest men in Greece.[4] This is certainly an exaggeration, but they must have had considerable fortunes. For instance, when Agis IV proposed an equalisation of wealth he promised his own fortune of six thousand talents, and Plutarch says his mother and grandmother were the wealthiest women in Sparta.

---

[1] Arist. *Pol.* 1271 A.   [2] Herod. VI, 57; Xen. *Hell.* V, 3, 20.

[3] Xen. *Resp. Lac.* XV, 3. The problem of the exact nature of the royal revenues is dealt with more fully hereafter; *vide infra*, p. 309.

[4] Plato, *Alcib.* I, 123.

In war they received a part of the spoils. We are told by Herodotus[1] that Pausanias after the victory of Plataea received one-tenth. But Cleomenes III after the capture of Megalopolis took one-third of six thousand talents.[2] Since Cleomenes was in complete control and had no ephors to fear, no doubt he could take anything he liked. At the public sacrifices they received the skins and chines of the victims, and a pig from every litter.[3] When dining at the *syssition* the kings received a double portion, not, Xenophon is careful to add, that they might eat more, but that they might honour anyone they chose by giving him an extra helping. Agesilaus went one better and gave both his portions away and apparently went without his own dinner.[4]

The kings were members *ex officio* of the *Gerousia*. Whether or not they could introduce bills into the house is doubtful. When Agis IV wanted the Senate to adopt his famous *rhetra* annulling debts and dividing lands and wealth, he did so through the ephor Lysander. This is not conclusive evidence, since it is possible that Agis, a very young man, may have considered it politic to put up one of the ephors to make so revolutionary a proposal, and the point must be left in doubt. It is certain, however, that the kings took part in debates.

The two royal houses were co-equal in power, and there is no evidence, as some writers have claimed, that the Agiad line was more renowned and powerful than the Eurypontid. Officially the one who had reigned longer was senior, and his name headed all official documents.[5]

On his accession a new king proclaimed the annulment of all debts due to him or to the State.[6] At the religious festivals they were accorded seats of honour, and on their entrances to the Assembly all rose, except the ephors.[7] Thucydides[8] is at some pains to explain that they did not have two votes in the

[1] Herod. IX, 81.   [2] Phylarchus, ap. Polyb. XI, 62.
[3] Herod. VI, 56.   [4] *Resp. Lac.* XV, 4; *Ages.* V, 1.
[5] E.g. Pleistoanax (Thuc. V. 24).   [6] Herod. VI, 59.
[7] Xen. *Resp. Lac.* XV, 6. Cf. Nicol. Damas. *F.H.G.* III, 44, 41.
[8] I, 20.

Gerousia as was generally supposed. This misapprehension seems to have arisen from a misunderstanding of a passage in Herodotus,[1] which certainly does not say they had double voting power, but says 'if they do not attend, those of the Senators most nearly connected with them enjoy the privileges of the kings, giving two votes, and a third their own'. The kings had their official headquarters,[2] where we may suppose they transacted business and held the royal *syssition*. It was evidently of great age; the doors at least were built by Aristodemus, an ancestor of both families; it was very unpretentious and doubtless uncomfortable. Besides their official residence or palace, they had each his own house.

Whatever honours and privileges appertained to the royal office, they hardly compensated for the complete subjection of the kings to the ephors. We are told[3] that they obeyed the ephors 'as children obey their parents', and certainly the slightest tendency on their part to disregard orders was punished. Some lingering signs of their independence did indeed remain, for instance, the formality of refusing to come at ephors' bidding until summoned three times.[4]

BURIAL OBSEQUIES

Herodotus[5] gives a long account of the elaborate mourning imposed upon the people on the death of one of the kings. The death was announced throughout the land, whereupon the women going through the city beat cauldrons. This curious proceeding, characteristic of primitive peoples, was probably prompted in remote times by an attempt through the noise to frighten away the evil spirits that might attack the country when the king, its protector, was dead; or possibly against the malignity of the spirit of the dead king himself.

[1] VI, 57.   [2] Xen. *Ages.* VIII; *Hell.* V, 3, 20; Plut. *Ages.* XIX.
[3] Polyb. XXIII, 11.   [4] Plut. *Cleom.* X.
[5] Herod. VI, 58; cf. Paus. IV, 14, 4. W. S. Ferguson, 'The Zulus and the Spartans', *Harvard African Studies*, II (1918), pp. 197 ff., draws a striking parallel between the mourning for a Zulu king and for a Spartan king.

Two free people, a man and a woman, from each household had to make themselves squalid in token of grief, failure to do so entailing a heavy fine; a custom which, he remarks, was shared by the barbarians of Asia. From the whole of Lacedaemon and the *perioeci*, delegations were summoned to attend the funeral to the number of many thousands. On assembling together for the ceremony, they struck their foreheads and gave themselves up to unbounded lamentations, affirming that the dead king was the best they ever had. It may be suggested, parenthetically, that possibly this mourning may have been designed to propitiate his *manes*, so that after death he might do no harm to the people.[1] Perhaps the old saying, *de mortuis nil nisi bonum*, may be traced to the same motive. If he had fallen in war, his body was embalmed and brought back to Sparta for burial. Cornelius Nepos[2] tells us that, when Agesilaus died before reaching Sparta on his way back from Egypt, his soldiers, having no honey—which was generally used for embalming—covered the body with wax. The effigy of the dead king, laid on a costly couch, was exposed to the public gaze. After the burial no assembly was held for ten days, nor an election of magistrates during the period of mourning.

THE CROWN PRINCE

Of the position and prerogatives of the crown prince we know very little. If Plutarch[3] is correct, he was not subject to the discipline through which the other Spartan boys went, for the reason, frankly stated, that so strict a training tended to make them too submissive and afraid to assume responsibility, characteristics unfitting for a king. He was, therefore, not technically a citizen of Sparta at all and presumably could

---

[1] E.g. the spirit of Pausanias, that had to be exorcised by necromancers, specially brought to Sparta from abroad—a significant touch (Plut. *de sera Num. vind.* 560 F). Numerous examples of driving spirits away by noise cited by Frazer, *The Golden Bough* ('The Scapegoat'), pp. 109, 147.

[2] XVII, 8, 7.

[3] Plut. *Ages.* 1. But this statement directly conflicts with that of Stob. *Flor.* XL, 8, where it is said that even kings' sons had to undergo the training.

fill no office other than that of king. It is doubtful if he carried on when his father could not. We do know that the State appointed Archidamus to take over when Agesilaus was sick; but this may have been a special appointment.[1] If we are to judge from the speech composed by Isocrates for Archidamus we might conclude that the crown prince had the special privilege of addressing the *Ecclesia*.[2]

THE END OF THE DYARCHY

That this peculiar system of dyarchy should have endured for centuries may be accounted for by the conservatism of the Spartan spirit. It may also be urged that, on the whole, the system did not work too badly. The quarrels of the rival houses were endless and used up the energies of the reigning kings so much, that they had little time or inclination to meddle dangerously with affairs of state, which suited the ephors exactly. We may surmise that often, when one king seemed disposed to give trouble, the ephors deliberately stirred up the other to oppose him; a simple and highly effective way of getting out of difficulties.

The prestige of the kingship was very great and no ephor dared to suggest its abolition. The incident related by Plutarch and Diodorus[3] of Lysander's plan to change the kingly office from an hereditary to an elective form is worth noting. Lysander, the victor over Athens, had evidently come to the conclusion that the hereditary kingship was ineffective and also that he himself was a highly suitable candidate if it were turned into an elective office. He seems to have hesitated as to whether the candidates should be members of the Heraclid family, to which he claimed to belong, or whether election should be thrown open to all Spartans. But, however that may be, he is said to have requested Cleon of Halicarnassus

---

[1] Xen. *Hell.* VI, 4, 18. Cf. Kahrstedt, *op. cit.* pp. 129f., 135f.

[2] *Vide* also Diod. XIX, 70, 4.

[3] Plut. *Lys.* XXX; *Ages.* XX; *Apoph. Lac.* 282; Diod. Sic. XIV, 3. Cf. Bazin, *La république des Lac. de Xen.* p. 178. Cicero, *De divin.* I, 43.

to compose a speech for him advocating his proposal. He also consulted, we are told, the oracles of Delphi, Dodona and Zeus Ammon, but got no encouragement, although he tried to bribe them. He even went so far as to favour an impostor who claimed divine parentage and who, under prompting, would profess to find in the archives at Delphi a prophecy of an elective kingship.[1] Whether Lysander actually was ready to go to these extreme lengths or not, is hard to say. It is safe to say, however, that the scheme broke down through the reluctance of the ephors to agree to it. It is related that Agesilaus found the speech of Cleon among Lysander's papers after his death and wished to publish it. He was prevented by Lacratidas, the eponymous ephor, who advised against an act which might have had serious repercussions and involved the ephorate.[2] The final downfall of the kingship came many years later, when the tyrant Nabis swept it away, and it was never revived.

THE EPHORATE

In the college of ephors, consisting of five magistrates elected annually, was vested the administrative power of the Spartan State. About the origin of this board of 'managers' or 'overseers' there has raged a prolonged controversy, which it must be acknowledged is still not finally decided.[3]

[1] *Lys.* XXVI.

[2] *Ibid.* XXX. W. K. Prentice, *American Journal of Archaeology*, XXXVIII (1934), pp. 39f., sweeps the whole story away as intrinsically impossible and out of line with Lysander's reputation for honesty.

[3] General references: Kahrstedt, *Griechisches Staatsrecht*, pp. 237ff; Kuchtner, *Die Entstehung u. ursprüngliche Bedeutung des spartanischen Ephorats*; Dum, *op. cit.* Stern, 'Zur Entstehung u. ursprünglichen Bedeutung d. Ephorats in Sparta', *Berl. Studien für klassische Philologie*; Meyer, *Forschungen zur alten Geschichte*, I, p. 244. The reference in Timaeus, *Soph. Lex. Plat.* CXXVIII, to five senior and five junior ephors is only explainable on the ground that the junior ephors were alternates who acted when any of the seniors were absent from Sparta, e.g. on a campaign. The point is incapable of solution. We must reject the statement in the *Etym. Mag. s.v.* 'Ephoroi' that they were nine in number. The evidence that there were five is quite conclusive. Cf. Solari, *Ricerche Spartane*, p. 191.

There are three theories as to the origin of the ephorate which merit careful consideration. These are:

(1) That the ephors were priests, or astrologers, whose office was of immemorial antiquity among the Dorian tribes. These, by slow degrees, came to exercise supreme power and usurp the position of the kings.

(2) That they were the creation of the kings, who appointed them to carry on the functions of government when they were in the field.

(3) That they were originally headmen of the five tribes, and so leaders of the democracy that overthrew the predominant nobility and gave to Sparta a 'democratic' form of government.

(1) It is quite possible that there was a college of priests who always had possessed occult powers, and had gradually usurped secular powers. Certainly it was of very ancient origin, since a similar institution was found in Cyrene, Thera, Heraclea and Messene.[1] Along with this view goes the problem as to the derivation of the word 'ephor'. It is generally supposed to denote an overseer or superintendent. But it is by no means impossible that originally it meant a seer, magician or medicine man, astrologer or watcher of the heavens, who by observing such phenomena as shooting stars and eclipses interpreted the will or displeasure of the gods.[2] They regulated the calendar and their president or high priest was eponymous, that is, he gave his name to his year of office.[3]

There is no compelling reason why this view of the ancient character of the ephorate should be rejected. That a priestly

[1] Cyrene, Herac. Pont. IV, 5; *F.H.G.* II, 212; Thera, *I.G.* XII, 3, 322, 326, 330, 336; Heraclea, *I.G.* XIV, 645; Messene, Polyb. IV, 4, 31. The evidence for the existence of ephors at Geronthrai, Amyclae, Gythium and Epidaurus is from Roman times and cannot be accepted as pointing to an ancient foundation. Cf. also Kuchtner, *op. cit.* p. 60; Stern, *loc. cit.* p. 15.

[2] S. Luria, 'Zum politischen Kampf in Sparta gegen Ende des 5. Jahrhds'., *Klio* (1927), p. 413. Cf. also Frazer, *The Golden Bough* ('The Dying God'), pp. 58ff. Hasebroek, *Griech. Wirtschafts- u. Gesellschaftsgeschichte*, p. 206.

[3] Apparently this was done by proclamation of the ephors, Plut. *Agis*, XVI. Eponymous ephor, Thuc. V, 19.

caste has again and again asserted itself and become the *de facto* ruler of the country has been seen in innumerable instances in almost every time and country. Where the chief or king is weak and the priesthood strong and able, through its claims to magical terrors, to dominate the people, a hierarchy can usurp almost complete control; although the *de jure* right of the king to rule may conveniently be retained. It is not to be denied that vestiges of the astrological character of the Spartan ephorate persisted, as, for instance, the watching of the heavens every ninth year for the decision of the gods upon the conduct of the kings, as already described. They pretended to obtain divine guidance by sleeping in the temple of Ino Pasiphae when the will of the gods was revealed to them in dreams.[1]

But while this ancient priestly character of the ephorate cannot be wholly ignored, yet it is pertinent to remark that with the exceptions given above, the ephors seem to have lost all their religious attributes. The one thing that a priestly caste will never do is to let these extraordinary functions lapse. It will cling to them with the utmost tenacity and strengthen them by every means in its power. It is, therefore, extremely unlikely that it would abandon most of its sacerdotal character in exchange for secular power. The former was much more effective than the latter, and so the less likely to be relinquished. As a theory of the rise of the ephorate to supreme power in Sparta it is obviously incomplete.

A much more prosaic explanation of their origin was first put forward by Müller,[2] who suggested they were originally overseers of the market. His argument that the ephors were judges in all cases involving contracts is hardly convincing in this case. It is very probable that one of their duties was to control the market; but that hardly explains their origin.

[1] Plut. *Cleom.* 7; Paus. III, 26, 1. Cf. Cicero, *De divin.* I, 43, 96. Dickins, *Class. Quart.* v, pp. 240f. suggests that Chilon brought Epimenides of Crete to Sparta to institute this cult as an offset to the royal influence at Delphi. The point is impossible to substantiate.

[2] *Doric Race*, II, p. 119. Also E. Meyer, *Rhein. Mus.* XLI (1886), p. 583. Cf. Stern, *loc. cit.* p. 25.

(2) That the ephors were the creation of the kings, who appointed them to perform judicial and administrative functions, when the chief executive in the person of one or both kings was absent on a campaign, rests upon a passage in Plutarch,[1] which merits careful examination. King Cleomenes III (c. 238–219), in his attempted reform of the Spartan constitution by the overthrow and murder of the ephors, justifies his action by saying:

By Lycurgus the council of elders was joined to the kings and that form of government had continued a long time and no other sort of magistracy had been wanted. But afterwards in the long war with the Messenians when the kings, having to command the army, found no time to administer justice, chose some of their friends and left them to determine the suits of the citizens in their stead. These were called Ephors and at first behaved themselves as servants of the kings. But afterwards by degrees they appropriated the power to themselves and erected a distinct magistracy. An evidence of the truth of this was the custom, still observed by the kings, who, when the Ephors send for them, refuse upon the first and second summons to go, but upon the third rise up and attend them. And Asteropus, the first that raised the Ephors to that height of power, lived a great many years after their institution. So long therefore as they confined themselves to their own proper sphere, it had been better to bear with them than to make a disturbance. But that an upstart power should so far subvert the ancient form of government as to banish some kings, murder others without hearing their defense and threaten those who desired to see the best and most divine constitution restored to Sparta, was not to be borne.

The whole speech, reported or invented by Plutarch, is, of course, a piece of special pleading and must, so far as that goes, be severely suspect. Cleomenes is excusing his violent *coup d'état* by saying that the ephorate was founded by royal decree and that, since it unconstitutionally usurped the royal prerogatives, he is justified in overthrowing it. In examining this

---

[1] *Cleom.* x.

it must be acknowledged that a royal foundation of the college of ephors was held by all ancient writers. Herodotus attributes it to Lycurgus, who was of the royal house,[1] as does also Xenophon,[2] Plato[3] and Diogenes Laertius.[4] Aristotle attributes it to King Theopompus[5] as does Plutarch in another passage,[6] who adds that this was 130 years after the death of Lycurgus. But since we know nothing whatever of the date of his death— if he ever existed, which is, to say the least, debatable—we, are not helped at all by this. There is certainly no convincing reason why we should reject a royal foundation.[7] It must be noted, however, that the accounts given by Plutarch differ radically. In the life of Lycurgus he says that King Theopompus gave way gracefully to the pressure put upon him by the ephors and, when upbraided by his wife for supineness, excused himself by saying that in fact he had saved kingship in Sparta by giving way to *force majeure*. This is a very different account from that in the life of Cleomenes, where the kings appoint their friends to carry on for them when they are occupied with the army. King Theopompus, it is agreed, led the Spartans in the war against Messenia,[8] which can be put at the latter half of the eighth century. It is pertinent to remark that the alleged action of Theopompus, coinciding with the long-drawn-out Messenian war, does give a certain amount of support to the idea that the power of the ephors increased, or perhaps was conferred upon them, in consequence of the preoccupation of the kings with war. But undoubtedly Theopompus did not 'create' the ephorate as a new college of officials. We have lists which may or may not be genuine, of eponymous ephors before the time of Theopompus; which at least does show that their position was one of dignity and importance even at so early a period.[9]

[1] I, 65.   [2] *Resp. Lac.* VIII, 3.   [3] *Ep.* VIII, 354B.
[4] I, 68 (Satyrus).   [5] *Pol.* 1313A.   [6] *Lyc.* VII.
[7] Szanto in art. 'Ephoroi' in P.W. concludes that this is by far the most likely explanation of their origin.
[8] Wade-Gery in *C.A.H.* III, p. 527.
[9] Meyer, *Forschungen*, I, pp. 245 f.

(3) Were the ephors head-men of the tribes? The five ephors must have some close connection with the five tribes or phyles. It cannot be merely a coincidence that there were five phyles, five *lochoi* and five ephors. Perhaps originally they were tribal chiefs, who formed the principal advisers of the kings.[1] We do not know how these headmen originally gained their position, possibly by election. But we do know that in historical times the ephors were elected by the people at large, and all traces of their representing their own tribes had been lost. The monthly oath taken by kings and ephors was a regularly renewed treaty between the kings and the tribes.[2] This treaty is significant in showing that the duly accredited representatives of the people were entering into an alliance with the divinely appointed kings.

From their original position as advisers to the kings and representatives of the five tribes in the constitutional system, the ephors slowly advanced in power until at last they had usurped all the significant powers of the kings and were *de facto* if not *de jure* the rulers of Sparta. This evolution must have been a slow process, reaching its climax towards the end of the sixth century. The ephors continued in supreme power until those in office at the time were murdered by Cleomenes III and their order, if not permanently suppressed, reduced to impotence and the second place in the Spartan constitution after the *patronomoi*. There is evidence that the order existed in Roman times and enjoyed considerable power.[3]

ASTEROPUS AND CHILON

We are now confronted with the further statement of King Cleomenes that the ephor Asteropus increased the power of the ephorate. Of Asteropus we know nothing whatever,

[1] Cf., on this view of the origin of the ephorate, Neumann, *Hist. Ztschr.* XCVI (1906), pp. 43 ff.; also Beloch, *Bevölkerung der griechisch-römischen Welt*, pp. 131 f.

[2] Stern, *loc. cit.* p. 61. Xen. *Resp. Lac.* XV, 7. Ehrenberg, 'Der Damos im archaischen Sparta', *Hermes*, LXVIII (1933), pp. 288 ff.

[3] Philostratus, *Vita Apoll.* IV, 31–3.

and even his existence is open to doubt. His name 'Star-gazer' excites suspicion, as it undoubtedly refers to the astrological functions of the ephors. All that can be said is that his existence can neither be denied or affirmed.[1] The problem of the founding of the ephorate is further complicated by Diogenes Laertius[2] who asserts that Chilon was the one who instituted the order. He alleges that he was an old man in the 52nd Olympiad (572) and was eponymous ephor in the 56th Olympiad (556). He was reckoned one of the 'Seven Sages' of Greece.[3] Herodotus says he was a contemporary of Hippocrates, father of Pisistratus, the tyrant of Athens.[4] Alcidamas the rhetorician[5] says he was a member of the *Gerousia*. Further than that we know nothing of Chilon. It seems practically certain that he was an historic personage, the evidence is too strong to disregard. That he founded the ephorate is far from certain; in fact we may reject the supposition. That he strengthened the order and gave it greater power and prestige is very likely indeed. It may very well be that a man of his prestige and wisdom did add to the office of ephor.

But whether or not Asteropus or Chilon, or perhaps a lawgiver identified with Lycurgus, 'founded' the ephorate (that is, gave it its commanding position in the Spartan constitution) is actually of little moment. What is obvious is that at some time—whether in the seventh or sixth century is uncertain,

---

[1] S. Luria, 'Asteropos', *Phil. Woch.* XLVI (1926), p. 701; V. Ehrenberg, 'Asteropos', *Phil. Woch.* XLVII (1927), p. 27; art. 'Asteropos' in P.W. by Niese. Opinions as to Asteropos differ widely among commentators. Stein, *Das spart. Ephor*, p. 20, holds that A. obtained for the ephors the presidency of the Assembly and a share in the discussions of the *Gerousia*. Frick, *De Ephoris Spartanis*, p. 21, thinks they were originally representatives of the Minyans and under A. took their foremost place in the Spartan constitution. Schaefer, *De Ephoris Spartanis*, p. 15, believes that A. threw the ephorate open to popular election. With this last opinion Gilbert, *Grk. Const. Ant.* p. 20, agrees. Luria (*ut supra*) denies the existence at any time of an individual named A. Ehrenberg, while agreeing, says that evidently Cleomenes believed, or affected to believe, in his existence.

[2] I, 68–73.   [3] Plato, *Protag.* 343.

[4] I, 59; cf. VII, 235.

[5] ap. Arist. *Rhet.* II, 23, 11. Cf. art. 'Chilon' (1), by Niese in P.W.

but most probably in the latter—the Spartan State became 'democratised' and the balance of power, taken from the kings and senators, was given to the ephors as representatives of the *Demos* popularly elected. It is quite clear that by the middle of the sixth century, which agrees with the date of Chilon, the ephors had arrived at considerable influence and that during the fifth century this influence became progressively greater. By 480 they had monopolised the conduct of foreign affairs and, by the end of the Peloponnesian war, that of military affairs also.[1] The story of Herodotus[2] of the ephors' commanding King Anaxandrides to take another wife is significant of their domination over the kings.

ELECTION

It seems undoubted that the ephors were elected from the people at large and were therefore entirely democratic. The reference to this by Aristotle,[3] while not very clear, is yet unmistakable:

ἔτι τῷ δύο τάς μεγίστας ἀρχὰς τὴν μὲν αἱρεῖσθαι τὸν δῆμον, τῆς δὲ μετέχειν (τοὺς μὲν γὰρ γέροντας αἱροῦνται, τῆς δ' ἐφορείας μετέχουσιν).

'Of the two greatest offices, the people at large elect to one and share in the other (they elect the gerontes and share in the ephorate).'

To 'share in the ephorate' can only mean that the commons, that is, the whole body of Spartan peers, could elect those of their own order; the ephors need not be senators. Gachon[4] has suggested that the *gerontes* nominated the candidates for whom the omens were favourable and from these the ephors were elected by popular vote. This is not impossible and indeed may be likely, but rests on no evidence. Aristotle[5]

---

[1] Cf. Solari, *op. cit.* p. 175.   [2] v, 39.

[3] *Pol.* 1294B.

[4] *de Ephoris Spartanis*, p. 78. Cf. Kahrstedt, *op. cit.* pp. 146ff., who leaves the problem unsolved but infers they were elected in the same way as the *gerontes*.   [5] *Pol.* 1271 A.

says the *gerontes* canvassed for office, a practice of which he greatly disapproved, but says nothing of the ephors' doing so. It is probable, however, that they did.

POWERS OF THE EPHORATE

Whatever doubts we may be in with regard to the origin and development of the ephorate, there are few as to their powers and functions in historic times. They formed an annually elected board of executive officers, which came into office at the beginning of winter.[1] It must be noted that they were not necessarily chosen from the members of the *Gerousia*, anybody could be selected from the people in general. The eponymous ephor was their chairman and presided when both houses met together in plenary session.[2] A majority vote decided their policy.[3] They had an official residence, the *ephoreion*, or perhaps merely an office in the market-place, where they took their meals together in the Spartan manner.[4] Upon entering office they somewhat surprisingly enjoined upon the people to shave their moustaches and obey the laws.[5]

How far they were empowered to carry out foreign policy on their own initiative is doubtful. Certainly the final decision on war,[6] peace[7] and the making of treaties[8] rested with the *Gerousia* and *Ecclesia* sitting together. Before a foreign embassy could enter the country it was halted at the border

---

[1] Thuc. v. 36. Xen. *Hell.* II, 3, 9. Cf. Busolt-Swoboda, *op. cit.* p. 686, n. 5.

[2] Plut. *Lys.* xxx; Thuc. v, 19.   [3] Xen. *Hell.* II, 3, 34, 29.

[4] Xen. *Ages.* I, 36; Paus. III, 11, 11; Plut. *Cleom.* VIII, *Apoph. Lac.* 232; Cf. Solari, *op. cit.* p. 209; or τὸ ἀρχεῖον, Plut. *Agis*, XVI.

[5] Plut. *Cleom.* IX. Plutarch's explanation of this remarkable command, that it was intended to show the power of the ephors both in great and small matters, is hardly plausible. It is not impossible that it may have had some ancient and forgotten ritual significance. Shaving or cutting the hair as a lustration is widely known. Cf. Arist. fr. 496; Plut. *de sera Num. vind.* IV; Antiphanes ap. Athen. IV, 143 A. Also Ridgeway, *Early Age of Greece* II, p. 145, with picture of early terra-cottas with upper lip shaved, from *A.B.S.A.* XII, Plate 10; Busolt-Swoboda, *op. cit.* p. 685, n. 1; Solari, *op. cit.* p. 289; Ehrenberg, *Aspects of the Ancient World*, p. 101.

[6] Thuc. I, 87; Xen. *Hell.* IV, 6, 3.   [7] Xen. *Hell.* VI, 3, 18.

[8] Thuc. V, 77.

and had to obtain the permission of the ephors to proceed.[1]
On arrival in Sparta, the ambassadors laid their proposals
before them and they decided whether they should go before
the assembly.[2] Once war was declared the power of the ephors
became still greater. They issued the order mobilising the
army and decided what classes should be called out.[3] They
gave orders to the generals[4] and recalled them if they failed in
the field.[5] When one of the kings went on a campaign, two of
the ephors accompanied him, like the political commissars of
Soviet Russia.[6]

King Agesilaus was wily enough to pretend to defer to
their judgement and obey their commands. This may have
been due to political sagacity, but we may also suppose that,
owing to the dispute over the succession when he came to the
throne, he was taking no chances in stirring up strife. So long
as he had the ephors on his side he was safe. Plutarch says:

Instead of contending with them he courted them. In all proceedings he commenced by taking their advice, and was always
ready to go, nay almost to run, when they called him. If he was
on his royal seat hearing causes and the Ephors came in, he rose to
them. When any man was elected to the Council of Elders, he
presented him with a gown and an ox. Thus, while he made a show
of deference and of a desire to extend their authority, he secretly
advanced his own and enlarged the prerogatives of the kings by
several liberties which their friendship to his person conceded.[7]

There is no evidence that the ephors themselves had the
power to inflict capital punishment, although they did so at
times, as in the execution of Cinadon and of Agis IV and his
family. The latter act was utterly unconstitutional and shocking
and clearly shook their prestige and power. The ease with
which Cleomenes did away with them is evidence of that.

[1] Xen. *Hell.* II, 2, 13.
[2] *Ibid.* v, 2, 11; Polyb. LV, 34, 5–6.   [3] Xen. *Hell*, VI, 4, 17.
[4] Thuc. VIII, 11; Xen. *Hell*. III, 1, 1.   [5] Thuc. I, 131; Plut. *Lys.* 19.
[6] Xen. *Hell*. II, 4, 36; *Resp. Lac.* XIII, 5.
[7] *Ages.* IV; cf. *Praec. reip. ger.* XXI.

Nor do we find any evidence that they could impose a sentence of banishment. Apparently all that the ephors could do was to fine a culprit. We know they imposed a penalty for bringing money into Sparta.[1] We also hear that they fined a man for being lazy[2] and, surprisingly, for being unpopular.[3] They fined King Agis for not sacrificing when he should.

As evidence of the great importance placed upon the education of the young Spartans, the ephors were in control of their training. Every ten days the youths appeared for a physical examination.[4] If any youth had been guilty of serious misconduct he was brought before them. They selected annually the three captains of the royal bodyguard or *hippeis*, who formed the *corps d'élite* of the Spartan army.[5]

Their power over the lesser magistrates was unlimited. 'They have power also to degrade magistrates, even while they are in office, to put them in prison and bring them to trial for their life.'[6] At the conclusion of a magistrate's term of office he was required to render account of it to the ephors.[7] The secret police, the *crypteia*, was under their orders.[8] They were in control of the finances of the State, they received all booty captured in war and imposed taxation.[9]

They summoned and presided over the sessions of the *Gerousia* and *Ecclesia*.[10] It seems probable that the right of initiating legislation belonged to them alone,[11] although admittedly the point is obscure.[12] We do not know how far they were directly responsible to the *Gerousia* or whether they could be indicted while in office or only on retirement.[13] In conjunction with the *Gerousia* they formed a court of

---

[1] Plut. *Lys.* xix.   [2] Schol. ad Thuc. I, 84.   [3] Plut. *Inst. Lac.* 254.
[4] Agatharchides ap. Athen. xii, 550c.
[5] Xen. *Resp. Lac.* iv, 3.   [6] *Ibid.* viii, 4.
[7] Arist. *Pol.* 1271 a; Plut. *Apoph. Lac.* 212 d.
[8] *Vide infra*, p. 162, for further comment on the *crypteia*.
[9] Plut. *Lys.* xvi; *Agis*, xvi; Diod. Sic. xiii, 106.
[10] Xen. *Hell.* ii, 2, 19; Plut. *Agis*, ix; Thuc. I, 87.
[11] Plut. *Agis*, v, 8.
[12] The point is further discussed, *vide infra*, p. 142.
[13] Arist. *Rhet.* iii, 18; Plut. *Agis*, xii; Arist. *Pol.* ii, 9.

criminal justice[1] and carried out the infliction of punishments.[2] Civil cases involving contracts were judged by the ephors alone, or by some of them.[3]

It is therefore evident that their powers were very great. They were limited only by the fact that their office was elective and they only held office for one year, which must have imposed a good deal of discretion when they knew that they would be called to account for their actions and vengeance would be wreaked upon them when they became private citizens once again. Aristotle disapproved highly of the system of election to the ephorate and has some severe things to say of them.[4]

These magistrates take cognizance of matters of the greatest importance and yet they are chosen out of the people in general; so that it often happens that a very poor person is elected to that office, who from that circumstance is easily bought...and these men being corrupted with money went as far as they could to ruin the city. Because, their power is too great and nearly tyrannical, their kings are obliged to flatter them, which contributes greatly to hurt the state.

One of their duties, carried out presumably in the name of the eponymous ephor, was to proclaim the intercalation of an extra month once every three years whereby the lunar and solar calendars were made to coincide. One of the charges against the ephor Agesilaus, uncle of the young reformer, King Agis IV, was that he proclaimed an intercalary month where it was not due, and collected the taxes thereon.[5] This passage leads to more than one conclusion of considerable importance. First, it distinctly suggests, although too much need not be made of the point, that the ancient role of 'seer' or 'star-gazer' still appertained to the ephoral office. As astronomers, or astrologers, it was their duty to scan the heavens and therefore they were the right people to know

---

[1] Arist. *Pol.* 1275 B.   [2] Plut. *Agis*, XIX.   [3] Arist. *Pol.* 1275 B.
[4] *Pol.* 1270 B. Cf. Plato, *Legg.* III, 692.   [5] Plut. *Agis*, XVI.

when the calendar needed revision. Second, Agesilaus, however culpable he may have been in proclaiming the extra month
when it was not due, at least was within his legal rights in
doing so. Third, that it was by the authority of the eponymous
ephor that the intercalation was made is a fair inference to
draw. If the year was named after him, then it is natural to
suppose that it was on his responsibility that the month was
added. There is evidence to show that it was the eponymous
archon at Athens who performed the same duty.[1] Fourth, if
our reasoning is correct, then Agesilaus was eponymous
ephor for his year of office, a piece of information that is
otherwise lacking. This is all the more likely when his high-
handed and illegal acts are observed.[2] The eponymous ephor
was the chief-ranking officer and in consequence was able to
exert considerable influence, which Agesilaus proceeded to do.
Fifth, the highly obscure reference to his collecting the taxes
for the month involves considerations which must be postponed
for further discussion hereafter.[3]

[1] This may be safely deduced, in Dr B. D. Meritt's opinion, from *I.G.* i², 76.
There is no evidence to suggest that it was the duty of the *archon basileus*.
The *archon eponymos* seems to have brought the matter before the *demos*, who
then voted him the authority to proclaim the extra month. The suggestion
of A. S. Gow, in *Companion to Greek Studies*, that it was done by authority
of the ἱερομνήμονες lacks confirmation. It is quite likely that these officials
'reminded' the archon that it was time.

[2] *Vide infra*, p. 319.

[3] *Vide infra*, p. 320. Dr E. T. Salmon suggests an apposite parallel to the
act of Agesilaus in the precisely similar attempt by Curio in Rome to intercalate a month in 50 B.C. Curio, one of the *pontifices*, undoubtedly was acting
secretly in Caesar's interest, while seeking at the same time to prolong his own
term as plebeian tribune. His fellow *pontifices* refused to sanction the proposal,
although the addition of a month was overdue from 51 B.C. In mock indignation, Curio openly changed sides in politics and went over to Caesar, who
thereupon paid his debts. It seems that at Rome in the last century B.C.,
although the normal practice was to intercalate a month after February every
third year, the actual choice of the year was legally at the discretion of the
pontifices. In Athens also it seems to have been carried out quite unsyste-
matically in the fifth and fourth centuries and we may suppose it was as
unsystematic at Sparta. The crime of Agesilaus was therefore not quite so
heinous as appears at first sight. For references to Curio, *vide* Dio Cass. XL,

Cavaignac,[1] who does not think much of the ephorate, remarks that, of those who held office during the Peloponnesian war, only three played an important part. Solari[2] points out that from 500 to 184 B.C. 1580 ephors had held office, of which the names of only seventy-two have been preserved. It is true enough that they were 'men of little renown'. It would have been a misfortune were they not. They acted as a body and sank their identities in their office. It is safe to say that no 'unsafe' man had much chance of election. The whole system of administration was 'admirably adapted to a government that was both oligarchic and military and that looked suspiciously on kings and populace and needed absolute discipline and time for speed and secrecy in making and executing decisions'.[3]

Comparisons between ancient and medieval or modern political institutions are always dangerous and of dubious efficacy. The ephorate has sometimes been likened to the Council of Ten of the Venetian Republic. There is, obviously, a certain superficial resemblance; but it is impossible to press the comparison very far. The two Spartan kings were certainly nothing like the Doge of Venice, and it was to keep the privileges of the kings in abeyance that the ephorate existed. 'It solved the dilemma of division of power between people and leaders by giving both a minimum of authority and by maintaining the traditional authoritarian character of the constitution.'[4]

DOWNFALL OF THE EPHORATE: *PATRONOMOI*

With the downfall of Agis and the expulsion of Agesilaus, who had dared in his insolent abuse of office as ephor to

62, 1; Cicero, *Epist. ad fam.* VIII, 5; Appian, *Bell. civ.* II, 27; Ed. Meyer, *Caesars Monarchie u. das Prinzipat Pompejus* (3rd ed. 1922), p. 260. For further discussion on intercalation, *vide* J. K. Fotheringham, 'Cleostratus', *J.H.S.* XL (1919), p. 179; G. Thomson, 'The Greek Calendar', *J.H.S.* LXIII (1943).

[1] *Revue de Paris* (1912), p. 339.   [2] *Ricerche Spartane.*
[3] Andreades, *Hist. Grk. Pub. Fin.* p. 45.   [4] Jaeger, *Paideia*, p. 79.

announce that he would hold office for a second year, an unheard-of assumption,[1] the ephors who displaced the nominees of Agis resumed their power and continued in their reactionary policy until the *coup d'état* of Cleomenes III, when four of them were murdered, only one managing to escape.[2] Apparently then Cleomenes set up a new board of magistrates, the *patronomoi*[3] (either six or twelve, the number being uncertain)[4], who displaced the ephors in power. With the defeat of Cleomenes at Sellasia and his flight and suicide in Egypt, the ancient constitution was restored by Antigonus Doson and the ephorate once more constituted.[5] The ephors showed all the characteristics of reactionaries and used as their tool, one Lycurgus, not of the royal line, whom they placed on the throne. If we are to believe Polybius[6] 'by giving a talent to each of the ephors, he became a descendant of Heracles and king of Sparta'. The ephors seem to have been in complete control and when they suspected Lycurgus of designs to make himself a tyrant he was obliged to flee. Later they discovered their mistake and recalled him.[7] We have no information as to their existence during the tyranny of Machanidas, but we may reasonably infer that he turned them out of office. Nabis abolished the college of ephors and may have used a restored board of *patronomoi*, although here we are in complete uncertainty. Later our information is very vague and nothing definite may be said. Certainly the *patronomoi* were functioning in Roman times, although what was their relationship to the ephors, who also existed, it is impossible to say.[8] A somewhat obscure reference in Philo-

---

[1] *Agis*, XVI.   [2] *Cleom.* VIII.

[3] Paus. II, 9, 1. Cf. Beloch, *Griech. Gesch*, IV, pt. 1, p. 703, n. 3.

[4] The point is obscure. Cf. art. 'Patronomoi' in P.W. for inconclusive discussion; also Solari, *op. cit.* p. 179 ff. Busolt-Swoboda, *op. cit.* II, pp. 645, 729, holds that Cleomenes abolished the kome Dyme, substituted that of Amyclae and added a sixth, Neapolis, with a sixth representative or *patronomos*. The evidence is insufficient to substantiate this view which may, or may not, be correct.

[5] *Cleom.* XXX.   [6] IV, 35.   [7] V, 91.

[8] *I.G.* V, 1, 65. Temp. Antoninus Pius, end of the first century A.D.

stratus¹ suggests that the ephors still held office in the second century A.D.

The origin and powers of these *patronomoi* are by no means clear, and a careful examination of the subject reveals several obscurities and difficulties which are difficult to resolve satisfactorily.² In the first place, did Cleomenes create these officials *de novo*? That can almost certainly be answered in the negative, if we accept the statements of Philostratus³ and Plutarch⁴ who say that the *patronomoi* were always among the principal magistrates ranking with the gymnasiarchs and ephors. According to Lucian,⁵ in Athens the function of similar officials was to look after the behaviour of the adolescents. While we cannot be sure that they exercised the same functions in Sparta, yet it would be in character if they did. Perhaps after the young boys had been under the care of their *paidonomoi* for some years they passed into a higher class, presumably that of the age group 12–18, and were under the discipline of the *patronomoi*. This is the purest conjecture and incapable of proof.

Secondly, what was their position after their elevation to power by Cleomenes? Pausanias⁶ says τὸ κράτος τῆς γερουσίας καταλύσας πατρονόμους τῷ λογῷ κατέστησεν ἀντ' αὐτῶν, that is, having taken away the powers of the *Gerousia*, he put the *patronomoi* in their place. Was the Senate entirely dissolved? Evidently not, as we hear of it again.⁷ Apparently Cleomenes wanted to get rid of both *Gerousia* and ephors, but did not dare to abolish them altogether, perhaps they merely changed places with the *patronomoi*. It is noteworthy that when in the middle of the second century B.C. Jonathan, the leader of the Jews in their struggle for freedom,

---

¹ *Vita Apoll.* IV, 32.
² Solari, *op. cit.* p. 179; Gilbert, *Grk. Const. Ant.* p. 25, n. 5.
³ IV, 32.
⁴ *An seni resp. ger. sit*, XXIV.
⁵ *Demosth. Encom.* XII; Photius, *s.v.*
⁶ II, p. 1; *C.I.G.* 1356.
⁷ Paus. III, 11, 2. Cf. Boeckh, *C.I.G.* I, p. 605.

sent a letter of friendship to the Spartans by the embassy returning from Rome it was addressed to 'the Senate, People and Ephors of Sparta'.[1]

The senior *patronomos* was made eponymous, although Pausanias[2] says that the senior ephor was still eponymous, a statement which is strongly open to doubt. Along with the senior *patronomoi* were six 'associates' (σύναρχοι).[3] What exactly were the functions of these associates is not clear, but it is probable that they acted as substitutes and while functioning possessed the same powers as the six seniors. Attached to the college was a clerk (γραμματεύς)[4] and a constable (ὑπηρέτας), who was probably in command of their bodyguard and acted as a chief of police.[5] Apparently, although not certainly, the *patronomoi* could hold office for more than one year.

[1] Joseph. *Jud. Antiq.* XIII, 5, 8.
[2] III, 11, 2.   [3] *I.G.* v[1], 74.
[4] *I.G.* v[1], 124.   [5] *Ibid.*

CHAPTER V

THE SPARTAN CONSTITUTION (II)

The Senate and General Assembly; Civil Service and Judiciary

Besides the hereditary dual monarchy and the elective college of ephors, the Spartan constitution provided for a Senate, whose members were elected for life and the General Assembly of all male Spartans who were of age and could prove full citizenship. There were, therefore, no fewer than four branches of government which functioned, if not always without friction—the rivalry between kings and ephors was unceasing —at least with tolerable efficiency.

THE *GEROUSIA*

The Senate of elders, the *Gerousia*, also called *Gerontia* and *Gerochia*,[1]* consisted of twenty-eight members and, with the two kings sitting *ex officio*, thirty in all. Membership was restricted to those among the Spartan peers who had reached the age of sixty, when they ceased to be liable for military service.[2] The method of election, of which Aristotle highly disapproved,[3] was that each candidate appeared before the assembled people, in an order determined by lot, and the volume of applause accorded to each was estimated by a board of judges shut up in a nearby house. He who was greeted with the greatest clamour was pronounced elected. Obviously

---

[1] *Gerousia*, Dem. *in Lept.* CVII; *Gerontia*, Xen. *Resp. Lac.* x, 1, 3; *Gerochia*, Aristoph. *Lys.* 980. For various forms cf. Busolt-Swoboda, *Griech. Staatsk.* p. 679, n. 4. Probably, if not certainly, the original or oldest form was *Gerochia*, the senators, γέροντες, being those who enjoyed honour and who were not necessarily elders. Plutarch adds that the Pythian Apollo first called them πρεσβυγενέες but later Lycurgus called them γέροντες. *An seni resp. ger. sit*, 789E. Cf. Wilamowitz Moellendorff, *Staat und Gesellschaft der Griechen*, p. 84.

[2] Plut. *Lyc.* XXVI.   [3] Arist. *Pol.* 1270B. Cf. Polyb. VI, 10.

such a method was open to abuse, since the noisiest claque could raise a stupendous uproar. But although Aristotle calls this method of election 'childish', failing election by secret ballot it was probably effective and secured the success of the best, or most popular, candidate. On being elected the successful candidate, crowned with a chaplet of flowers, and followed by an applauding throng of young men and maidens made a round of the temples. Lastly he went to his *syssition* where, in honour of the occasion, he was given a double portion. At the door were congregated the women of his family, and to the one he deemed most worthy he presented one of the portions.

We have already quoted in part the *rhetra* whereby having set up sanctuaries and confirmed the existence of the phyles and obes, the next step was to establish thirty men as a Senate or *Gerousia* including the two kings. When that had been done, season after season, the people must keep *Apellai* (that is, assemble on a certain day of each month, presumably at the full moon)[1] between Babyca and Gnacion. These senators or *gerontes* shall bring proposals (to the *demos*) or shall decline to bring proposals; the demos shall have the right to criticise and the final voice. And if the demos formulate crooked judgements, the senators and kings shall decline to accept them.[2] The meaning here is plain. To use modern phraseology, bills must originate in the Senate or Upper House, but did not reach final enactment until they had received the approval of the Lower House. The Senate was therefore a probouleutic body.

---

[1] Schol. ad Thuc. I, 67, Mr Wade-Gery (*Class. Quart.* XXXVII (1943), p. 67) suggests 'with due reserve' that there were μεγάλαι ἀπελλαί annually in the month Apellaios, as an inference from the inscription at Gythium (*I.G.* v, 1, 1144–6), and lesser *apellai* every month. Boisacq, *Dict. Etym. s.v.* 'ἀπελλαί' connects the word with Apollo, and we know that sacrifices were made monthly to him.

[2] This seems to contradict the view that bills could only be initiated by the ephors (*supra*, p. 128). Possibly the ephors introduced their proposals in the Senate, and upon these being approved they were taken to the *Ecclesia* for final ratification. To propose a motion, εἰπεῖν γνώμην, cf. Thuc. VIII, 68.

It formulated proposed bills, and put them into shape before submitting them to final debate. The same system was followed in Athens where the *Boule* discussed proposals before submitting them to the people (τῷ δήμῳ).[1] This perfectly understandable procedure is obviously different from modern usage, where bills may originate in either House of the legislature. If the senators found their proposals unacceptable to the *Ecclesia*, they could adjourn the House and, presumably, withdraw the bill altogether or bring it in again with amendments.

Why the *Gerousia* should have consisted, along with the two kings, of thirty members presents a problem which has taxed the ingenuity of all commentators and remains unsolved. Why were there twenty-eight senators or *gerontes*? Perhaps, as Plutarch suggests, there was some mystical significance in that number, since it is the sum of its own factors.[2] This is not an impossible explanation, knowing as we do the fascination that numbers held for all the ancient peoples.[3] A suggestion that there were four phyles, each of which was represented by seven senators[4] has already been made and rejected, on the ground that the probability is greatly in favour of there having been five. Another suggestion, which merits attention, is that each of the five phyles were represented in the *Gerousia* by five senators. That would make twenty-five *gerontes*, and the 'leaders' must have been the five ephors and not the two kings who sat with, but were not officially numbered among, them. This would provide a neat mathematical solution, if it were not for the fact that there is no indication in the *rhetra* of the participation of the ephors in the government at that epoch;

[1] Dem. *in Timoc.* II, 20.

[2] I.e. $1+2+4+7+14$. Cf. Plato, *Legg.* v, 8, 738 A. Plut. *Lyc.* v. The number 28 is a 'perfect' number.

[3] E.g. the mathematical puzzles presented in Plato's *Republic* and *Laws* and in the Book of Daniel. Plutarch, *Lyc.* v, rather half-heartedly mentions that Aristotle, presumably in the lost treatise on Laconia, was the author of the statement that originally Lycurgus had chosen thirty senators but that two had been afraid to assume office. This seems even more unlikely. Cf. Neumann, *Hist. Ztschr.* XCVI (1906), p. 42.

[4] *Supra*, p. 97.

nor have we any grounds for supposing that at the time of the 'Lycurgan' settlement the college of ephors had advanced to the power that it subsequently enjoyed owing to the actions, supposedly, of Asteropus and Chilon.

Aside from these obscurities, we are well informed as to the status and duties of the Senate. The principal function of the *Gerousia* was to deliberate upon measures to be submitted to the Lower House or *Ecclesia*. Originally, if we are to judge from the Lycurgan *rhetra*, the *Gerousia* was bound to accept the decision of the Lower House. This was changed, and if the Senate disagreed with the decision of the *Ecclesia*, it would adjourn, thus leaving the vote unratified.[1] Along with the two kings and the five ephors, the senators formed the executive branch of government.[2] They were the court of criminal jurisdiction; tried murder cases[3] and treason against the State; could impose money fines;[4] *atimia*;[5] banishment or death.[6] The ephors were the supreme court of appeal.[7] The procedure in capital cases before the *Gerousia*, if a Spartan was involved, was of great deliberation and solemnity, the trial occupying several days.[8] Once judgement had been pronounced and the accused condemned, he was handed over to the ephors to see that the sentence of the court was carried out. Although the powers of the *Gerousia* were great, Andreades[9] is scarcely correct when he says it 'had succeeded in appropriating to itself the right to choose those officers

---

[1] Plut. *Lyc.* VI. Cf. *Agis*, VIII–XI, where the *Gerousia* vetoed the proposed land reforms which had been approved by the lower house.

[2] Polyb. VI, 45, 5; Dion. Hal. II, 14; Isocr. XII, 154.

[3] Arist. *Pol.* 1275 B.   [4] Plut. *Inst. Lac.* 239 C.

[5] Plut. *Inst. Lac.* VII, 237 B, C.

[6] Evidently the ephors did at times take this prerogative to themselves when the case involved treason against the State; e.g. Gylippus, Diod. XIII, 106; Thorax, Plut. *Lys.* XIX; Cinadon, Xen. *Hell.* III, 3, and King Agis and his family. Perhaps the ephors had deprived the *Gerousia* altogether of its function as a criminal court; *vide* Solari, *Ricerche Spartane*, p. 207; Dum, *Entstehung u. Entwick. des Spart. Eph.* p. 121.

[7] Arist. *Pol.* 1270 B.   [8] Plut. *Apoph. Lac.* 217 B. Cf. Thuc. I, 132.

[9] *Greek Public Finance*, p. 44.

into whose hands all power was concentrated, namely the ephors'. As we have already seen, election to the ephorate was by popular vote.

A most ingenious explanation of the composition of the *Gerousia* has been made by Mr Toynbee.[1] Each phyle was subdivided into ten phratries, the royal phratries and nine others and each phratry into ten γένη, making 300 in all. The twenty-seven 'commoner' phratries were represented in the Senate by their headmen to make up the thirty members with the three kings. These twenty-seven phratries celebrated the feast of the Carneia, in which each phratry was represented by three men and the eighty-one celebrants were grouped in nine *skiades* or 'tabernacles' of nine men each, each *skias* containing the representatives of three phratries, one from each phyle.[2] Finally, each γένος equipped a horseman in war, and the corps of *hippeis* always retained its original numbers, even after its constitution and duties were transformed.

As is so often the case in examining such neat and mathematical demonstrations, unfortunately, there is no certain evidence to support them. Mr Toynbee's calculations rest upon the assumption that, before their expulsion, the Aegeidai were on an equality with the other two royal houses, for which there is no evidence. Nor is there any evidence that the two, or three royal houses were subdivided into γένη. It also does not satisfactorily explain why, after the expulsion of the Aegeidai, the number of the senators was increased to twenty-eight. What phratry did the additional senator represent? It must be acknowledged that Mr Toynbee does give an explanation of the nine Tabernacles of the Carneia, which is more than anyone else has attempted to do. But again, his assumption is entirely conjectural. Finally, although the point is not immediately pertinent, his statement that the 300 γένη each equipped a horseman, while not impossible, cannot be substantiated.

J.H.S. xxxiii, p. 255.   [2] Dem. Sceps. ap. Athen. iv, 141

A senator held office for life and could not be called to account for his conduct, a practice of which Aristotle strongly disapproves:[1]

> If they were fitly trained to the practice of every human virtue everyone would readily admit that they would be useful to the government. But still it might be debated whether they should be continued judges for life and so determine matters of the greatest importance, since the mind has its old age as well as the body. Since they are brought up in such fashion that even the legislator could not depend upon them as good men, their power must be inconsistent with the safety of the state. For it is known that the members of that body have been guilty of both bribery and partiality in many public affairs. For which reason it would have been much better if they had been made answerable for their conduct, which they are not. It may indeed be said that the Ephors have a check upon them. They have, in truth, in this particular very great power, but I affirm that they should not be entrusted with this control in the way they are.... By making his citizens ambitious for honours, the legislator has filled his senate with men of that sort for no others will seek election to that body. Yet most of these crimes of which men are guilty arise from ambition and avarice.

THE *ECCLESIA*[2]

The *Ecclesia* or General Assembly of the Spartan people was simply the muster of the tribesmen, the warriors who met

---

[1] Arist. *Pol.* 1270 B, 1271 A; Plut. *Lyc.* XXVI; Polyb. VI, 45, 5.

[2] Mr Wade-Gery, *Class. Quart.* XXXVII (1943), p. 66, points out that there is no evidence of the use of the word *apella* as denoting the popular assembly or *Ecclesia*. The word is never used in the singular. In an early Roman inscription at Gythium in Laconia (*I.G.* V, 1, 1144, 1146) the word in the plural applies to annual religious festivals. Cf. Nilsson, *Griechische Feste*, p. 464. In the plural it is also used by Hesychius. Gilbert, *Grk. Const. Ant.* p. 50, while dubious of the word *apella*, objects that *ecclesia* was not a technical term. That is probably true, but at least it is the only one used by Xenophon (*Hell.* III, 2, 23, V, 2, 11) to denote the popular assembly, and in default of a better is the only one that we can use. While we cannot say for certain that *apella* was not used, neither can we affirm it. In the dilemma it is better to speak of *ecclesia*. There is no evidence to warrant the use of the word ἁλία in this connection, although it is used constantly in Doric inscriptions. The use of the word in Herod. VII, 134, is not conclusive.

to settle questions of great moment to the whole nation. Its membership was composed of all free-born Spartans who, presumably, had not lost their political rights through a sentence of disgrace or *atimia*, or from inability to keep up their dues to the *syssitia*.[1] Sessions of this body were held in the open air 'between Babyca and Gnacion'. This place is unidentifiable and even puzzled Plutarch to fix with certainty, who says in his time it was called Oenus. Aristotle says, 'Gnacion is a river and Babyca a bridge.'[2]

Evidently the powers of the *Ecclesia* were circumscribed.

The people were assembled in the open air, it was not allowed to any of them to give his advice, but only to ratify or reject what was propounded to them by king or Senate. But since afterwards the people by adding or omitting words distorted the sense of the proposals laid before the kings, Polydorus and Theopompus added to the covenant or *rhetra* the following clause: 'That if the people decide crookedly it shall be lawful for the leaders to prorogue the Assembly,' that is to say refuse ratification of its will and dismiss the people as depravers and perverters of their counsel.

It is pertinent to note that the kings, according to Plutarch's statement, 'persuaded the people to accept this *rhetra* in the belief that it was the command of the God', which is sufficient to indicate it was a 'put-up job', whereby the mass of the Spartans was denied all real power. The analogy between this and the summoning of the Reichstag and Italian Parliament to hear and applaud the decisions of the dictators is apposite.

Every Spartan of good standing who had attained his thirtieth year had the right to attend. In earlier times the kings presided, but later the ephors,[3] under the chairmanship, presumably, of the eponymous ephor. A problem of considerable obscurity, upon which it seems impossible to come to a definite conclusion, is whether or no an ordinary member

---

[1] Arist. *Pol.* 1271 A. But doubtful; for further on this cf. p. 38.
[2] Plut. *Lyc.* VI, 2; *Pelopidas*, XVII. Probably a general term for the whole Eurotas valley, like Dan and Beersheba of ancient Canaan.
[3] Thuc. I, 87.

(that is, one who was neither an ephor nor a senator) could address the House. Plutarch explicitly states that he could not,[1] and it seems hard to get away from that. Mr Wade-Gery,[2] however, suggests that Plutarch was mistaken and that debates were held in which members of both Houses took part. Aeschines[3] tells of a man of bad character who almost carried the Assembly with him. Plutarch[4] also tells of a dissolute man named Demosthenes who made a desirable motion in the Assembly which the people rejected. Rather than let it go, the ephors put up one of their own number to reintroduce the motion. In neither case are we told that the speaker was not a senator. In the great debate on the proposal to declare war on Athens[5] we must suppose that many speakers took part, we know that King Archidamus and the Ephor Sthenelaidas spoke; but we do not know for certain that any of the Lower House did.

The words of the *rhetra* as given by the manuscripts are evidently corrupt.

γαμωδᾶν γορίαν ἤ μὴν καὶ κράτος.

Mr Wade-Gery proposes to emend this to δάμω δ'ἀνταγορίαν ἦμεν καὶ κράτος, that is, the people have the power to criticise or speak against any proposal brought before them. If we accept this reading (and it seems a reasonable one), it appears that debate was permissible, although it is unlikely that motions could be put from the floor of the House. That was certainly impossible in Athens.[6] The procedure was evidently that a motion was proposed by a spokesman of the ephors and thrown open to debate. Amendments were out of order; all that could be done was either to accept or reject the motion, and this was done by shouting 'Yes' or 'No'; in case of uncertainty the House divided.[7] If the ephors and Senate

---

[1] *Lyc.* VI.
[2] *Class. Quart.* XXXVIII (1944), p. 8.
[3] *In Timarch.* CLXXX.
[4] *Praec. ger. resp.* 800 C.
[5] Thuc. I, 87.
[6] *Ath. Pol.* XLV, 4.
[7] Thuc. I, 87.

disapproved of what they considered a 'crooked judgement' in the defeat of the motion, they could withdraw it—they were not bound to accept the decision as final and could presumably bring it up again at a subsequent meeting of the Assembly.

If we accept this emendation, we are then confronted with another difficulty in the passage where Aristotle comments unfavourably on parliamentary practice in Sparta, comparing it with Carthaginian. In the latter State he says

the kings and elders, if unanimous, may determine whether they will or will not bring a matter before the people, but when they are not unanimous the people may decide whether or not the matter shall be brought forward. And whatever the kings and elders bring before the people is not only heard but also determined by them and anyone who likes may oppose it; now this is not permitted in Sparta and Crete.

It must be acknowledged that, if Aristotle is correct in this passage, the conclusion that debate in the *Ecclesia* was allowed cannot stand. Mr Wade-Gery[1] boldly asserts that either Aristotle made a mistake, or else a copyist has transposed the order of the sentence. As he proposes to read it, the words 'this is not permitted in Sparta or Crete' should be transposed to come immediately after 'the people shall decide whether or not the matter shall be brought forward'. The sense of the passage therefore is that in Carthage unanimity in the Senate is necessary before a proposal is brought up in the *Ecclesia*. If the vote is not unanimous, then it is referred to the *Ecclesia*, a procedure not known in Sparta or Crete. When a proposal is before the Lower House it is debated and the final decision rests there. This is a somewhat violent emendation, but there is a good deal to be said in its favour. So far as is known unanimity in the Senate was not necessary in Sparta, and there is not a hint of the procedure in Carthage of taking a debatable measure to the *Ecclesia* for final settlement. The point must be left open, no final decision being possible upon it.

[1] *Class. Quart.* XXXVII, p. 71.

We are left with one more problem, namely, whether, if a bill was introduced into the *Ecclesia* and rejected, the administration could still go ahead and defy the Lower House. This is a supposition which might be inferred from the passage in Plutarch quoted above concerning the 'crooked' decisions which might be rejected or ignored by the administration. This view is taken by Gilbert[1] and Oncken,[2] but it seems a little difficult to accept. If the administration could do exactly as it saw fit, simply ignoring the adverse vote in the *Ecclesia*, it is obvious that only a shadow of parliamentary procedure was preserved in Sparta.

It would depend upon whether the ephors in office at the moment were strong and resolute men, whose decision to defy the *Ecclesia* was backed by the Senate, and who were willing to face popular displeasure and the risk of indictment when their term expired. This seems unlikely. Disregard of the wishes of the Lower House is only possible in a system of government where the dictators cannot be removed and reference of administrative acts to a 'democratic' assembly is a more or less empty form, as was the case in Italy and Germany under the Fascist and Nazi regimes and is still so in Russia. It is true that the senators could not be removed from office during good behaviour, but the ephors were elected annually, and it is unlikely they would risk popular displeasure. It is much more likely that when they found their proposals disapproved they modified them and brought them forward again in a more acceptable form, or abandoned altogether the attempt to have them approved by the people.

The *Ecclesia* decided on questions of peace or war and foreign policy.[3] It appointed the generals[4] and elected the *gerontes*,[5] decided claims to the throne[6] and voted on proposed laws.[7] It also freed such helots as had displayed conspicuous valour in battle.[8]

[1] Gilbert, *op. cit.* p. 51.   [2] *Staatslehre Aristoteles*, I, pp. 279 f.
[3] Xen. *Hell.* II, 4, 38; V, 2, 32.   [4] *Ibid.* IV, 2, 9; VI, 5, 10.
[5] Plut. *Lyc.* XXVI.
[6] Herod. VI, 65–66; Xen. *Hell.* III, 3, 4.
[7] Plut. *Agis*, IX, X.   [8] Thuc. V, 34.

The curious reference in Xenophon[1] to 'the so-called Little Ecclesia' has led some commentators to suppose there was a smaller assembly, or a kind of executive committee. The phrase is found nowhere else and appears unintelligible, unless it refers to kings, ephors and *gerontes*. It may have been a kind of 'inner cabinet' that the ephors could call at short notice; but no satisfactory explanation can be given and it must be left in doubt. If it was a committee of the executive, the fact that it met in secret accounts for our lack of knowledge of its functions.

The conclusion to which we may reasonably arrive is that, in spite of the various obscurities, the constitution of Sparta was, in Cicero's phrase, 'mixed'. It was an oligarchy, in so far as the number of enfranchised Spartans was very small and this privileged body ruled the *perioeci* and helots, who had no say in the central government whatever. In this Sparta did not notably differ from any other Greek city-state, where citizenship formed a 'close corporation', and reflection will reveal that Sparta only differed from Attica in the fact that the Spartan peers were far fewer in number than the Athenian citizens. It was a democracy in the limited sense that any Spartan who submitted himself to the discipline imposed and was of good standing in his mess, could claim, as of right, membership in the General Assembly. It was also democratic in the fact that the college of ephors was elective, holding office for one year, ineligible for a second term and accountable for its actions on leaving office. The Senate was also elected by popular vote, although its members held office for life.

Lastly, it is difficult to agree with Ehrenberg when he says that the *Ecclesia* 'had lost all effective political influence'. It is evident that if the popular assembly of all enfranchised citizens

---

[1] *Hell.* III, 3, 8. Cf. Gilbert, *op. cit.* p. 50, n. 2. Busolt-Swoboda, *op. cit.* p. 693, n. 5. Schömann-Lipsius, *Griech. Altert.* I, 4, p. 240. Ollier, *Le Mirage Spartiate*, p. 26; Glotz, *Histoire Grecque*, I, p. 364. Art. 'Ekklesia' in D.S. by Glotz, who puts forward the suggestion that it consisted of kings, senators, ephors and a select number of men of renown and wealth.

refused to agree to the proposals of the ephors and senators, a deadlock must have been reached until some compromise could be arrived at.

PLACES OF ASSEMBLY

The *Gerousia* met in their own senate chamber in the market-place, which was near, or formed part of the executive offices of the ephors (ἀρχεῖα).[1] As being so small a body, it could be accommodated in the crowded market-place and doubtless it was wise that it should be near the government offices and in constant touch with the ephors. The meeting place of the General Assembly, on the other hand, was purposely situated outside the city, not only because of crowded conditions within the town, but also no doubt because the distractions and noise of the market-place would prevent clear thought and calm deliberation.

Plutarch[2] says that the all-wise Lycurgus would allow no kind of hall or any other building, or any statues or scenic embellishments or extravagantly decorated roofs of council halls. Pausanias[3] speaks apparently of a parliament house called the Skias, that is, the 'canopy', where the Spartans hold the meetings of their Assembly. 'This canopy they say was made by Theodorus of Samos.' It must be acknowledged that we here encounter very serious difficulties. Did the Spartan Assembly meet in the open air or in a building called the Skias? Perhaps the simplest thing is to imagine a building without sides with a 'canopy' or roof upheld on pillars to shade the Assembly from the sun. Or perhaps the kings and ephors sat on a daïs with a canopy above their heads, while the commons sat or stood in the open air. No conclusion is possible on this point.

The *Ecclesia* apparently met monthly, either at the new or the full moon, but more probably the latter.[4] The fact that it met so constantly indicates that it must have had considerable

---

[1] Paus. III, 11, 2; W. A. Macdonald, *Political Meeting Places of the Greeks*.
[2] *Lyc.* VI.   [3] III, 12, 10.   [4] Schol. ad Thuc. I, 67.

power and that the acts of the ephors were always under review. In so small a community secrets were hard to keep, and we cannot envisage an ephorate working below the surface and imposing obedience to its orders through a secret police without the members of the *Ecclesia* knowing all about it.

It would seem reasonable to suppose that generally *Gerousia* and *Ecclesia* met together in plenary session. Mr Wade-Gery,[1] however, points out that they could meet separately. In the course of the development of the constitutional crisis at the time of Agis IV,[2] the *Ecclesia* apparently met and discussed the bill before the *Gerousia* had voted upon it. While the debate in the *Gerousia* was still going on, and there were signs that it would probably be rejected, Lysander summoned the *Ecclesia* and Agis spoke before it, opposed by Leonidas. Subsequently the bill was thrown out by the *Gerousia*. Mr Wade-Gery acknowledges that this 'may be a symptom of revolution' and it would seem unsafe to base any conclusion upon the incident. Everything was in a turmoil and the fate of the measure hung in the balance. Lysander, to intimidate the *gerontes*, appealed to the people. Another famous incident early in the fifth century was connected with the name of the senator Hetoimaridas and reported by Diodorus.[3] The two Houses assembled, apparently apart, although it must be acknowledged that the narration is far from clear, and Hetoimaridas persuaded both *Gerousia* and *Ecclesia* to adopt his view.

Neither of these instances is conclusive and it would seem that ordinarily both Houses met together, although there was no reason why they should not meet separately and we may suppose that they occasionally did so. It might be conjectured, although here we are on very unsafe ground, that the practice of meeting separately is implied in the power of the *Gerousia* to refuse to bring a motion before the plenary session and refers to one that had already been approved by the *Ecclesia*.

[1] *Class. Quart.* XXXVIII, p. 8.
[2] Plut. *Agis*, IX–XI.   [3] Diod. XI, 50.

But it might equally well refer to a motion introduced into the *Gerousia* by one of the senators. The point must be left unsettled.

Grote's conclusion[1] that in actual practice the *Ecclesia* was seldom convened and that the business of the State was carried on by ephors and senators without reference, or at best with only occasional reference, to the people at large, cannot be sustained. How far ephors and Senate took the general body into their confidence is quite another matter. Probably they did not consult them in the less important problems of day-to-day administration; but in matters of vital importance they must have done so.

The generic term for all members of both Houses was οἱ ἔκκλητοι, that is, those who were summoned to confer upon matters of government.[2]

THE CIVIL SERVICE

We are ill-informed with regard to the minor officials and magistrates. We do not know whether there was an elective body of officers whose duty it was to carry on the civil administration under the supervision of the ephors. It seems more likely that in so small a community the five ephors were sufficient in themselves to administer the ordinary affairs of the town and country.

We hear of an *empeloros* in Roman times, according to Hesychius an official corresponding with the *agoranomos* of Athens, whose duties were to manage and maintain order and fair dealing in the market. There seems to have been an official overseer or 'curator' in the city of Sparta, who bore the title of *epimeletes*, with five assistants (σύναρχοι).[3] What his duties were we do not know, but probably he was city marshal or chief of police and had as his assistants the *eructeres*, slave policemen, of whom we have already spoken, charged with preserving order.[4] Hesychius says that there were *harmosunoi*,

---

[1] II, p. 357. [2] Xen. *Hell.* v, 2, 11; vi, 3, 3.
[3] *I.G.* v, 1. 133–5. Cf. Ehrenberg, *Hermes*, LIX (1924), p. 27. This seems a reasonable inference from the title ἐπιμελετὴς τῆς πόλεως, but very uncertain.
[4] Uncertain; cf. art. 'Epimeletes' by Glotz in D.S.

a kind of *police des mœurs*, who, like the *gynaikonomoi* of Athens, saw that the women behaved themselves. Nothing more is known of these, and they may have been a late development of Roman times. There were four *pythioi*, whose duty it was to consult the Delphic oracle when its decision was required by the people.[1]

Officials of whom we know very little, and whose very existence in Laconia and Messenia has been questioned, were the *harmosts*. They were apparently governors or representatives sent to outlying districts. We know of a governor of Cythera,[2] and a somewhat doubtful source[3] says there were twenty such harmosts, supposedly stationed on the lands of the *perioeci*. Parke[4] accepts the evidence of their existence, faulty though it is, and surmises they received orders from the home government through the medium of the *scytale*, or message tally. But we know very well that in foreign countries the harmosts were governors, civil or military, representing the Spartan government. It was their conduct, their arrogance, harshness and corruption that aroused hatred against Sparta among other nations, who had looked to her to be a true leader of the Greeks and who were bitterly disappointed by this conduct. We know where a good many were stationed,[5]

---

[1] Herod. VI, 57; Xen. *Resp. Lac.* XV, 5.

[2] Thuc. IV, 53.   [3] Schol. ad Pind. *Ol.* VI, 154.

[4] H. W. Parke, 'The Evidence for Harmosts in Laconia', *Hermathena*, XLVI (1931), p. 31. Cf. also Gilbert, *op. cit.* p. 36, n. 2. Schömann-Lipsius, *Griech. Altert.* p. 216, supposes that the whole of Laconia was divided into twenty military districts each under its governor, like England under Cromwell's major-generals. Not impossible, but without evidence. Busolt-Swoboda, *op. cit.* p. 664, leaves the problem open. Cf. art. 'Harmostai' in P.W. by Oehler. H. Schaefer, *Staatsform u. Politik*, p. 232, suggests that when the ephors usurped the powers of the Kings the personal tie between kings and *perioeci* was dissolved and the harmosts were sent to the perioecic districts to represent the ephors in their relations with the *perioeci*. Cf. also Kahrstedt, *Griech. Staatsr.* p. 75.

[5] E.g. Cythera, Thuc. IV, 53; Methone (Brasidas), Thuc. II, 25; Thyrea (Tantalus), Thuc. IV, 57; Ionia (Thibron and Dercyllidas), Xen. *Hell.* III, 1, 4; Attica (Lysander), *Hell.* II, 4, 28; Olynthus (Polybiades), *Hell.* V, 3, 20; in the Hellespont, *Hell.* III, 2, 20; IV, 1, 8, 5, 39.

but the list is far from complete; there must have been others. They were appointed 'by the Lacedaemonians', that elusive phrase that causes so much uncertainty. It is hard to believe they were elected by the people; the truth probably is they were nominated by the ephors and the appointment ratified by the *Ecclesia*.[1]

The functions of another official, the *kreodaites*, provide a puzzle which is not easy to solve. He seems to have been head carver or, perhaps more likely, the distributor of the portions of meat at the public festivals. This must have been a post of honour; but we are told that when Agesilaus appointed Lysander his *kreodaites* Lysander was insulted.[2] It is also possible, although there is scanty evidence to support it, that the *kreodaites* was mess president and presided over the dinners at the *syssitia*.

Hesychius tells us the names of some other officials in Roman times of which nothing is known. The ἄμπαιδες οἱ τῶν παίδων ἐπιμελούμενοι παρὰ Λάκωσιν were obviously supervisors of the boys or assistants to the *paidonomus*. Perhaps they supplemented the *bidaioi*, who were exclusively in charge of the athletic exercises of the boys and young men. Nor is anything known of the γεροάκται· οἱ δήμαρχοι παρὰ Λάκωσιν, nor of the ἐμπεσάντας ἀρχεῖόν τι ἐν Λακεδαίμονι. If Hesychius is correct in naming them among Spartan officials, they were probably late innovations in Roman times. The *boonetai* were probably those whose duty it was to purchase oxen for sacrifices.[3]

PROXENIA

The word *proxenia*, as used in all Greek cities as well as in Sparta, must be understood in two senses. In the first, the

---

[1] Thuc. IV, 132; Xen. *Hell.* III, 1, 4.

[2] Pollux, VI, 34; Plut. *Quaest. Conv.* II, 10, 2 (644B); *Lys.* XXIII. Cf. Herod. VI, 60; Bielschowsky, *De Spartanorum Syssitiis*, pp. 21 f., where the problem is discussed inconclusively. It is pertinent to remember that the office of chief butler to the kings of England is held by the Duke of Norfolk, the highest noble in the land.   [3] Paus. III, 12, 1.

person called *proxenos* was a duly appointed official whose
duty it was to look after merchants of other cities. In the
second sense, a decree of *proxenia* was an honour accorded to
a foreigner conferring upon him the 'freedom of the city'.
In every great city there was what may be called a sort of
consular service, whereby the duty of looking after strangers
was allotted to various citizens. Visiting merchants and
travellers from other cities could find entertainment and,
presumably to a certain limited extent, protection at the hands
of the *proxenos* of his city in Athens or Corinth or Sparta.
Sometimes this *proxenia* was hereditary, as for instance that
of Sparta in the family of Alcibiades, but generally the duty
seems to have been imposed by the State on a rich man as
a liturgy, a service to the State compulsorily imposed upon
him.[1] Such *proxenoi* in Sparta were appointed by the kings.[2]
A good deal of controversy has taken place among commentators over the exact status and powers of these *proxenoi*.
Gilbert,[3] following Boeckh, thinks that they were magistrates
who combined with their judicial powers the duty of looking
after strangers. The evidence for this is scanty and not too
clear and Boeckh himself was ready to abandon it.[4] Gilbert
also puts forward the view that the kings themselves were
ex officio proxenoi for all strangers, but appointed various
Spartan citizens as their deputies. On that point we cannot
be definite and it is not of great importance.

Using the term *proxenia* in its second sense, that of an
honorific decree conferring the freedom of the city upon
a distinguished foreigner, we find that the Spartans, with that
lack of graciousness which characterised them, were not as
fond of granting privileges to strangers as was Athens or other
cities. It is curious to note that the only two inscriptions[5]
extant granting the honour of *proxenia* to a foreigner are

---

[1] P. Monceaux, *Les Proxénies grecques*, pp. 146 ff. J. d'André, *La Proxénie*,
pp. 149 f.
[2] Herod. VI, 57.   [3] *Op. cit.* p. 59, n. 3.
[4] Monceaux, *ut supra*, p. 147.   [5] *I.G.* V, 1, 4, 5.

presumably, if not certainly, of the period from about 188–4, when Sparta had been forced to join the Achaean League and to abandon her ancient 'Lycurgan' constitution. Once she had received back her own constitution, we have no more decrees of *proxenia*. It is amusing to note from the two inscriptions that the person to be honoured had to make the application himself and urge his own qualifications. This rule, perhaps purely Laconian, may very well be a token of the bluntness of Spartan manners. In other states some friendly citizen moved the vote of thanks; at Sparta the candidate for the proxeny was forced to sue in person.[1]

We know the names of a good many Spartans who served as *proxenoi* for various cities: for instance, the famous Lichas, who was *proxenos* of Argos;[2] Clearchus, *proxenos* of Byzantium;[3] Pharax, of Boeotia;[4] Coroebus, of Athens.[5]

THE *XENELASIA*[6]

The fact that the Spartan government regularly appointed *proxenoi* to look after strangers casts a light upon the generally accepted idea that foreigners were invariably expelled, and that Sparta deliberately kept them out, in order that the land and its customs might not be spied upon. Actually this was not so, and there is no evidence that under ordinary circumstances strangers were prevented from visiting Laconia. The ephors could, and did, expel any foreigner whose presence was obnoxious to them. But this prerogative is exercised by every government, and is very far from being the wholesale expulsion that it is often thought to be. In the same category was the custom in Sparta to forbid any man of military age to leave the country,[7] a rule that is strictly enforced by governments in modern times. But while we need not exaggerate the

---

[1] H. Swoboda, *Griech. Volksbeschlüsse*, p. 140. H. J. W. Tillyard, in *A.B.S.A.* XII, p. 441. Art. 'Proxénie' in D.S. by Monceaux.

[2] Thuc. v, 74.　　　[3] Xen. *Hell.* I, 1, 35.　　　[4] *Ibid.* III, 2; VI, 5.

[5] *C.I.A.* II, 50.　　　[6] Art. 'Xenelasia' by Krebs in D.S.

[7] Isocrates, XI (Busiris), 17, 18. Cf. *Class. Rev.* XLIII (1929), pp. 52, 114, referring to Thucydides. IV, 132.

exclusiveness of the Spartans, yet we cannot overlook it nor unduly minimize its effects. It was notorious all over Greece and always aroused interest.[1] To the inhabitants of Athens, the cosmopolitan city with its swarms of foreign sailors in the harbours and its metics taking so large a part in the business world of Greece, it seemed an extraordinary thing and one worthy of censure. Pericles,[2] in his great funeral oration, refers to the Spartan *xenelasia* contemptuously when he said that the Athenians threw their city open to the whole world and never expelled those who might seek to spy upon them in time of war.

But whether the idea of *xenelasia* was to keep strangers from spying on the Spartans, or from corrupting them, seems to have puzzled observers. Lycurgus,[3] to whom inevitably the practice was ascribed, not only would not allow Spartans to travel abroad and so learn evil ways, but he expelled all strangers from Sparta who might corrupt his citizens.

For along with strange people strange doctrines must come in and novel doctrines bring novel decisions, from which there must arise many feelings and resolutions which destroy the harmony of the existing political order. Therefore, he thought it more necessary to keep bad manners and customs from invading and filling the city than it was to keep out infectious diseases.

With the end of the Peloponnesian war and the expansion of Spartan policy to wide areas outside of the Peloponnese, the practice of forbidding residence abroad, if it ever obtained to any degree, seems to have dropped.[4] Xenophon deplores this and notes that all the evils which Lycurgus sought to avoid had fastened on the Spartans, love of money and power, and that the greatest ambition of a leading man was to obtain a foreign governorship whereby he could enrich himself. It might not unfairly be asked whether the corruption of Spartan

---

[1] Many references, e.g. Aristoph. *Aves*, 1012; Frag. Aristot. 543 (ed. Rose).
[2] Thuc. II, 39. [3] Plut. *Lyc.* XXVII.
[4] *Resp. Lac.* XIV, 4.

life might not have been avoided if they had mixed more freely with other peoples. The comparison between Sparta and Japan seems inevitable in almost every instance, and it is easy to remember the jealous seclusion of Japan from foreign influence which expelled all foreigners for several centuries.

THE ADMINISTRATION OF JUSTICE[1]

The Spartans seem, so far as we can surmise, to have been markedly non-litigious. This admirable trait is in striking contrast with the passion for litigation which characterised the Athenians, wasted so much of their time, and provided so disturbing a factor in the life of their city. So anxious were the Spartans to avoid civil suits that there was a regular system of arbitration in case of disputes.[2] An arbitrator having been agreed upon by both parties, he took them into the Bronze Temple and there imposed an oath upon them that they would abide by his decision, and they were not allowed to leave the temple until the dispute had been settled. There were no professional advocates[3] nor record of cases. We can well believe that their 'laconic' brevity of speech would have made impossible in Sparta such famous cases as have been recorded in the Athenian courts.

We have, however, records of numerous state-trials in which the conduct of kings or generals was in question. When errors in judgement in the conduct of campaigns were not charged, generally the accusation was of having been bribed by the enemy. For instance, Cleomenes I was accused of not having captured Argos because of bribery.[4] Pleistoanax was charged with accepting a bribe from Pericles in 446, was fined fifteen talents and went into exile.[5] In 418 Agis[6] was accused

---

[1] Bonner and Smith, *Class. Phil.* XXXVII (1942), p. 113.

[2] Plut. *Apoph. Lac.* 218 D.

[3] The reference of Plut. *Apoph. Lac.* 231 C to a συνήγορος may mean either an advocate or a judge, but probably the latter.

[4] Herod. VI, 82.   [5] Thuc. I, 114; II, 21.   [6] *Idem*, V, 63.

of having failed before Argos. He was fined 10,000 drachmas and his house in Sparta was to be razed. The sentence was remitted, on his begging to be given the chance to perform some service to the State which would wipe out the disgrace. In 403 Pausanias II,[1] grandson of the victor of Plataea, was charged with having failed to carry out the orders of the ephors. This case is interesting since we have some particulars of the procedure. He was tried before his fellow king, the five ephors and the twenty-eight *gerontes*, or thirty-four judges in all. Of those, fifteen voted against him and nineteen for acquittal.[2] In 395 he was accused a second time but failed to appear before the court, fled to Tegea and was condemned *in absentia*.[3] It is to be noted that an accused person could be tried a second time on a charge on which he had been formerly found innocent. The rule of *exceptio rei judicatae*,* or *autrefois acquit*, did not hold in the Spartan law system,[4] on the ground that additional evidence might subsequently prove the accused guilty.

The case of Cinadon, who conspired against the State in 398, is an interesting one.[5] The plot was reported by an informer to the ephors, who were greatly alarmed and, not trusting to the discretion of the full *Gerousia*, spoke privately to some of the *gerontes*. A plan was concocted to get rid of Cinadon which was highly successful. He was sent off to Aulon, ostensibly to arrest certain people and helots, among them a woman 'who was the handsomest in the place and was thought to corrupt all the Lacedaemonians old as well as young that went thither'. Cinadon had executed similar commissions for the ephors already and was unsuspecting; so he set out, only to be arrested and brought back when the names of his co-conspirators were revealed. Under examination he made a full confession. We are not told what form this examination

---

[1] Paus. III, 5, 2.
[2] *Ibid.* 5. Cf. Beloch, *Griech. Gesch.* III, 1, p. 71.
[3] Xen. *Hell.* III, 5, 25. [4] Plut. *Apoph. Lac.* 217B.
[5] Xen. *Hell.* III, 3, 4.

took, whether he was put to the torture. We may surmise, however, that the ephors would stick at nothing and, since Cinadon was an 'inferior', would not hesitate to examine him under torture, a thing they would hardly dare to do to a Spartan peer. On his conviction, he and his partners in the conspiracy were led to execution through the streets, 'with arms and neck fastened in a wooden collar and scourged and pricked with lances'. Criminals in early times were executed by being thrown into a chasm.[1] Later they were hanged[2] and their bodies buried in a ravine called Caiadas.[3]

In 382 Phoebidas was condemned to a fine of 100,000 drachmas and dismissed from his command, on the charge of acting in the field without the authorisation of the government.[4] In 379 three harmosts were brought to trial for not resisting the enemy with sufficient vigour. Two were put to death and the third heavily fined.[5] In 378 Sphodrias was indicted on a charge of having been bribed by the enemy. Fearing for his life he failed to appear before the court, but was acquitted, rather unexpectedly, in his absence.[6] The Sphodrias case was an interesting one and we shall have occasion to speak of it again. The tragedy of King Agis IV and his unsuccessful attempt to upset the authority of the ephors hardly comes within the category of justice, since the ephors were fighting for their existence and took revenge upon the young king and his family without due process of law. No king of Sparta had ever been put to death before,[7] and no doubt this outrage upon the sacrosanct character of the kingship was a very shocking thing to Spartan sentiment.

[1] Paus. IV, 18, 4.

[2] Plut. *Agis*, XIX. The assertion of Herod. IV, 146, that executions always took place at night evidently refers to the older form. The fate of Cinadon and his fellow conspirators (Xen. *Hell.* III, 3, 11) was particularly severe, no doubt to impress the disaffected mob.

[3] Thuc. I, 134; Paus. IV, 18, 4; Strabo, 233, 367.

[4] Plut. *Pelop.* VI; Diod. Sic. XV, 20; Xen. *Hell.* V, 2, 32.

[5] Diod. Sic. XV, 24; Xen. *Hell.* V, 4, 13; Plut. *Pelop.* XIII.

[6] Xen. *Hell.* V, 4, 24, 32; Plut. *Pelop.* XIV; *Ages.* XXIV.

[7] Plut. *Agis*, XXI.

It explains the ease with which Cleomenes III later was able to overthrow the Ephorate and put four of them to death.[1]

Constitutional issues involving rival claims to the throne were judged by the people as a whole. We have no positive evidence, but we must suppose the cases were heard by ephors, *Gerousia* and *Ecclesia* sitting together. We hear of several such cases, for instance that of Leotychidas and Demaratus, in 491, which turned on the legitimacy of the latter. Leotychidas, another member of the royal family, proceeded by formal indictment, making a declaration on oath with regard to the circumstances surrounding the birth of Demaratus. His most powerful witnesses were the ephors who had been present when the father, King Ariston, declared that the child could not possibly be by him. The court could come to no decision and referred the matter to Delphi where, the priestess having been bribed as Herodotus dryly remarks, Demaratus was declared illegitimate.[2]

In 398 an even more famous case of disputed succession to the throne, involving another Leotychidas, turned on the alleged seduction of Timaea, wife of King Agis III, by Alcibiades. Xenophon reports the case[3] with several interesting details. Lysander wanted to put Agesilaus, brother of the deceased Agis, on the throne instead of the youthful Leotychidas. The latter quoted the law that a son, not a brother, should succeed a king. If, however, there should happen to be no son, then a brother should succeed. Agesilaus retorted that there was no legitimate son and therefore he was the rightful claimant. Leotychidas cited his mother's evidence as

---

[1] Plut. *Cleom.* VIII.   [2] Herod. VI, 62 ff.

[3] *Hell.* III, 3, 1 f; Plut. *Ages.* III; *Alc.* XXIII; *Lys.* XXII; Paus. III, 8, 7; Justin, V. 2. For modern treatment of this notorious incident *vide* Beloch, *Griech. Gesch.* I, 2, p. 188. Beloch dismissed the whole affair as a trumped-up charge to deprive the rightful heir. Art. 'Agis' in P.W. by Niese; Luria, *Klio*, XXI (1927), pp. 404 ff; H. D. Westlake, in *J.H.S.* LVIII (1938) pp. 31 f; J. Hatzfeld, in *Revue des études anciennes*, XXXV (1933), pp. 381 f. Grote, who is ready to believe anything to the discredit of Alcibiades, accepts the story entire. Modern scholars are doubtful and inclined to consider the evidence untrustworthy.

to his paternity and the fact that his father Agis on his deathbed had acknowledged him. Agesilaus countered this by alleging that Leotychidas was born ten months after Agis had left Timaea, fixing the time by the occurrence of an earthquake. Diopeithes is put in the witness box to testify to an oracle warning Sparta against a lame King, and draws the obvious inference that this must refer to Agesilaus who is lame. Lysander, who is conducting the case on behalf of his nominee, ingeniously twists this to refer not to physical lameness but rather to the alleged illegitimacy of Leotychidas. The people gave their verdict in favour of Agesilaus. It may be remarked that the whole case was an unsatisfactory one. The alleged seduction of Timaea by Alcibiades is in doubt and has been rejected by many of the best historians.

A third case of rival claims to the throne, that of Cleonymus and Areus, is mentioned by Pausanias,[1] who says the case came before the *Gerousia*. This raises the question whether Pausanias is correct in assigning the case to that body. If it came before the senators, it certainly was unique in not having been brought before the people assembled in the *Ecclesia*.

The most outstanding aspect of Spartan justice was that the ephors acted both as prosecutors and judges in all criminal cases. This explains the statement by Isocrates[2] that *perioeci* were condemned 'unheard' (ἀκρίτους). This passage, which has been a stumbling-block for all commentators, if taken literally and at its face value, is startling enough to cast doubt upon the knowledge of the speaker and his good faith in criticising Spartan constitutional law. If he means that the *perioeci* were in a different category altogether from that of the Spartans, then we must revise our ideas of the relations between the two classes in the Spartan State. It seems altogether

---

[1] Paus. III, 6, 2, Cf. Busolt-Swoboda, *op. cit.* p. 673, who accept the account of Pausanias. Bonner and Smith, *loc. cit.* p. 129, reject it and hold that Pausanias was in error.

[2] *Panath.* CLXXXI.

monstrous that freemen should be treated in such a manner, and that *perioeci* should be arrested and condemned without legal process. The only explanation of the word 'unheard' is that it means that such cases were not brought before the full court of kings, ephors and *gerontes*, the ephors were the sole judges.[1] Isocrates is suspect in his condemnation of the judicial system of the Spartans since in another passage he alleges that 'the Lacedaemonians have executed without trial more Greeks than we have brought to trial since the foundation of Athens'.[2] A curious passage in Dionysius of Halicarnassus[3] asserts that the Lacedaemonians had given to the 'elders' (πρεσβύτατοι) the right to order a beating to anyone misbehaving in a public place. Who these 'elders' are is hard to say, except that presumably senators are meant. This would seem to indicate that summary punishment could be administered to the unruly, probably helots, without the formality of prosecution.

It is evident that the Spartan courts handled cases involving any of the *homoioi* very gingerly.[4] We hear of a rich man being condemned to go without dessert for dinner. If this was a permanent deprivation, it seems rather a severe sentence, since the *epaikla* or dessert was the best part of the dinner. We also hear of poor men being sentenced to go out and bring back a reed or a handful of laurel leaves.[5] *Homoioi*, so far as we know, were never imprisoned and only for the worst crimes condemned to death. They stuck by their friends and were loyal to their own class. When Sphodrias was in serious trouble in 378 for having, contrary to orders, invaded Attica and tried to seize the Piraeus, his guilt was apparent and his condemnation sure. But Agesilaus saved him on the general principle of his being a Spartan.

[1] Cf. art. 'Perioiki' in P.W. by Larsen. Busolt-Swoboda, *op. cit.* p. 664, n. 2. Larsen rejects the evidence of Isocrates, Busolt accepts it. Ringnalda, *De exerc. Laced.* p. 64, proposes, over-boldly, to read helots for *perioeci*.

[2] *Panath.* LXVI. [3] *Antiq. Rom.* XX, 13, 2.
[4] Cf. Thuc. I, 132. [5] Athen. IV, 140E, 141A.

When as a child, boy and young man one has continually performed all the duties of a Spartan, it is a hard thing to put such a one to death, for Sparta has need of such soldiers.[1]

For cowardice they were subject to *atimia*, a very severe sentence. For serious offences they were condemned to banishment. The two polemarchs, Hipponoidas and Aristocles, who disobeyed orders at First Mantinea were banished.[2] Clearchus, who was a mercenary leader under Cyrus, prudently kept out of Sparta for fear of being condemned for not obeying orders.[3] Thimbron was fined and banished on the charge of allowing his troops to plunder the friends of Sparta.[4] There was probably much more behind this, since Thimbron had been giving a good deal of anxiety by his high-handed actions.

Cases involving civil contracts were judged by the ephors. Aristotle says 'some of the ephors',[5] which, if correct, suggests that they did not sit as a body in all cases but constituted a panel from which individual members would serve as judges as cases came up. We do not know if there was any appeal to a higher court consisting of all five ephors sitting together. Aristotle disapproves of the system:

> The ephors are the supreme judges in causes of the last consequence; but as it is quite accidental what sort of persons they may be, it is not right that they should give judgement according to their own opinion, but by a written law or established custom.[6]

It is pertinent to remark that Aristotle is hardly fair here. It is inconceivable that there should not have been a corpus of legal precedents to guide them. Perhaps later in Roman times this lack of expert lawyers was felt. We hear of an 'interpreter of the laws of Lycurgus' (ἐξηγητὴς τῶν Λυκουργείων) but know nothing of his status or functions.[7] The land system of Sparta was not sufficiently simple to allow of the

---

[1] Xen. *Hell.* v, 4, 32.   [2] Thuc. v, 72.
[3] Xen. *Anab.* I, 1, 9; II, 6, 4.   [4] *Hell.* III, 1, 8.
[5] *Pol.* 1275 B. Plut. *Apoph. Lac.* 221 B, says they sat every day.
[6] *Pol.* 1270 B.   [7] In *C.I.G.* 1364.

ephors giving their decisions solely in the light of reason. There must have been some recognised principles that would bind them. Otherwise, as Aristotle alleges, bribery of judges would have made things intolerable.

Our knowledge of the Spartan judicial system is obviously imperfect. We actually know very little indeed about it. It seems to have been primitive and, judged by Athenian or modern standards, amateur and unsatisfactory. The recurring accusation by Aristotle and the known or, perhaps we should better say, alleged cases of bribery and corruption seem to suggest an unsatisfactory state of affairs.

Lycurgus would never reduce his laws to writing. Indeed there is a Rhetra expressly forbidding it. He thought that the most important points, and such as most directly tended to the public welfare, being imprinted on the hearts of their youth by good discipline, would be sure to remain, and would find a stronger security than any compulsion would secure in the example afforded by the best lawgiver, education. And as for things of lesser importance, such as pecuniary contracts, the forms of which have to be changed as occasion requires, he thought it best to prescribe no positive rule or inviolable usage in such cases. He was rather willing that their manner and form alter according to time and the opinion of men of wisdom. Every end and object of law and enactment it was his design that education should effect.[1]

This special pleading on the part of Plutarch does not ring true. If Spartan education was designed solely to make good soldiers and submissive subjects of the State, it could hardly be thought of as making good lawyers. Plutarch, for all his idealisation of the wise lawgiver, is well aware that the legal system of the Spartan State had been severely criticised. He sees 'no sign of injustice or want of equity in the laws of Lycurgus, although some who admit them to be well contrived to make good soldiers, pronounce them defective in point of justice'.[2] In conclusion, it may be remarked that the unwritten

[1] Plut. *Lyc.* XIII.   [2] *Lyc.* XXVIII.

state of the law, gave enormous power to the ephors, who were the official interpreters of the traditions. They had only to retire to the temple of Ino Pasiphae for a night, and emerge with a divinely inspired pronouncement from which there was no appeal.

THE *CRYPTEIA*[1]

A Spartan institution, which has invariably horrified both ancient and modern commentators, was that of the secret police or *crypteia*. According to the account given by Plutarch,[2] the ephors 'from time to time' sent out young Spartans armed with daggers into the country parts. Hiding by day, they sallied out at night and murdered indiscriminately any unsuspecting and helpless helot they could find. Apparently this was done on the principle of thereby encouraging the other helots to a submissive state of mind. The *crypteia* was, therefore, a secret police of the most tyrannical and vicious description for the express purpose of terrorism, in which, if our information can be relied upon, they must have been singularly successful.

Secret assassination has always been a favourite weapon of all tyrannies, and we need not hesitate to attribute such means to the Spartan ephors when dealing with a disaffected and, at times, mutinous helotry. It is altogether probable that they did send out assassins to 'liquidate' particularly obnoxious helots. But that is not to say that indiscriminate murder was regularly resorted to. It is to be noted that Plutarch carefully says 'from time to time', and we may infer therefrom that this drastic measure was only resorted to on extraordinary occasions. There is nothing whatever to show that every young Spartan took a course in murder as part of his regular training.

---

[1] Arts. 'Krypteia' in P.W. by Oehler and in D.S. by Girard. A. Koechly, *de Lacedaemoniorum Cryptia*; Jeanmaire, 'La Cryptie Lacédémonienne', in *Rev. ét. gr.* XXVI (1913), p. 121; H. Wallon, *Explication d'un passage de Plutarque sur une loi de Lycurgue nommée la Cryptie.*

[2] *Lyc.* XXVIII.

But, however that may be, there does seem to have been some secret body—the name *crypteia* implies that—which was at the disposal of the ephors for special service, a kind of 'commando' corps made up of picked youths. Pompeius Trogus says that every Spartan either served in it, or was liable to be called up to the age of thirty.[1] Regular service in it seems to have been for two years, and Giraud[2] suggests that possibly recruits were melleirens, youths from eighteen to twenty, after which they might be called up at any time for special service. We hear of the corps again when it was employed at the battle of Sellasia,[3] which suggests that at least at that date, it was a regularly constituted part of the army.

Several explanations of the existence of this singular body have been given. Jeanmaire,[4] in an important study of the *crypteia*, seeks to show that it was part of the long series of initiations through which youths had to pass before entering the status of full manhood. Numerous examples drawn from primitive peoples at the present go to support his argument. A withdrawing from the rest of the tribe for a period, hiding outside the settlement and living on whatever theft or ingenuity can provide, are all to be found in the primitive savages in Australia, South Africa and the North American Indians. The parallels drawn by Jeanmaire are so exact that it is impossible to deny the strength of the argument. There is little doubt that service in the *crypteia* was part of the arduous training that went to the making of a Spartan.

Giraud[5] puts forward the theory that we have in Plato's[6] description of the rural guardians or *agronomoi* an account of the *crypteia* as it actually did function. These youths, who were to serve for two years, were to busy themselves, somewhat on the pattern of the boy scouts, in all sorts of 'good deeds' in the rural parts and in making themselves generally useful. Certainly it is hard to suppose that the Spartan youths

[1] Justin, III, 3.
[2] *Rev. ét. gr.* XI (1898), pp. 31 ff.
[3] Plut. *Cleom.* XXVIII.
[4] *Rev. ét. gr.* XXVI (1913), p. 121.
[5] Art. 'Krypteia' in D.S.
[6] *Legg.* VI, 760 ff.

busied themselves in mending watercourses and broken down walls, as Plato would have his *agronomoi*. Such manual labour would have been utterly alien to the whole spirit of Spartan philosophy in the training of the warrior caste. We know that the ephebes of Attica were employed as rural patrols.[1] It is not unlikely that the *crypteia* was made similar use of.

One pertinent suggestion is that the *crypteia* was used as a kind of guard against the thieving of the boys.[2] The contest between this body of secret police and the hungry boys, who were forced to supplement their meagre fare by theft, came to be a kind of game played between them, designed to sharpen the wits of both sides. Perhaps this was so; nothing definite can be said on that score. The only conclusion to which we can arrive is that service in the *crypteia* was a part of the training of Spartan youths, who were used by the ephors at their discretion, and that sometimes the removal of undesirable people was carried out through its agency. We are not expressly told so, but it is reasonable to suppose that the arrest of Cinadon was carried out by members of the *crypteia*.[3] It is also obvious that as a check upon the helots it was useful. That the youths were sent out to commit murder indiscriminately is so monstrous as to be incredible.

[1] Pollux, VIII, 105; Aesch. *de Falsa Leg.* 167 (two-year service); Thuc. IV, 67; VIII, 92; Aristoph. *Aves*, 1167.

[2] Meier, *Klio*, XII, p. 336.

[3] Xen. *Hell.* III, 3, 8–9. We are told here that the young men charged with the arrest of Cinadon were selected by the *hippagretae*, i.e. the commanders of the royal bodyguard. It is not impossible that they were also in command of the *crypteia*.

CHAPTER VI

THE SPARTAN DISCIPLINE

The whole way of life, the constitution of the State, the system of education of ancient Sparta were calculated to one end—the maintenance of an army of experts who were ready and able at any moment to suppress sedition within the State or repel invasion from without. The Spartan was a professional soldier and nothing else, and his education was directed entirely to two ends—physical fitness and obedience to authority. Within these two narrow limits he was superbly capable. From the moment of his birth to the day he was too old to be of any further active use in the field, the Spartan was subject to discipline. He was under orders, his individuality was submerged to a degree seldom if ever matched in any other country.

According to Plutarch,[1] at birth the male infant was brought before the elders of his tribe at an unidentified place called Lesche,* where he was inspected. If he appeared healthy and not deformed, he was then given into the care of the parents. If he did not pass this physical test, the infant was exposed and left to die at a place called Apothetae, a chasm at the foot of Mount Taÿgetus. Even when an infant the hardening process was well under way, for Spartan nurses were famous for their

[1] *Lyc.* XVI, 1. It seems best to take Plutarch's words at their face value, and to reject Humbert's elaborate argument in art. 'Expositio' in D.S. that the underlying meaning of this passage is that the Spartan father could limit the size of his family by these means to one or at most two sons, any others that were born could be got rid of. To this practice Humbert attributes the dwindling number of Spartans. The whole question of exposure of infants in ancient Greece is obscure. It is certain that it was not practised on any considerable scale. The small numbers of the Spartans make it sure that no male infant was exposed unless hopelessly deformed. Ehrenberg's assertion that 'a large proportion of the girls were exposed' cannot be substantiated; *Aspects of the Ancient World*, p. 98 (Oxford, 1946). For further on the general subject of infanticide *vide* A. Cameron, 'The exposure of children and Greek ethics', *Class. Rev.* XVI (1932), p. 105; H. Bolkestein, *Class. Phil.* XVII (1922), p. 222.

severity and refusal to spoil their charges. They taught them to be content with plain food, unafraid of the dark or of being left alone and without peevishness or ill-humour or crying.

A remarkable and trying ordeal for the infant was the practice of bathing new-born children in wine 'to improve the temper and complexion of their bodies; from a notion that epileptic and weakly children faint and waste away upon being thus bathed, while those of a strong and vigorous habit acquire firmness and get a temper by it like steel'. It may be parenthetically remarked that it is not impossible that this custom of washing the new-born infant in wine was prompted by primitive hygienic motives, the wine acting as a mild antiseptic. Plutarch goes on to say that Spartan nurses were famous and sought after by parents of other countries.[1] Amycla, the nurse of Alcibiades, was one; but unfortunately she had little success with him since her good endeavours were frustrated by his preceptor, the contemptible Zopyrus.[2] It may be surmised that women who left Sparta to act as nurses in other countries must have belonged to the helots. It is unthinkable that a free-born Spartan woman should have demeaned herself to so lowly a calling.

AGE GROUPS

The male Spartan from the day of his birth until he reached the age of sixty was under the discipline and regimentation of the State. That during these years of active life he was placed in different age categories is quite certain: what exactly these groups were and what nomenclature was applied to them is less certain, and has given rise to considerable controversy and difference of opinion among commentators. It is not impossible, however, to arrive at tolerably satisfactory conclusions with regard to them which, while not positively definitive, at least are so likely as to admit of not too serious doubt about their accuracy.

[1] From a funerary inscription we know the name of another Spartan nurse, Malicha, *I.G.* II, 3, 3111. [2] Plut. *Alc.* I.

In the first place, it must always be borne in mind that modern usage differs from ancient in the names of birthdays. To-day we say that a child has its first birthday on the completion of twelve months of life. The Greeks, more logically perhaps, spoke of the first year of life. The day the child was born was to them its first birthday and the modern first birthday was its second. This confusion in ancient and modern usage is prolific in misunderstandings and must be very carefully guarded against.

It is quite certain that the male infant for the first six years of his life lived under the care of his mother.[1] During this stage of infancy he was in what may conjecturally be termed the προπαίδιον class. At the end of his sixth year, or as the Greeks would say, on his seventh birthday, he left home and went to live in barracks along with other children of his age group. That also seems certain, although Fustel de Coulanges[2] has argued that although he was under some form of mild discipline and was being trained in the earlier stages of the Spartan educational system, he still lived at home. This must be rejected. M. de Coulanges has sought to prove his point by evidence that is far from convincing. We have, he says, a picture, surely the most human in all Spartan history, of Agesilaus playing with his children by riding on a stick.[3] But this would suggest that they were very young to be able to enjoy so simple a game. He also cites the instance of Antalcidas' sending his family to Cythera at a time of danger.[4] Again this is far from convincing, and it is surely easier to suppose that whatever male children he had were infants. We need not think that this was an impossibly early

---

[1] Plut. *Lyc.* xvi. Toynbee, 'The growth of Sparta', *J.H.S.* xxxiii, p. 261, asserts that, the years were counted from the beginning of the official year within which the boy was born, not from his birthday. There is no evidence to support this.

[2] *Nouvelles recherches sur quelques problèmes d'histoire*, p. 75.

[3] Plut. *Ages.* xxv; *Apoph. Lac.* 213 E. Unfortunately for the credibility of this story, Val. Max. viii, 8, 1 (Ext.), tells the same story of Socrates, adding that he was laughed at by Alcibiades.   [4] Plut. *Ages.* xxxii, 1.

age for the child to leave his mother, and we can easily imagine that he visited her frequently and that she looked after his clothes and kept a watchful eye on his health. There is nothing in Spartan life to suggest that the influence of the mother was at any time lacking, or that once having left home her son was lost to her for ever. Rather, on the contrary, we see from numerous anecdotes that the mother's influence was at all times very strong.

For the next six years of his life, the boy was in what we may call the παιδίον class. He was enrolled in one of the juvenile platoons or *ilai*[1] which probably were subdivisions of the companies or *bouai*, to make up the full regiment or *agele*. During these six years he was under the tutelage of masters and began his introduction into the severe Spartan system of education. It is reasonable to suppose that his training was fitted to his tender years and that the full rigour of the discipline was only gradually imposed upon him. For one thing, we know that he did not take part in competitive exercises in music, dancing or athletics until he was ten. It is hard to suppose that his clothing was as scanty as it became later, or that he was sent out stealing to supplement his meagre fare. We must credit the Spartans with some wisdom in their treatment of children. As a matter of fact, it is quite evident that the regimen was calculated with minute care and though rough, at least by modern standards, was healthful and well fitted for steady growth. Among a people who prized bodily vigour above all things, the question of health was of paramount importance and we may well credit them with wise foresight in their system of training.

On the completion of his twelfth year the boy entered on the full exercise of the training. His hair was cut short, he went barefoot, without underclothing and only a single

[1] Xen. *Resp. Lac.* II, 11. This division into regiments, companies, platoons, seems preferable to making the *agele* and the *boua* the same. But for another view cf. Gilbert, *op. cit.* p. 63. Nilsson, *Klio*, XII, p. 313, surmises that the *ile* was a battalion made up of an indeterminate number of *agelai*. It is impossible to come to a definite conclusion on this.

garment and played and exercised naked. His bed was of rushes plucked by hand from the river Eurotas; he was not allowed to cut them in order to make the task of gathering them more difficult. In winter he was allowed to add thistledown which was supposed, as Plutarch dryly remarks, to give added warmth. The boys did all the housekeeping of their barracks themselves and, according to Plutarch, supplemented their unappetising diet by stealing. If they were caught they got one beating from the owner of their booty and another from their master for allowing themselves to be caught.[1] One punishment that does not seem to have been quite so severe was to walk round and round the altar of Artemis Orthia.[2] But perhaps this mild correction for wrong doing was accompanied by the jeers and insults of the spectators, or perhaps the culprit had to keep it up until he dropped from exhaustion.

Up to this point our comprehension of the system of training and the age classes presents no very great difficulty and we may be tolerably satisfied that we are on safe ground. It is during the third six-year period that we begin to encounter difficulties of nomenclature that are hard to dissolve and have led to sharp differences of opinion among commentators.[3] That the various ages from thirteen to eighteen inclusive were called by specific names is quite sure; the question is rather to fix these names with certainty. So far as can be ascertained—and we must speak with caution—the following names were applied:

13th year	ῥωβίδας.
14th year	προμικιζόμενος.
15th year	μικιζόμενος (μικιχιζόμενος).
16th year	πρόπαις (σιδεῦναι(?)).
17th year	παῖς.
18th year	μελλείρην.

---

[1] Plut. *Lyc.* XVI. For further comment on this alleged practice of stealing *vide infra*, p. 177.   [2] Plut. *Inst. Lac.* 237 C.

[3] Diller, 'A New Source on the Spartan *Ephebia*', *American Journal of Philology*, LXII, 4 (1941), p. 499.

The difficulty here arises from the word μικιӡόμενος or μικιχιӡόμενος. The older explanation, which is rather surprisingly followed by the new edition of Liddell and Scott, was that this term was applied to a Spartan infant in the third year of its life.[1] Later commentators,[2] and it must be candidly admitted among the very best, following Plutarch's statement that a boy was enrolled in a company on the completion of his sixth year, have applied the word to his ninth year. But in rebuttal of this view we have a reference in an inscription[3] which clearly puts it as late as the fifteenth year. This agrees with the evidence adduced by Prof. Diller based on a gloss on Herodotus, which need not be quoted here at length. Interesting, not to say tantalising, as the problem is with regard to this elusive word μικιӡόμενος, it is not of great importance and may be left with the strong presumption that it applied to a boy in the fifteenth year of his age.

The general title of the age-class 13–18 seems to have been ἡβῶν which may be translated 'adolescent'; or perhaps, but very doubtfully, σιδεῦναι. The word ἥβη[4] denotes 'majority'

---

[1] Stein (ed.), Herod. II, p. 465.

[2] Woodward, *A.B.S.A.* xv, pp. 45–8; Nilsson, *Klio*, XII, pp. 309–11; Busolt-Swoboda, *Griech. Staatsk.* pp. 695–7; Kretschner, *Glotta*, III (1911), p. 269.

[3] *I.G.* v[1], 296. ἀπὸ μικιχιӡομένων μέχρι μελλειρενείας. We are on safe ground in putting the μελλείρην in the eighteenth year, therefore the μικιӡόμενος must clearly be the fifteenth.

[4] Xen. H. III, 4, 23 οἱ δέκα ἀφ᾿ ἥβης, i.e. 28; VI, 4, 17, οἱ τετταράκοντα ἀφ᾿ ἥβης, i.e. 58. σιδεῦναι Müller, *Doric Race*, II, p. 309. Photius, *s.v.* συνέφηβος. Albert Billheimer in art. 'τὰ δέκα ἀφ᾿ ἥβης' in *Trans. Am. Philol. Assoc.* LXXVII (1946), p. 214, argues that a youth became a *hebōn* at twenty. Although Mr Billheimer's arguments are weighty, it seems almost impossible to come to a conclusion on the point. Woodward, *A.B.S.A.* xv, p. 48, says that in the inscriptions recording the victories of the boys in the various contests it is surprising how often μικιӡόμενοι are the winners, if they were only ten years old, and supposes that a victory at that age was so remarkable as to be invariably recorded. But if the μικιӡόμενοι were fifteen and not ten, there would be nothing remarkable about the older boys winning. The younger would have little chance, as Woodward acknowledges. The exact meaning of πρατοπάμπαις, and ἀτροπάμπαις found in the inscriptions (*I.G.* vi[1], 278, 279) is quite obscure. Woodward, *ut supra*, p. 46, suggests that they mean

or 'coming of age' which, apparently, was fixed in Sparta at 18. Presumably this was in a legal, but not military sense, although the point is not perfectly clear. At this age the boy reached the status of μελλείρην which may be called 'postulant'. He was a candidate for the rank of εἴρην, and it is likely that he was tried out in the army in non-combatant service, or as a cadet or 'squire' to see how he shaped.

In his nineteenth year the young Spartan entered the class of eiren.[1] He was now a combatant but not a first line soldier. In this six-year age group the succeeding years were probably, but far from certainly, named as follows;

19th year	εἴρην.
20th year	πρωτείρης.
21st year	διείρης.
22nd year	τριττείρης.
23rd year	τεττείρης.
24th year	πεντείρης.

Admittedly the names of the various year classes are conjectural but appear quite reasonable, following Beloch's[2] suggestion that mention of τριτίρενες in an inscription prompts the adoption of the other names.

It is at this point that we arrive at a problem that has puzzled all commentators. Herodotus,[3] in his account of the battle of Plataea, says that the Spartan dead were buried on the battlefield according to their legal and social status, each

---

a boy in the first (πρωτο) and second (ἑτερο) years of his παῖς class. This suggestion seems to hold the field and no better has been put forward. The truth about all these different names of the boys' classes is probably that in all languages there are different, more or less slangy, words; just as we say 'kid', 'youngster', 'lad', etc. without any definite meaning other than an adolescent boy.

[1] Plut. *Lyc.* XVII, 'on his twentieth birthday', i.e. by modern usage his nineteenth.

[2] *Bevölkerung*, p. 148, referring to *I.G.* v[1], 1386. The inscription is from Thuria, second century. Cf. arts. Μελλήφοβος (by Poland) in P.W. and 'Agelai' (by Caillemer) in D.S.   [3] IX, 85.

class being assigned a common grave. In the first were buried the eirens, among whom were Poseidonius, Amompharetus, Phylocion and Callicrates; in the second the rest of the Lacedaemonians and in the third the helots. But these four officers most certainly were not eirens; they were old and experienced and had long since passed from that class. The puzzle is made more perplexing from the fact that the manuscripts read ἱρέες or ἱρέας, and this has been emended, probably correctly, to ἱρένες. If we were to accept the word ἱρέες, we would be confronted with the problem as to what they were. It can only mean those who held, or had held, sacred office. But we have no idea as to what that office may have been. It appears most probable that the emendation to ἱρένες is correct, and that Herodotus made a mistake, not knowing exactly what an eiren was. There seems no other way out of this tantalising puzzle.[1]

On the completion of his twenty-fourth year the young Spartan graduated from the eiren class and became a first-line soldier. If we accept Pausanias[2] (and we may do so somewhat doubtfully), this class was called σφαιρεῖς* and took part in the particularly strenuous ball-game of which mention is made hereafter. Further than this we have no information with regard to this class, but we presume that the picked corps of 'knights' or ἱππεῖς were chosen from them.[3] On the completion of his thirtieth year he entered upon full citizenship and took his place in the General Assembly or *Ecclesia*. He no longer lived in barracks but set up his own establishment and lived with his wife and family. He was allowed to enter

[1] Macan's note on this passage in his edition of Herodotus sums up the difficulties very well. He agrees that the emendation must be accepted. It must be candidly acknowledged that our understanding of this tantalising word is not helped by Hesychius who, *s.v.* ἱρανες, says that it means ἄρχοντες or διώκοντες εἰρηνάξει which equals κρατεῖ. Hesychius must have had this passage of Herodotus in mind and concluded that the mention of the three commanders justified his definition. If so, it arouses an interesting problem regarding the text used.

[2] III, 14, 6.   [3] Xen. *Resp. Lac.* IV, 3.

the market place and do his own shopping, obviously a necessity for a family man; hitherto his wants had been supplied by his family or 'lovers'.[1] Perhaps for the first time since he left home as a small boy the Spartan at last enjoyed some privacy and was able to lead a normal family life into which the prying eyes of his superiors did not reach. Dionysius of Halicarnassus[2] remarks that the home of the Spartan was at least his own and that the door of his house was a barrier that kept out the supervision of others.

On reaching the age of manhood the Spartan was allowed to let his hair grow. He then appeared 'taller, more manly and more terrible to the enemy'.[3] On campaign the young men were allowed to curl and adorn their hair[4] and we remember the heroic band under Leonidas attending to their coiffures before Thermopylae. But at all times they took great care to have it properly parted and trimmed, believing that 'a large head of hair added beauty to a good face and terror to an ugly'. It may be surmised that it is not impossible that in this custom of allowing the hair to grow after manhood was attained there was a ritual significance, quite apart from the terrifying appearance it gave them. The boys were close-cropped because they had not grown to their full strength. When they had done so the length of their hair denoted their physical vigour and became a sacred symbol. Instances of the sacredness of the hair among primitive tribes are innumerable.[5]

Although they took great pains in the care of their coiffure, they do not seem to have been particularly attentive to personal cleanliness. An anecdote recounted by Plutarch[6] which sounds as if it might be true, tells of a Spartan who observed a slave drawing water for Alcibiades' bath and remarked he must be

---

[1] Plut. *Lyc.* xxv.   [2] *Antiq. Rom.* xx, 13, 2.
[3] Xen. *Resp. Lac.* xi, 3.   [4] Plut. *Lyc.* xxi.
[5] Frazer, *The Golden Bough* ('Balder the Beautiful'), ii, p. 158; Robertson Smith, *Religion of Semites*, p. 329.
[6] *Inst. Lac.* 237B.

a very dirty person to need so much water. Doubtless the young men washed and anointed themselves after the exercises in the gymnasia; but we know nothing of any public baths.

MUSICAL AND ATHLETIC CONTESTS

The competitive spirit was early introduced into the curriculum.[1] By the time they were ten years old they were taking part in public contests. What these were is not altogether clear, but two of them were musical (the κελοῖα and μῶα[2]) and one athletic καθθηρατόριον. The musical competitions were vocal, not instrumental, and probably carried out by choruses of the various companies or βοῦαι. The leader, or βούαγος, of the winning company was honoured by a stele or inscribed stone. Evidently the prize was one of those mysterious 'sickles' or iron instruments which look like an Australian boomerang, the cult significance of which is unknown to us. On the stele the sickle was mounted as a dedication to Artemis Orthia, and at least one of these strange objects has been found still in position.[3]

It may be remarked that we have no information as to whether the boys, or girls, were taught to play the lyre or flute. We know that there was a military band that played the Spartan army into battle on their flutes. But whether or not these were professionals is very hard to say. Playing either instrument would seem to be an honourable occupation, and, with their devotion to choric exercises, a very necessary and important one. But we may surmise that the proud young Spartan would despise them. He was willing enough to sing

---

[1] *A.B.S.A.* XII, p. 380; *Artemis Orthia* (Dawkins *et al.*), pp. 285 ff.

[2] κελοῖα or κελῆα, *I.G.* v[1], 264; μῶα, probably a variant of μοῦσα. Cf. Baunack, *Rhein. Mus.* XXXVIII, p. 293. Both were certainly musical, but their form is unknown.

[3] *I.G.* v[1], 258, 316. What these things are is almost impossible to determine. They have been identified as scrapers, tall caps and sickles, *A.B.S.A.* XII, p. 384. It is quite possible that they were identical with the ξυήλη, a curved dagger, which seems to have been very like the Gurkha kukri. It is not clear if this was carried as a side-arm by the Spartan soldier.

in choruses; but to play the tunes was another matter which could appropriately be relegated to inferiors, helots perhaps or *perioeci*.

What the καθθηρατόριον was is hard to say. It was 'some kind of rough game', and at least we may be sure it was rough. The most likely suggestion is that it was a θηρομαχία or simulated wild animal hunt which the boys enacted. We can easily imagine some more or less harmless play-acting, or that perhaps they chased an animal. Mr Tod[1] has even suggested that it may have been that form of bull-fighting with which the finds at Cnossus have made us familiar. That, certainly would have been strenuous enough even for the Spartans; but since the participants in it were only ten-year-olds, it is hard to imagine they could have been strong enough' to take part in a game which must have been very dangerous. There is no evidence that the Cretan bull-fighting ever was practised in Sparta.

FLOGGING AT THE ALTAR OF ARTEMIS ORTHIA

The most notorious of all their contests was the ceremonial flogging of young men at the altar of Artemis Orthia. Pausanias[2] tells a story of a quarrel between Spartan tribesmen sacrificing at the altar when it was defiled by human blood. The sacrilege could only be expiated, according to the oracle, by more human blood, and so an annual human sacrifice was instituted. This practice Lycurgus stopped, substituting a flogging of youths so that the blood from the lash should fall upon the altar. The youth who endured it longest was called βωμονίκης[3] and his endurance celebrated by a statue of honour. Frequently, we are told, the contestants died under the ordeal.[4]

---

[1] *Ath. Mitt.* XXIX (1904), p. 50. Cf. Baunack, *loc. cit.*
[2] Paus. III, 16, 10.
[3] Hyginus, *Fabulae*, CCLXI; *Artemis Orthia* (Dawkins *et al.*), pp. 356 ff.
[4] Plut. *Lyc.* XVIII; *Inst. Lac.* 239 D; Lucian, *Anach.* XXXVIII; Nicol. Damas. *F.H.G.* III, p. 458, 114, 11.

It may be remarked that the infliction of pain through floggings or tortures upon young men to test their endurance is a common practice everywhere among primitive peoples and is part of the ceremonies accompanying initiation into manhood.[1] But in this case there is little doubt that the sprinkling of the blood of the participants in this ceremony was of the nature of a 'blood-bond' between gods and human beings, and not a substitution for human sacrifice.[2] Bosanquet[3] gives good reasons to suppose that the ceremony in its most brutal form was a product of Roman times, a part of the 'Lycurgan revival'. It seems fairly certain that the idea of a contest of endurance was very late, and the building of a theatre about the altar was undoubtedly of Roman origin. The miserable affair aroused enormous interest and references to it are numerous.[4] The sadistic pleasure taken in watching the spectacle is well expressed by Apollonius of Tyana who says: 'The Greeks assemble just as they do at the Hyacinthia and the Gymnopaediae to look on with enjoyment and eager interest.' Tertullian says that 'the festival which in our day ranks highest at Sparta, the *diamastigosis*—that is the scourging—is notorious'. So popular and famous was it that it continued until the second half of the fourth century A.D.

Xenophon[5] tells of a kind of game in which youths tried to steal cheeses from the altar, and were kept off by whips and sticks. The passage in his *Government of the Lacedaemonians* is confused, and it is difficult to determine whether he is referring to another thing altogether, or whether he means

[1] Cf. Frazer's note in his edition of Pausanias, III, 16, 10, giving several examples.

[2] Robertson Smith, *op. cit.* p. 321. Toynbee, *op. cit.* III, p. 77; VI, p. 50, traces its origin to a primitive fertility ritual.

[3] *A.B.S.A.* XII, p. 314; *Artemis Orthia* (Dawkins *et al.*), p. 404.

[4] Philostratus, *Vita Apoll.* IV, 31–3; Libanius, *Orat.* I, 23 (p. 18, Reiske); Greg. Naz. *Orat.* IV, p. 109 and XXXIX, p. 679; Themistius, *Orat.* XXI, 250A; Tertullian, *ad. mart.* IV; cf. also Anton Thomsen in *Archiv für Religionswissenschaft*, IX, p. 397; Nilsson, *Griechische Feste*, p. 109.

[5] *Resp. Lac.* II, 9; cf. Plut. *Arist.* XVII; Plato, *Legg.* I, 633 B.

the scourging at the altar. As is remarked elsewhere,[1] it is not impossible that Xenophon is confusing the scourging with what was known as the 'mimetic' dance which was a kind of game in which hungry boys tried to steal food. If Hesychius (*s.v.* φούαξιρ) is to be trusted, the boys underwent a long preparation for this test of endurance, a statement which we may accept as probably true. It was the culmination of a protracted training in which they were fitted for initiation and the shedding of their blood on the altar was the last act: they became united with the divinity in a bond sealed with their own blood.

STEALING BY BOYS

A custom which aroused the astonishment of all writers was that of the boys' supplementing their meagre fare by stealing. Plutarch[2] says:

This young man [the eiren] was their captain when they fought and their master at home, using them for the offices of his house, sending the eldest of them to fetch wood and the weaker and less able to gather salads and herbs. And these they must either go without or steal, which they did by creeping into the gardens or crawling cunningly into the eating-houses. If they were taken in the act, they were whipped without mercy for thieving so ill and awkwardly. They stole also all other meat they could lay their hands on, looking out and watching for any opportunity when people were asleep or more careless than usual. If they were caught, they not only suffered a whipping but went hungry as well, being reduced to their ordinary rations which were very slender and contrived so that they were forced to look out for themselves and exercise their energy and ingenuity.

It seems incredible to us, and to their contemporaries as well, that such a state of affairs should have existed. Even Xenophon[3] was astonished at this custom and thinks it necessary to defend

[1] *Vide* p. 189.   [2] *Lyc.* XVII.
[3] *Resp. Lac.* II, 7–8.

it, in what must be regarded as a laboured and by no means convincing manner:

It was not on account of a difficulty in providing for them that he encouraged them to get their food by their own cunning. No one, I suppose, can fail to see that. Obviously a man who intends to take to thieving must spend sleepless nights and play the deceiver and lie in ambush by day, and moreover, if he means to make a capture, he must have spies ready. There can be no doubt then, that all this education was planned by him in order to make the boys more resourceful in getting supplies and better fighting men. Someone may ask: But why, if he believed stealing to be a fine thing, did he have the boy who was caught beaten with many stripes? I reply: Because in all cases men punish a learner for not carrying out whatever he is taught to do.

This alleged custom of stealing severely shocked all observers. It is hard to believe that such a state of affairs should have existed as to require that the boys should be deliberately taught and encouraged to thieve, and that all over the city of Sparta they should be continually creeping into back-yards, uprooting vegetables, snatching at edibles when the owners were for a moment off their guard. Life would be intolerable both for citizens, who wanted to live in peace and reasonable security, and for the miserable, half-starved boys, continually driven to satisfy their hunger by pilfering and afraid of severe punishment if detected.

But is this a right picture of the actual state of affairs? Careful consideration of the various scattered references will reveal that it is not. First, it must be observed that the boys 'at a certain period' were banished from the town and all contacts with citizens. They led a wandering life in the forests and mountains supporting themselves as best they could from whatever source was available to them. What they could take for their own support was carefully laid down: 'Such things as the law does not forbid' (ὅσα μὴ κωλύει νόμος).[1] It is quite

---

[1] Xen. *Anab.* IV, 6, 14.

evident that this refers to the bare necessities of life which were always available in caches to any hunter who had run short of supplies. He could legally help himself to an amount sufficient to satisfy his hunger for the time being, just as he could call on any helot to come to his aid.[1]

Viewed in this light, the whole thing takes on a perfectly different aspect. It was not a case of indiscriminate theft carried on at all times by boys deliberately kept on short rations to encourage thieving. It was a part of their training for a certain time, far away from the city be it carefully noted, they should be compelled to learn the art of scouting and patrolling the outer marches, spying and tracking, creeping through the undergrowth, learning woodcraft much as the present day boy scout does. He was cast entirely on his own: he took no rations with him, and if he could find nothing to eat he starved. The story of the Spartan boy who had concealed a live fox under his cloak and, rather than acknowledge its possession, allowed it to tear out his vitals, ridiculous as it is, surely gives us a picture of this part of the education of the young Spartan. He had been out hunting and caught a fox. Obviously the animal was nobody's private property, he had not stolen it. But why he did not kill the animal, and why he should not have owned up to having it, is hard to say. The story, as told, is nonsensical. The whole figment of stealing as part of the curriculum falls down. Perhaps sometimes hungry boys went too far and actually did commit serious theft for which they were severely punished. But generally speaking it was carried on according to rule and may have had some small educational value.

It may be surmised that these scouting exercises were closely connected with the *crypteia*, that other misunderstood part of the Spartan system. If the boys were creeping about under cover, it was most likely that they observed many things which the authorities would be glad to hear about. We need not imagine these boys murdering innocent helots; but since

[1] Xen. *Resp. Lac.* VI, 3.

accurate observation was highly necessary to the trained soldier, no doubt they did a lot of spying and communicated what they saw to the ephors.

FORMAL EDUCATION

We know little of formal education in Sparta, perhaps because there was very little imparted. Plutarch[1] says:

> They learned to read and write for purely practical reasons, but all other forms of education they barred from the country, books and treatises being included in this as much as men. All their education was directed towards prompt obedience to authority, stout endurance of hardship and victory or death in battle.

Isocrates[2] accused them of being entirely illiterate, but that may be put down rather to malice than actual truth. We must believe that Plutarch was correct in saying that at least they could read and write; the service of the State, the necessity for sending military dispatches and diplomatic instructions through the medium of the primitive code of the *scytale*[3] must have demanded it.

But that their literary training went no further we may certainly believe. It is not hard to imagine the contempt with which they looked on the endless logic-chopping of the philosophers and rhetoricians, who were banished from Sparta, Chamaeleon tells us,[4] 'because of the envious strife and unprofitable arguments that arise in their discussions'. There is an amusing passage in Plato's dialogue called the *Hippias Major*.[5] Hippias, the sophist of Elis, had visited Sparta and returned discomfited, having utterly failed to make any impression on the people there. Socrates, with gentle irony, wants to know why they should have spurned so eminent a teacher. Did they not

---

[1] *Inst. Lac.* 237 A; *Lyc.* XVI. It is difficult to reconcile this with Ehrenberg's assertion, 'Very few of the boys could read and write'. *Aspects of the Ancient World*, p. 99.   [2] *Panath.* 209.

[3] *Vide infra*, p. 273, for further comment on the *scytale*.

[4] ap. Athen. XIII, 611 A.   [5] 285 C (trans. of Loeb ed.).

want to hear Hippias discourse about the stars and the phenomena of the heavens, a subject on which Hippias was highly qualified to speak?

Hipp. Not in the least: they won't even endure these.

Soc. But they enjoy hearing about geometry?

Hipp. Not at all, since one might say that many of them do not even know how to count.

Soc. Then they are far from enduring a lecture by you on the processes of thought?

Hipp. Far from it indeed, by Zeus.

Soc. Well, then, these matters which you of all men know best how to discuss, concerning the value of letters and syllables and rhythms and harmonies?

Hipp. Harmonies, indeed, my good fellow, and letters!

Soc. But then what are the things about which they like to listen to you and applaud? Tell me yourself for I cannot discover them.

Hipp. They are very fond of hearing about the genealogies of heroes and men, Socrates, and the foundations of cities in ancient times and, in short, about antiquity in general, so that for their sake I have been obliged to learn all that sort of thing by heart and practise it thoroughly.

It is not difficult from the foregoing to guess why so distinguished a sophist, with his tortuous dialectical arguments, found the going hard and could make no money in Sparta. The art of oratory was forbidden, and we are told that a youth who had learned it abroad and brought it to Sparta was punished by the ephors.[1] The Athenians regarded them as uneducated, and Plutarch says that when a Spartan was reproached for this he replied, 'At least we learned no evil from you.'[2] But perhaps, after all, they were not so insensible to the deeper emotions. Plutarch[3] tells the story that when the Spartans proposed to destroy Athens completely, 'they were melted with compassion' when a man from Phocis recited a chorus from the *Electra* of Euripides.

---

[1] Sextus Empiricus, II, 21. [2] *Apoph. Lac.* 217 D. [3] *Lys.* XV.

MUSIC

The art of music, both vocal and instrumental, was cultivated assiduously in Sparta, a fact that was frequently remarked upon by ancient authors, who seem to have been rather surprised that a people, otherwise so uncultured, should have attained to such a degree of excellence in it. 'The Spartans', says Plutarch,[1] 'are at the same time the most musical and the most warlike. "In equal poise to match the sword hangs the sweet art of the harpist" as their poet says.' Pratinas[2] frankly puts this love of music down to what the moderns call 'escapism'.

For people were glad to turn from the soberness and austerity of life to the solace of music, because the art has the power to charm and with good reason the listeners liked it.

Aristotle[3] somewhat grudgingly acknowledges that the Spartans 'without ever having learned music are yet able to judge what is good and what is bad'. This rather surprising statement seems explainable only on the ground that he means that there were in Sparta no professional music teachers or rhetoricians, and that Aristotle is unable to understand how competent musicians, either vocal or instrumental, can possibly exist if they have not been trained by professionals. This seems a narrow and prejudiced view to take, when we reflect that a very notable school of native music did undoubtedly exist in Sparta.[4] Perhaps it was more as preservers of ancient and honourable forms of music that the Spartans were most highly honoured. Pratinas says of them[5]

Of all the Greeks the Spartans have most faithfully preserved the art of music, employing it most extensively and many composers of lyrics have arisen among them. Even to this day they carefully retain the ancient songs and are very well taught in them and strict in holding to them.

---

[1] *Lyc.* XXI, 4.   [2] ap. Athen. XIV, 633 A.   [3] *Pol.* 1339 B.
[4] Aristotle's words seem to find an echo in Athen. XIV, 628 B.
[5] ap. Athen. XIV, 632 F.

Mention has already been made of the place of Terpander in the development of Greek music.[1] As usual, the accounts given of his accomplishments are highly confused; but whatever he did, or did not do, it is certain that in him the Greeks found an innovator of genius whose influence was of the greatest possible importance.[2] It seems certain that he added three strings to the four-stringed 'Dorian' lyre. But why he added three and not a fourth in order to produce an octave is not clear. The story was that soon after he arrived in Sparta he was playing one day in the presence of the ephors when one of them started up and, seizing a hatchet, cut one of the strings from his lyre, accusing him of being an impious innovator in the ancient Spartan music.[3] Does this mean that his lyre had eight strings and was forcibly reduced to seven? And why did the ephor object to eight and allow him seven, when to add three to the original four was already an innovation in the ancient mode? The whole story is confused and evidentially worthless. Perhaps people were puzzled at there being only seven strings and the story of the ephor was invented to account for it. If it was not true, it was just the kind of thing a Spartan ephor would do. It may be remarked that to add to the confusion the story is also told of Timotheus and Phrynis who came after Terpander.[4] Perhaps they also tried to introduce the eighth string and were restrained in similar violent fashion.

[1] *Supra*, p. 14.   [2] Art. 'Musik' by Vetter in P.W. xvi, 861.

[3] Plutarch, *de Musica*, xix. J. Curtis, 'Greek Music' in *J.H.S.* xxxiii (1913), p. 35. The so-called 'defective scale' of Terpander was really a tuning of the strings of the cithara, E F G A B – D E. Mr Curtis answers the question of how a seven-stringed instrument could play an eight-note scale by following Plutarch that the upper octave of the lowest note was played as a harmonic on the lowest string. It may be remarked that, while this is practicable on a violin, it would be difficult and unsatisfactory on a lyre played with a plectrum.

[4] Terpander, Plut. *Inst. Lac.* 238 c; Timotheus, *ibid.*; Athen. xiv, 636 E; Dio Chrys. *Orat.* xxxii; Paus. iii, 12, 8. Boethius, *de Mus.* i, 1, a curious passage professing to give the actual decree of the ephors against Timotheus. Worthless evidentially. Phrynis, Plut. *Apoph. Lac.* 220 c; *vide* art. 'Lyra' in D.S. by Th. Reinach. Curt Sachs, *Rise of Music in the Ancient World*, p. 216.

Beyond enlarging the compass of the lyre, it is difficult to determine what was Terpander's contribution to music in Sparta. The most ancient mode was the Phrygian, which was supposed to have come into Sparta with the legendary Pelops.[1] Evidently Terpander and his successors taught the Spartans something better than this archaic form. It is altogether likely that the Spartans were glad enough to be taught, since the Phrygian was hardly suitable for the quite elaborate dancing and drilling which they were anxious to practice and improve. It is generally thought that Terpander favoured the Lydian mode of music;[2] but since this was always considered effeminate and enervating, more suitable for women's voices than men's, it is not easy to understand how he introduced it into Sparta, unless it was adopted especially for women's choruses. Perhaps Terpander arrived in Sparta playing this Lydian mode and found himself confronted with official displeasure and hastily changed. He was said to have introduced a 'Boeotian' harmony, but of this nothing is known.[3] In any case the puzzles with regard to Greek music are so baffling that we need not concern ourselves more with them.

Whatever actually were the contributions to music made by Terpander and his followers, there is no doubt that the Spartans were good pupils and profited by their lessons. They may have been ultra-conservative; but they did see that music was of value in the dancing exercises upon which they put so great store. We are told by Polybius[4] that the ancient Cretans and Lacedaemonians introduced the flute and a marching rhythm in place of the trumpet. Obviously the rhythmical tones of the flute were much more suitable for marching exercises than the sound of the trumpet. The flute seems to have been the Spartans' favourite instrument and in its playing they reached a high degree of excellence.[5] The lyre

---

[1] Athen. XIV, 625 F.   [2] Athen. XIV, 635 D; Paus. IX, 5, 4.
[3] Schol. ad Aristoph. *Acharn.* 14; Plut. *De mus.* XVI; Schol. ad Pindar, *Ol.* XI, 117.   [4] ap. Athen. XIV, 626 A.
[5] Chamaeleon, ap. Athen. 184 D.

was more suitable for dances, especially those of the maidens as Alcman says.[1] Plutarch[2] mentions a little incident, which may or may not be true, saying that a visiting harp-player was fined by the ephors because he plucked the strings with his fingers instead of with a plectrum. Apparently they did not like their music played softly; perhaps the visitor was the ancient equivalent of a 'crooner'! Plato[3] did not seem to think much of Spartan choral singing. When he asked his Laconian friend what song was best fitted for heroes, the Laconian answered innocently that the only songs he knew were those of the choruses he was taught in Sparta; which was a perfectly good answer. But Socrates catches him up and says choral singing is not the noblest form of music, and that the education in Sparta is too much like the herd system, in which no one can ever hope to be singled out from the rest. It is not a very polite comment and draws a mild protest from the Spartan. The passage is amusing, as showing Socrates at his most irritating trick of catching up his unfortunate friends on an unguarded answer to one of his innumerable questions.

DANCING

Dancing to the sound of flutes or lyres was practised assiduously in Sparta. Generally, but not always, these dances were more like drilling or moving in complicated evolutions and often like mimic warfare. Excellence in the dance was valued highly and there was keen rivalry between the squads or platoons of boys and young men who took part in the public displays.

The most famous was the pyrrhic dance,[4] which represented in a sort of pantomime a sham fight. It was danced to the flute, very quickly and lightly, imitating both defence and offence, retreating, springing up, crouching, attacking, thrusting with

---

[1] *Lyra Graeca* (ed. J. M. Edmonds), Alcman, fr. XXXVII, p. 79.
[2] *Apoph. Lac.* 233 F.   [3] *Legg.* 666 D.
[4] Plato, *Legg.* VII, 815; Athen. XIV, 631 A; Lucian, *De salt.* VIII; Strabo, X (C. 467); Pollux, IV, 99; Paus. III, 25.

the lance and shooting arrows. This dance was known in other parts of Greece, but had degenerated into a kind of slap-stick knockabout, of a not over-refined character. In Sparta, characteristically, it had been preserved in its original character, and was thought so highly of that every boy, when he reached the age of fifteen,[1] began to learn its complicated steps and figures.

At the festival of the Gymnopaediae, dancing and gymnastics were the principal features. The festival[2] was a tremendous affair in which all male Spartans took part and provided, as Mr Wade-Gery remarks, 'the most brilliant of those solemn revels that sweetened the austerity of the new Spartan life', commemorating the slain at the battle of Thyrea, 'the battle of the champions'. Troops of boys, young men and old men sang one after the other, the children singing of what they would do when they were grown up, the young men boasting of their strength and prowess, and the old men telling of their deeds in their prime. Often whole battalions were led out by the ephors.[3] There were posts of honour and dishonour in the line, a fact which Agesilaus very neatly turned to his own account. When placed in a lowly position by the *choregus*, he remarked that no doubt the intention was to give honour to the place by putting him there.[4]

The festival was so famous that we know a good deal about it. An excellent article by Bölte for a full treatment of certain aspects may be consulted.[5] Evidently the boys led off in the early morning before the heat of the sun became too exhausting. The able-bodied men followed in the afternoon after lunch and showed their endurance in the heat. We may presume that the old men came on in the evening or when the field was in shade. The leader of each troop, or file, was distinguished by an elaborate head-dress woven from palm leaves.[6] Mr Wade-Gery advances the suggestion that these were made of feathers

---

[1] Athen. XIV, 631 A. Not at five as some commentators suppose.
[2] Plut. *Lyc.* 21; *Inst. Lac.* 238 B; Pollux, IV, 107.   [3] Xen. *Hell.* VI, 4, 16.
[4] Xen. *Ages.* II, 17. A favourite story and told of several others.
[5] *Rhein. Mus.* LXXVIII (1929), pp. 124 ff.
[6] Sosibius, ap. Athen. 678 B.

and not palm leaves.[1] In this he may well be correct, although feathered head-dresses are not mentioned anywhere in ancient writings. The composition of this barbaric head-dress must therefore be left in doubt. The troop behind the leader kept time by him. The festival lasted for several days, Mr Wade-Gery supposes five, each *oba* having a day to itself. It is easy to suppose that the last day was climaxed by a grand parade of all taking part, led by the ephors. It may be added that the often asserted meaning of *gymnopaedia* as 'dance of the naked youths,' cannot be correct. The word comes from γυμνός, which rather means 'unarmed' than 'nude', and παίζειν meaning to 'dance' or 'exercise'.

One of the most popular dances at this festival was the *Anapale*[2] or wrestling dance, in which the boys moved in time to the music 'with graceful motions of the hands, displaying the practices of the wrestling-school and the pancratium'. Moving in ranks one behind the other to the sound of flutes they performed their evolutions, and when these were done they broke into song bidding Aphrodite and Eros join them and encouraging one another in their tasks.[3]

The *Embaterion*[4] was not strictly a dance, but rather a quick-step march to the sound of flutes and the chanting of Castor's Song, an anapaestic measure 'lively and invigorating', to which they marched into battle. It would seem that the 'Messenian measure' was another name for this.[5] *Embateria* and *Enoplia*[6] were probably marching songs, just as soldiers sing to-day when on the march.

Lucian[7] gives a spirited picture of the young men in their *palaestra*.

[1] 'A note on the origin of the Spartan Gymnopaediai', *Class. Quart.* XLIII (Jan–April 1949), p. 79.
[2] Plut. *De mus.* XXVI; Pollux, V, 79. Athen. XIV, 631 B; J. Jüthner, 'Der spartanische Nackttanz', *Wiener Studien*, XXXIV (1912), p. 43.
[3] Lucian, *De salt.* X, 11.
[4] Art. 'Embaterion' in P.W. by Crusius.
[5] Doubtful. Only used by Marius Victorinus, *Art. Gramm.* I, II.
[6] Athen. XIV, 630 F.   [7] *De salt.* X–XII.

Even now you may see their young men studying dancing quite as much as fighting under arms. When they have stopped sparring and exchanging blow for blow with each other, their contest ends in dancing and a flute player sits in the middle playing them a tune and marking time with his foot, while they, following one another in line, perform figures of all sorts in rhythmic steps, now those of war and presently those of the choral dance that are dear to Dionysus and Aphrodite.

Religious dances, in which girls as well as men took part, were common, such as the *Hyporchema*, apparently in honour of Apollo.[1] This seems to have been particularly effective, the dancers circling about a blazing fire on the altar. Probably this dance came originally from Crete and was introduced thence into Sparta, where it was much admired.

The *Hormos*[2] or 'String of Beads' was performed by youths and maidens together. 'The boy goes first, doing the steps and postures of young manhood and those which later he will practise in war. The maiden follows after him, showing how to do the women's dance with propriety, and so the string is beaded with modesty and manliness.' Another dance performed by girls was the *Dipoda*, 'a stately Spartan measure', of which we know nothing beyond its name.[3]

The *Bryallicha*[4] seems to have been a women's dance in honour of Apollo and Artemis, if it was not a burlesque performance by men with masks of women's faces. It seems impossible to decide definitely which it was. Another dance, of which we have no particulars, was the *Caryatid* performed by women in honour of Artemis at Caryae.[5]

Pollux[6] mentions several others by name of which we know little more. The *Deimalea* was performed by men dressed as

[1] Lucian, *De salt.* XVI; Athen. XIV, 630 D, E; Sandys, *Pindar* (in Loeb ed.), pp. 547 ff.   [2] Lucian, *De salt.* II.

[3] Cratinus in Meineke, *Fragmenta Comicorum Graecorum*, II, 1, 109; Schol. ad Aristoph. *Lys.* 1245.

[4] Pollux, IV, 104; Hesych, *s.v.* βόλλιχαι χωρόι; *vide* also Bölte in Hermes, LXXIX (1930), p. 141.

[5] Pollux, *ut supra*; Paus. III, 10, 7.   [6] IV, 104.

satyrs dancing in a circle. The *Ithymbi* was performed in honour of *Bacchus*. The *Hypogypones* imitated old men leaning on sticks and the *Gypones* was danced on stilts, the performers wearing 'transparent Tarentine dress'. There was a Bacchanalian dance called the *Tyrbasia*, and another, the 'Mimetic', in which were mimicked those who were caught stealing the remains of the public meals, by which we may understand the unfortunate half-starved boys; it was probably a fairly vigorous and rough affair.[1]

There may have been—but here we are on very debatable ground—a vulgar dance called the *Mothon*[2] performed by helots imitating drunkenness, which may possibly explain the legend that the Spartans intoxicated slaves to act as a salutary warning to the boys against insobriety. The point is quite incapable of proof. We may be sure that many of these dances, when not of a religious or military character, were fairly unrefined, to put it mildly, as country dances always have been.

Sosibius[3] speaks of 'an ancient variety of comic pastime, not taken very seriously because in such matters Sparta follows simplicity'. This was the *Deikelistes* which apparently was a kind of pantomime played by masked performers called *deikelistai*. The exact purport of this is not known, nor whether it had religious significance, although the latter seems probable. Apparently these masks were dedicated to Artemis Orthia, and specimens of them have been unearthed.[4]

There is a joyousness in all these dances which belies the otherwise over-gloomy picture we have of Spartan life. They certainly had their moments of relaxation; perhaps the austerity of their discipline when relaxed contributed to the other extreme and, as is so often found, licence was the result. There are too many hints and even open accusations of

---

[1] Perhaps this is what Xenophon is referring to in *Resp. Lac.* II, 9.

[2] Athen. XIV, 618 C; Schol. ad Aristoph. *Plutus*, 279; Eurip. *Bacchae*, 1060; Aristoph. *Equites*, 697.

[3] ap. Athen. XIV, 621 D.

[4] *A.B.S.A.* XII, pp. 338 ff., and plates X–XII; also Thiele, *Neue Jahrbücher f.d. klassische Altertum*, IX (1902), p. 411.

immorality among the Spartans to be wholly groundless. But, however that may be, the closing lines of Aristophanes' *Lysistrata*, sung by a chorus of Spartan girls, are very pleasing.

> Now then, now the step begin,
> Twisting light the fleecy skin;
> So we join our blithesome voices,
> Praising Sparta loud and long,
> Sparta who of old rejoices
> In the choral dance and song.
> O to watch her pretty daughters
> Sport along Eurotas' waters,
> Winsome feet for ever plying
> Fleet as fillies, wild and gay,
> Winsome tresses, tossing, flying,
> As of Bacchanals at play.

FIGHTS AND GAMES

The annual fight of the youths as described by Pausanias and Cicero[1] was certainly strenuous enough to satisfy anyone —nothing was barred. The accounts of this annual combat are so interesting that it is worth while to recount them in some detail, and it will be found that further consideration will reveal implications in the custom not at first apparent. The fight between two bands of young men was preceded the night before by a drawing of lots to decide which should represent the band of Lycurgus and which that of Heracles. This ceremony took place at the Phoibaion near Therapne[2] and after it was done a puppy was sacrificed to Ares or Enyalius. Then a boar fight took place between two animals representing the opposing sides, the outcome of which presaged the decision on the morrow.

Next day the two bands marched on to the place of combat, an island in the river, approached by two bridges named Lycurgus and Heracles. Thereupon they fell on each other

---

[1] Paus. III, 14, 8; Cicero, *Tusc. Disp.* V, 27, 77; Lucian, *Anach.* XXXVIII; Plut. *Quaest. Rom.* 290 D. [2] Herod. VI, 61.

with astonishing ferocity 'using their hands, kicking with their feet, biting and gouging out the eyes of their opponents in the attempt to drive the opposing side into the river'.

If this were merely another example of Spartan ferocity it would not afford more than passing interest. But it will be found that there is much more in it than at first appears. Hermann Usener, in his article 'Heilige Handlung',[1] has demonstrated that fights of this description were widespread, and indeed the gladiatorial combats of the Etruscans and later of the Romans may be traced to the same motive. What is more extraordinary is to realise that fights between bands of youths were observed in different places, notably Pisa, Siena and Florence, until well into the seventeenth century. Usener gives evidence to show that these fights were symbolic of the victory of spring over winter—they took place in the early spring—although the original significance had long since been forgotten.

The sacrifice of a dog to Enyalius–Ares–Thereitas was certainly a lustration, a φαρμακός or κάθαρμα, of apotropaic significance, a purification and turning away of the gods' wrath.[2] The dog was sacred to Ares, or Enyalius as he was called in Laconia. In some unexplained way this cult came from Caria[3] and Pausanias[4] is probably correct in saying that the Greeks did not offer dogs to any Olympian deity. But the point is obscure. Possibly the sacrifice of a dog took the place of human sacrifice, although this is not certain. Plutarch's statement that a dog was sacrificed, as being the most courageous animal, to the fiercest of the gods is certainly without foundation.[5] The boar fight[6] was obviously for the purpose of foretelling the outcome of the battle on the morrow;

---

[1] *Archiv f. Religionswissenschaft*, VII (1904), pp. 281 ff., reprinted in *Kleine Schriften*, IV, pp. 422 ff.

[2] H. Scholz, *Der Hund in d. griech.-röm. Magie u. Religion* (Phil. Diss. 1937), pp. 17f.; Nilsson, *Griech. Feste*, p. 405, n. 3.

[3] Arnobius, *adv. Nationes*, IV, 25. Clem. Alex. *Cohort. ad Gentes*, II, 8.

[4] III, 14, 9.　　　　　　　　[5] *Quaest. Rom.* (111), 290 D.

[6] Nilsson, *op. cit.* p. 403.

a pig was a sacred animal. It would seem that a fight between opposing bands was looked upon as an omen of victory or defeat in a forthcoming battle. For instance, before the battle of Gaugamela[1] two bands of Alexander's soldiers, representing Greeks and Persians, had a fight. The victory of the Greeks so encouraged the army that it went into battle on the morrow confident of victory, and one is tempted to suspect that Alexander had the fight 'fixed' beforehand.

The annual ball-game was hardly less strenuous and seems to have been played with no rules whatever. So far as we can gather from the very scanty details left to us[2] the opposing teams of about fifteen players each lined up on the Plane Tree Ground. At a given signal they threw themselves on the ball and the team found to be in possession of it when time was called was the winner. Apparently there was no kicking of goals or scoring of points; it was a straight fight for the possession of the ball and must have been one of the most primitive and strenuous games ever played.

Plutarch[3] tells us that Lycurgus would allow no games involving 'a stretching forth of hands'. This curious rule can only be explained, somewhat doubtfully, by supposing it means a stretching forth in the manner of suppliants begging for mercy. Apparently the opponent had to be beaten into complete insensibility before the game was over. Somewhat surprisingly we are told that he forbade all boxing, 'so that even in sport the people might not acquire the habit of crying off'. We might have thought that, if the fight went on to a knock-out, it would have satisfied all requirements. But whether Lycurgus forbade it or not, they affected to despise boxing, although they claimed to have invented it, and never competed in it at any of the great games.[4] It looks as if this prohibition of

---

[1] Plut. *Alex.* XXXI. Cf. Livy, XL, 6. Many instances of human sacrifice before battle, e.g. Salamis, Plut. *Them.* XIII. Cf. Robertson Smith, *op. cit.* p. 309.

[2] Lucian, *Anach.* XXXVIII; Demet. Phal. *De eloc.* CXXII; Schol. ad Plato, *Legg.* I, 63 C; Tod, *A.B.S.A.* X (1903), pp. 63 ff.

[3] *Lyc.* XIX, 4; *Apoph. Lac.* 228 D. Cf. E. Gardiner, *Greek Athletic Sports*, p. 415.   [4] Philostratus, *Gym.* IX.

boxing sprang rather from a desire to maintain order in the streets than from any dislike of the sport. Xenophon tells us:[1]

They must also attend to their health, for in consequence of this emulation they engage in fist fights with one another whenever they chance to meet. But any person who comes upon them fighting has full power to separate the combatants. And if either of them disobeys him, the paidonomus takes him before the Ephors who punish him severely to prevent anger from going so far as to cause a breach of the law.

Any fighting, therefore, must be organised and private grudges must not be paid off individually, an admirable sentiment but likely to present difficulties in enforcement. But at least they liked to do their own fighting; gladiators were not tolerated in Sparta.[2] In wrestling they despised, or affected to despise, science and relied solely on brute force. A Spartan who had been defeated excused himself on the ground that, although his opponent was a better wrestler, he was not a better man than himself; which may have been true but hardly seems an adequate excuse for his failure.[3] These fights and games were under the supervision of five officials called *bidaioi*.[4] Later in Roman times a special official, the διαβέτης, was in charge of the ball-game. He seems to have been a kind of *magister ludorum*, an honour bestowed, or imposed, on a rich man, who probably spent a lot of money on it during his term of office.

ATHLETIC CONTESTS IN ROMAN TIMES

Although the evidence is late, there are one or two little items with regard to the contests which are interesting enough to record.[5] The games probably took place at the feast of the Hyacinthia and evidently a big crowd was expected and careful preparations were made. Special magistrates, νομο-

---

[1] *Resp. Lac.* IV, 6.   [2] Plato, *Laches*, CLXXXIII.

[3] Plut. *Quaest. Conviv.* 639 F. Cf. *Pelopidas*, VII, 3. No wrestling instructors in Sparta, *Apoph. Lac.* 233 E.

[4] Paus. III, 11, 2; *C.I.G.* 1241, 42, 54, 55. Referees or judges almost certainly connected with ἴδυοι or ϝίδυοι.   [5] *A.B.S.A.* XII, pp. 450 ff.

φύλακες, are sworn in to handle any disputes that might arise. The athletes are under the special discipline of officials named ἀθλοθέται. Ordinary lawsuits are suspended, freedom of import and sale of goods is to be allowed and the bank managers are to be put under bond in the sum of 30,000 *denarii*: all of which is curiously like the provisions laid down for the conduct of the medieval fairs.

The athletes must obey orders and failure to do so entailed a fine of five *denarii*. The fact that a contestant has put down his name for a certain event is evidence that he will abide by the rules and accept the umpire's decision as final. The gymnasiarch shall provide every day four *cyathi* of oil for adult contestants, three for youths and two for boys. The *cyathus*, it may be mentioned, was a small fluid measure of about one-twelfth of a pint.[1] In another inscription[2] we find the generosity of a gymnasiarch named Theophrastus recorded in about the year A.D. 132. Evidently by then the office of gymnasiarch had become a liturgy, that is an office laid upon some rich man who paid for the expenses out of his own pocket. In this case he is particularly generous since he provides large jars of oil from which the contestants can take whatever they want for anointing themselves, instead of the carefully measured quantities usually allotted to them. Another curious item is that Theophrastus also provided linen towels, λέντια ξῦστρα, for their convenience. Evidently they provided their own strigils or scrapers. In conclusion, it may be remarked that the same Theophrastus paid for distributions of grain (σεπωνεία), which is a new thing in Spartan economy. Hitherto the rich valley of the Eurotas had been able to support the population easily.

THE DARKER SIDE

There was another and, to modern susceptibilities, a very dark side to all this training of the boys. It is quite amusing

---

[1] Hultsch, *Griechische und römische Metrologie*, p. 104, and table, p. 703.
[2] *A.B.S.A.* xxvii, p. 231.

to read the elaborate and strained defence by Xenophon[1] of the system by which each Spartan boy had a 'guardian' who was responsible for his conduct (a system which he claims is much superior to that of other Greeks, who entrust them to pedagogues, who might be, and often were, quite worthless, an opinion shared by Plato).[2] These Spartan guardians were called 'lovers', and there can be little doubt that the relationship degenerated in many, if not in most, cases into gross sensuality. The boys and young men were leading an extraordinary life of hardship under a discipline that denied them any ameliorative circumstances, or gave any respite in the rigour of the conditions under which they lived. It has been the constant experience of humanity that, when discipline and hardship imposed upon persons have reached a climax, as they had under the Spartan system, they work their own destruction and particularly virulent manifestations of sensuality ensue.[3] This aspect of Greek morals is an extraordinary one into which, for the sake of our own equanimity, it is unprofitable to pry too closely. The best thinkers among the Greeks themselves condemned it; the remarks of both Aristotle[4] and Plato[5] show that they were fully alive to the evils arising from what was in the ancient world an almost universal practice. Plutarch tried to put the best interpretation upon it:

Their lovers had a share in the young boys' honour or disgrace; and there is a story that one of them was fined by the magistrate because the lad whom he loved cried out effeminately as he was fighting. And though this sort of love was so approved among

---

[1] *Resp. Lac.* II, 12. Cf. also Plut. *Lyc.* XVIII, 4; *Inst. Lac.* 237B; Aelian, *V.H.* III, 10, 12.   [2] *Prot.* 225D.

[3] For the view that *paiderastia* was distinctively a Dorian propensity, cf. Bethe, 'Dorische Knabenliebe', *Rhein. Mus.* LXII (1907), p. 438; Semenov, 'Zur dorischen Knabenliebe', *Philologus*, LXX (1911), p. 146; Wilamowitz-Moellendorff, *Staat u. Gesell. d. Griechen*, p. 90. For discussion of terms εἰσπνήλας 'lover' and ἄϊτας 'loved' cf. Gilbert, *Grk. Const. Ant.* p. 65, n. 1.

[4] *Pol.* 1272A, and Ruppersberg in *Philologus*, LXX (1911), p. 151.

[5] *Legg.* 636E.

them that the most virtuous matrons would make professions of it to young girls, yet rivalry did not exist. If several men's fancies met in one person, it was rather the beginning of an intimate friendship whilst they all jointly conspired to render the object of their affection as accomplished as possible.[1]

If so lofty and pure a passion was degraded to sensuality the lapse was punished by lifelong disgrace or *atimia*; even to be seen kissing a boy was a heavily punished offence.[2] Xenophon[3] is painfully aware that his account of this pure affection is incredible.

That such a state of things is disbelieved by some I am not surprised, for in many states the laws are not opposed to the indulgence of these appetites.

We are left to wonder how far Xenophon believed what he was saying himself. But since he was writing a panegyric on all things Spartan, he had to do the best he could with a difficult subject.

The same system that sought to toughen them physically was used to harden them intellectually. We are told that, when the dinner at the boys' mess was done, the eiren who presided would call upon one of the boys to sing a song or would put questions to them, such as who was the noblest citizen. If they failed to give sensible replies, they were ridiculed and punished, rather curiously, by having their thumbs bitten by the eiren.[4] The code of punishments was a severe one, floggings for even small offences; but it is at least reassuring to know that an eiren could be called to account if his infliction of punishment went beyond reasonable bounds. But however that may be, there must have been a lot of

---

[1] Plut. *Lyc.* XVIII.   [2] Plut. *Inst. Lac.* 237C; Ael. *V.H.* III, 12.
[3] *Resp. Lac.* II, 14.
[4] Cf. H. Volkmann, 'Ein verkannter Strafbrauch der Spartaner', in *Archiv für Religionswissenschaft*, XXXII (1935), p. 188. It is probable that a magical significance pertained to this practice, and that biting the thumb imparted strength or wisdom to the boy who had failed to answer properly. Volkmann supplies evidence of similar practices among primitive peoples.

bullying. The system was a hard one, in some ways an extra-ordinary one, and if carried out to its logical extremity an impossible one in which the wastage must have been high. If a boy went through it he emerged into manhood mentally and physically tough and hardened, an automaton trained to obey orders, taciturn, with a 'laconic' brevity of speech, a first-class fighting man but nothing more.

TRAINING OF THE GIRLS

Nor were the girls allowed to escape similar drastic methods of upbringing.[1] Athletic exercises of a vigorous nature were imposed upon them, running, wrestling, throwing the discus and casting the javelin. Hippasus[2] tells of a ball-game played by Spartan girls, but gives no particulars. One particularly strenuous form of exercise, the *bibasis*, in which the girls jumped up and down, touching the buttocks with their heels at each leap, seems to have been celebrated. The Spartan woman in Aristophanes' *Lysistrata*[3] is proud to boast she can perform it. Perhaps an exhibition was given then and there on the stage. Pollux[4] refers to this 'kind of dance' and quotes an epigram to the effect that to do the *bibasis* a thousand times would be to do it more times than anyone ever had, in which we may heartily agree.

If we may trust a fragment of Pindar preserved in Athenaeus[5] the girls were organised into bands (Λάκαινα παρθένων ἀγέλα) like the boys, but not under such strict discipline since they lived at home. Theocritus[6] speaks of a band of four times sixty maidens who anoint themselves like the men and run races beside the Eurotas. Later in the same idyll he talks of their skill in weaving wool and playing the lyre, which somewhat spoils the picture since we know that Spartan

---

[1] Plut. *Lyc.* xiv; Nicol. Damas. *F.H.G.* iii, p. 458, 114, 4.
[2] ap. Athen. i, 14E.   [3] *Lysist.* 82.
[4] iv, 102.   [5] xiv, 631 c.
[6] xviii, 23. Vergil, *Georg.* ii, 487, speaks of Bacchic rites of Spartan women on the banks of the Taÿgetus, probably an echo of the preceding.

women did not do wool work in their homes. No doubt also in their choral singing the rivalry was very great, although we have no records of contests or prizes. It is curious to note in Alcman how this or that girl is praised as leader of the chorus. Their harmless jealousies and ambitions are touched up and gentle fun poked at them. But it shows that rivalry and the spirit of competition were as potent among the girls as among the men. It is not without its significance to reflect that 'team-play' among the Spartans, men and women, had been taken to the point where it could go no further, and that to relieve it and make it bearable the competitive spirit in individuals had to be introduced. These sports they carried out often in the presence of the youths, who looked on also while they danced and sang. The same invariable spirit of rivalry went through all their training. They mocked and railed ('good-naturedly', Plutarch tells us) at any youth who had been guilty of some fault, 'and again they would sing the praises of those who had shown themselves worthy, and so inspire the young men with great ambition and ardour'.

At home the girls were not taught the traditional and universal task of the woman—spinning and weaving wool.[1] Such occupations were good enough for slaves; mothers of Spartan warriors must not enervate their bodies by tasks that kept them all day at the loom. By athleticism they made sure that their children would be up to the standard of physical fitness demanded by the Spartan system. It may be remarked that Plato is not quite sure that he approves of the Spartan girls' upbringing; although he acknowledges that it is half-way between the life of the savage woman and that of the Athenian.

THE PHILOSOPHERS ON SPARTAN EDUCATION

Interest in the Spartan educational system, as in everything that came out of that mysterious and intriguing land, was very great in those who observed from outside. Approval of it was general; mingled with a little wonder at its rigour and some

[1] Plato, *Legg.* 806 A.

disapproval of its neglect of the Arts so dear to the Greek nature. To all Greek philosophers of the fourth century 'the problem of education was ultimately the problem of finding an absolute standard for the human behaviour. In Sparta this had been solved.'[1] Individualism had run wild in Greece and democracy was evidently dying; indeed, by Aristotle's time it had met its end. Only by training, by discipline, by the subordination of the errant individual to the State, could the Greek world be saved from the tyranny it so fiercely hated and to which it was inevitably doomed. Was not the Spartan constitution blessed by the Delphic God himself? That the Spartan system of education and polity imposed a greater tyranny than any man-made despot ever imposed was hidden to them; or if not hidden, misunderstood or wilfully ignored.

The chorus of praise was not unbroken, however, and the closest observers, Plato and Aristotle, have some severe criticisms of it. Plato[2] puts his finger on the failure of the Spartan educational system in saying that they had neglected 'her who is the true Muse, the companion of reason and philosophy, and have honoured gymnastic more than music'. Their system is a mixture of good and evil and 'where there is a mixture there is seen but one thing only, the spirit of contention and ambition, and that is due to the prevalence of the passionate or spirited element'. In other words, Plato is saying that in Spartan education the spiritual is starved and the physical is exalted. In the never-ending struggle between good and evil, the highest and the lowest in man's nature, the evil attributes have triumphed.

Aristotle says of States which are trained for nothing but war that, 'after they have acquired supreme power over those around them, they are ruined; for during peace, like a sword, they lose their brightness. This fault lies in the legislator who never taught them how to be at rest.'[3] His final judgement of the Spartan educational system is very severe.

[1] Jaeger, *Paideia*, p. 81. [2] *Rep.* 548.
[3] *Pol.* 1234A.

What is fair and honourable ought to take the place in education of what is fierce and cruel; for it is not a wolf nor any other wild beast which will brave any noble danger, but rather a good man. So that those who permit boys to engage too earnestly in these exercises without instructing them in what they ought to do, render them mean and vile, trained for only one duty of a citizen and good for nothing in every other respect, as reason shows.[1]

The study of Spartan institutions always fascinated the Greek philosophers, who found in them what might be called a laboratory experiment in a planned economic and political system. Philo-Laconianism was traditional in the Socratic school, Plato himself being a warm admirer of the Spartan polity which he essayed to reproduce, more or less, in his ideal Republic. Xenophon was as ardent in his admiration, and when exiled went to Laconia, where he was treated with exceptional generosity, at least for Sparta, and given an estate at Scillus near Olympia in Elis,[2] no doubt through the influence of King Agesilaus who was his personal friend. Not only the philosophers but the oligarchs in Athens were whole-heartedly philo-Laconian, as might well be expected since to them the government of Sparta was the model of all that an oligarchic rule should be. Critias, one of the thirty tyrants of Athens and in his early days a pupil of Socrates, wrote a treatise on Sparta praising it as the ideal State.[3] Aristotle, as was to be expected, devoted considerable attention to Sparta, but not, as we have seen, invariably favourably; indeed, often his judgements are very severe in condemnation of what he considers to be faulty. The Stoics were great admirers of everything Spartan and Zeno modelled his ideal State upon it. Sphaerus the Stoic was deeply involved in the reforms of Agis and Cleomenes, not with the happiest results.[4]

[1] *Ibid.* 1338 A.

[2] Xen. *Anab.* VII, 3, 7; Paus. v, 6, 5; Diog. Laert. II, 6, 52.

[3] *F.H.G.* II, p. 69. Cf. Köhler, in *Sitzungsberichte d. preussischen Akademie d. Wissenschaft zu Berlin* (1896), p. 361, in which it is argued that Xenophon based much of his own *Government of the Lacedaemonians* on the earlier work of Critias.   [4] *Vide infra*, p. 322.

The order and discipline of the 'Lycurgan' system seemed to Plato an admirable thing, and in his *Republic*, written, it must be understood, before the defeat of Leuctra, he essays a sketch, a ground plan, of the ideal State which in some, but not all, ways resembles the Spartan. For instance, he will have no money in his Republic; just as Lycurgus would have only the clumsy and practically unusable iron money for his Spartans. Of course he has to confess that through the frailties of human nature and the greed for possessions they have fallen from the ideal, as he sadly acknowledges in the *Alcibiades*.[1] He takes the Spartan system as his pattern for the training of his military caste, the guardians of the State who shall devote their whole lives and energies to their task. But he by no means thinks that all his citizens should be absorbed in a single duty. The guardians of the Republic are specialists, they are not typical of everyone, for his system is to be a balanced one and he clearly sees that in the Spartan State there is a lack of balance, which brings its own evils with it. Control by a military caste cannot be allowed, and in his ideal State the guardians must be kept in their place by the rulers.

In Sparta he found that equality of the sexes which was lacking in any other Greek State. Not that he altogether approves of the freedom given to the Spartan women. Like everyone else he is shocked at some of their practices, which he certainly would not allow in his Republic. But he likes the theoretical community of property with its mathematical division of the land into equal lots, although he must have known that it had broken down in Sparta.

But Plato was an Athenian not a Spartan. He delighted in the grace and freedom of the philosophic and literary way of life which was dear to him and was so utterly lacking in the Spartan mode. In the actual Sparta of Lycurgus he would have been acutely unhappy, and therefore he invents an ideal State which would combine what he conceives as the best of

[1] *Alcib.* I, 122 D.

both the Athenian and Spartan ways of life. It is an impossible one he knows, but at least well worth consideration and perhaps, if modified and brought down to earth as he shows in the *Laws*, not altogether impossible. He is hard put to it to classify the Spartan polity[1] and does not know whether to call it a democracy or a tyranny since it partook of both systems. But in any case, he thinks, the more vicious aspects of both were wanting and what was best of democracy and tyranny were happily blended.

The eclipse of Sparta was for Plato a great blow, a grievous disappointment. He had thought that from Sparta might come the unifying force, the leadership that would save Greece from the internal strife that was tearing her to pieces, and impose, by force of arms, a sanity that was otherwise impossible to attain in the hopelessly divided Hellas with her irreconcilable jealousies and animosities. Only force would do that, and with the triumph of Sparta in the Peloponnesian war it looked as if that force had been found. And then at Leuctra, after a brief thirty years of ineffective leadership, Sparta was ruined and the old weary and dispiriting struggle between the divisive elements began all over again; for it was evident that with the death of Epaminondas Thebes was no adequate successor to Sparta. No wonder Plato despaired and Aristotle, with truer vision than most, turned to the rising power of Macedon. It was the tragedy of Demosthenes that he was totally unable to rise above the petty politics of a divided Greece and to grasp the fact that the city-state was done, worn out and ruined by exactly the spirit which Demosthenes tried in vain to arouse once more in the hearts of his fellow citizens, grown weary in the hopeless struggle.

Plato wrote his *Laws*, a kind of revised *Republic*, after the catastrophe of Leuctra and the book is to a large extent a post-mortem examination of the failure of Sparta.[2] It is not hard, he thinks, to find the causes which had led to that failure. It was not caused by lack of courage or determination,

---

[1] *Legg.* IV, 712 D.   [2] Jaeger, *Paideia*, III, p. 321.

nobody ever dreamed of accusing the Spartans of a deficiency in that, but rather they fell through ignorance (ἀμαθία) of the vital things in human life, through a lack of culture.[1] There was lacking in the Spartans the faculty of reconciling desire with intellect and achieving that 'symphony' (ξυμφωνία) of the desires that, in the last analysis, is alone virtuous.[2]

The downfall of Sparta was due to something much more vital than mere defeat on the battlefield. The virtue of courage is good enough, but to put it first of the four virtues, before wisdom, prudence and justice, is fatal; to do so is merely to invite spiritual bankruptcy, that 'collapse of the state within the soul of the ruler which is confirmed by the outward overthrow of his power'.

Xenophon, in his little treatise on the *Government of the Lacedaemonians*, speaks enthusiastically of the laws of Lycurgus, which he considers to be the best and wisest ever devised for the government of a State and people. Admittedly he owes a great deal to the lost treatise on Sparta by Critias, who was a strong philo-Laconian. However, even without that, Xenophon finds enough to praise; perhaps he had one eye on his Spartan hosts as he wrote it, at least as far as his thirteenth chapter. But he is acute enough to realise that if the laws of Lycurgus were what had made Sparta great, a departure from them must have in it the seeds of dissolution and downfall. The Spartans have not lived up to the ideals and have fallen into sadly degenerate ways; that is to say, if we accept his fourteenth chapter as genuine, which is conjectural.[3] He says

---

[1] *Legg.* 688 c.   [2] 653 B.

[3] Cf. Köhler, *loc. cit.* pp. 365 ff. Köhler accepts the authenticity of this chapter. Jaeger, *Paideia*, III, p. 326, points out the similarity between cap. XIV of the *Resp. Lac.* and the *Cyropaedia*, VIII, 8, where Xenophon blames the Persians for lapsing from their earlier ideals. The comparison between the two passages is very striking, and it would be extraordinary if both were later interpolations. Marchant, in his preface to the Loeb edition of the *Resp. Lac.*, suggests that this chapter was written after the scandalous seizure of the Theban citadel by Phoebidas in 381 (Xen. *Hell.* v, 2, 22 ff.), and the equally outrageous attempt of Sphodrias to occupy the Piraeus in 378. Sphodrias was tried at Sparta for this but was acquitted. The whole affair was called 'most

that the Spartans have abandoned their former simple and noble life. They have grown corrupt by governing foreign cities and listening to flatterers. They are ostentatious in their wealth and want to go abroad to govern other people in order that they may enrich themselves. Whereas formerly other Greeks were eager that they should lead them, now the rest of Greece will do anything to avoid such a thing. 'We must not feel surprised that such reproach is thrown upon them, since they evidently show themselves neither obedient to God nor to the laws of Lycurgus.'

Aristotle[1] puts his finger on the root cause of the defects in Spartan polity. The way of life is 'too severe, so that they cannot support it, but are obliged privately to act contrary to law that they may enjoy some of the pleasures of the senses'.

The whole constitution was calculated only for the business of war. It is indeed excellent to make them conquerors; for which reason the preservation of the state depended thereon. The destruction of it commenced with their victories, for they knew not how to be idle, or engage in any other employment than war.

The judgement of all three is unanimous. They all found the same answer to the question why the Spartan system had failed. It was not capable of adapting itself to new conditions; it lacked the resilience necessary to carry it through a change with which it was not fitted to deal. The Spartan system of education inculcated the discipline of the drill sergeant, and when confronted with other conditions than those to be found in the camp and on the field, it broke down and left them a prey to all the frailties against which it had so carefully and elaborately sought to guard them. It was the supreme example of a system theoretically conceived and practically impossible to carry out. Human nature was too strong for it.

iniquitous' by Xenophon, *Hell.* v, 4, 22. Xenophon was deeply shocked, as indeed was all Greece, and it is quite likely that this chapter was added as a protest against the abuse of power by the Spartans.

[1] *Pol.* 1294B.

CHAPTER VII

THE SPARTAN SYSTEM OF LAND TENURE

THE PUBLIC LAND

The Spartan *homoios* or 'peer' devoted himself to the noble profession of arms, untroubled by worldly cares: being a Spartan warrior was a whole-time job. He was trained for nothing else than physical prowess; he knew no trade or other occupation. As servant and guardian of the State to which he owed implicit obedience, he must look to the State to support him, just as an enlisted soldier must draw his pay and rations. In order that the Spartan might be able to pursue this career of public service, he was granted a certain amount of land, a *cleros*, with which went a number of helots, who cultivated it and provided the lord to whom they had been allotted a sufficient amount of natural products to support him and his family, and to make the monthly contribution to the *syssition* to which he belonged. This lot, we are told by Polybius[1] was assigned to him from the πολιτικὴ χώρα, the public land or *ager publicus*. It was his by right of citizenship, but was not held in fee simple. That is to say, he was not the absolute owner of the land[2] and, until the famous law of Epitadeus was passed, he could dispose of it neither by sale nor by will. He held it, in medieval legal phraseology, on the basis of knight's service. In return for liability for military service at the behest of the State he enjoyed the usufruct for life.

As to the origin of this public land, we are ill-informed and are left to infer that it must have comprised the original land of Laconia conquered by the invading Dorian tribes, who divided it among themselves. In the same fashion we may safely conclude that Messenia was divided among the conquering Spartans. We are told that when King Polydorus was

---

[1] VI, 45, 3. Cf. Guiraud, *Propriété foncière*, p. 161; Pöhlmann, *Gesch. d. soz. Frage*, I, p. 83.　　　　[2] *Vide infra*, p. 211.

about to make war upon Messene and was asked if he was fighting his brothers, he replied 'No', he was going against 'unassigned land' that had not been divided into *cleroi*, ἐπὶ τὴν ἀκλήρωτον τῆς χώρας βαδίζειν.[1] Pareti's[2] suggestion that the terms πολιτικὴ χώρα and ἀρχαῖα μοῖρα refer only to the land in the Eurotas valley and not in Messenia, and the prohibition against selling it referred only to the former, remains a conjecture that may very well be true, but for lack of definite evidence must remain uncertain.

THE EQUAL DIVISION OF LAND IN SPARTA

'The most learned writers of antiquity,' says Polybius,[3] 'Ephorus, Xenophon, Callisthenes and Plato, have said that the political institutions of Crete were similar to those of Sparta. These same authors say that in Sparta no one can possess a greater estate in land than another and that all the citizens have an equal share in the public land.' He goes on to say that, however alike the two countries were in their institutions, yet there were marked differences, the principal being that in Sparta Lycurgus had abolished all money, while in Crete it was freely used and its possession accounted honourable, and the law allowed a citizen to have as much land as he could acquire.

It must be admitted that Polybius presents here a formidable list of authorities. But it is to be particularly noticed that one, the greatest of all, is omitted, namely Aristotle. We know that he was particularly interested and observant of Sparta and, in addition to his observations on the Spartan constitution in his *Politics*, he is known to have written a special treatise on the government of the Lacedaemonians, which is unfortunately lost. While of course it is impossible to speak of the latter, yet in his *Politics* he says nothing of any equality in land-holding. The *argumentum ex silentio* is not always a valid one and may indeed lead into serious error; but all the same it is intriguing, although it is not conclusive, that Aristotle says nothing.

[1] Plut. *Inst. Lac.* 231 E.   [2] *Storia di Sparta arcaica*, I, p. 197.   [3] VI, 46–7.

Was there ever, as a matter of actual fact, equality in possessions in Sparta? The answer is emphatically no. There were always rich and poor, and never at any time was there equality in land-holding—for instance, we know that the kings had large estates. We are therefore confronted with this quite strange contradiction. What was meant by the division of land by Lycurgus? The weight of evidence on the subject of the *cleroi* is too great to allow us to dismiss the whole thing as a fairy story; or, as Grote seeks to make out, a concoction of the self-styled 'reformers' of the third century to bolster up their own confiscatory ideas. We have got to make sense of this 'equal' division of land somehow.

ENDOWMENT WITH A *CLEROS*

Plutarch[1] is quite explicit in his statement that, when a male infant had been approved by the 'triers' as likely to grow up to vigorous manhood, he was then endowed with a *cleros*. But was Plutarch correct? The statement has been the cause of much discussion and admittedly is involved in serious difficulties. Kahrstedt[2] objects that these 'triers' could not have had the authority to apportion a lot to the infant. This hardly seems a valid point, for it is entirely likely that, when he had been certified eligible, his father could then go to the ephors and claim his lot. It does not seem a very important point as to what authority gave the lot to the child. Another objection that Kahrstedt raises is that there could not have been sufficient land to endow each male Spartan with a lot at birth. This seems very unlikely, in view of the small and steadily diminishing number of eligible Spartans, as Meyer[3] long ago pointed out. Fustel de Coulanges[4] rejects the whole statement of Plutarch. Busolt,[5] while not entirely rejecting it, points out that it raises serious difficulties with regard to the

---

[1] *Lyc.* XVI. [2] *Griech. Staatsr.* p. 16, n. 3.
[3] *Geschichte des Altertums*, II, p. 194.
[4] *Étude sur la propriété foncière à Sparte*, pp. 14f.
[5] Busolt-Swoboda, *Griech. Staatsk.* II, p. 636, n. 3.

law of succession. Suppose a Spartan had two or three sons who all received a *cleros* at birth, what happened to his own when he died? Was this the πατρῷος κλῆρος to which Plato referred in the *Laws*?[1] And did the eldest son inherit it at his father's death? If so, did he hold it in addition to his own? or did the father's *cleros* revert to the State? Perhaps the eldest son surrendered his own *cleros* on inheriting that of his father. If he held both, it might explain the accumulation of large estates.

The question is a serious one, and it must be admitted that no perfectly satisfactory solution can be arrived at. Reflection will reveal that, if we accept Plutarch's statement, tempting though it may be to do so, we are at once confronted with more difficulties than it solves. Busolt's objection is a real one and can only be got over in the manner suggested above, and for that we have no evidence whatever. Secondly, if every Spartan male infant was endowed at birth with a *cleros*, how could he fall into indigence and, through failure to keep up his dues to his *syssition*, lose his status as a peer? The only plausible explanation must be that, through bad management or misfortune, he had been obliged to mortgage his land and the interest he had to pay ate up his income. That is quite likely; as is seen in every country where the law of entail obtains. The life tenant cannot lose his land outright;[2] it must descend to his heir, but so encumbered with debt as to be

[1] *Legg.* 923 C, D. Mr Toynbee asserts, 'The Growth of Sparta', *J.H.S.* XXXIII, p. 260, that if there was no adult son to step into a deceased holder's place the *cleros* could not be left vacant till the son grew up, a competent successor must be put in at once and the child must take his chance of finding a vacancy when he came of age. It is very hard to accept this view in the face of Plutarch's statement that the boy was endowed with a *cleros* at birth. This latter view, beset with difficulties though it is, seems the more plausible. If the boy were an infant at his father's death it would be to the advantage of the State that his mother should be supported with a sort of widow's pension in her task of rearing the child for the public service.

[2] Toynbee, *loc. cit.* p. 259, asserts that, if the owner failed to make his regular contribution to the *syssition*, his *cleros* was sequestrated by the State. There is no evidence for this. Nor is there for his further assertion that each *cleros* was bound to provide one hoplite to the army.

a *damnosa haereditas*. And thirdly, if *cleroi* reverted to the State, how could large estates be accumulated? It would seem obvious that such a system would very effectively prevent this. In answer to that objection, it might be urged that, with a dwindling number of peers eligible for *cleroi*, there must have been a good deal of land falling in and at the disposal of the ephors who could, illegally no doubt, sell it to those rich enough to bribe them. It is quite possible that in this we find the explanation of the notorious peculation and venality of the ephorate, which Aristotle so severely condemned.

Formidable as these difficulties are, yet we are forced back to the point that, if the State demanded the lifelong service of its citizen, it must find some means of providing for him and the easiest, in fact the only, way it could do so was to endow him with a portion of land. This right the Spartan peers could claim and that fact explains a good deal. It was a very valuable right; therefore they were chary of admitting newcomers to their ranks. This is illuminating when one remembers how exclusive the citizenry of all Greek states was; to be a citizen meant participation in substantial benefits from the State.

But, once having bestowed the *cleros* on the Spartan peer, the State could not guarantee its good management by him. It could guarantee it should not be taken away from him, but not that it should be debt-free. Unless a Spartan could contract a favourable marriage with some heiress, probably the daughter of a rich *perioecus*, all he had to live on was the small estate bestowed on him by right of his citizenship, a poor prospect for an ambitious young man. He might, and most likely did, get into serious difficulties and have to raise money on his *cleros*, or rather on the security of the products of his land, paying, no doubt, a ruinous rate of interest. In view of the land reverting to the State at the death of the mortgagor, the mortgagee would protect himself against loss by charging extortionate rates.

LAW OF INHERITANCE

We are seriously at fault in our knowledge of the law of inheritance in Sparta, and all we can do is to make certain reasonable inferences from the laws in Athens, of which we are well informed. Of one thing at least we can be certain, there was a community of possession in land shared by the sons of the family. The law of primogeniture, an invention of the Middle Ages and the feudal system, was unknown in the Greek world, or indeed anywhere in ancient times. It is true that the eldest son was given certain honours; he was the 'keeper of the hearth' (ἑστιοπάμων)[1] and administered the estate for the benefit of the family as a whole. He also, it seems, had certain spiritual attributes as the avenger of wrongs done to parents—'The Erinyes are ever at the command of the first-born'.[2] But beyond these religious or mystical attributes, he had no right of succession superior to that of younger brothers.

As Müller[3] very justly remarks, 'In Sparta the principle of community of goods was carried to a further extent than in any other nation, although it was the principle on which the legislation of many other Grecian states was founded.' The extraordinary statement by Polybius as to several brothers marrying the same wife and living together on the estate, to which reference has already been made,[4] can only be explained, if indeed it is explainable, on this ground. The evidence of the closest intermarriage within families in order to hold the estates together is fairly abundant and need not be enlarged upon here.[5] If there was to be community in goods and

---

[1] Pollux, I, 74.

[2] *Il.* xv, 204. The idea of magical powers pertaining to the first-born is widespread; *vide* Frazer, *The Golden Bough* ('Balder the Beautiful'), I, p. 295.

[3] *Doric Race*, II, p. 208.   [4] XII, 6B, 8; *vide supra*, p. 59.

[5] Several examples, e.g. Anaxandrides, Herod. v, 39; Archidamus and Lampito, Herod. vi, 71; Leonidas, Herod. vii, 205; Hippomedon, Polyb. iv, 35; Cleonymus and Chelidonis, Plut. *Pyrrhus*, xxvi; Agiatis and Cleomenes, Plut. *Cleom.* i.

estates, then these must be in sufficient abundance to support those who shared in them. At all costs, therefore, they must be kept intact and marriage alliances were the easiest and most effective means of accomplishing it. This was all the more necessary, since the endowment *cleros* reverted to the State, the original donor, on the death of its holder and the land was thus lost to the family.

TENURE IN FEE-TAIL IN SPARTA

The conclusions at which we have at least tentatively arrived may be summarised as follows. The *cleros* was entailed; that seems clear and no other explanation can reasonably be regarded as tenable. Each Spartan only held a life interest in it and enjoyed the usufruct, that is to say he received the fruits of the land during his lifetime. But he could not alienate it during his lifetime, nor dispose of it freely by will, at least until the law of Epitadeus was passed. It belonged not to him but to the State. In return he was bound to submit to the Spartan discipline and way of life and serve in the army when called upon. He could be, and no doubt often was, 'land-poor', just as we have already noted the Samurai of Japan were. Although he could not legally be dispossessed of his *cleros*, he could mortgage it, whereby the entire income was eaten up. The eagerness with which landowners agreed to the plan of Agis to burn the mortgages, but would not agree to a division of lands, is very illuminating. The law of entail may prevent a landed aristocracy from being actually deprived of its land; it cannot protect it against the encroachments of a newly enriched commercial class, which in the long run must replace the old 'land-poor' aristocracy. The only occupation that a Spartan peer could follow with befitting dignity and without the loss of social prestige was the profession of arms, coupled, no doubt, with management of his *cleros*, when he was not otherwise engaged in the public service. To increase his fortune he married an heiress, if he could find one, and we know that 'dowry-hunting' became a public scandal.

The Spartan *homoios* was all right as long as he had his *cleros* unencumbered by debt. As numbers dwindled he was able, we may well imagine, to improve his position by bribery of the ephors, from whom he could obtain land that should have reverted to the State. There must have been a great deal of jobbery going on all the time, that dishonesty which Aristotle[1] inveighs against, whereby the various *cleroi*, which, failing an heir, would normally revert to the State, were diverted to persons who could bribe the officials. Rich Spartans could, with a show of legality or even without it, claim certain lands and so increase their estates. To obtain the money they borrowed from the newly enriched merchant class and their land was heavily mortgaged. No doubt rich perioecic merchants and land speculators could buy up vacant *cleroi* from ephors, who were only too glad to receive bribes. Aristotle was writing after the law of Epitadeus, which must have thrown the archaic land system into confusion. The opportunities for official peculation must have been numerous and the ephors, poor men as Aristotle says, must have been open to many temptations to abuse their powers with regard to the allocation of lands. It is quite clear that Aristotle was writing of a bad state of affairs, well known to everyone, and since property in land is the only form of wealth that an aristocracy can interest itself in, these scandals were obviously the outcome of 'graft' in the disposition of estates. It may also be surmised that probably the kings were involved in the same business through their prerogative of betrothing orphan heiresses. It is easy to imagine the bribery and corruption attendant upon this, and the fortunes accumulated by the royal families probably came from these dishonest sources. As the newly enriched merchant class encroached more and more upon the old landed aristocracy, buying estates and lending money craftily on mortgage with a view to subsequent foreclosure, so did the Spartan nobility cling more desperately to what it had, and by every means in its power

[1] *Pol.* 1270 B.

defend itself against impoverishment and extinction. The world has seen the same struggle many times and in many countries.

This conclusion is inescapable; we return to it again and again. We see a privileged class of Spartan peers clinging tenaciously to its land and, as time passes, adding to its holdings. As numbers diminish estates increase in size, and much land passes into the possession of women. To possess land is all that the Spartan can do to maintain his position and dignity. Commerce is denied him, and to get the land he covets he borrows at ruinous rates of interest. A few rich families become richer; others, burdened with debt, sink. Discontent increases, and those outside the circle of peers hate, and do all they can to thwart and defeat, those who so arrogantly take everything to themselves and by bribery and corruption of officials create scandals in the State. Social unrest becomes more and more serious and there arises what the Greeks called *stasis*, that sickness of the State, the quarrelling of rich and poor, the privileged with the unprivileged, that in the end works destruction. Sparta's internal troubles and discontents can be traced from the earliest to the latest times to exactly the same cause—the perennial and never settled land question. To it can be traced the troubles that Lycurgus tried to compose, the never ending dangers from the helots, Cinadon's conspiracy, the attempted reforms of Agis and Cleomenes and the tyrannies of Machanidas and Nabis. When a class of landed proprietors, which diminishes in numbers and is not recruited from without, tries to perpetuate itself and does so by bribing officials, then the downfall of the State is sure, however long it may be postponed.

Aristotle[1] saw the dangers very clearly:

[In an oligarchy] provision should be made that estates pass by inheritance and not by gift, and no person should have more than one inheritance, for in this way properties will be equalised and more of the poor rise to competency.

[1] *Pol.* 1309 A.

He knew quite well that the law of entail was necessary to maintain an aristocracy; but he also saw the danger of a landed aristocracy dwindling in numbers and entrenching itself within its own possessions.

TENURE IN FEE-TAIL ELSEWHERE

It is to be noted that holding land by fee-tail was well known and widely practised among the Greeks. Aristotle[1] gives several examples. In Athens, the laws of Solon forbade a father to disinherit his son. He could only leave his property to others outside his immediate family if he had no sons.[2] If he left only a daughter, then her inheritance passed to her husband as a dowry. According to the law of Gortyn in Crete, which may be regarded as 'Dorian' and accordingly significant for Spartan analogies, gifts at death were only recognised as from a husband to his wife and a son to his mother.[3] The very serious punishment of *atimia* was inflicted on those who dissipated the inheritance received from a father.[4] Polybius[5] speaks of the evils that had arisen in Boeotia through breaking the entail. The law of Locris only allowed selling of land under certain circumstances.[6] Meier[7] seeks to show that this law of fee-tail was founded on religious grounds with the idea of not allowing the family to die out nor be separated from its land,[8] and points to the analogy of the corresponding Roman law.[9] Doubtless Meier is correct in finding a family cult connected with the land in early times; but probably that had been forgotten and it had become wholly juristic.

Although not strictly applying to Sparta, it is apposite to look at the law of succession that Plato laid down for his ideal

---

[1] *Pol.* 1319A.

[2] Cf. Dem. *in Lept.* CII; Plut. *Solon,* XXI; Wilamowitz-Moellendorff, *Aristoteles u. Athen,* II, p. 47.

[3] Cf. Meier-Schömann-Lipsius, *Das attische Recht,* II, p. 52.

[4] Diog. Laert. I, 2, 7.   [5] XX, 6, 5.

[6] Arist. *Pol.* 1266B.   [7] *Klio,* Beih. XLII (1939), p. 36.

[8] Isaeus, *de Apoll. Her.* XXX; Demos. *in Macart.* LXXVI.

[9] Dion. Hal. IX, 22.

republic in the *Laws*.[1] The whole land has been divided into the 'ideal' number of 5040 *cleroi*,[2] and when one of the citizens wishes to make his will he first names his heir-at-law (κληρο-νόμος), and to him goes the ancestral lot (ὁ πατρῷος κλῆρος), which is entailed and must go to the heir. If he has any other son who is not entitled to a *cleros* (μὴ ἐπί τινι κλήρῳ πεποιημένος), and who cannot be provided for by sending him away to a colony, he can leave any other property he may have to him. If after the testator's death a legatee, son or daughter, be found to possess a *cleros* already, he must renounce his inheritance. It is evident here that Plato has Sparta in mind, and is anxious to avoid the accumulation of large estates. It is true that we have no hint of a younger son being entitled to a *cleros* at birth; but we do find the inalienable *cleros* descending to the legal heir.

THE LAW OF EPITADEUS

Such an explanation of the Spartan system of land tenure is perfectly rational, and indeed is the only one that covers it in a satisfactory manner. But at some time or other a change was made in the land laws which was to have very serious consequences. All that we know of this is contained in a single passage in Plutarch's *Life of Agis*.[3]

The Lacedaemonian state began to suffer distemper and corruption soon after its subversion of the Athenian supremacy filled it with gold and silver. However, since the number of families instituted by Lycurgus was still preserved in the transmission of estates and father left to his son his inheritance, to some extent the continuance of this order and equality sustained the state in spite of its errors in other respects. But when a certain powerful man came to be Ephor, headstrong and of a violent temper, Epitadeus

---

[1] *Legg.* XI, 923 C.

[2] 737 C. The number 5040 has the greatest possible number of divisors (59) including all the digits from 1 to 10.

[3] *Agis*, v. E. Meyer, *Rhein. Mus.* XLI, p. 589, sweeps the whole story of Epitadeus and his law away, calling it 'an aetiological anecdote', invented *ad hoc* to explain the breakdown of the old system of inalienable lots.

by name, he had a quarrel with his son and introduced a law permitting a man during his lifetime to give his estate and allotment to anyone he wished or to leave it so in his will.... Men of power and influence at once began to acquire estates without scruple, ejecting the rightful heirs from their inheritance; and speedily the wealth of the state went into the hands of a few men and poverty became the general rule, bringing with it lack of leisure for noble pursuits and occupations unworthy of freemen, along with envy and hatred towards the men of property. Thus there were left of the old Spartan families not more than seven hundred and of these perhaps a hundred possessed land and allotments.

The purport of this account is quite plain. The *rhetra* or law introduced by the ephor Epitadeus put an end to the rule of entail.[1] It changed possession by the individual Spartan of his *cleros* from fee tail to fee simple; he could sell or leave his *cleros* to anyone he liked. The suggestion that the law of Epitadeus permitted only the disposal of the *cleros* by will and not by sale during the lifetime of the holder seems difficult to sustain. The statement that 'men of power and influence at once began to acquire estates' points unmistakably to purchase. Undoubtedly by the time of Aristotle purchase was legal, but held to be disgraceful, and we have no evidence that the law of Epitadeus was followed by another and still more drastic departure from ancient custom.

So far the account is tolerably clear; but unfortunately there are some very grave difficulties involved in this passage. In the first place, who was Epitadeus? He is mentioned nowhere else, and it seems strange that so revolutionary a change in the Spartan land system should have been carried out by an unknown man. To identify him with the ephor Epitadas, who

---

[1] The word *rhetra* is used loosely to mean either 'bill'—a proposal introduced to the legislature which may, or may not, become law, or 'act'—a law placed on the statute book. Plutarch, in *Agis*, v, 8–11, uses it in both senses. The *rhetra* of Epitadeus became law; that of King Agis IV did not. To translate the word 'oracle', as in Plut. *Lyc.* vi, cannot be sustained; *vide* Wade-Gery, *Class. Quart.* XXXVIII (1944), p. 6. It may be remarked that modern usage also errs in accuracy, e.g. the Bill of Rights of 1688, and the Reform Bill of 1832.

was killed at Sphacteria in 424,[1] is quite out of the question and may be dismissed at once. Secondly, when did this momentous change take place? It was one that struck at the foundation of the whole Spartan way of life and system of military service. It will be noted that Plutarch puts it down to the 'distemper and corruption' that had assailed the Spartans with the spoils that had come to them after the downfall of Athens. We know well enough that these had had their effect and the old austerity and simplicity of life had been irreparably impaired. But even then, it is hard to grasp why the growing luxury induced by money should have broken down the old system of granting an inalienable *cleros* to each Spartan.

Neither of the explanations given by Plutarch—increase of wealth and the quarrel of Epitadeus with his son—suffices. There must have been another reason. Everything goes to show that at least no outward and acknowledged change in the old traditional Spartan way of life took place until after the defeat at Leuctra in 371 and the loss of Messenia, whereby the Spartan peers lost their estates in that country. The ruin that this caused was very great, and we may well imagine many previously well-to-do families reduced to penury. We know that many went off as mercenaries simply to keep themselves. Toynbee[2] has suggested that the law of Epitadeus was passed to induce these mercenaries who had enriched themselves abroad to return and buy *cleroi* in the Eurotas valley. This is at least a possible explanation; but Cary[3] has suggested an even more likely one. If there were any mercenaries who had made fortunes, and these were probably few in number, they could easily have acquired land from the holders of large estates without encroaching upon that allotted as *cleroi*. It is

[1] Thuc. IV, 8 ff. Cf. art. 'Epitadeus' by Niese in P.W.; also Meyer, *Forschungen*, I, p. 258; Hermann-Thümser, *Lehrbuch d. Griech. Antiq.* I, 6, p. 259. There is some doubt as to whether Epitadeus was actually an ephor when he introduced his bill. The use of the word ἐφορεύσας suggests that he had completed his year of office.

[2] *J.H.S.* (1913), pp. 272–3.   [3] *Class. Quart.* XX, p. 186.

far more likely, he says, that the Spartans who wanted to leave for foreign service were anxious to sell their *cleroi* before they went, in order to leave their wives and families provided for while they were away.

It must be acknowledged that this is an attractive and highly plausible explanation of the motives that induced the passing of this famous law. It is, of course, entirely conjectural and cannot be substantiated by any evidence whatever. On the other hand, it might be argued that, if a Spartan wanted to provide for his wife and family, the best way to do that would be to leave them on the *cleros*. It would be a very unwise thing to sell the land and leave the wife with the money to spend. In any case, it would be the younger Spartans who enlisted as mercenaries and they probably were still unmarried or had no family.

These suggestions, while not affording a complete explanation of the law of Epitadeus, at least add to our idea of a land system which had fallen into confusion and was completely out of date. An ultra-conservatism that is oblivious of the passage of time and fails to adapt itself to new conditions is foredoomed to extinction. As the number of Spartan peers dwindled, the number of *cleroi* destined for their upkeep diminished *pari passu*. The vacant *cleroi* went back to the State, and the law of Epitadeus was designed to correct an anomalous and economically unsound state of affairs. Hitherto inalienable estates, *cleroi* granted to Spartans, could by this law be alienated, and we may suppose that the State could also sell those lands that had returned to it through failure of heirs.[1] It is not to be wondered at that, as the number of Spartan peers diminished, the lands formerly held by them fell into the hands of the 'new rich' or of heiresses. The evils, which Plutarch deplores as arising from the wealth that poured into

---

[1] Andreades, *op. cit.* p. 53, makes the suggestion that the enrichment of the helots was due to this law whereby they could acquire real estate. This may be true, but it seems more likely that they made their money in trade, which was beneath the dignity of a Spartan but highly lucrative to others.

Sparta after the downfall of Athens, might with greater truth be traced to a dwindling population of Spartan warriors.

With the increase of wealth and the aggregation of large estates went the invariable reverse of growing poverty and 'landless men', the 'inferiors' who were shut off from the land and who were galled by their lowly social position and resentful of the privileged Spartans. To such as these Agis, Cleomenes and Nabis appealed. To sweep the whole thing away, as Grote does, and say that the appeal of Agis to the 'Lycurgan' division of land was merely an appeal to something that had never existed, and that there never had been any 'equal' division, gets one nowhere. What bothers Grote is the word 'equal'. The Spartans were equals and each had the right to a *cleros*. But the land was never divided into equal shares for everybody. Once having grasped that point, the puzzle becomes explicable and Grote's objections fall to the ground. It is altogether too drastic to deny that there ever was a system whereby *cleroi* were granted to support the Spartan peers.

We simply ask, if a Spartan could not support himself by any gainful occupation nor marry a rich wife, how could he live, unless the State provided him with land sufficient to support him? And if the State did that, was it not essential that this land should be inalienable? When the number of Spartans had fallen to a negligible quantity the law of Epitadeus altered the anachronism. Whether that was for good or evil is another thing. It was inevitably the outcome of a diminished population.

ARISTOTLE AND THE SPARTAN LAND SYSTEM

It now remains to examine a passage in which Aristotle speaks of the Lycurgan land system in Sparta.[1]

He made it infamous for anyone either to buy or sell his possessions (τὴν ὑπάρχουσαν), in which he did right; but he permitted anyone who chose to give them away or bequeath them,

---

[1] *Pol.* 1270A.

although nearly the same consequence will arise from the one practice as from the other. It is supposed that near two parts in five of the whole country is the property of women owing to their being so often sole heirs.... Now everyone is permitted to make a woman his sole heir if he pleases. And if he dies intestate, he who succeeds as heir-at-law gives it to whom he pleases.

Properly understood this passage does not offer any insuperable difficulty. Aristotle says that Lycurgus made it 'infamous' for a Spartan to get rid of his possessions. It must be clearly understood that there is no actual legal prohibition of selling land, only that it was thought to be a disgraceful thing to do. That can easily be understood among a landed nobility whose ownership of land was the one safeguard it possessed. The spectacle of an extravagant and reckless young man dissipating the family fortune has always been a painful one. For a Spartan peer, to get rid of his land was 'infamous'; it degraded him in the sight of his fellows.

It will be noticed that Aristotle uses the term ἡ ὑπάρχουσα, meaning his possessions or real and personal estate. At this point we must note a very important statement by Heracleides Ponticus[1] who, in commenting on this, adds the significant words τῆς δ' ἀρχείας μοίρας οὐδὲ ἔξεστιν, i.e. the 'ancient lot', the *cleros*, could under no circumstances be alienated. It was a disgraceful thing for a Spartan to sell his land; it was legally impossible for him to sell his *cleros*.

It must be admitted that this leaves one thing unsolved, a difficulty which has been pointed out by Susemihl,[2] who asks why Aristotle has said nothing whatever about an inalienable *cleros*. Surely so important a thing as that could not have escaped Aristotle's attention; and so careful a writer would not ignore it if he knew of it. Moreover, in a subsequent passage[3] he says, 'formerly also in some states no one was allowed to sell his original lots of land' (τοὺς πρώτους κλήρους). Why

---

[1] *F.H.G.* II, p. 211, 7.
[2] Susemihl and Hicks, *The Politics of Aristotle*, p. 287.
[3] *Pol.* 1319A.

does he not specifically name Sparta among these, especially when he mentions one Oxylus and the customs of the Aphyteans?

The answers to these rather difficult questions can only be found in the fact that Aristotle was writing after the law of Epitadeus had made alienation of the *cleros* legal, and he did not bother to mention this fact. He says that formerly in some states alienation of land was forbidden by law, but simply omits to specify Sparta. This seems to be the only rational explanation of what is, admittedly, a somewhat formidable difficulty. To brush aside the evidence of Heracleides Ponticus altogether is impossible. First, because to do so is altogether too violent. He did not invent it himself, but must have got it from some unknown *Laconica*. And secondly, to ignore Heracleides is to encounter serious difficulties, which otherwise would not bother us. To accept what he says may be the easy way out; it is, nevertheless, the obviously rational way out. The difficulties which beset the path of those who try and understand the Spartan system of land tenure are too many and too formidable to allow of ignoring any assistance from ancient sources.

When the Dorian invaders conquered Laconia they divided the land among themselves; and again when Messenia was overrun there was a systematic sharing up of the new territory. It is quite likely that the Eurotas valley was divided equitably, but not 'equally', among the three conquering tribes; just as the land of Canaan was divided among the tribes of Israel,[1] and Saxon England among the conquering Normans. Upon what basis this division was made we have no idea; but it is

---

[1] A comparison between the Spartan and Jewish land systems reveals some similarities. When the land of Canaan was conquered it was divided according to clans and families, Jos. xiv. 1–5. The family was bound very closely to its ancestral lot which was inalienable, any purchase of land being restricted to a lease for fifty years, i.e. the year of Jubilee, Lev. xxv. A kinsman could always pre-empt the land of his family, Jer. xxxii. 6. The laws of inheritance are set out in Num. xxvii. 5–10. Where there are no sons, property goes to daughters, failing them to paternal uncles.

reasonable to conjecture that every man had at least a minimum allotment. Some may have had considerably more because of their fame and prowess—we know the kings received more. This minimum allotment was the *cleros*, the 'ancestral lot'; it was inalienable and held by the grantee as a life tenant. He could not dispose of it either in his lifetime or by will; it must descend to his eldest son or male heir-at-law. In default of any heir, it reverted to the original grantor, in this instance the State.[1] But, while each male Spartan received this minimum *cleros*, there was nothing to prevent him receiving more, either as an original grant at the time of conquest, or as a dowry brought to him by his wife, or by purchase. With regard to the last it must be emphasised that there is not a scrap of evidence to show that there was at any time any restriction upon the Spartan peers buying and selling land or any other article, or using money other than the impossibly clumsy iron money they were supposed to, but did not actually, use.[2]

THE LANDLESS CLASSES

Who, then, comprised the landless classes in Sparta? The artisans and workers and a mob of nondescripts, 'inferiors' who, for one reason or another, could prove no legal claim to a *cleros*, bitterly resentful of the scorn of the Spartan landed gentry who, in true Spartan fashion, treated them as riff-raff and denied them any participation in the conduct of public affairs. To men like these Cinadon had appealed, and it is not hard to imagine how eagerly they welcomed the proposed reforms of Agis and Cleomenes and were even content with

[1] It must be admitted that the use of the term 'State' here is far from satisfactory. It is tempting to identify State and kings in this connection, on the analogy of the royal disposition of heiresses. But this would be unsafe, because we do not know how estates left without any heirs were disposed of. The State of the Spartans meant the kings, ephors, *Gerousia* and *Ecclesia* legislating in plenary session. In practice it is highly probable the ephors disposed of any lands that reverted to the State, thereby enriching themselves.

[2] The whole problem of the Spartan monetary system is dealt with at length hereafter.

the tyranny of Nabis. Explosive elements within the State, it is a marvel they were kept in subjection so long. The Spartan peers may have deteriorated in character and dwindled in numbers; but at least they had a first-class police system to keep the 'inferiors' in order.

Were any of the true Spartans included among the landless? Almost certainly not, at least before Leuctra. But with the loss of Messenia the answer is much less emphatic. It would be natural to suppose that so close-knit a caste would be loth to see members of aristocratic families sink into indigence and, by granting them *cleroi*, would seek to buttress their own fast diminishing numbers. But with the short-sighted selfishness that afflicts every degenerating aristocracy, the growth of large estates owned by women and the severely restricted area of Laconia, it is not hard to imagine that the lucky ones should have callously let their unfortunate brethren sink into indigence. After Leuctra, it was everyone for himself, and any Spartan peer who had lost everything in Messenia must have found it difficult or even impossible to re-establish himself in face of those who still possessed estates in Laconia. The Spartan State was going downhill fast, which explains why after Leuctra it was never able to put up an effective front again. One defeat on the battlefield alone could not have had so devastating an effect. It was the economic disaster of the loss of Messenia that paralysed the Spartans and turned them into an effete aristocracy, greedy for their own gain.

SIZE OF THE *CLEROS*

If we encounter difficulties in our understanding of the Spartan system of land tenure, it must be admitted that we suffer complete defeat in attempting any elucidation of the basis on which the division of the land into lots or *cleroi* was made. Only one thing is quite certain and that is that each Spartan received a *cleros*. Starting with that one basic fact all our subsequent conclusions must be based solely on conjecture.

In the idealised account of the 'Lycurgan' settlement given us by Plutarch[1] we are told that the whole State had fallen into a bad way because of the inequality in the distribution of land, whereby the city was burdened with indigent and help-less people and wealth was concentrated in the hands of a few.

Determined, therefore, to banish insolence and envy and crime and luxury, and those yet more deep-seated and afflictive diseases of the state, poverty and wealth, he persuaded his fellow-citizens to make one parcel of all their territory and divide it up anew and to live with one another on a basis of entire uniformity and equality in the means of subsistence, seeking pre-eminence through virtue alone, assured that there was no other difference or inequality between man and man than that which was established by blame for base actions and praise for good ones.

It is noteworthy that the earlier writers, Plato[2] and Isocrates,[3] say nothing about any redivision, but only of an equal division, both quite evidently referring to a pre-Lycurgan allotment.[4] Ephorus is the author of the Lycurgan attribution,[5] in which he is followed by Trogus Pompeius.[6] But for our purposes it really does not matter much. Some division must have been made so that the system of individual *cleroi* should be established. This division according to Plutarch was as follows:

Lycurgus distributed the last of the Laconian land among the Perioeci or free provincials in 30,000 lots and that which belonged to the City of Sparta in 9000 lots to as many genuine Spartans. But some say that Lycurgus distributed only 6000 lots among the Spartans and that 3000 were afterwards added by Polydorus; others again that Polydorus added half of 9000 to the half distri-buted [by Lycurgus]. The lot of each was large enough to produce annually 70 medimni of barley for a man and 12 for his wife, with a proportionate amount of fluids.

---

[1] *Lyc.* VIII.　　　　　　　　　　　　[2] *Legg.* 684 D, E.
[3] *Archidamus*, XX; *Panath.* CLVII ff.
[4] Cf. Kessler, *Plutarchs Leben des Lykurgos*, p. 38; K. J. Neumann, *Hist. Ztschr.* XCVI (1905), p. 7. Hermann-Thümser, *Lehrbuch*, p. 191.
[5] ap. Polyb. VI, 48; Strabo, X, 4, 16 (C. 480).　　　[6] Justin, III, 3.

Contrasted with this we have the passage in the *Life of Agis* in which that reformer sought to return to the 'Lycurgan' system and to redivide the land.

All the lands were to be divided into equal portions, those that lay between the water-course near Pellene and Mount Taygetus and as far as the cities of Malea and Sellasia into 4500 lots, the remainder into 15,000; these last to be shared out among those of the country people who were fit for service as heavy-armed soldiers, the first among the natural-born Spartans.

It is apparent at once that the 'Lycurgan' distribution was into 30,000 and 9000 lots and the Agian into exactly half 15,000 and 4500. However little reliance may be placed on these figures (and we shall shortly see that they are absolutely impossible), we can at least explain the halving of the Lycurgan figures by Agis on the ground of the loss of Messenia, which contained the richest land available for distribution.

According to the latest available reports of the present Greek Government's Department of Agriculture, there are in Laconia about 250,000 acres of cultivable land and in Messenia 350,000 or 600,000 acres in all. If 'Lycurgus' divided this land into 39,000 shares, each would receive about fifteen acres. Under the Agian scheme of distribution each of the 19,500 lots in Laconia would contain somewhat less than thirteen acres. At the very outset, therefore, we encounter what can only be called an absurdity. Each *cleros* was to support the Spartan and his family and the helots living thereon and to provide the landlord's contribution to his *syssition*. If we assume that one acre, which is the barest minimum, was allocated to vines, olives and figs, farm buildings, footpaths etc., fourteen acres were left for the growing of barley or other grains. Inefficient ancient agriculture demanded an annual fallow, therefore no more than seven acres would be under cultivation at any time. A liberal average production of twenty bushels of barley to the acre would give a maximum annual production of 140 bushels to the *cleros*. We know that the annual dues to the Spartan lord were eighty-two medimni of barley or 170 bushels. There is something so palpably wrong that it is needless to continue further by asking what the helots lived on. If we follow up the Agian distribution of Laconia we find the figures even more impossible, and we are forced to discard Plutarch's statements *in toto*.

In fairness to him it must be pointed out that he knows quite well his figures are unsatisfactory and admits that other versions of the basis of distribution are extant. Lycurgus gave the Spartans 6000 *cleroi* and Polydorus added 3000, to make 9000. Another version is that 'Polydorus added half of 9000 to the half distributed' (by Lycurgus). This can only be explained on the supposition that the original 'Lycurgan' distribution was 4500, and this was doubled by Polydorus. The passage as it stands appears to be corrupt; but this explanation is at least intelligible. Whether 'Lycurgus' gave the Spartans 9000, 6000 or 4500, the two latter being supplemented by Polydorus, does not matter very much, for we arrive at 9000 in all three versions. What matters is that this figure is impossibly high and must be rejected. The passage in the life of Agis is quite straightforward and admits of no emendation. From the strictly statistical standpoint these passages are palpably impossible. Can we then emend them or submit an 'ideal' scheme of distribution? The answer is very decidedly in the negative; we have not enough evidence to go on, and what is available is unreliable and even absurd.

There seems to be only one explanation and that is that the word *cleros* as used in Sparta did not refer to a self-contained parcel of land sufficient to support a Spartan lord, but to some unit of so many acres, several of which, when combined together, sufficed to give him a living. We have the idea of the available lands of Laconia and Messenia divided neatly into so many small estates each carefully calculated to produce so much subsistence. But was that possible? It seems so unlikely that we must reject it. Some land was better than others. Some was more suitable for grain growing, others for vines or olives and some was pasture land which could not profitably be cultivated but must be left under grass.

If then the term *cleros* be understood as a unit of land of indeterminate extent, perhaps fifteen acres more or less, then it is not impossible that Plutarch's figures may have some significance. Laconia under the 'Lycurgan' division was divided into 9000 of these units which were then combined, according to some system of which we have no details, into small estates, each of which was calculated to support a Spartan lord and his family and the suitable number of helots to till the land. It is not hard to envisage such a system and to conclude that it could work effectively. We may imagine a Spartan who had ten or fifteen acres near the city, with another *cleros* further out, and perhaps another still further away which was suitable only for pasturage. If we are to find any significance whatever in Plutarch's figures and are not to reject them entirely, some such explanation seems forced upon us.

It would be very easy, and quite useless, to let our imagination play with an ideal *cleros*, to which we can easily assign any number of Spartans and helots we choose, and this has been done with quite startlingly diverse results by various commentators.[1] There is no way whatever by which we can arrive at any rational conclusion either as to the size or the number of *cleroi*, and the cautious student of demography must acknowledge himself defeated. Practically every ancient author when dealing with numbers of any kind—population figures, size of armies, etc.—is hopelessly inaccurate and cannot be relied upon. Even when a census was taken, as for

---

[1] Jardé, *Céréales*, p. 113, reckons the size of the *cleros* at from 27 to 36 hectares (62·7 to 89 acres). Kahrstedt, *Hermes*, LIV, p. 283, says 30 hectares (74 acres). Fustel de Coulanges, *Nouvelles Recherches sur quelques problèmes d'histoire*, p. 99, 17–20 acres. Busolt-Swoboda, *Griech. Staatsk.* II, p. 641, 25 hectares (62 acres); Müller, *Doric Race*, II, p. 31, 45 acres. Hildebrand, *Jahrb. f. Naturalökon.* XII (1869), p. 14, 33 acres. E. Meyer, *Gesch. d. Altertums*, II, p. 297, 22 acres. Beloch, *Griech. Gesch.* I, 2, 1, p. 304, 38 acres of barley-producing land. Niccolini, 'Per la storia di Sparta', *Rend. Ist. Lomb.* XXXVIII (1904), p. 538, 35½ acres. Duncker, *Über die Hufen der Spartaner*, 25 acres.

instance by Demetrius of Phalerum in Attica, the results reported were grotesque, if our information is correct.[1] The problem is all the more tantalising when we reflect that accurate records, constantly kept up-to-date, of men fit for military service must of necessity have been kept. There must also have been some sort of Registry Offices, where records of land titles were preserved. Indeed, we are safe in asserting there was, on the evidence of the demand for the destruction of the mortgages, when Agis and Cleomenes made their abortive attempts at redistribution of the land. The pertinent documents must have been preserved in the city of Sparta. But however that may be, the fact remains that we are totally at fault in any estimate, and in that unsatisfactory state we must leave the problem.

THE DIMINISHING NUMBER OF SPARTANS

Among the many things in Sparta that Aristotle did not approve of, their land system seemed to him the worst and suffered his severest disapproval. In a passage in the *Politics*[2] he deplores the way in which large estates have multiplied and the land fallen into the hands of women.

Whereby although the country is able to support fifteen hundred horse and thirty thousand foot, the number does not exceed one thousand. From this it is evident that their affairs are badly regulated for the city could not support even one disaster, but was ruined for lack of men. It is said that during the reigns of their ancient kings they used to present the freedom of their city to foreigners to prevent a want of men while engaged in long wars. It is also affirmed that the number of Spartans was formerly ten thousand. However that may be, an equality of property conduces greatly to increase the number of people. The law which he made to encourage population was not calculated to correct this inequality. Wanting to make the Spartans as numerous as possible by inducing them to have large families, he ordered that he who had

[1] Athen. VI, 272 B, C, D. Cf. Michell, *Economics of Ancient Greece*, pp. 19 ff.
[2] 1270 A.

three children should be excused the night watch and that he who had four should pay no taxes. But it is evident that while the land was divided in this manner, if the people increased in number many of them must be very poor.

Aristotle here, as always, has put his finger unerringly on the fundamental trouble that lay at the heart of Spartan degeneracy —a system of land tenure that kept the commonalty from the soil and fostered the growth of large estates. As the rich became richer their desire to hold their estates together led to a restriction of the size of families and their numbers steadily decreased, a phenomenon familiar to all countries and times.

Consideration of Aristotle's figures with regard to potential manpower will reveal several obscurities which are difficult to resolve. He says the country will support 31,500 foot and horse. Does he mean Messenia and Laconia? If so, he is approximately correct. According to the last available census of the modern departments, the population of Messenia is 247,907 and of Laconia 144,336 or 392,243 together. Beloch estimated the population in ancient times at 248,000. This we may regard as a minimum, and although present-day figures are certainly in excess of ancient, we may very well estimate the combined populations in Aristotle's time as not far short of 300,000. The proportion of one man fit for active service in ten of the population is the accepted ratio in both ancient and modern times, and on that basis we arrive at a potential manpower of about 30,000 which agrees with Aristotle's 31,500 fairly closely.

But Aristotle was writing after the loss of Messenia, and a comparison between pre- and post-Leuctra conditions is impossible on the grounds that he puts forward—a fall in population. If Aristotle had said 'In the days when the Spartan State included Messenia it could put 30,000 foot and 1500 horse into the field. But now Messenia is lost, Laconia can barely raise 1000', his estimate would have been not very far from the truth, if we suppose that by 1000 he means Spartans alone and not *perioeci* and helots. If the latter, he is certainly in error, for Laconia could easily raise an army greatly in excess of that number. A full century after Aristotle, at Sellasia in 222, Cleomenes is said to have had 13,000 men from Laconia, of whom 4000 were 'Spartans'.[1] At Third Mantinea in 207 Plutarch[2] says that 4000 'Spartans' fell, which is almost certainly an exaggeration. In 195 Nabis had 10,000 'Laconians', mostly freed helots and *perioeci*.[3]

But while the evidence clearly shows that there was no fall in the numbers of the Lacedaemonians but, if anything, an increase, it is also quite clear that the *homoioi* were diminishing in number, and at an increasing pace after the disaster of Leuctra and the loss of Messenia. Plutarch[4] says that in the second half of the third century there did not remain more than 700 of the old Spartan families, of whom perhaps only 100 had any possessions in land. That under the Romans all Greece decayed and numbers shrank is of course well known. Strabo gives a melancholy picture of Laconia where, outside the city of Sparta, the country is well-nigh deserted and says that where there were a hundred populous towns now barely thirty exist.[5]

An aristocracy that is not constantly recruited from below invariably diminishes in numbers. This fact is strikingly evident in the British peerage, which is kept up to strength by new creations from the commonalty as older families die out and titles become extinct. This renewal from below was impossible in Sparta, where inclusion into the ranks of the jealously guarded order of *homoioi* was so difficult as to be practically impossible. The Spartans doomed themselves to extinction by their own mistaken policy of exclusiveness.

And along with this policy of maintaining their order as a 'close corporation' there went, we must suppose, although

---

[1] Polyb. II, 65, 7–10; 69, 3. Macrobius, *Saturn.* I, 11, 34, says Nabis found 15,000 men fit to take the field on his accession, a not impossible figure.

[2] *Philop.* x.   [3] Livy, xxxiv, 27, 36.

[4] *Agis*, v.   [5] Strabo, viii, 4 11 (C. 362).

the evidence is not direct, a widespread practice of 'birth-control', limitation of the size of families, and, to a certain extent, of celibacy among the male Spartans. It is very evident that they were well aware of the dangers of diminishing numbers. Special privileges were granted to the fathers of sons, and it is not impossible that the very peculiar customs with regard to sharing wives were prompted thereby. Bachelors were held up to scorn and insult, as also those who made late or unsuitable marriages. References in the ancient authors to this are numerous.[1] Small families among an aristocracy is the invariable rule when the law of entail gives the land to the eldest son.[2] The suggestion that the practices of *paiderastia* had anything to do with the falling numbers of Spartans may be disregarded, despite what Aristotle says of the effects of the practice in Crete.[3]

In conclusion it may be affirmed that this particular 'mystery', when carefully examined, is no mystery at all, but may be explained on economic grounds. An increase of wealth and luxury invariably brings with it a declining birth-rate, not from any biological causes but simply because, as is seen so strikingly at the present time, parents desire a higher standard of living for their children and the preservation of their own comforts. That so wise a man as Lycurgus ever advocated a Spartan having only one son, as Plutarch asserts, is hard to believe.[4]

A suggestion put forward by Ziehen[5] is worthy of careful attention. He traces the decline of population back to the earthquake of 464, which we know caused great destruction and loss of life. This explanation would not be impossible, if we supposed that at that early date the birth-rate had already

---

[1] Plut. *Lyc.* xv; *Lys.* xxx; *De amor. prol.* 11; *Apoph. Lac.* CCLXXX; Pollux, III, 48, VIII, 40; Aelian, *V.H.* vi, 6.

[2] Andreades finds an exactly similar state of affairs among the Japanese Samurai in the eighteenth century. *Revue économique internationale*, Jan. 1931, pp. 19 ff.　　　　[3] *Pol.* 1272 A.

[4] *Ex comment. Hesiodis*, xx.

[5] 'Das spart. Bevölkerungsproblem', *Hermes*, LXVIII (1933), pp. 218 ff.

begun to drop fairly drastically. If that were so, then a natural disaster, earthquake, famine, plague, might very well give an added impetus to the decline, which would from that moment be accelerated. Otherwise losses occasioned by such disasters are usually, if not always, made good in a comparatively few years. But there is no evidence to suggest that the birth-rate was falling before the end of the fifth century; it was either stationary or even slightly rising. Ziehen's suggestion, therefore, attractive though it is, must be rejected.

Darré[1] seeks to explain the phenomenon on the ground that the Dorians were 'Nordics' who, in a Mediterranean environment, had degenerated and eventually died out under conditions unfavourable to them. This hypothesis is totally untenable, since there is no evidence to show that the Dorians were Nordics, nor that their environment proved to be a degenerative factor. It may be observed that this is another instance of the curious and very marked interest in Sparta evinced by Germans who found there an object lesson for Nazi ideology.

[1] *Das Bauerntum*, p. 162.

CHAPTER VIII

SPARTAN MILITARY
AND NAVAL ORGANISATION[1]

THE MYSTERY OF SPARTAN MILITARY ORGANISATION

One of the most baffling of all the 'mysteries' that surround the Spartan State is that of its military establishment. This arises not so much from any supposed desire on the part of the Spartans to keep their affairs secret, but rather from the vagueness of the historians and their many inconsistencies. The other Greeks had met the Spartans often enough on the battlefield to know the disposition of their forces; there was no mystery about that. The trouble arises from a confusion of nomenclature. Herodotus uses certain terms to describe units of the army, while Thucydides uses others. Xenophon is apparently inconsistent in his use of names and involves us in the worst difficulties. So far as tactics in the field and the deploying of troops in battle formation are concerned, we are not on too unsafe ground if we work them out in the light of reason. The Spartans were highly skilled soldiers, none more so, and their movements in the field were actuated by the soundest tactical reasons. The problems of manœuvring infantry units to bring them most expeditiously into position are the same to-day as they always were. But even here we

---

[1] General references: All the historians have dealt with the various problems as they arise from the description of battles. More particularly the following special treatments may be cited. Rüstow u. Köchly, *Gesch. d. griech. Kriegswesen*; Beloch, *Bevölkerung d. griech.-röm. Welt*; Busolt, 'Spartas Heer und Leuktra', *Hermes*, XL, p. 387; Cavaignac, *Klio*, XII (1912), p. 261; Kromayer, 'Die Wehrkraft Lakoniens u. seine Wehrverfassung', *Klio*, III (1903), p. 173; Ringnalda, *de Exerc. Lacedaem.*; Stehfen, *de Spart. re militari*; G. C. Stein, *Das Kriegswesen d. Spartaner*; Trieber, *Zum Kriegswesen d. Spartaner*. The nearest approach to the military organisation of Sparta is to be found in that of the Zulus under their warrior kings, *vide* W.S. Ferguson, 'The Zulus and the Spartans', *Harvard African Studies*, II (1918), p. 197ff.

find some confusing problems. Xenophon, as we shall see later, sets out with an engaging air of lucidity to explain the tactics of the Spartan army in the field, and only succeeds in perplexing the careful reader.

That the analysis of the military organisation given in the following pages is definitive on the subject is too much to hope. Doubtless other writers in the future will exercise their ingenuity, as have many in the past, on what Cavaignac has aptly termed 'l'éternelle et irritante question' of the military dispositions of the Spartan State. Probably no final conclusion can ever by arrived at. All that can be claimed for our treatment of this problem is that in all probability it is the most likely reconstruction to which, in the present state of our knowledge, we may reasonably attain.

EVOLUTION OF THE SPARTAN ARMY

It seems fairly certain that the Lacedaemonian army went through a series of changes corresponding with the events of prime importance in their history. As new conditions arose, the military establishment was changed of necessity, and, although we have no specific information as to when these successive reorganisations took place, yet it is by no means impossible to fix them with reasonable certainty. The history of Sparta falls into five well-defined periods, and in each of them the army was organised upon a system appropriate to the conditions prevailing therein. These five periods may be enumerated as follows:

1. The primitive or early period up to the close of the second Messenian war.

2. From the second Messenian war to the middle of the fifth century, including the Persian wars.

3. The second half of the fifth century, including the Peloponnesian war.

4. From the close of the Peloponnesian war to the battle of Leuctra.

5. The period after Leuctra.

The early period. Originally the Spartan army was brigaded according to the ancient three tribes, the Hylleis, Dymanes and Pamphyloi.[1] Of its organisation we have no exact knowledge, and except from what we can draw from reasonable inference, we can only speak of it with uncertainty. It might even be argued that there was no Spartan army in the sense of a regularly organised and disciplined force, but rather a host of tribesmen, who fought in three groups corresponding with their clans. When an emergency arose there was a *levée en masse*, and all those who were capable of bearing arms gathered and went to battle in a more or less undisciplined rabble under their tribal chieftains, who were themselves under the leadership of one or both of the two kings.

The second period. The stern lessons that were learned during the perilous second Messenian war, and the emergence of the Spartan State as we know it, necessitated a radical reorganisation and a discipline such as Sparta had never up till then been subjected to. This new organisation is traditionally connected with the name of Lycurgus, and if we accept him as a historical personage, it is by no means unreasonable to suppose that it was accomplished by his acts.[2] The Spartan army emerged as a highly disciplined and closely co-ordinated battle army, divided into regiments which were recruited according to locality and not according to birth or tribal affiliation. These regiments were called *lochoi* and were five in number, which apparently bore the names of Aidolios, Sines, Sarinas, Ploas and Mesoates.[3] Seemingly these cor-

---

[1] Tyrtaeus, in *Elegy and Iambus* (Loeb ed.), p. 59; Tyrtaios, fr. 1, Diehl, *Anthologia Lyrica Graeca.* Cf. Ehrenberg in *Hermes,* LIX (1924), p. 24; Wilamowitz-Moellendorff, *Sitz.-ber. d. Berl. Akad.* (1918), pp. 728 ff.

[2] Cf. Wade-Gery in *C.A.H.* III, p. 560. In *Class. Quart.* XXXVIII (1944), p. 117, Mr Wade-Gery calls this 'new-model army' the 'obal' army, identifying the five regional divisions with the obes.

[3] Schol. ad Thuc. IV, 8. Or Edolos and Mesoages. Sarinas may be Arimas according to Schol. ad Aristoph. *Lysist.* 453. Whether or not there was a Pitanatan *lochos* has puzzled all commentators. Herodotus (IX, 53) says its commander at Plataea was Amompharetus; but Thucydides (I, 20) emphatically denies that such a *lochos* ever existed. Gilbert, *Grk. Const. Ant.*

responded with the five new territorial divisions into which
the Lacedaemonian State had been reorganised, namely
Edolos, Konosoura or Konooura, Limnai, Pitanes and Mesoates.
Two of them are obviously the same, and we must suppose
the other three were variants of the remaining territorial
divisions.[1]

At this point our difficulties commence, and we are involved
in obscurities which are almost impossible to resolve with any
satisfactory degree of certainty. Herodotus,[2] in a passage that
has puzzled all commentators, says that Lycurgus instituted
enomotiae, *triecades* and *syssitia*. The word *enomotia* is recognisable as a regular term denoting a platoon, and we shall have
a good deal to say about it hereafter. *Triecas* was, at least in
Attica, apparently a division of the people containing thirty
families.[3] Whatever it denoted in Sparta, it certainly had, at
one time or another, something to do with the number thirty.
Syssition was, of course, the mess in which the Spartan men
ate together. We are left with the problem, therefore, of
trying to determine, if Herodotus is correct, what the terms
triecas and *syssition* denoted in the military system.

What was the *triecas*? Suidas says it was a mess that convened
on the thirtieth day of each month. Was it the same as the
syssition, or did it denote some special feast or assembly that
took place each month? If so, what had it to do with the army?
Almost certainly it was an archaic term, later dropped, to
denote the *enomotia* which, as we shall see hereafter, consisted
of thirty men and two officers.

p. 68, n. 4, discusses the point and cites references. There certainly was
a Pitanatan *oba*, since this has been identified in an inscription: *A.B.S.A.*
XIII, p. 213. But that does not say there was a Pitanatan *lochos*. Cf. Neumann,
in *Hist. Ztschr.* XCVI (1906), pp. 42f. Wade-Gery, *Class. Quart.* XXXVIII,
p. 131. holds that Thucydides is correct when he says there was no Pitanatan
lochos in his day, but incorrect in denying there had ever been one. The name
was obsolete, but certainly had been in use at the time of Plataea and therefore
Herodotus was right.

[1] Cf. Ringnalda, *de Exerc. Lac.* pp. 9ff.
[2] I, 65. Cf. Polyaenus II, 3, 11.
[3] But doubtful. Cf. Pollux, VIII, 111.

We are as greatly puzzled over Herodotus' allusion to the *syssition*. Was it a unit of the army in the second phase of its evolution? Quite a good case may be made of this view. The life of the Spartan was regimented on a military system, of which the *syssition* was an integral and very important part. What more likely than that the members of each *syssition* marched together as a unit? A significant passage of Plutarch[1] may be considered in this connection. When Lycurgus was asked why he had divided the citizens into small companies 'under arms' (μεθ' ὅπλων), he replied 'So that they may be ready to get orders promptly', i.e. be ready to march fully equipped at a moment's notice. We know that the *syssitia* were under the control of the polemarchs and not of the ephors, and since we know that each *syssition* had 'about fifteen' members,[2] it would not be unreasonable to suppose that two *syssitia* went to one *triecas*.

It must, however, be frankly acknowledged that this view is entirely conjectural and has been severely criticised. Stehfen[3] has rejected it altogether on the ground that the term *syssition* used in this sense is found nowhere else and Xenophon never alludes to it. A curious passage in Polyaenus,[4] which describes the Spartans bivouacking after an inconclusive engagement with the Thebans, says that they did so κατὰ λόχους καὶ μόρας καὶ ἐνωμοτίας καὶ συσσιτία. Everything seems to be collected here, but the sense of the passage can be seen from the context. The Spartans in their regular messes saw the serious gaps in their ranks and were correspondingly disheartened. Epaminondas being wiser mixed his Thebans up on purpose so that they did not realise their losses. The word *syssition* here must be understood to refer to the field mess, of which sixteen members was a convenient number, i.e. fifteen

---

[1] *Apoph. Lac.* 226E.   [2] Plut. *Lyc.* XII.

[3] *de Spart. re milit.* p. 23. The same view is expressed in Ringnalda, *de Exerc. Lac.* pp. 1ff. Cf. also Rüstow u. Kochly, *Gesch. d. Griech. Kriegswesen*, p. 38; Stein, *Kriegsw. d. Spart.* p. 6; Bielschowsky, *de Spart. Syss.* pp. 32ff.; Kahrstedt, *Griech. Staatsr.* p. 299.

[4] *Strat.* II, 3, 11.

men and one officer and two *syssitia* made up one *enomotia* of thirty men and two officers. No definitive conclusion may be reached on this problem; but on the whole it seems probable that, in the second period of the organisation of the Spartan army, the words *syssition* and *triecas* were used to denote half platoons and quarter companies and that later these archaic terms were dropped.

Another question arises with regard to the position of the *perioeci* in this second period. Were they brigaded separately? The inference that they were is very strong and may be supported by the account given by Herodotus[1] of the army that fought at Plataea. Pausanias marched with 5000 Spartans, each of them attended by seven helots. These were followed by another contingent 'of the neighbouring Lacedaemonians', i.e. the *perioeci*. At the battle the whole army of 10,000 'Lacedaemonians' occupied the right wing and Herodotus is careful to repeat his statement that of these only 5000 were Spartans. It seems certain that the *perioeci* were drawn up in their own regimental formations.

Third period. Towards the middle of the fifth century indications point to a reorganisation of the army for the second time. Probably, if not certainly, this was soon after the great earthquake of 464, which had caused such serious loss of life that the Spartan army was depleted of men. The ranks had to be filled up with *perioeci*, who were no longer brigaded separately but served in the same battalions as the Spartans. So much is certain, and we may go farther and surmise that *perioeci* were carefully distributed among the various regiments so that men from the same town or district did not serve together, a wise policy if the Spartans were not invariably sure of them. The incident of the Amyclaeans insisting upon going home to celebrate the festival of the Hyacinthia immediately before the battle of Lechaeum seems fairly satisfactory proof of this careful intermingling. Agesilaus had let the Amyclaeans 'out of all his army' (ἐκ πάσης τῆς στρατιᾶς) drop out of the

[1] IX, 10, 11, 28.

ranks.[1] As will be seen more fully hereafter, the perioecic Sciritai served as a separate unit, a fact so carefully recorded as to point to its being unique. We may also surmise that when the *perioeci* came to outnumber considerably the Spartans this rule could not have been insisted upon.

The next reference we have comes from the account in Thucydides[2] of the first battle of Mantinea, fought in 418.

There were engaged in the battle seven lochoi, exclusive of the Sciritai, who numbered six hundred. In each lochos there were four pentecostyes, and in each pentecostys four enomotiai. In the first rank of the enomotia there were four men. In depth, although they had not all been drawn up alike but as each lochagus chose, they took their position on the field eight deep. Thus along the whole line the first rank consisted of four hundred and forty-eight men besides the Sciritai.

Beginning with the smallest unit, the enomotia or platoon, it is evident that it must have consisted of thirty-two men. It is not unreasonable to suppose that here we have, under another name, the *triecas* of thirty men and two officers, that is, fifteen and an officer from each *syssition*.[3] Four *enomotiai* made up the *pentecostys* or company, which numbered 120 men and eight officers. It is perfectly sure that the word *pentecostys* has something to do with fifty, but it is as sure that it does not mean a company of fifty men. It must mean a fiftieth part. As will be seen later, the entiré establishment at First

[1] Xen. *Hell.* IV, 5, 11.

[2] v, 68. All commentators listed in the general references at the beginning of this chapter have dealt at length with this battle. To them may be added W. J. Woodhouse, *King Agis of Sparta and his Campaign in Arkadia in* 418 B.C. (Oxford, 1933); A. W. Gomme, *Essays in Greek History and Literature* (Oxford, 1937), pp. 132 ff.; Kromayer, *Antike Schlachtfelder*, IV, pp. 207 ff.; *idem, Klio*, III, pp. 47 ff., 173 ff.

[3] What may, perhaps fancifully, be called a geometric progression—16, 32, 64, 128—was general in ancient armies; *vide* Asclepiodotus, *Tactica*, II, 8; Aelian, *Tact.* IX, 3; Arrian, *Ars. tact.* X, 2. the smallest unit that could conveniently be handled was sixteen.

Mantinea consisted of approximately 6475. The *pentecostys* consisted of four platoons or *enomotiai* of thirty-two men, or 128 in all, and 128 × 50 equals 6400. While not too much must be made of these tempting mathematical proofs, this does seem sufficiently clear to allow of our regarding it as practically conclusive. Four companies went to the *lochos* or regiment which numbered 512, or 480 men and thirty-two officers. According to this computation, the seven regiments in the field at the battle consisted of 3584. But Thucydides tells us that the front rank consisted of 448 men and the files were eight deep. That makes 3840, or 266 more than the first computation. This surplus obviously must be accounted for by the *hippeis* or royal bodyguard. This corps normally numbered 300, but it is not necessary to suppose it was always kept at full strength, or was not present at this battle. To these heavy-armed hoplites must be added the Sciritai, a picked corps of *perioeci* numbering normally 600 men, a regiment of Brasideioi and *neodamodeis*, 700 strong,[1] and two troops of cavalry to the number of about 400.[2] The battle array therefore was as follows:

Hoplites	3584
Royal Guard	300
Sciritai	600
Brasideioi	700
Cavalry	400
	5584

To these were added an indeterminate number of Maenalians, Heraeans and Tegeans. If we reckon each contingent at about five hundred, we should probably not be far out and certainly that estimate is a liberal one.[3] The entire allied army at First

[1] Thuc. VII. 19.

[2] Thuc. IV, 55; V. 67. Ringnalda's estimate of 4234 in *de Exerc. Lac.* pp. 18 f. cannot be accepted. He persists in assuming there were only six *lochoi* in the field.

[3] I.e. exactly half of Diodorus' estimate of 3000 (XII, 78, 4). It is impossible to accept this figure.

Mantinea therefore amounted to approximately 7000 men.[1] It must be noted that the 5550 Lacedaemonians were all first-class men, the older men and boys had already been sent home.[2] We are told that these numbered one-sixth of the entire army, or about 975, so that we may conclude that the entire Lacedaemonian army in 418 amounted to about 6475 men.

The account given by Thucydides of the singular battle of First Mantinea is interesting and raises several problems which are far from easy to elucidate. He tells us that the army under Agis was drawn up in the following order: cavalry, Sciritai, Brasideioi, Lacedaemonians, allies, 'a few Lacedaemonians', cavalry.

He is most explicit in stating that there were seven *lochoi* 'beside the Sciritai'. This statement involves us in two problems. First, were the Brasideioi reckoned as a *lochos*? It seems fairly obvious that they were, otherwise Thucydides would have said 'beside the Sciritai and Brasideioi'. There is no evidence that these liberated helots were not included in the regular military establishment. That leaves, therefore, six *lochoi* of Lacedaemonians, that is, mixed Spartans and *perioeci*[3]

[1] This estimate agrees almost exactly with that of Busolt in *Hermes*, XL, p. 418, where he arrives at 6800 all told, including the allies. Bury's estimate (*History of Greece* p. 461) of 10,000 is impossibly large, and even more so Woodhouse's 13,060 and Gomme's 'rather more than 11,000'. Kromayer, *Antike Schlachtfelder*, IV, p. 213, reckons 8000–9000 'at the very outside'. Cf. also Beloch, *Klio*, VI (1900), p. 69, who agrees closely with the above, but accepts Diodorus' figures for the allies.

[2] Thuc. v, 64.

[3] This is the conclusion of Stein, *Kriegsw. d. Spartaner*, p. 8. Stehfen, *de Spart. re mil.* p. 15, thinks there were ten, i.e. one on the left, seven in the centre and two on the right, or perhaps even three on the right if two could safely be withdrawn. Busolt, *Griech. Gesch.* p. 535, objects that three *lochoi* on the right wing could hardly be called 'a few'. Ringnalda (*de Exerc. Spart.* p. 20) suggests the emendation οἱ λοίποι for ὀλίγοι, which he says will remove all difficulties. But any difficulty can be removed to the satisfaction of the commentator by sufficiently drastic changes in the text. On all counts Thucydides' explicit statement that seven *lochoi* were engaged must be accepted. Their actual disposition in the battle array is a minor point which need not occupy our attention over-much. Kromayer (*Klio*, III, p. 192, n. 5)

and the Brasideioi to make the seventh. The second problem is, how were these drawn up? It seems plain that the main body under the direct command of Agis was in the centre, the Sciritai and Brasideioi on the left wing and an undetermined number on the right wing. It is with regard to those on the right that the difficulty arises and opinions of commentators differ sharply thereon. Thucydides says the right wing consisted of 'a few Lacedaemonians', and we are left to conjecture what he means by 'few'. Were these the two *lochoi* under Hipponoidas and Aristocles, which Agis at the crisis of the battle ordered to move over to the left to fill the gap caused by his ill-judged order to the Sciritai and Brasideioi to wheel to the left to prevent his left wing being outflanked? It seems very likely that they were. It is almost impossible to imagine that Agis, incompetent general as he was, should deliberately leave so gaping a place in his centre by moving out two whole *lochoi* while the fighting was at its height. If we accept the view that these two *lochoi* constituted the 'few', then we must conclude that Agis had under his personal command four Lacedaemonian *lochoi* in the centre.[1]

That the Spartans won the battle at all was a miracle. Only the remarkable fighting qualities of the Lacedaemonians redeemed the day from complete disaster. Agis was a bungler of the worst description and no attempts at making him any-

argues with considerable force that the two *lochoi* on the right wing were not wholly composed of Spartans but a mixed force stiffened by a few Spartans. The fact that they were commanded by polemarchs and *lochagi*, he says, indicates this. It is impossible to arrive at a definite conclusion upon this point. Beloch, *Bevölkerung*, pp. 133 ff. advances the theory that the *mora* consisted of two *lochoi*, one of Spartans the other of *perioeci*. At First Mantinea there were six Spartan and six perioecic *lochoi*, the seventh was composed of the Brasideioi, and the Sciritai formed a separate body. There is no evidence that the *mora* consisted of two *lochoi*.

[1] Both Woodhouse and Gomme put these two *lochoi* on the right centre, Henderson puts them on the extreme right. The latter, however, does not number the Brasideioi among the seven *lochoi* and therefore makes the number under the command of Agis five *lochoi*.

thing else can succeed.[1] The otherwise inexplicable refusal of
Hipponoidas and Aristocles to obey his order can only be
explained on the ground that they were utterly distrustful of
his leadership, and were called upon to execute a manœuvre
of the greatest danger at a critical moment when they could
see that obedience would inevitably bring disaster. Agis had
made a terrible blunder and was trying to retrieve his mistake
by giving an impossible order. How else can we explain this
lapse in the famous Spartan code of discipline on the battlefield?[2]

Fourth period: *the* lochos *and the* mora. Up to First
Mantinea the evolution of the Spartan army is not difficult to
follow. Subsequently our understanding of the system by
which the cadres of the army were organised becomes greatly
confused, because we hear for the first time of the *mora* as
a unit in 404, when Xenophon[3] tells us that Lysander took
two *morai* of Spartan infantry and some Athenian cavalry to
get the rebels out of the Piraeus. Evidently during the fourteen
years that had elapsed between First Mantinea and the end of
the war, some new system of army organisation had been
introduced. That this must be so is attested by Xenophon's
careful description of the army in his *Government of the
Lacedaemonians*.[4]

He [Lycurgus] divided them into six morai of cavalry and
heavy armed infantry. Each of these morai of the citizens[5] has one

---

[1] Woodhouse does his best to rehabilitate poor Agis and calls him 'one
of the ablest commanders that Greece produced'. In view of his record it is
impossible to accept this.

[2] Another famous case of disobedience on the battlefield was when
Amompharetus refused to obey the order to retreat before the battle of
Plataea. Herod. IX, 53. The two battles were curiously alike in that troops
were shifted in the battle line immediately before the engagement began,
the Spartans at Plataea insisting on changing places with the Athenians.
Herod. IX, 46.

[3] *Hell.* II, 4, 31. Hesychius, *s.v.* μόρα, says it was an alternative word for
lochos.

[4] *Resp. Lac.* XI, 4.

[5] Reading τῶν πολιτῶν instead of ὁπλιτικῶν as in Stobaeus.

polemarch, four lochagi, eight penteconters and sixteen enomotarchs. The men of these *morai* are sometimes, according to the
command issued, formed in enomotiai, sometimes by threes,
sometimes by sixes.[1]

The reference to Lycurgus is, of course, absurd and only put
in by Xenophon to give an air of antiquity to the composition
of the army. What has happened is fairly evident. With the
close of the Peloponnesian war the Spartan army was reorganised on a peace footing. Instead of the seven that fought
at First Mantinea, there are now six regiments and a completely new nomenclature has been introduced.[2] The old name
of *lochos* to denote the battalion is no longer used, instead it is
called the *mora*. Why this change? Is it to be attributed merely
to the fact that Xenophon uses the word *mora* where Thucydides uses *lochos*? That is hard to credit, more especially as we
shall see later, in the last book of his *Hellenica*, Xenophon
suddenly reverts to the use of the term *lochos* to denote the
battalion. No completely satisfactory explanation of this has
been put forward by the commentators. Adolph Bauer[3]
suggests that there was no actual change in organisation but
that the *lochos* was the tactical, the *mora* the administrative
unit. Stehfen[4] suggests that when the *perioeci* were numbered
in the army the battalions were called *morai*, when only
Spartans were referred to they were called *lochoi*, and with
this conclusion Kromayer agrees.[5] These are no more than

---

[1] τότε μὲν εἰς ἐνωμοτίας, τότε δὲ εἰς τρεῖς, τότε δὲ εἰς ἕξ, a puzzle to
all commentators. It probably means that the company marched either in
single file or three abreast or six abreast.

[2] For a contrary view cf. Beloch. *Bevölkerung*, p. 132, and *Klio*, VI (1906),
pp. 58 ff., where he characterises any reorganisation of the Spartan army as
so foreign to the intensely conservative character of the Spartans as to be
unbelievable. Gilbert, *Grk. Const. Ant.* p. 71, n. 1, accepts the hypothesis of
a reorganisation, but can offer no explanation of the 'extraordinary phenomenon' of the change in nomenclature in the last book of the *Hellenica*, for
a discussion of which *vide infra*, p. 246. The view expressed above is substantially that of Busolt, *Hermes*, XL, pp. 419 ff.

[3] 'Kriegsaltertümer', p. 313, in Müller's *Handbuch der klass. Altertums-
wissenschaft*, IV, I.   [4] *de Spart. re mil.* p. 10.   [5] *Klio*, III, p. 187.

conjectures and the problem must perforce be left unsolved. It may be added that Xenophon's use of the term ἄγημα to denote a division of the Spartan army admits of no satisfactory explanation.[1] Evidently these words were used loosely and without great accuracy.

If we are correct in assuming that there was a reorganisation of the army at the close of the Peloponnesian war—and it seems reasonable to suppose that this was the case—we may also assume that this new order was adhered to for the next thirty years until the battle of Leuctra in 371, when four out of the six battalions were engaged.

We may safely assume that between First Mantinea and Leuctra the size of the army remained substantially the same. At First Mantinea 3584 composed the battle array; at Leuctra, if all six *morai* had been engaged instead of the four that were actually present, there would have been 3456, a reduction of 128[2] which is so small as to be without significance. There was no increase in numbers,[3] but certainly there was no decrease. Any idea that a dwindling population in Laconia was the cause of the downfall of the State must be dismissed at once. The privileged caste of peers did decrease; but the 'Lacedae-monians' did not. In fact, as Beloch[4] remarks, between 371 and 230 B.C. they actually increased.

Fifth period: later army organisation. The patient reader who tries to follow Xenophon's account of the organisation of the

[1] *Resp. Lac.* XI, 9; XIII, 6. In the Macedonian army the term ἄγημα was generally used to denote the royal bodyguard. This prompts Beloch, *Bevölke-rung*, p. 134, and *Klio*, VI, p. 64, to suggest that in Sparta it refers to the *hippeis*. Kahrstedt, *Griech. Staatsr.* p. 307, n. 2, suggests that this ἄγημα τῆς πρώτης μόρας served as the bodyguard if the *hippeis* were not present. More probably it refers to the 100 picked men (λογάδες) who surrounded the king on the battlefield. Toynbee, *J.H.S.* XXXIII, p. 262, suggests that the leading *enomotia* in column of route was called the *agema*. This is possible but lacks confirmatory evidence. No satisfactory conclusion is possible. Cf. art. *s.v.* by Droysen in P.W.

[2] It is curious to observe that 128 represents four *enomotiai* or a double *penticostia* of the old army. But this is probably no more than a coincidence.

[3] As Kromayer in *Klio*, III, p. 199, supposes.

[4] *Bevölkerung*, p. 144.

Spartan army reaches a point of complete bewilderment, not to say exasperation, when he finds that, having once already mystified him with the *mora* and its composition, Xenophon suddenly changes his nomenclature and speaks of the *lochos*.

In the first six books of the *Hellenica* the word *lochos* is never used. But in the seventh and last book it is introduced and used three times.[1] What has happened to the *mora*, and why does Xenophon use the word *lochos*? To that question only one answer can be given, namely that after the disaster of Leuctra the Spartan army once more underwent a drastic reorganisation. Great numbers of the *perioeci* were gone from the army with the loss of Messenia, and Agesilaus had taken the unprecedented and almost reckless step of freeing 6000 helots and drafting them into the army.[2] For some reason which we do not know, the word *mora* was dropped and the older *lochos* readopted. Perhaps this was from patriotic motives, more than that we cannot say.

It is evident that the names given to various units of the Spartan army puzzled the historians and commentators in ancient times, and even so careful an observer as Xenophon flounders hopelessly. At Tegaeum in 392 he speaks of a *mora* of 600 men.[3] Plutarch,[4] when speaking of the battle of Tegyra in 375, says the Spartans had two *morai*, 'the mora consisting, as Ephorus states, of 500; Callisthenes 700 and others, as Polybius, 900'. The word *lochos* is used by various authors in a bewildering fashion. Suidas defines it as a cohort consisting of eight, twelve or sixteen men. Xenophon in one passage refers to a *lochos* of twenty-four men[5] and in two other places of 100 men.[6] Evidently the word referred to a detachment which might vary in strength within wide limits.

---

[1] *Hell.* VII, 1, 30; 4, 20; 5, 10.
[2] *Hell.* VI, 5, 29. Kromayer, *Klio*, III, p. 187, regards this rightly as an astonishing step and asks how Agesilaus could have induced the Spartans to agree to it? The obvious answer is that only stern necessity could have done so. Sparta was ruined and drastic measures were necessary.
[3] *Hell.* IV, 5, 12.
[4] *Pel.* XVII.
[5] *Cyr.* VI, 3, 21.
[6] *Anab.* III, 4, 21; IV, 8, 15.

In the same way there is considerable variation in the number of regiments in the Spartan army either permanently on the establishment or actually in the field at any particular engagement. How many battalions the Spartans put into the field in any one campaign, or how many were actually engaged at any particular battle and how many were in reserve naturally depended upon the exigencies of the situation. This fact explains the wide discrepancies to be met with in various authors. For instance, Photius[1] states that Aristophanes gave four *lochoi* in the Spartan army, Thucydides five and Aristotle seven. But Hesychius states that Aristotle says there were five. This leads to a confusion into which it is unprofitable to go. The Spartan army undoubtedly underwent more than one reorganisation. To say more than that is not possible, so difficult and obscure is the problem.

LIABILITY FOR MILITARY SERVICE

As soon as a Spartan youth entered on his eighteenth year he was enrolled in the roster (κατάλογος)[2] of those liable for military service, and that liability continued until the completion of his sixtieth year. There were, therefore, forty-two year-classes which might at need be called to the colours; but actually, except at moments of great danger, the younger and older men were not enrolled. So far as is known, the only occasion on which all forty-two classes were called up was in 418, when youths from eighteen to twenty and men up to sixty were included, but before the first battle of Mantinea these were discharged and sent back to Sparta.[3] Even after the disaster of Leuctra only forty year-classes were called up, the youths were exempted.[4] Generally thirty classes were enrolled, that is, men from twenty to fifty; but when the need

---

[1] *s.v.* 'Lochoi'. The reference in Aristophanes, *Lysist.* 453, *sensu obsceno*, et schol., to four *lochoi*, may be disregarded. For comments on this passage cf. Ringnalda, *de Exerc. Lac.* p. 10; Stehfen, *de Spart. re mil.* p. 2.

[2] Thuc. VI, 43 (Athenian).   [3] *Ibid.* V, 64.

[4] Xen. *Hell.* VI, 4, 17.

was great five more classes, men from fifty to fifty-five were added. In any case it seems that after fifty-five a Spartan could not be compelled to serve on foreign campaigns. Agesilaus pleaded he was fifty-eight, and so not liable for service outside Sparta.[1]

Apparently those actually called up to serve were called συντεταγμένοι.[2] Less certainly they were called λογάδες, although this word may apply only to those picked for special operations or forming the king's bodyguard in battle.[3] Although we have no certain information on that subject, it is safe to suppose that the same rules of obligatory service applied to the *perioeci*.[4] Apparently the Spartan high command called upon them to supply so many men, and they sent those whom they selected themselves. During the Persian wars the *perioeci* were brigaded separately; but by the time of Leuctra the number of Spartans in the army had fallen so far that *perioeci* were in the great majority. The various classes of 'inferiors'—*hypomeiones* and *neodamodeis*—served in the army according to the same rules as the Spartans.

Aristotle[5] says that fathers of three sons were exempted from the night watch, but does not say they were excused from military service altogether. Indeed, a passage in Hero-

---

[1] *Ibid.* v, 4, 13. We are left with the difficult, even exasperating, expression τὰ δέκα ἀφ' ἥβης. It is agreed that a youth became a ἥβων at twenty; does τὰ δέκα mean all classes from twenty to twenty-nine, or the twenty-nine year old class? Mr Billheimer, *Transactions of the American Philological Association*, LXXVII (1946), p. 74, favours the former. In Xen. *Hell.* IV, 14–16, where the Acarnians were harassing the Spartans on the march, τὰ πεντεκαίδεκα ἀφ' ἥβης were sent out to beat them off. Were there all classes from twenty to thirty-four, or the age-class thirty-four alone? If it means all classes, then they represented the bulk of the contingent and the whole line would have been dispersed, which seems hard to credit.

[2] But doubtful, this may not be the technical term; *vide* Xen. *Hell.* III, 3, 7; VI, 5, 29.

[3] Uncertain, Herod. VI, 56.

[4] Ringnalda, *De Exerc. Lac.* p. 35, points out that the anecdote in Plut. *Ages.* XXVI, shows that possession of a *cleros* was also necessary for service among the *perioeci*. If not, some of them would have stood up. Those who did not possess a *cleros* served, presumably, in other battalions, among the *neodamodeis* perhaps.　　　　　　　　　[5] *Pol.* 1270B.

dotus[1] seems to suggest that men who had sons to take their place after them were selected for particularly dangerous undertakings. The three hundred chosen by Leonidas to accompany him to Thermopylae were all fathers of sons.

A *corps d'élite* of 300 ἱππεῖς served as a brigade of guards. Although their name would suggest it, apparently they were not mounted.[2] Selection for service in this corps was counted a great honour. They served for one year, the ephors choosing three *hippagretai*, or commanders of companies, who each selected, according to his own choice, a hundred young men.[3] As being specially trustworthy, they were employed by the ephors in peace-time on particular missions of a difficult character.[4] We are not specifically told so, but we may reasonably suppose that the secret police, or *crypteia*, was recruited from them; or perhaps only those who were required for a special duty of a dangerous and highly confidential character. In battle the kings were surrounded by a corps of 100 picked men, ἄνδρες λογάδες.[5] Inclusion in this number was accounted the greatest honour of all and included winners in the Olympic Games. We are told an improving story[6] of a Spartan who was offered a large bribe to default in a wrestling match at the games. He refused and, on being asked in what way he had benefited himself, replied that now he would always fight by the side of his king.

In earlier times, before the number of Spartans had dwindled, the helots were employed as 'batmen' and shield-carriers or light-armed skirmishers.[7] Later, when the lessening numbers

---

[1] VII, 205.

[2] Herod. I, 67; later unmounted. Strabo, x, 4, 18 (C. 481–2). Cf. Thuc. v, 72. Dion. Hal. II, 13, 4, says they sometimes were mounted. This is not impossible but seems unlikely, since cavalry were little used and were ineffective, as will be seen later.

[3] Xen. *Resp. Lac.* IV, 3. Cf. Plut. *Lyc. Apoph. Lac.* 231 B; Herod. VIII, 124. Mr Toynbee's suggestion (*J.H.S.* XXXIII, p. 255) that each of 300 γένη was originally charged with the duty of equipping a horseman must be rejected for lack of evidence.

[4] E.g. Xen. *Hell.* III, 3, 9.
[5] Herod. VI, 56.
[6] Plut. *Lyc.* 22; *Quaest. Conviv.* II, 5.
[7] Herod. IX, 28.

made it necessary to seek men wherever they could be found, helots served as hoplites when, if they distinguished themselves in battle, they were set free from servitude and joined the class of *neodamodeis*.[1]

The great pains taken to keep Spartans from leaving the country is shown by the statement of Isocrates that to do so involved the penalty of death.[2] Plutarch[3] says that this was to prevent their being corrupted by foreign peoples; but it is quite certain that the motive was to prevent desertions from the army.

The Sciritai, who came originally from Sciritis on the borders of Arcadia, formed a separate *lochos* of about 600 men.[4] They seem to have been a picked corps which was used in particularly hazardous undertakings;[5] they fought in the vanguard,[6] began and ended the battle, and were always on the left wing,[7] the position of greatest danger, since the left side was always liable to edge towards the right to gain protection from the shield of the right-hand man. A particularly steady body which would check that tendency was therefore needed on the left flank. Originally, no doubt, they were Arcadians[8] and won fame as scouts in the early wars of Sparta. The importance to the Spartans of the region of Sciritis was that the two roads from Megalopolis and Tegea passed through it into the Eurotas valley. It was very necessary, therefore, that this strategic point should be held strongly. It is not without significance that immediately after Leuctra

---

[1] Thuc. VII, 19.

[2] *Orat.* XI, 18 (Busiris). Cf. Plut. *Agis*, 11; *Lyc.* XXVII; Trieber, *Quaestiones Laconicae*, p. 57.

[3] *Inst. Lac.* 238 D, E. Cf. also Nicol. Damas. *F.H.G.* III, p. 458, 114, 5.

[4] Thuc. V, 68.   [5] Xen. *Cyr.* IV, 2, 1.

[6] Xen. *Resp. Lac.* XIII, 6.

[7] Thuc. V, 67; Diod. Sic. XV, 32. It is unnecessary to suppose that the Sciritai were recruited exclusively from Sciritis. One is reminded of the British Coldstream Guards, which derive their name from a small village where they were originally raised.

[8] Art. 'Skiritis' in P.W. by Geyer; Hesychius, *s.v.* 'Skiros'; Wade-Gery in *Class. Quart.* XXXVIII (1944), p. 119; *C.A.H.* III, 365; Herod. I, 66.

the Sciritai were seeking their independence at the hands of Epaminondas. That may have been merely good policy on their part; or it may have arisen from resentment at their treatment by Sparta. We do not know how they were armed. Fighting at the point of extreme danger on the left wing, we should naturally expect them to be heavily armed with the full panoply. But if they were used as scouts they must have laid aside their armour. Probably they were adaptable for any task.

THE *NEODAMODEIS*[*]

Helots who served in the army as hoplites belonged to the class of freedmen called *neodamodeis*. Mr Toynbee's suggestion,[1] that they formed 'a standing force of hoplites raised from the helots for oversea service, in order to set free the whole of the Lacedaemonian army for service on the Greek mainland', while lacking positive proof, may be true. They were first raised in 425 to the number of 2000[2] but seem to have got out of hand and the alleged infamous murder of the whole, or majority, of them followed; although, as previously remarked, this incident may be looked on with suspicion at least as recorded by Thucydides. In 413, 600 of them were sent to Sicily[3] and in 412 they formed an expeditionary force of 300.[4] Thibron took 1000 *neodamodeis* to Asia in 400[5] and Agesilaus had 2000 with him in 396.[6] In 394, these were all in garrison in Asia,[7] or marching round the Aegean coast with Agesilaus.[8] We hear of them again in 382, when Eudamidas had an unspecified number with him.[9] The 6000 helots who were freed in 370–369[10] were probably classed among the *neodamodeis*, although we have no certain information on that point. Nor do we know how they were financed. Mr Toynbee's guess that they were paid out of the war fund of the

[1] *J.H.S.* XXXIII, p. 266, n. 80.
[2] Thuc. IV, 80.
[3] *Ibid.* VII, 19.
[4] *Ibid.* VIII, 8.
[5] Xen. *Hell.* III, 1, 4.
[6] *Ibid.* III, 4, 2.
[7] *Ibid.* IV, 25.
[8] *Ibid.* III, 15.
[9] *Ibid.* V, 2, 24.
[10] *Ibid.* VI, 5, 29.

Peloponnesian League, and later out of the tribute paid by the allies when it was transferred to Sparta from Athens may very well be true. In any case their upkeep must have cost a large sum. Nor do we know on what system they were selected for service nor how they were armed, whether each man provided his own panoply or was fitted out by the State. It is likely that their ranks were voluntarily recruited from the sons of well-to-do helots who wanted to escape from their galling social inferiority and the hard manual labour on their master's *cleroi*. They proved themselves excellent soldiers, not perhaps trained to that pitch of efficiency attained by the Spartans, but at least good enough for all practical purposes, as the success of those under Brasidas in Thrace proved.

THE PHALANX

It is probably true to say that the Spartan heavy-armed hoplite was the most formidable soldier of the ancient world. Indeed, we might go so far as to say that, so far as physique, endurance and training go, he has never been matched in any army or at any time. In its prime the Spartan army was unbeatable, as Pericles and the Athenians very well knew, and never risked a decisive encounter with it.

The main body fought in close order, shoulder to shoulder in the 'phalanx'. This was the traditional, age-long form of line of battle among all the Greeks. Homer says of the Achaean host:

As a man joins the compacted wall-stones of a high house and shuts out the raging winds; so was joined the wall of helmets and bossy shields. Shield pressed on shield, and helmet upon helmet, and man on man. And the horse-hair plumes of the bright crests touched as they tossed about; so close stood the men together.[1]

When the battle was joined and the two opposing phalanxes clashed, it was simply a matter of which pushed the harder. Once the phalanx was broken then all was lost, since it was

[1] *Il.* XVI, 212–5. Cf. also XIII, 130.

impossible to rally. Formidable as the phalanx was, it suffered from almost complete lack of mobility. It was not until Alexander introduced the smaller and more mobile cohort that the most ancient form of battle array was changed, and afforded him his greatest victories.

So inflexible and unwieldy was the phalanx that it was utterly useless in an assault upon a walled town or even a stockade. Lycurgus evidently made a virtue of necessity and forbade them to attack walled towns, so that brave men should not die at the hands of women and children.[1] At Plataea the Spartans could do nothing against the stockade round the Persian camp.

So long as the Athenians were absent the barbarians defended themselves and had much the advantage over the Lacedaemonians, as they were not skilled in attacking fortifications. But when the Athenians came up, then a vehement fight at the walls took place and continued for a long time. But at length the Athenians by their valour and constancy surmounted the wall and made a breach and there at length the Greeks poured in.[2]

At Third Mantinea the phalanx of Machanidas was thrown into confusion in trying to cross a wide ditch or ravine and was unable to form up again or resist the charge of Philopoemen's ordered ranks.

The phalanx formed the hard core of the army, the battle was won or lost by it alone. As will be seen later, cavalry never formed an important part of the military establishment. Light-armed troops, the *euzonoi*, hoplites without their heavy shields, armed with javelins, were extensively used, but they

---

[1] Plut. *Apoph. Lac.* 228 D; *Comp. Lysand. et Sulla*, 477 D. But cf. a lively criticism of this view of the phalanx in battle by A. D. Fraser, 'The myth of the Phalanx Scrimmage', *Classical Weekly*, XXXVI, 2, 12 Oct. 1942. Mr Fraser suggests that the phalanx was not so compact as usually imagined, that each man in the front rank singled out an opponent and engaged him. If a front-rank man was killed the man behind came up to take his place. The suggestion is ingenious but hardly convincing. The whole strength of the phalanx was in its compactness and impenetrable front.

[2] Herod. IX, 70.

were little more than skirmishers who hung on the flanks.[1]
If the opposing phalanx was broken, these light-armed men
ran in to augment the confusion and cut off stragglers, in
which action the cavalry, if there were any on the field, took
a part.

The reason for the preponderating importance in warfare of
the heavy-armed hoplite fighting in the phalanx has been well
explained by Polybius.[2] The phalanx was only effective on the
plains, the fertile pockets between the mountain ranges which
formed but a fifth of the area of Greece. The light-armed men
and the cavalry played very little part in the battle, there was
not room for them to manœuvre effectively. The only
opportunity for them to strike was when the heavy-armed
were caught on rugged ground and could not retain their
close formation, and under these circumstances both could be
very effective indeed.[3] But that was seldom enough 'because
the hoplites could always compel the enemy to meet it on the
plain, otherwise it could devastate that plain and the lower
slopes of the hills which were the only cultivable ground,
destroying crops and, what was far more serious, olive trees
and vines and thereby reducing the population to a position
in which they could have no food supply for the next year and
no means of purchasing a supply from abroad'.[4] The stratagem
of Pericles in abandoning the countryside of Attica and taking
all the people within the long walls of Athens, where they
could be provisioned by sea, was correct. He knew that if he
met the Spartan phalanx in the open he was doomed; nothing
could stand against it.

---

[1] At the battle of Sellasia by both sides. Polyb. II, 67, 2; 69, 3. Cf. Xen.
Anab. VII, 3, 46.   [2] XVIII, 29–32.

[3] A notable example of such a disaster was the action fought at Lechaeum
in 390, when the Athenians under Iphicrates cut to pieces a Spartan *mora* on
the march with flanks unprotected by cavalry. The account given by Xenophon, *Hell.* IV, 5, 11–17, shows the ineffectiveness of the heavy-armed hoplite
when out of formation and how deadly the attacks of light-armed peltasts
could be.

[4] G. B. Grundy, *History of the Greek and Roman World*, p. 189.

It was a fundamental principle of Spartan military training that, if the line was broken and the formation thrown into confusion, the men should be able to re-form as soon as possible with whomever they found nearest to them (μετὰ τοῦ παρα-τυχόντος).[1] Evidently this was the outcome of special training, since it would be natural for them to look out for their friends or relations in the confusion of the moment. For that reason it appears that sons, brothers and fathers were separated and served in different regiments,[2] thus breaking the age-long 'Nestor's rule'[3] that kin should fight alongside kin, which in an undisciplined mob would certainly be found. This training was not enough to save them at Leuctra when the formation was broken, 'though the Spartans used to train themselves to nothing so much as to keep from confusion upon any change of position and to follow any leader or right-hand man and form in order and fight wherever danger pressed'.[4]

If the phalanx were broken, the battle was over. The genius of Epaminondas at Leuctra was to crumple the Spartan phalanx in an entirely unexpected manner. The account given by Plutarch in his *Life of Pelopidas* is much fuller than that of Xenophon in the *Hellenica* and may conveniently be followed here.[5] Cleombrotus, the Spartan king, had drawn up his army in the conventional battle array, his allies on his left wing, the Lacedaemonian phalanx, twelve deep, on his right, with his cavalry, a negligible and utterly ineffective force, in the van. Epaminondas, the Theban commander, who was greatly out-numbered but possessed military genius of a high order, determined on a bold and hitherto undreamed-of manoeuvre.

---

[1] Xen. *Resp. Lac.* XI, 7.

[2] A reasonable inference, according to Wade-Gery, *Class. Quart.* XXXVIII, p. 119; cf. Xen. *Hell.* IV, 5, 10.

[3] *Il.* ii, 362. 'Separate the men by families and by tribes, that family may help family, and tribe tribe.' Evidently this was not considered a wise rule in Thebes as well as Sparta since the Sacred Band was not made up of men related to each other but of 'lovers'. 'For men of the same tribe or family little value one another when dangers press.' Plut. *Pelop.* XVIII.

[4] *Pelop.* XXIII.   [5] *Pelop.* XXIII; *Hell.* VI, 4, 5.

Massing the pick of his army in ranks fifty deep he struck suddenly on the left of the Spartan phalanx at the point where it joined 'the other Greeks'. Obviously the correct movement of Cleombrotus was to swing round on his left, keeping the closest formation, and to bring up his right to take the charging Thebans in the flank. This is what he tried to do, and if the manœuvre had been carried out in close formation it seems likely it would have succeeded. But the Spartans made a fatal mistake, 'they opened and extended their right wing changing their order'. Pelopidas with three hundred picked men seeing what was happening 'came rapidly up before Cleombrotus could extend his line and close up his division, and so fell upon the Spartans while in disorder'. As always, once the close formation of the phalanx was broken confusion followed. The Spartans were helpless and 'there began such a flight and slaughter among them as never before was known'.

Epaminondas had introduced a new 'shock tactic' which was astoundingly successful. We may be sure that Alexander studied this battle, for it is precisely what he did himself many years later at Gaugamela when, outnumbered as Epaminondas had been, he split the Persian host in two, thus exposing the left flank of the enemy's centre and, turning obliquely, fell upon the Persian contingent drawn up around Darius. The Persian king fled in his chariot from the field, and his army, bereft of their leader, broke and the battle was over.

The tactics of Alexander, with certain modifications, were essentially those of Epaminondas—the crushing blow delivered at the vital spot which paralysed the opposing force and threw everything into confusion. Alexander introduced a longer spear, which was highly effective, and made great play with his cavalry, which he could do on the plains of Asia.

It is curious to see how the Spartans never recovered from the disaster of Leuctra. Second and Third Mantinea and Sellasia were defeats of the first magnitude which blotted Sparta out as a first-class military power for ever.

ARCHERS: MERCENARIES

We do not hear of archers until 424, when 'contrary to their custom they raised four hundred horse and some bow-men'.[1] It is to be noted that this was after the occupation of Pylus and Cythera and 'then if ever they were decidedly more timid than usual in military matters, being engaged in a conflict opposed to the usual character of their forces'. It seems they regarded, or affected to regard, the bow as a 'womanish weapon'.[2] Evidently the Persian archers were not much good, as the jest testifies which Leonidas made when he was told that the Persian arrows darkened the sky.[3] Agesilaus seems to have been the only Spartan who appreciated their usefulness. In his Asiatic campaign he offered prizes for the best turned-out companies of archers[4] and at the battle of Corinth he had 300 Cretans.[5]

It may be observed parenthetically that the Spartans in disregarding the bow were following sound military practice. At no time in ancient warfare was the bow a really effective weapon, and no battles were ever won by archers. The first effective use of bows and arrows in battle was that of the English six-foot long bow, which discharged an arrow of thirty-seven inches (the cloth-yard or ell). This weapon was deadly against chain-mail but was defeated by plate-armour and finally superseded by the gun.

Plutarch[6] tells us that the sling or catapult was brought from Sicily for the first time during the reign of King Archidamus III (361–338). This is absurd, since the sling was used in Homeric times.[7] The defeat of the Spartans at Pylus had been largely due to their being harassed by slingers.[8] We have no information as to whether the Spartans ever adopted the weapon themselves, but may be fairly certain they did not. Agesilaus had 400 slingers from the Marganians, Litvians and

---

[1] Thuc. IV, 55.
[2] Plut. *Apoph. Lac.* 234 E.
[3] *Ibid.* 225 B.
[4] Xen. *Hell.* IV, 2, 5.
[5] *Ibid.* IV, 2, 16.
[6] *Reg. et Imp. Apoph.* 191 E.
[7] *Il.* XIII, 600.
[8] Thuc. IV, 32.

Amphidolians at Corinth in 394.[1] We also know that Machanidas used mercenary slingers at Third Mantinea.[2]

An evidence of the heavy drain on Spartan man-power
quite early in the Peloponnesian war, the first mention we
have of mercenaries was in 426 in the campaign in Acarnania.[3]
Brasidas frequently used them.[4] We have no information about
the disposition of the mercenary troops. Certainly they were
not brigaded with the Spartan or perioecic battalions. Probably
they were in smaller units, which may possibly have been
called *taxeis* under a taxiarch.[5]

CAVALRY

In the Spartan army cavalry formed a minor and unim-
portant part. This is hardly to be wondered at, since the
mountainous and narrow defiles made their effective use very
difficult. Only in Thessaly, where suitable open country made
their use possible, were cavalry ever employed largely by any
Greek state. Plutarch, quoting from Philostephanus, attributes
the formation of a cavalry corps to Lycurgus, who formed
them in troops of fifty each, drawn up in a square. Like most
things attributed to Lycurgus this is more than doubtful,
Plutarch acknowledging that Demetrius of Phalerum denied
it on the ground that Lycurgus lived in a time of peace and
never engaged himself in an organisation of the army.[6]
Xenophon, however, follows the same tradition.[7] In the first
Messenian war, according to Pausanias,[8] both the Spartans and
Messenians had each 500 horsemen and light-armed troops.
In one of the battles the heavy-armed foot regiments were
separated by a ravine and could not come to close-quarters

---

[1] Xen. *Hell.* IV, 2, 16.   [2] Polyb. XI, 11, 3; 12, 4.
[3] Thuc. III, 109. Cf. H. W. Parke, *Greek Mercenary Soldiers*, p. 16;
G. T. Griffith, *Mercenaries of the Hellenistic World*, p. 238; B. Müller,
Beiträge zur Gesch. d. griech. Söldnerwesens, p. 17.
[4] Thuc. IV, 80; v, 6.
[5] Very doubtful; cf. Xen. *Hell.* IV, 1, 26; v, 2, 3.
[6] Plut. *Lyc.* XXIII; *F.H.G.* III, 23.   [7] *Resp. Lac.* XI, 4.
[8] Paus. IV, 7, 4.

while the cavalry and light-armed troops alone were engaged.[1]
In another battle he says the cavalry on both sides were few in
number and did nothing memorable, adding that the people
of the Peloponnesus were not skilful at that time in the use of
cavalry.[2] Their failure to employ cavalry seems to have arisen
from a genuine inability to master the technique of their use.
Certainly they had a highly effective lesson at Plataea, when
the Persian cavalry harassed them continually and nearly
defeated them.[3]

*At the opening of the Peloponnesian war the Spartans either
had no cavalry or regarded them as so inferior as to be of
negligible use. Such as they had came from their allies in
Boeotia, Phocis and Locris.[4] In the attack upon Corinth the
Athenians had a small force of 200 cavalry, which gave them
the advantage since the Corinthians had none.[5] By the time
of the battle of Delium in 424[6] it seems that the importance of
cavalry had been learned by the Spartans, since it was the
manœuvre of Pagondas that won the victory. He sent two
troops of horse round a hill to fall upon the Athenians who
were till then victorious. The Athenians, imagining a new
army was coming up, were panic-striken and fled. In this
battle the cavalry and light-armed troops on both sides were
drawn up on the two wings.[7] At First Mantinea in 418, they
do not appear to have had any important influence.[8]

At the beginning of the fourth century, the Spartan cavalry
were 600 strong, divided into a *mora* and twelve *oulamoi* or
troops.[9] Agesilaus, who almost alone among Spartan generals
was an innovator, seems to have been the only one who could

---

[1] Paus. IV, 7, 5.   [2] *Ibid.* 8, 12.   [3] Herod. IX, 49 ff.
[4] Thuc. II, 9.   [5] *Ibid.* IV, 44.
[6] Toynbee, *loc. cit.* XXXIII, p. 264, suggests that the seizure by the Athenians
of the island of Cythera forced the Spartans to raise a force of cavalry to
patrol the coast. This is not impossible, but rests on no evidence.
[7] Thuc. IV, 96.   [8] *Ibid.* V, 67.
[9] Toynbee's assertion, *loc. cit.* p. 264, that the infantry *mora* was a composite
force of foot and horse cannot be sustained. Xen. *Hell.* IV, 5, 11; Plut. *Lyc.*
XXIII.

make effective use of cavalry.[1] When, greatly to his surprise, at the head of 500 horsemen he had routed the Pharsalian cavalry 'this victory gave him special pleasure, because with horsemen of his own mustering and training, and with no other force he had conquered those whose chief pride was placed in their cavalry'.[2]

Evidently the Spartans did not consistently appreciate their use, or take care to keep them efficient. This neglect was to cost them dear at the battle of Leuctra.[3] As Xenophon says:

The Lacedaemonian cavalry was at that time in a very inefficient condition, for the richest men maintained the horses and when notice of an expedition was given, the men appointed came to ride them and each taking his horse and whatever arms were given him proceeded at once to the field, and thus the worst and least spirited of the men were mounted on horseback.

The Theban cavalry were only about 500 strong, but were veteran troops, well organised and rapid in movement. They at once fell upon the Spartan horse, defeated them and drove them in confusion upon the ranks of their infantry, thus preparing the way for the assault of the heavy-armed phalanx. There is a curious passage in Xenophon's *Hipparchus*[4] in which he says that the fame of Spartan cavalry dated from the introduction of foreign mercenaries. This was written probably about 365, and shows that the miserable display at Leuctra had had its effect. But the improvement, if any, was short-lived, for, at Second Mantinea, once more the Spartan horse was driven ignominiously from the field by the Thebans.[5]

This failure to develop an effective use of mounted troops appears the more remarkable at first sight when it is remembered that their remote ancestors were nomads, horsemen from the grassy steppes of Eurasia. But on the other hand, it must also

---

[1] The story told by Polyaenus, *Strat.* II, 1, 17, of how he tricked the Macedonians into thinking he had a large force of cavalry by mounting men on asses, mules and baggage horses is almost beyond belief.

[2] Plut. *Ages.* XVI; Xen. *Hell.* IV, 3, 9. Cf. Plut. *Apoph. Lac.* 209 B, 211 F.

[3] Xen. *Hell.* VI, 4, 10. [4] IX, 4. [5] *Hell.* VII, 5, 23.

be remembered that in the battles of Homer the heroes fought on foot. They drove to the battlefield in their chariots and then dismounted. Greek horses were unshod and their riders were chary in using them over rough stony ground. The Romans used a leather shoe enveloping the whole hoof; the iron shoe nailed to the hoof was a very late improvement.

The fact that stirrups were unknown made an effective charge against masses of foot-soldiers impossible.[1] Once an enemy was broken, cavalry could be used to pursue and cut down a disordered retreat. Otherwise their effectiveness was very limited. It is probably true to say that among ancient generals Alexander and Hannibal were the only ones who made skilful use of their cavalry.

ENGINEERS

The army in the field was accompanied by a corps of engineers and handicraftsmen with a baggage train under the command of the ἄρχων τῶν σκευοφόρων or quartermaster-general, who superintended the construction of the camp.[2]

The Lacedaemonians provide themselves in the field with an abundance of all those things which people use in the city; and, of whatsoever instruments an army may require, orders are given to bring some on waggons and others on beasts of burden as by this arrangement anything left behind is least likely to escape notice.

The speech of Cyrus[3] to his soldiers before setting out on the adventure to Babylon gives an excellent picture of the organisation of an army on the march.

MANŒUVRES ON THE BATTLEFIELD

Xenophon, in his *Government of the Lacedaemonians*,[4] remarks that many people do not understand the manner in

---

[1] The stirrup is first recorded in the *Strategikon* of the Emperor Maurice of Constantinople (A.D. 582–602); Oman, *History of the Art of War*, p. 185. It is not improbable that it came from China, since the first mention of it is found in Chinese literature in A.D. 477; Toynbee, *Study of History*, II, p. 164, n. 2.

[2] Xen. *Resp. Lac.* XI, 2; *Hell.* III, 4, 22.

[3] *Cyrop.* VI, 2, 26 ff.   [4] *Resp. Lac.* XI, 5 ff.

which the Spartan army executes its evolutions on the field of battle and imagine to be difficult what is really very easy to grasp. He then, with an air of engaging lucidity, proceeds to explain these evolutions. Unfortunately, however, his exposition is far from clear, and every commentator upon the passage has encountered difficulties which have led to a conflict of opinions.[1] There seems to be no reason to suppose that the passage is corrupt, and it would seem that Xenophon's powers of exposition failed to make clear what he had so confidently declared to be simple, a failure which is surprising in so experienced a soldier.

The key to the whole passage lies in two fundamental points that must be grasped before it is understood. First, the phalanx was formed of ranks of four and files of eight. That was the formation at First Mantinea, and we may assume it was the regular order during the Peloponnesian war. It is true that at Leuctra it was twelve deep, but, as already remarked, this was probably assumed to meet the impact of the Thebans who were advancing fifty deep. Otherwise the eight-deep formation was invariably maintained. Second, on the field of battle the regiments, companies and platoons, when executing a turning movement, unless compelled to the opposite, as will be seen hereafter, always wheeled clockwise, that is, they wheeled round towards the right, in order that the left hand on which the shield was carried should be presented to the enemy. If they wheeled counter-clockwise, the right side would be exposed, which would be dangerous.

Keeping these points clearly in mind, therefore, we may understand Xenophon's obscure exposition in the following manner:

1. When the army is marching forward to battle they are in column 'one *enomotia* following another'. When the enemy is about to attack this formation on the front, each company forms up on the left of the one in front thus forming a line

[1] Cf. Grote, II, pp. 456f. Boucher, 'La tactique grecque à l'origine de l'histoire militaire; *Rev. ét. gr.* XXV (1912), p. 302.

eight deep. This movement is made throughout the whole army, until it presents itself in full array against the enemy.

2. When the enemy shows himself against this formation in the rear 'each rank performs an evolution so that the strongest may always be presented to the enemy'. In this case 'to perform an evolution' (ἐξελίττω) can only mean to about-turn,[1] and the strongest (οἱ κράτιστοι), who always march in the front rank, must then come forward through the ranks from the rear to the front. The suggestion that the 'strongest' always marched in the rear, or that they were divided between front and rear, cannot be correct. The only reasonable supposition must be that the best fighters were invariably in the front rank and came to the front when the line about-faced.[2]

3. If the enemy attempts an encircling movement the whole line wheels round 'not on the defenceless but on the armed side', led by the commander, whose position is always on the left.[3] The wheeling movement is always clockwise.

4. 'If on any occasion it should appear advantageous for a particular object that the commander should occupy the right wing they wheel the troop towards the wing and manœuvre the main body until the commander is on the right and the rear becomes the left.' That is to say, pivoting on the left company, they have made a movement of 90°, the leading company with the commander is then on the right

---

[1] The manœuvre was called ἐξελιγμός and was employed successfully by Agesilaus at the battle of Coronea, Xen. *Hell*. IV, 3, 18. Cf. also Arrian, *Ars tactica*, XXIII, XXIV, XXVII. Themistius, I, 2b (ed. Dindorf).

[2] The manœuvre is described by Asclepiodotus, *Tactics*, X, 14 (Loeb ed.), as the Laconian counter-march. 'They would seem to those who have appeared in the rear to be making for and charging upon them. So that they dismay the enemy and arouse fear among them.' That this manœuvre was very difficult is strikingly shown at the battle of Cynoscephalae when the Macedonian phalanx was attacked in the rear by a small force of Romans. Unable to turn round quickly and also attacked strongly in front, the phalanx was thrown into confusion.

[3] The commander is always on the left of the company because he is protected by his shield on his left arm. If he were on the right his unprotected right side would be open to attack.

and the rear company is on the left. The expression 'the commander is on the right' does not mean, as some have supposed, that the commander then changes his position and takes up his position on the right of his *lochos*, but that the commander's company is on the right wing of the regiment.

5. 'If a body of the enemy appear on the right marching in column, they do nothing else but turn each company round like a ship' (τὸν λόχον ἕκαστον ὥσπερ τριήρη ἀντίπρῳρον). It is at this point that Xenophon's narrative becomes obscure. The regiment is in column of route, marching by fours when the enemy appears on the right flank. The first four ranks of the *enomotia* then make a right wheel, and the next four form up in their rear to form the eight-deep phalanx. The third then closes in on the first and the fourth forms up in its rear. The whole *enomotia* is then in battle formation. This seems the only explanation of this difficult passage. If the whole column of route simply halted and right-turned the phalanx would be only four deep. Of course it is quite possible that, if they were caught unawares and had not time to take up their usual positions, they would have to do that and risk having their extended line broken.

6. 'But if the enemy approach on the left, they do not allow them to come near but repulse them or turn their companies round to face the enemy and thus again the company that was in the rear takes its place on the left.' The manœuvre is exactly similar to the preceding one, except that the whole column makes a left wheel when the rear company is then on the left flank. The exigency of the attack on the left flank has thus forced them to wheel to the left, the only manœuvre that departs from their otherwise invariable rule of wheeling to the right.

On the march the king leads the van of the main body of hoplites, preceded only by the Sciritai and mounted scouts. On taking up battle formation 'the king, taking the foremost troop of the first *mora* and wheeling it round, leads off to the right until he reaches the space between two morae and two polemarchs'.[1] The foremost troop obviously indicates the royal bodyguard on the field of battle, the ἄνδρες λογάδες. From this brief description we can see exactly how the combat formation was formed. As soon as the enemy is sighted the cavalry scouts wheel to right and left, taking up positions on both wings, ready to charge in should the enemy break and become disordered. The Sciritai wheel to the left and invariably take up their station on the extreme left wing. The king's bodyguard wheels to the right and when it has reached its position halts while the first *mora* forms on its right, the second *mora* on its left and the other *morai* on its left until the entire battle line is formed between the first *mora* on the extreme right and the Sciritai on the extreme left.

ARMY COMMAND

One of the kings was always commander-in-chief in the field when the main Spartan army was engaged. Other expeditions were under the command of harmosts.[2] The polemarchs, six in number in command of the six *morai* or *lochoi* were the highest ranking officers and messed with the king. Each had a staff of συμφορεῖς or aides-de-camp of an unspecified number.[3] If the king fell in battle, presumably the senior polemarch took command.[4] The *lochagi* were apparently second in command, perhaps major would correspond to that rank; the *penteconteres*, captains of companies, and the enomotarchs, lieutenants of platoons; hipparmosts were captains of cavalry regiments.[5]

The king's staff (δαμοσία σκηνή) consisted of the polemarchs, the *pythioi* or diviners, surgeons, flute-players, the *kreodaites*, of whose duties we are not fully informed but who

[1] Xen. *Resp. Lac.* XIII, 6.   [2] Xen. *Hell.* II, 4, 28; III, 1, 4; IV, 2, 5.
[3] *Ibid.* VI, 4, 14; Xen. *Resp. Lac.* XII, 6.   [4] *Hell.* VI, 4, 15, 25.
[5] It is curious to note that when a council of war was summoned the polemarchs and *penteconteres* were present (Xen. *Hell.* III, 5, 22; IV, 5, 7). But there is no mention of the *lochagi*, who were undoubtedly ranking officers to the latter. This omission evidently agrees with Xenophon's use of *mora* instead of *lochos*. The rank of *lochagus* must have been abolished.

may have been quarter-masters; two ephors who went along to keep an eye on the king and report back to Sparta if dissatisfied; the *lathyropolai* who took charge of all booty captured; the *pyrphorus* or bearer of the sacred fire; three commissariat officers[1] and a personal squire or protector, chosen from among those who had been crowned in the games.[2] It is not perfectly clear what were the functions of the *hellanodicae* mentioned by Xenophon,[3] but in any case they were legal. They seem to have constituted what may be called the Judge-Advocate-General's department and may have constituted a court of appeal from courts martial on Spartan soldiers who appealed to the king for justice, and were by him referred to these judges. On the other hand, it is not impossible that their special sphere was the composing of disputes in the field between the Spartans and their allies. No definite conclusion seems possible on this point.

When Agis was in disfavour with the ephors in 418 after his return from Argolis, a special number of ten councillors (σύμβουλοι) were sent along with him.[4] However, this does not seem to have been a regular practice although we hear again of a similar council that accompanied Agesipolis to Olynthus.[5] Agesilaus appointed thirty σύμβουλοι to go with him on his Asiatic expedition.[6] Evidently these councillors were not part of the regular army system, but were occasionally appointed when the ephors were distrustful of the king, or as in the case of Agesilaus, he needed a staff of trusted friends around him. But in any case the government in Sparta was not willing to trust too much to the king's discretion. Couriers were going back and forth between the front and the capital the whole time with despatches, bearing the *scytale* or message stick with them.[7]

[1] Xen. *Resp. Lac.* XIII, 1. *Vide* p. 150, for further comment upon the *kreodaites*.
[2] Plut. *Lyc.* XXII; *Quaest. Conviv.* II, 5.
[3] *Resp. Lac.* XIII, 11.   [4] Thuc. V, 63.   [5] Xen. *Hell.* v, 3, 8.
[6] Diod. XIV, 79; Xen. *Hell.* III, 4, 20; IV, 1, 5, 30, 34.
[7] Arts., *s.v.*, by Martin in D.S. and by Oehler in P.W.

THE CAMP[1]

If the configuration of the ground allowed, the camp was circular in shape, unless its back was on a mountain or there was a river behind to protect it. The circular shape was most suitable, since if it was square, there would be useless space at the four corners. A curious passage in Xenophon's account says that during the day guards were posted close to the camp, not for the purpose of guarding against the approach of the enemy, which was provided for by cavalry vedettes, but to keep a watch on the camp and its inmates. We must suppose this was to prevent desertions or straying from the camp, absence without leave. Formerly anyone leaving the camp at night was watched by the Sciritai, who seem to have had the duty of night-guard allocated to them at first. But later this was taken over by any of the mercenary troops that happened to be with the Spartans. Evidently the Sciritai, by their valour, had earned for themselves relief from this troublesome task.

The position of the camp was changed frequently 'in order to do damage to their enemies and serve their friends', and also, we may suspect, because their somewhat primitive sanitary arrangements made a shift necessary. Athletic exercises were carried out every day,[2] 'and they thus acquire a finer appearance than they had before and a more manly air than other men'. These exercises were not more strenuous than were necessary to keep them fit, because, Plutarch[3] tells us, while on campaign the athletic requirements of their training were much modified 'so that they were the only people to whom war gave repose'. Wandering from the camp was strictly forbidden and no one was allowed on foot or on horseback to leave the place where his regiment was situated.[4]

---

[1] Xen. *Resp. Lac.* XII.　　　　[2] Cf. Herod. VII, 208.

[3] *Lyc.* XXII.

[4] *Resp. Lac.* XII, 5. δεῖ δὲ οὔτε περίπατον οὔτε δρόμον μάσσω ποιεῖσθαι ἢ ὅσον ἂν ἡ μόρα ἐφήκῃ, ὅπως μηδεὶς τῶν αὐτοῦ ὅπλων πόρρω γίγνηται. This curious, and possibly corrupt, passage has been a stumbling-block to all translators and commentators. Marchant (in Loeb ed.) renders it: 'Neither

'When the exercises are over, the senior polemarch orders the men to sit down. This serves as a review and then the order is given to take breakfast and soon afterwards to relieve the advance pickets. The men then amuse themselves and rest before the evening exercises. After these they are ordered to take supper, and when they have sung a hymn to the gods from whom they have had favourable omens when sacrificing, they may repose themselves on their arms.' Philochorus[1] adds that after the Spartans had overcome the Messenians through Tyrtaeus's leadership, they instituted the following custom in their military campaigns. When they had finished dinner and sung the hymn of thanksgiving (the paean), each one in turn had to sing something by Tyrtaeus; their polemarch acted as judge and awarded a prize of meat to the victor.

Xenophon[2] says that while in camp the soldiers were never permitted to be without their spears, a rule which was imposed 'for the same reason as led them to prohibit slaves from entering the camp'. This statement is not very clear, since Xenophon knew that large numbers of helots and 'slaves' followed the army as 'batmen' and doubtless as transport workers, labourers who dug trenches and put up stockades. Are we to conclude from this that these 'labour battalions' were never allowed inside the fortified camp? It hardly seems possible, since it is easy to imagine that an attack on these unfortunates, unarmed and unprotected, might be very serious to the Spartan warriors behind the stockades. We may perhaps surmise that what Xenophon means is that these slaves were only allowed inside the camp unarmed.

walk nor race course may exceed in length the space covered by the regiment, so that no one may get far away from his own arms.' This is far from illuminating, in fact it is unintelligible. Ollier (*La République des Lacédémoniens*) renders it: 'Mais on ne doit, ni en marchant, ni en courant, sortir de l'emplacement attribué à la *more* afin que personne ne s'éloigne de ses armes.' This at least makes sense.

[1] ap. Athen. XIV 630F.
[2] *Resp. Lac.* XII, 3. Cf. Libanius, *Orat. de serv.* II, p. 85.

EQUIPMENT

The heavy-armed hoplite had a short sword, so short indeed that many stories are related concerning it. 'A Spartan in answer to the inquiry "Why do you use short swords?" said "So that we may get close to the enemy".'[1] As a matter of fact this answer is perfectly correct. In close battle formation, a long sword would be useless once the spear had been dropped. Swordsmanship consisted in stabbing; slashing in the phalanx was impossible. His other equipment was a spear and probably, although we are not certain of it, the ξυήλη, a curved dagger worn as a side-arm. He also carried a large bronze shield. This was a cumbersome affair, designed to cover the body from shoulder to knee. It was suspended by a thong (τελαμών) from the neck and held by a handle fastened on the concave side.[2] Cleomenes III, in order to allow both hands free to grasp the longer pike he introduced, made the shield much lighter and less unwieldy, did away with the handle, and supported it entirely by the thong round the neck.[3] This was tantamount to abolishing the shield altogether and substituting a sort of cuirass. The clumsiness of these shields was so great that, once the line was broken, the hoplite was almost helplessly encumbered with this enormous covering. It is easy to understand that in a retreat or rout it was absolutely necessary to get rid of it. It bore on it a large Λ to denote Lacedaemonian, and possibly it also bore personal insignia painted on it, as Plutarch's[4] story of the man who had painted a 'life-size bee' on his would suggest. When some mockingly said that he had done this to escape being noticed, he said. 'Rather that I may be noticeable; for I come so close to the enemy that my emblem is seen by them in its true size'.

We are told that 'Lycurgus' ordained that a bright red tunic should be the distinguishing uniform of the soldier,

---

[1] *Apoph. Lac.* 232 E; also 217 E, 191 E.
[2] Aristoph. *Lys.* 107; *Equites*, 848.
[3] Plut. *Cleom.* 11.   [4] *Apoph. Lac.* 234 D.

'because such a dress had least resemblance to that of women and was well adapted for the field of battle, as it is soonest made splendid and is longest in growing soiled'.[1] It may be remarked that if the same Lycurgus had banished the dyer's art* from Sparta 'because it was a flattery of the senses'[2] these red coats must have been the only bit of colour in Sparta, which is rather hard to believe. In these tunics they were buried.[3] They also wore a large coarse cloak and single-soled shoes.[4]

FEAR IN SPARTAN CHARACTER

That the Spartans were courageous beyond all other peoples, and by such feats as that of Leonidas and his three hundred at Thermopylae gave to the world examples of devotion to duty and intrepidity in the face of certain death, has generally been accepted. That there was another side to their character, a far less courageous and admirable one, which shows them to have been a people full of fear, continually mistrustful of their own powers, and ready to collapse when things went against them, has not often been recognised. A careful appraisal of the facts leads Mr Preston H. Epps[5] to the conclusion that, in the last analysis, the whole elaborate system of statecraft and training of the Spartan citizen was designed to one end—the bolstering up of a naturally timorous people through a discipline which would make them able to withstand the frailty of human nature in the face of danger and death.

It is characteristic of a fearful people to distrust themselves and to trust the more in something external to save them—in some science, system or panacea the mechanics of which will inevitably bring unerring salvation. The prospect of powerful enemies will readily incline a fearful people to yield themselves to a military system, and the greater the fear, the more will they be prone to

---

[1] Xen. *Resp. Lac.* XI, 3; Aristoph. *Lys.* 1140; Schol. ad *Acharn.* 320.
[2] *Apoph. Lac.* 228 B.   [3] Plut. *Lyc.* XXVII.
[4] Demosth. *in Conon.* XXXIV.
[5] 'Fear in Spartan Character', *Class. Phil.* XXVIII (Jan. 1933), p. 12.

yield to a system even if its exactions be incredibly severe. More-over such a people are capable of much confidence as long as every-thing progresses as the system demands. But let any unexpected exigency arise and their innate fear reasserts itself with increased severity.

But however that may be, it is curious to note the many references to the fears that swayed the Spartans both in peace and war. Perhaps the most extraordinary incident of all was at the battle of Plataea, when the Spartans found themselves confronted with the Persians and insisted on changing places with the Athenians, who had fought the enemy at Marathon, since they were afraid of a foe they had never encountered before.[1] Once outside the Peloponnese they became so nervous that they were for ever scuttling back again. Immedi-ately after Plataea they returned to their own land.[2] Whenever they gained a victory they did the same.[3] Invasion of Sparta terrified them and they put up a poor resistance. The almost complete collapse of morale after Leuctra is astonishing. When Epaminondas was threatening the city, 'collaborationists' were found even among the pick of the younger warriors. Cornelius Nepos[4] tells a strange story of this which may, or may not, be true, for admittedly his evidence is none too trustworthy. After Leuctra, he says, some of the young men in panic wanted to go over to Epaminondas and so occupied a hill outside the city. Agesilaus, knowing how disastrous this would be, joined them with some of his own men, praising them for their wisdom in seizing the hill, and so infiltrated

[1] Herod. IX, 46. Grote's astonishment at this extraordinary manœuvre is boundless. 'No incident similar to this will be found throughout the whole course of Lacedaemonian history' (cap. 42). W. J. Woodhouse, in *J.H.S.* XVIII (1898), p. 44, totally rejects the whole story as being incredible and absurd. On the other hand, there seems no ground, other than our modern incredulity, to doubt the authenticity of the incident.

[2] Herod. IX, 77; Thuc. I, 89.

[3] Many instances: Thuc. I, 108, 114; Herod, VI, 81; VII, 148; Xen. *Hell.* IV, 4, 19; VII, 4, 20.

[4] *Ages.* XVII, 6. Polyaenus, *Strat.* II, 1, 14, tells very much the same story.

among them that the deserters did not dare go over to the Thebans. Whenever their carefully laid plans went wrong they flew into a panic, their curiously obstinate minds lacking the necessary resilience to snatch victory from defeat and unable to improvise a new plan to cope with an unexpected situation.

In the city of Sparta next to the *syssition* of the ephors they built a temple to Fear.[1]

> For they worship Fear, not as they do supernatural powers which they dread, esteeming it hurtful, but thinking their polity is chiefly kept up by fear.... The ancients, I think, did not imagine bravery to be plain fearlessness, but a cautious fear of blame and disgrace. For those that show most timidity towards the laws are most bold against their enemies, and those are least afraid of any danger who are most afraid of a just reproach.

Reflection upon these examples will induce a conclusion not quite so severe as that of Mr Epps. As Socrates[2] long ago recognised, the soldier in battle is kept steadfast by the support of his comrades, and his fear of an exhibition of cowardice which would be disgraceful and unendurable. The whole system of military discipline in every army has always been designed to the same end. The endless drillings, the subordination of the private soldier to his officers, the insistence upon implicit obedience, the sinking of the individuality of each to the spirit of the whole, are all calculated to create a habit of mind that will stand the test of the dangers of battle. The automatic and instant reaction of the normal human mind to a sudden danger is to run away. This instinctive prompting of human nature can only be overcome by a long course of discipline, fortified by traditions of glory, praise of valour and condemnation of cowardice. To say, therefore, that the whole way of life of the Spartan was designed solely to conquer an innate fearfulness peculiar to himself is hardly fair. It is surely a curious argument that will seek to prove that so notably

---

[1] Plut. *Cleom.* IX.   [2] *Phaedo*, 68 D.

warlike a people was, in actual fact, cowardly and timid. If the Spartans were not courageous in battle, who were?

The reluctance of the Spartans to venture outside of Sparta and their anxiety to get back again are certainly explainable, as Mr Epps quite fairly admits, on the ground of their peculiar situation at home, where they were for ever confronted with the helots on the look-out to profit by their masters' misfortunes and if possible to rise against them. With the whole of the Spartan first-line army away, the temptation to do so must have been very great, and it was imperative that the guardian army should be brought home as soon as possible. That they had 'one-track' minds, that could not quickly be readjusted to a new and startling situation has always been recognised. The Spartans were undoubtedly apt to fly into a panic; but there is no evidence to show that they did not rally. On the contrary, they pulled themselves together and acquitted themselves courageously.

THE *SCYTALE*

This famous means of conveying secret messages is explained by Aulus Gellius[1] as consisting of two sticks, one in the possession of the sender the other of the recipient. The sender twisted a strip of parchment round his stick writing his message thereon. The strip was then unwound and sent to the holder of the other stick who rewound it and the message appeared as originally written. The excessive simplicity of this form of cryptogram[2] and the ease with which by only a little experimenting the message could be reconstituted by anyone into whose hands it fell seems to have occurred to very few. As a matter of fact, was this the actual form of the *scytale*? J. H. Leopold,[3] in a thorough examination of the

---

[1] *Noct. Att.* XVII, 9.

[2] E.g. when the despatch announcing, in true 'laconic' style, the defeat of the Spartan fleet at Cynossema was captured, the Athenians readily deciphered it. Plut. *Alcib.* XXVIII.

[3] 'De Scytala Laconica', *Mnemosyne*, XXVIII (1900), pp. 365 ff. Numerous references: Thuc. I, 131; Plut. *Lys.* XIX; Aristoph. *Lys.* 991; Xen. *Hell.* III,

whole subject, concludes that it was not. Before an army left Sparta a stick with appropriate markings was split lengthwise, the halves being retained by the ephors and the general in the field respectively. The despatch, either oral or written, was then sent by messenger who carried half of the stick with him. On arrival the two halves were fitted together and served as the credential of the messenger. This explanation is far more reasonable than the other. We must credit the Spartans with intelligence in military affairs, in fact with a high degree of intelligence, and a childishly simple means of transmitting messages which rendered these liable to be deciphered with ease if they fell into the hands of the enemy would hardly appeal to them.

THE SPARTAN NAVY[1]

We have already given reason to suppose that in the 'golden age' the Spartans were, if not a sea-going people, at least not averse from the sea. The various references in the poems of Alcman give unmistakable evidence of that.[2] From various events it is safe to say that the Spartans either possessed ships before the Persian wars or perhaps hired them. We have, for instance, the colonisation of Tarentum, the expedition of Dorieus to Sicily and Libya and the assault upon Samos at the time of the tyranny of Polycrates. Probably, however, their naval establishment was not then organised as it was later.

3, 8; Arist. frag. 466; Schol. ad Pind. *Ol.* vi, 154. The use of tallies for identification and as receipts for money paid was widespread and not finally abandoned in exchequer accounts in England until 1826; *vide* art. 'Tally' in *Encyclop. Britannica.*

[1] Busolt-Swoboda, *Griech. Staatsk.* ii, p. 714; Beloch, 'Die Nauarchie in Sparta', *Rhein. Mus.* xxxiv (1879), p. 117; Bauer, 'Die spart. Nauarchen', *Wiener Studien* (1910), p. 226; Pareti, 'Ricerche sulla potenza maritima degli Spartani', *Memorie d. Accad. d. scienze di Torino,* 59, p. 71; Solari, *Ricerche Spartane,* pp. 1, 231; art. 'Nauarchos' in P.W. by Kiessling; 'Navarchus' in D.S. by Martin; Brownson, 'The succession of Spartan nauarchs in *Hellen.* i', *Trans. Am. Philol. Ass.* xxxiv (1903), p. 33; B. Fleischanderl, *Die spart. Verfass. bei Xen.* p. 56 (all refs. in Xen. cited); Kahrstedt, *Griech. Staatsr.* p. 319. [2] *Supra* p. 15.

With greater cares at home and their unending preoccupation with the helot problem, it is clear that they turned deliberately from any sea-going activities and became almost exclusively a land power. Plutarch[1] says that at first they forbade their people to be sailors, but later made themselves masters of the sea. Later again, observing the deterioration of morale which came from mixing with other peoples, they reimposed the prohibition, but still later they changed about again. It is not easy to relate these statements to the known facts of Spartan history. We can only suppose that the prohibition in the first instance came after the change-over in Spartan policy after the Messenian revolt, and that the reference to making themselves 'masters of the sea' has to do with the defeat of the Athenians in the last stage of the Peloponnesian war. The last two changes do not admit of any certain identification.

In any case it is safe to say that there never was at any time a Spartan navy of any significant size. At the battle of Artemisium there were only ten Spartan ships,[2] at Salamis sixteen.[3] In 478 Pausanias had twenty.[4] In 413 they built twenty-five for the Decelean war.[5] At Arginusae they had ten ships.[6] For such naval operations as they undertook, they invariably relied on their allies to supply the ships, their own squadrons were always inconsiderable. So far as is known they had only one shipyard of their own, that at Gythium, and such ships as they possessed themselves were probably mostly built in allies' yards. The squadrons with which they opposed the Athenians in the last phase of the war in the Hellespont were built with Persian supplies of timber from Asia Minor in the dockyards at Antandros[7] and were paid for with Persian money. Spartans did not take kindly to the sea. Their sailors were *perioeci*; their rowers helots or hired foreigners;[8] the Spartans themselves fought in the ships.

[1] *Inst. Lac.* 239 E.　　[2] Herod. VIII, 1.
[3] *Ibid.* 43.　　　　　[4] Thuc. I, 94.
[5] *Ibid.* VIII, 3.　　　[6] Xen. *Hell.* I, 6, 34.
[7] *Ibid.* I, 24.　　　　[8] *Ibid.* VII, 1, 12.

Whether or not the outfitting of a warship was imposed upon a rich man according to the Athenian custom of the trierarchy is uncertain. We do not know if 'liturgies' were practised although, as noticed elsewhere,[1] there seems evidence, doubtful though it is, that wealthy men paid for the cavalry, or at least provided the horses. But whether these contributions in money were imposed or not, we know that captains of ships, trierarchs, were appointed, and that these invariably were Spartans or *perioeci*.[2] As the Spartan captains certainly were not sailors they had a skilled 'steersman' (κυβερνήτης) or rather, navigating officer, who held a highly important post and one of great distinction. Hermon, the 'steersman' of Lysander's ship, had a statue in his honour put up to him at Delphi.[3] The *keleustes* or boatswain was in command of the rowers and called the time for the oars. In a particularly spirited action in 388,[4] Gorgopas, the Spartan commander, attacked an Athenian squadron off Cape Zoster creeping up on them in the dark with muffled oars, the boatswain giving the time to the rowers not, as usually, with his voice but by clinking stones together. A term which has puzzled all commentators and of which the meaning is admittedly not perfectly clear, at least as applied to the Spartan navy, is πρωτόπλοι.[5] This can only mean 'the vanguard' and probably, if not certainly, was a ship, or perhaps several ships, that led the way in navigating or in attack. As the other ships of the squadron would follow its lead, naturally a first-class sailor would have to be in command.

And lastly, there was attached to the admiral's ship an auxiliary craft[6] (ὑπηρετικὸς κέλης). Evidently this was a despatch boat, but there are no further details available.

The Spartans themselves were poor sailors and made no pretence to be anything else than soldiers. But they certainly

---

[1] *Vide* p. 260.

[2] Xen. *Hell.* II, 1, 12; VII, 1, 12; Thuc. IV, 11, 4. They were not as in Athens, the persons who paid for the fitting-out of the ships.

[3] Paus. X, 9, 7.

[4] Xen. *Hell.* V, 1, 8.

[5] *Ibid.* V, 1, 27.

[6] *Ibid.* I, 6, 36.

were able to command the services of skilled navigators. The dash of Mindarus from Miletus to the Hellespont, as recorded by Thucydides,[1] was a spirited bit of work. High pay, the money being provided by the Persians in the closing years of the Peloponnesian war, enabled them to hire the best rowers and seamen[2] and, although beaten over and over again by the superb Athenian navies, they won out in the end through the astounding carelessness of the Athenians at Aegospotami.

THE NAUARCH

The most important consideration for the historian of their naval system is the character and mode of appointment of the admiral or nauarch and his lieutenants. Evidently during the era of the Persian wars the nauarchia was a royal office. Possibly, but far from certainly, if one king was in the field as leader of the army, the other was with the fleet. King Leotychidas fought at Mycale in 479, Pausanias with the fleet liberated the Greeks on the coasts of Asia Minor in 478. Eurybiades, the admiral at Artemisium and Salamis, was not of either of the royal houses and was evidently an exception, as Herodotus is careful to mention.[3] We must conclude that the position of nauarch was not a regular one in the Spartan war establishment, and that an appointment was made only for a particular emergency. There is no record of nauarchs from 477 to 430 and, curiously, none from 426 to 413. This is the more extraordinary when we reflect that this latter period covered the greater part of the Peloponnesian war, and we should naturally expect that nauarchs would have been regularly appointed. Either the records are missing or none was appointed.

By 430 the prerogative of the kings to assume the office or appoint the nauarch had evidently been usurped by the ephors; if we interpret correctly the reference to the appointment of Cnemus 'by the Lacedaemonians'.[4] In 395 Agesilaus, in his

---

[1] VIII, 99 ff. [2] Plut. *Alc.* xxxv, 4.
[3] Herod. VIII, 42. [4] Thuc. II, 66, 80.

eastern campaign was specially appointed nauarch, being the first Spartan king, we are told, to hold the office of commander-in-chief of both army and navy.[1] Agesilaus thereupon nominated successively to the command two relatives, the first year Pisander[2] and next year Teleutias.[3] Pisander was his brother-in-law 'a man of ambition and great natural abilities, but too little skilled in the proper management of a fleet'. Teleutias was brother of Agesilaus and seems to have been more successful. Possibly he made them acting nauarchs, retaining the office of supreme commander himself.

Appointment was for one year[4] and could not be extended for a second term. That this was so is apparent from the fact that when Lysander had completed his year of office he was appointed second in command or *epistoleus* to Aracus 'for it is not lawful with them for the same man to be admiral twice'. Aracus was, however, merely a figurehead and Lysander still exercised full powers.[5] These powers were very extensive, indeed they were so great that Aristotle[6] disapproves.

Other persons have censured his [Lycurgus'] laws concerning naval affairs and not without reason, as it gives rise to disputes. For the commander of the fleet is in a manner set up in opposition to the kings who are generals of the army for life.

It may be remarked that this criticism is hardly just. It was manifestly impossible for the nauarch to be under the orders of the king in the field when he was absent on a distant expedition. It does, however, afford additional evidence that

[1] Plut. *Ages.* x.   [2] Xen. *Hell.* III, 4, 29; Plut. *Ages.* x.
[3] Xen. *Hell.* IV, 4, 19.
[4] Cf. Beloch, *loc. cit.* p. 119. But, for the view that the appointment was held for the duration of a campaign, cf. Solari, *Ric. Spart.* p. 8. C. L. Brownson, 'The succession of Spartan nauarchs in *Hellen.* I,' *Am. Philol. Ass.* XXXIV (1903), pp. 33 f., agrees with Beloch that the tenure of office was annual.
[5] Xen. *Hell.* II, 1, 7; Plut. *Lys.* VII. The case of Teleutias is a difficult one to decide. Apparently he was appointed nauarch three times. Cf. Xen. *Hell.* IV, 4, 19; V, 1, 2; VIII, 2, 3. But very uncertain. Cf. Kahrstedt, *Griech. Staatsr.* p. 161.   [6] *Pol.* 1271 A.

the ephors had usurped the powers of the kings in the appointment and control of the nauarch.

As being commander-in-chief of the navy and sole representative of Sparta in distant waters, his powers were considerable. His task was to keep the allies faithful—by no means an easy one—to punish those who rebelled, and to make truces and treaties. The case of Antalcidas who negotiated the momentous treaty of 387 is very apposite in this connection. He was nauarch, and a singularly successful one, as his manœuvres against the Athenians testify; but he also seems to have exercised specific diplomatic functions. In any case he could not conclude a regular peace on his own authority, and later the treaty was ratified by a special assembly of the Spartans and their allies.[1]

At the end of his term the nauarch was required to give account of his actions to the ephors. Pasippidas got into serious trouble and was banished from Sparta,[2] and Lysander, through the treachery of Pharnabazus, was in great peril when he returned to Sparta.[3] To keep some control over the nauarch the ephors sent political 'commissars' to keep an eye on him.[4] Were his conduct of a campaign unsatisfactory to the government in Sparta the nauarch could be recalled, as was Astyochus after he had served for eight months,[5] and Ecdicus who was superseded by Teleutias and sent back to Sparta.[6]

The *epistoleus*[7] or *epistoliaphorus*[8] must, as the name implies, have been originally the secretary or despatch-bearer of the nauarch. Later he was the second in command, or chief of the naval staff. In certain cases, if not in all, there were two appointed to the nauarch during his year of office, a senior

---

[1] Diod. xiv, 110. Agesilaus was careful to deny his ability to make peace, a power which belonged exclusively to the Lacedaemonians. Plut. *Ages.* x.

[2] Xen. *Hell.* i, 1, 32.   [3] Plut. *Lys.* xx.

[4] Thuc. ii, 85; iii, 69, 76; viii, 39.

[5] *Ibid.* viii, 39.

[6] Xen. *Hell.* iv, 8, 23; Diod. xiv, 79, 97.

[7] Xen. *Hell.* i, 1, 23.   [8] *Ibid.* vi, 2, 25.

and a junior.[1] Should the nauarch die or be killed in action the *epistoleus* took over his duties until a new nauarch was appointed and arrived with the fleet, as when Hippocrates carried on after the death of Mindarus. Apparently the senior *epistoleus* did not succeed to the office of nauarch by right. We have no information as to the length of term of his office although it is natural to suppose that it was also for one year. The fact, however, that he carried on after the death or departure of the nauarch seems to suggest that his term of office was of indefinite length. The point is, however, incapable of exact proof.

The naval base was at the port of Gythium, where were the dockyard and arsenal.[2] Situated twenty-seven miles from Sparta on a small plain enclosed by hills and sea, the place must have been very small since the harbour, of which no trace remains, was evidently constructed by human labour, as Strabo quite correctly asserts.[3] As a shipbuilding and repairing dockyard, its facilities must have been negligible in comparison with the first-class installations at Piraeus. All traces of the ancient dockyard are lost.

[1] E.g. Hippocrates and Philippus for Mindarus, Thuc. VIII, 99; Hippocrates was the senior. Clearchus and Eteonicus for Callicratidas, Diod. XIII, 98, 2. When Podanemus the nauarch was killed and Pollis the second in command wounded, Herippidas, who was evidently the junior *epistoleus*, took over. Xen. *Hell.* IV, 8, 11.

[2] Diod. XI, 84; Paus. I, 27, 5; Thuc. I, 108. Cf. Frazer's description of Gythium in his ed. of Pausanias, III, p. 376.

[3] Strabo, VIII, 5, 2 (C. 363).

CHAPTER IX

THE PUBLIC MEALS

Almost the most celebrated custom of the Spartans was their practice of eating together in public messes.[1] As a matter of fact, as will be seen later, this was by no means peculiar to them and was found in a number of other places as well. Certainly it was of very ancient origin and most probably was part of the customs of the early Doric race,[2] which on its march to conquer a new home would naturally fall into the habit of military messes as is inevitable in all armies. In any case it seems undoubted that they had a military origin and retained that character for centuries. We hear of the Homeric heroes messing together, both in the field and in peace-time in the halls of the kings,[3] and we are reminded of the Vikings dining together in the royal palaces. But although the custom was certainly not unique to the Spartans, yet there were some features of peculiar interest which call for particular attention and have exercised the ingenuity of all commentators.

The Spartans themselves of course attributed, quite erroneously, the foundation of these messes to Lycurgus, who made a law:

That they should all eat in common, of the same bread and meat of specified kinds, and should not spend their lives at home, laid on costly couches at splendid tables, delivering themselves up into the hands of their tradesmen and cooks, to fatten them in corners, like greedy brutes, and to ruin not their minds only but their very

---

[1] Every writer has commented upon them. Although old, the best and most detailed examination is still that of Bielschowsky, *De Spartanorum Syssitiis*.

[2] Müller, *Doric Race*, pp. 260f., 283.

[3] Numerous refs., e.g. *Il.* XI, 257; XVII, 248; *Od.* IV, 621; XI, 184. *Vide* Finsler, *Neue Jahrbücher für d. klassische Altertum*, XVII (1906), pp. 313ff., for full discussion of the Homeric parallels. Also Poehlmann, *Gesch. d. soz. Frage*, pp. 46ff.

bodies which, enfeebled by indulgence and excess, would stand in need of long sleep, warm bathing, freedom from work, and, in a word, of as much care and attendance as if they were continually sick.[1]

'It was certainly an extraordinary thing to have brought about such a result as this', Plutarch, with perfect justice, remarks. 'For, as Theophrastus observes, he had taken away from wealth not merely the property of being coveted, but its very nature of being wealth.'

The name *syssition* was generally applied to them but the older name was *andreion*, or gathering of men, *cenae virorum*, by which they were known in Crete, where the custom also obtained.[2] The Spartans themselves called them *pheidition*, *phidition*,[3] or *philition*.[4] It is not improbable that the last is the more correct name as denoting love feast and that *pheidition*, derived from φείδομαι, 'to be sparing', was applied to them more or less jokingly.[5] Xenophon, in several places in his *Government of the Lacedaemonians*,[6] calls them *syskeniae*, i.e. mess-tent gatherings. Obviously they went by several names, and it is unnecessary to try and arrive at any conclusion as to which was the most correct. There seems to be little doubt that originally the *syssition* was a military mess in which the members met 'under arms' and that the fifteen members formed a half company in the Spartan army. Later, however, this purely military character was lost, since men over military age belonged, and the *syssition* as a military unit was abandoned. It must be admitted, however, that Xenophon uses the word *syskenia* in no military sense whatever, in which he seems to be following Critias, who regarded them simply as social gatherings. The point is somewhat obscure and is discussed more fully hereafter.

---

[1] Plut. *Lyc.* x.　　　　　　　　[2] Arist. *Pol.* 1272 A.

[3] Arist. *ut supra*; Athen. v, 186 B; Xen. *Resp. Lac.* III, 5, 5; *Hell.* v, 4, 28; Dio Chrys. *De regno*, LXXXVII; Cicero, *Tusc. Disp.* v, 34.

[4] *Lyc.* XII.

[5] Bielschowsky, *De Spart. Syss.* p. 12.

[6] *Resp. Lac.* v, 2; also VII, 4; IX, 4; XIII, 7; XV, 5.

The Spartan boy when he left home was enrolled in a junior mess. It seems practically certain that the boys messed together under the supervision of their eirens. Xenophon[1] says Lycurgus introduced 'mixed companies', so that boys should hear the improving conversation of their elders. We must suppose the boys were allowed in after dinner was finished. We have no details about how these junior *syssitia* were provisioned; but it seems likely, as will be seen hereafter,[2] that the contributions made to the commissariat every month by the adult occupier of a *cleros* were designed to cover the requirements of the *syssitia* and the boys' messes. At the age of twenty[3] the Spartan youth became a candidate for membership in a senior *syssition*. Election, we are told by Plutarch,[4] was by unanimous vote, one 'black ball' being sufficient to disqualify him. The method of voting was simple and effective:

Each man in the company took a little ball of soft bread which he threw into a deep basin which a slave carried round on his head. Those that were in favour of the candidate's election dropped their ball into the basin without altering its shape, but those who disliked him pressed the ball flat between their fingers to signify a negative vote. If there was only one such flattened piece in the basin the candidate was rejected, so anxious were they that all members of the gathering should be agreeable to each other. The basin was called *caddichus* and rejected candidates were called by a name derived therefrom.

That there was a waiting list of young men, and that it was difficult to obtain admission, as Mr Toynbee has supposed,[5] seems a trifle unlikely in view of the steadily diminishing numbers of Spartans. We should rather expect keen competition among the various *syssitia* to obtain new members, whose contributions to the common larder would be acceptable.

[1] *Resp. Lac.* v, 5.   [2] *Vide infra*, p. 288.
[3] Doubtful; possibly at twenty-four when he entered the class of *sphaireis*. Bielschowsky, *De Spart. Syss.* p. 14, concludes that he became eligible at twenty.   [4] *Lyc.* XII.
[5] *J.H.S.* XXXIII (1913), p. 261. A comparison of the *syssition* with a college fraternity is amusing.

Presumably, although it is impossible to be sure, the Spartan *homoios* only ate dinner at his *syssition*, other meals were taken at home. Certainly we may suppose that the frugal breakfast—bread dipped in wine (ἀκράτισμα)—was eaten at home. We have no information with regard to lunch (ἄριστον): this was a substantial meal and he may have eaten it at his mess. The only meal we are sure of was the dinner (δεῖπνον, in Sparta called αἶκλον[1]) and that certainly was eaten in the mess, which, as time went on and as the warlike spirit of the Spartans diminished, became an exclusive dining club and totally lost its primitive warlike character.

Attendance every day was compulsory upon everyone from the highest to the lowest among the Spartan peers. In early times, we are told, the kings were allowed to dine in their own homes, when their rations were sent to them.[2] In this connection there is a significant incident which merits careful attention. It is related by Plutarch[3] that King Agis, on his return to Sparta 'after having conquered the Athenians', wanted to dine at home and sent to his *syssition* for his rations, as he had every right to do. The polemarchs refused to send them and Agis was so angry that next day he refused to offer the sacrifice usual upon the completion of a successful campaign, and was promptly fined by the ephors. It is evident from this that the *syssitia*, being military messes, were under the control of the polemarchs, not of the ephors. Agis was fined, not for refusing to go to his *syssition*, but for failing in his priestly duties, and in this he came into collision with the ephors. As commander-in-chief he could not have been punished by the polemarchs, who were his subordinate officers.

That the *syssition* contained fifteen or 'about fifteen' members, as Plutarch[4] says, seems to be fairly certain. It is true that a scholiast on a pertinent passage in Plato's *Laws*[5] says there were ten. But this may be rejected as extremely

---

[1] Polemon, ap. Athen. IV, 140 C.
[2] Herod. VI, 57.   [3] *Lyc.* XII.
[4] *Ibid.*   [5] Schol. ad *Legg.* 633 A.

unlikely. Bielschowsky,[1] who is nothing if not bold in his emendations, considers this a copyist's error of δέκα for πεντεκαίδεκα. Ringnalda,[2] however, says that 'undoubtedly' the number ten was taken from Xenophon's *Government of the Lacedaemonians*[3] where it is mentioned that on campaign 'the polemarchs pitch their tents close by the king, that being always at hand they may the better take counsel with him if they require to do so. Three others also of the equally privileged citizens pitch their tents with him'. Since there were six polemarchs this makes up the number ten. It is to be noted, however, that later on[4] Xenophon says that two *Pythii* also shared the king's quarters. This would make the number twelve, and we must reject the number ten as quite impossible and merely suppose that the scholiast made a mistake. We may reasonably infer that when not in the field the same arrangements of membership were carried on. The kings belonged to what might be called the royal *syssition*, to which the polemarchs and other high officials belonged. The incident of Agis just referred to is sufficient to prove that. We also know that the ephors messed together. When Cleomenes murdered four out of the five of them we are told they were at dinner in their own *syssition*.[5] We have no idea whether there were ten other members who also belonged to this mess. It is not unreasonable to conjecture that the lesser magistrates dined with them. But it is equally possible that the ephors desired privacy and nobody else was admitted. The dinner table is always a favourite place for discussion and it is not hard to imagine that they talked of policy and political problems in secrecy and comfort, a practice of which Cleomenes was very well aware.

Nilsson[6] has made the interesting suggestion that the otherwise rather mysterious official, the κρεοδαίτης, was the

[1] *De Spart. Syss.* p. 15, ι′ for ιε′. [2] *De exerc. Laced.* p. 6.
[3] *Resp. Lac.* XIII, 1. [4] XV, 5.
[5] Plut. *Cleom.* VIII.
[6] *Klio*, XII, p. 317. Mr Nilsson cites Pollux, VI, 34, and Plut. *Quaest. Conviv.* 644 B; but quite uncertain.

mess-president and had the duty of apportioning the shares of meat and, no doubt, of dessert. This is certainly possible, but lacks direct confirmation.

Excuses for non-attendance of ordinary members were strictly limited to sickness, absence on hunting expeditions, or attendance at a public sacrifice.[1] On feast days during the great public festivals the *syssitia* were not held. At the great feast of the Cleaver the Spartans dined at home, when they entertained strangers and slaves.[2] That strangers were regularly admitted to a *syssition* is doubtful, in view of the privacy in which they were conducted. But that sometimes they were invited seems indicated by several references. For instance, we hear of a Sybarite visiting one, and of his disgust at the plain fare he found there.[3] Alcibiades evidently was made a regular member.[4] We are told also that Hecateus[5] enjoyed the same privilege, coupled with the amusing information that he was found fault with for not speaking during the meal. Perhaps his feelings were too much for him. But since strangers were rare in Sparta we may safely suppose that their visits were not frequent. Distinguished visitors, such as ambassadors, were specially provided for in the kings' mess.[6]

SYSSITIA IN OTHER COUNTRIES

Exactly similar messes were the custom in Crete,[7] from which the Spartans may have derived theirs. They were also found in Miletus and Thurii,[8] Megara,[9] Thebes,[10] Oenotria,[11] Carthage (according to Aristotle),[12] and on the island of Lipara.[13] In his description of the communistic practices of the sect of the Essenes, Philo-Judaeus[14] uses the word *syssition* to denote the common meals of the sectaries. Possibly a relic

---

[1] Plut. *Lyc.* XII.
[2] Athen. IV, 139.
[3] Athen. IV, 138D.
[4] Plut. *Alcib.* XXIII.
[5] Plut. *Lyc.* XX; *Apoph. Lac.* 218B.
[6] Xen. *Resp. Lac.* XV, 4.
[7] Arist. *Pol.* 1272A.
[8] Plato, *Legg.* 636.
[9] Theognis, CCCIX.
[10] Polyaenus, II, 3, 11.
[11] Arist. *Pol.* 1329B.
[12] *Ibid.* 1272A.
[13] Diod. Sic. V, 9, 4.
[14] *Quod omnis. probus,* XII, 86 (458).

of the practice may be seen in the *agape* or love-feast of the early Christians. Nor is the custom of the men of a tribe messing together unknown at the present day. Mr H. J. Rose[1] has pointed out the analogy of the 'bachelors' house' which is still the rule in many of the Pacific Islands, and in Africa the young Masai warriors live together until marriage.

Whether the Spartans held their gatherings in tents or permanent structures is uncertain. Since the *syssition* numbered about fifteen members more or less, it is not impossible that a moderately sized tent would have served, which perhaps they took with them when campaigning. But it is a little difficult to suppose that tents would have served during times of peace, when serious deterioration would have ensued over protracted periods and permanent structures would have been necessary. What happened when the army was mobilised and those members of *syssitia* who were on the active list left, we do not know. Since they probably took the cooks with them, or as many as were necessary, perhaps the regular *syssitia* were suspended or several were combined.

It is practically certain that the place of meeting was a large open space by the side of the Hyacinthine way. The evidence of Demetrius of Scepsis[2] and of Pausanias[3] supports this very strongly. Pausanias says he saw the tomb of Tisamenus 'in the place where the Spartans eat their meals'.

UPKEEP OF THE *SYSSITIA*

The expenses of the kings' messing were defrayed by the public exchequer,[4] but other members were bound to make regular monthly contributions. According to Plutarch,[5] who gives Attic measures, these consisted of 1½ *medimni* of barley

[1] *Primitive Culture in Greece*, p. 122.
[2] Athen. IV, 173 F; cf. II, 39 C.
[3] VII, 1, 8. Bielschowsky, *De Spart. Syss.* p. 22, hesitates to accept this identification and leaves the place of meeting unknown.
[4] Xen. *Resp. Lac.* XV, 4.
[5] *Lyc.* XII. Also dates, according to Schol. ad Plato, *Legg.* I, 223.

meal, 11 or 12 *choes* of wine, a certain weight of cheese and figs, and ten Acginetan obols in money for the purchase of meat. According to Dicaearchus,[1] who gives Spartan measures, it was a *medimnus* of barley meal, 8 *choes* of wine, 5 minas of cheese, 2½ minas of figs and a small sum of money. The Attic *medimnus* contained approximately 1½ bushels,[2] and therefore the contribution of barley meal amounted to 2¼ bushels a month, or 27 bushels a year. We know that the daily ration of a Spartan soldier in the field was 2 *choinices* of barley meal a day,[3] and that was a liberal allowance as befitting men engaged in hard physical exertion. There were 48 *choinices* to the *medimnus*, and a *choinix* was equal almost precisely to one quart. If each member of the *syssition* was allowed the same amount as a field ration, he would consume 730 *choinices* a year. But his contribution amounted to 864, and it is quite apparent that there was a surplus of something like 134 *choinices* over and above what was necessary for his own upkeep. To what use was this surplus put? We can only suppose that it went to a central distributing warehouse for what may be called the 'junior *syssitia*' for boys;[4] or perhaps each adult mess had a junior one attached to it and the same kitchen served both. Some such explanation is clearly necessary to account for the very large contribution of meal, far more than was adequate for individual needs.

The same difficulty is found in the amount of wine contributed by each member, which amounted to 12 *choes* or 144 cotyles a month, which were equal to about 9 gallons. His annual contribution therefore amounted to 1728 cotyles or

---

[1] ap. Athen. IV, 141.

[2] The equation of Greek measures with modern is beset with almost insuperable difficulties. F. Hultsch, *Griech. u. röm. Metrologie*, pp. 99 ff. makes the Attic *medimnus* equal 52–53 litres. O. Viedebantt, in art. 'Medimnos' in P.W. makes it equal 40·93 litres. For further on this by the same author cf. 'Die athenischen Hohlmasse' in *Festschrift für Aug. Oxe*. (Darmstadt, 1938), pp. 135 ff.

[3] Thuc. IV, 16; cf. Herod. VII, 187; Diog. Laert. VIII, 18.

[4] Kahrstedt, 'Die spart. Agrarwirtschaft', *Hermes*, LIV (1919), p. 284.

108 gallons. Herodotus[1] tells us that the kings got a double portion of 2 cotyles a day, if they dined at the mess. Obviously, therefore, the daily ration of the ordinary member must have been one cotyle, half a pint, or 365 per annum at the time when Herodotus wrote. We are left with the enormous surplus of 1363 cotyles a year unaccounted for. The allowance was doubled later, as Thucydides[2] tells us that the Spartan prisoners captured at Sphacteria were allowed a daily ration of two cotyles or a pint.

Phylarchus,[3] in his description of the entertainment offered his guests by King Cleomenes III, is anxious to emphasize the strict moderation exercised. A silver bowl holding 2 cotyles of wine was placed on the tripod by each guest. Evidently that was the amount allotted to him for dinner. The servant filled the goblet of the diner with a ladle that presumably contained a *cyathos* which, in Attic measure at least, was about one-twelfth of a pint; 'but no drink was offered unless someone asked for it'. Critias, in his *Elegies* and again in his *Constitution of the Lacedaemonians*,[4] is enthusiastic over the strict moderation of the Spartans in their drinking, very different from the vicious practice in other countries of passing the bowl round from hand to hand (always passing, he is careful to say, from left to right), from which each guest is in honour bound to drink, a custom which leads to drunkenness and depravity. This custom we are told by Plutarch[5] was strictly forbidden by Agesilaus as a bad foreign habit that must not be allowed to corrupt the sober Spartans.[6]

---

[1] Herod. VI, 57.   [2] IV, 16.

[3] ap. Athen. IV, 142 D. The passage is somewhat obscure but the above seems to be the best explanation. It must be acknowledged, however, that this hardly agrees with Athen. X, 432 D, where it is said that jugs of wine were placed on the table for anyone to help himself when thirsty. *Vide* on this passage Mueller-Struebing, *Neue Jahrbücher für Philologie* (1878), p. 471.

[4] ap. Athen. X. 432 D ff.; XI, 463 E.   [5] *Apoph. Lac.* 208, 73.

[6] Mueller-Struebing, *loc. cit.* p. 471; K. Kircher, *Sakrale Bedeutung d. Weines im Altertum*, pp. 59 ff.

Bielschowsky[1] accuses the Spartans of heavy drinking if each member of the mess consumed the whole amount of his contribution every month. This seems unnecessary as the evidence of the small daily ration is quite clear. Sobriety was insisted on, at least in the best days of the system, although perhaps in their degenerate days the excellent precepts were departed from. If their elders were restricted to a small amount of wine, much more so were the juniors and we are told that what they had was liberally mixed with water.[2] It is probable that Plutarch has exaggerated his figures, those of Herodotus and Thucydides appear much more reliable. Otherwise the disposition of the surplus contributed by each member remains unexplained.

We are left to infer that the wine was not particularly palatable from the somewhat pert remark of Gorgo, daughter of King Cleomenes. When her father told her that someone had showed him how to make the wine taste good, she said, 'Then, father, there will be more wine drunk, and the drinkers will become more intemperate and depraved'.[3] Evidently the strict sobriety of the Spartans at their meals did not extend to their guests, as the story of the disgusting behaviour of the Chians shows. Having got very drunk when entertained at the *ephoreion* they vomited over the seats of the ephors. Having satisfied themselves that no Spartans were involved in this scandalous scene, the ephors proclaimed that the Spartans granted permission to the Chians to be filthy.[4]

The district of Deuthiades was celebrated for wine-making, and Leake tells us that in his time it was still produced there.[5] Strabo[6] says that the wine of Carystus was celebrated by Alcman. Possibly the name of the river Oenus betokens a wine-producing locality.

---

[1] *De Spart. Syss.* p. 26.   [2] Xen. *Resp. Lac.* I, 2.

[3] *Apoph. Lac.* 240 D. But the same story is told of King Archidamus. *Apoph. Lac.* 218 D.

[4] Plut. *Apoph. Lac.* 232 F. But Aelian, *V.H.* II, 15, tells the same story of the Clazomenians.

[5] *Travels in the Morea*, II, p. 532.   [6] X, 1, 6 (C. 446).

The monthly contribution of cheese weighed 5 minas and of figs 2½. A mina weighed about 15¼ oz. The annual contribution of cheese, therefore, amounted to a trifle over 57 lb. and the daily ration was about 2¾ oz. while the ration of figs was half that. This is so small an amount that we are left in doubt once more as to the accuracy of Plutarch's figures. If the meal and wine were in such abundance, why were the cheese and figs so restricted? Figs might be regarded as a luxury, but cheese could hardly come under that head. Evidently the juniors got none from their seniors, and we are left to surmise that these were the dainties that the boys had to steal if they wanted them.

The monthly dues of ten Aeginetan obols provide another puzzle. Where did this money come from, and how did a Spartan in good standing become possessed of it, when we are told that, according to the 'Lycurgan' discipline, the use of money, other than that of iron, was strictly forbidden? Of course the answer is that the use of money was never forbidden in Sparta and that the so-called 'iron money' was seldom employed. Sparta did not mint its own coins until very late, therefore foreign money was used.[1] But however that may be, there was a money payment, and we can only suppose that this fund was expended on the purchase of meat, from which was made the famous 'black broth', variously called βάφα or αἱμάτια or μέλας ζωμός. This was made of pork, cooked in blood and seasoned with salt and vinegar.[2] Plutarch[3] tells the improving story of a king of Pontus who was curious to taste this famous dish of which he had heard so much. He procured a Spartan cook to make it for him and on tasting it found it extremely bad. The cook, on observing his displeasure, said: 'Sir, to enjoy this broth you should have bathed first in the river Eurotas.' It must have taken all the resolution at his command for Alcibiades to eat and pretend to enjoy so strange a dish. No doubt it was an acquired taste, because we are told

---

[1] The point is discussed at length hereafter; vide p. 302.
[2] Plut. De san. praec. 128 C. Cf. De esu carnis, 995 B; Pollux, VI, 57; Plut. Lyc. XII.   [3] Lyc. XII.

that the older men were so fond of it that they ate nothing else, leaving what meat there was to the younger.[1]

Dicaearchus[2] gives us the following account of the meal which is interesting enough to quote in full.

> The dinner is at first served separately to each member, and there is no sharing of any kind with one's neighbour. Afterwards there is a barley cake as large as each desires, and for drinking again a cup is set beside him to use whenever he is thirsty. The same meat dish is given to all on every occasion, a piece of boiled pork; sometimes, however, not even so much as that is served, beyond a small bit of meat weighing not over a quarter of a pound. Besides this there is nothing whatsoever, except of course the broth made from this meat, enough to go round among the entire company throughout the whole dinner; there may possibly be an olive or a cheese or a fig, or they may even get something especially added, a fish or a hare or a ring-dove or something similar. Afterwards, when they have finished their dinner in haste, there are passed round the so-called *epaikla*....Sphaerus, in the third book of his *Spartan State*, writes: The members of the mess also contribute *epaikla* to them. Sometimes the common people bring whatever is caught in the chase; but the rich contribute wheat bread and anything from the fields which the season permits, in quantities sufficient for the one meeting alone, because they believe that to provide more than is enough is uncalled for, if the food is not going to be eaten.

With regard to these extra contributions (παράλογα)[3] there is some difference of opinion. Liddell and Scott, *s.v.*, define them as 'the over-portions of food given to guests which were not to be reckoned upon'. This explanation is not impossible and may indeed be correct. If guests were expected, it became necessary to have an increased supply of food ready for them.

---

[1] Neumann, *Hist. Ztschr.* xcvi (1906), p. 46, remarks that the military character of the *syssition* is shown in the fare provided which was pretty good field-kitchen cooking. If they wanted more, there was no objection to their providing it at their own expense.

[2] ap. Athen. iv, 131. Cf. Xen. *Resp. Lac.* v, 2.

[3] Xen. *Resp. Lac.* v, 3.

It seems, however, that generally these extra contributions were made by the members for the benefit of the mess generally and were not specially designed to provide for guests; although they certainly would be useful if any were present. A curious phrase in Xenophon seems to indicate that the richer members added a contribution of bread (ἄρτον ἀντιπαραβάλλουσι) to whatever supplies of game were brought in. It is not perfectly clear what is meant here, but the simplest explanation is that, not to be outdone in generosity, whenever game is brought in, the rich provide the bread necessary to eat with it.

The meals were cooked and served by slaves, wine-mixers, bread-makers and meat cooks. This raises a difficulty which is hard to explain, since we are told that there were hereditary cooks[1] who followed in the profession of their fathers, and were presumably freemen. Perhaps these were head chefs and the slaves worked under their direction. According to Polemon[2] and Demetrius of Scepsis[3] the cooks had set up a shrine to the 'heroes', Matten (the kneader) and Keraon (the mixer). Evidently these were the tutelary deities of those who 'make the barley cakes and mix the wine at the Phiditia'.

Even the Spartans at times had to relax.[4] The solemnity of the festival of the Hyacinthia was broken by a kind of *mi-carême* which lightened the gloom of the mourning for Hyacinthus. A choir of boys, 'running the whole gamut of the strings of the lyre with the plectrum' or accompanied by the flute, sang the praises of the god 'in a high pitch'. A mounted procession on gaily adorned horses marched through the theatre; choirs of young men sang the national songs and the dancers went through the figures of the ancient style. The girls were carried about in wicker carts sumptuously

---

[1] I.e. among the τεχνῖται Athenaeus gives us the names of many famous cooks among the Greeks and the recipes for which they were distinguished. In Crete each mess had a manageress with cooks and waiters under her. It is not impossible that the same custom prevailed at Sparta. Athen. IV, 143 B.

[2] ap. Athen. IV, 39 C.

[3] ap. Athen. IV, 173 F. S. Wide, *Lakonische Külte*, p. 278.

[4] Athen. IV, 139 D, E.

ornamented, while others paraded about in chariots yoked to two horses which they raced, 'while the entire city was given over to a bustle and joy of the festival'. Many victims were sacrificed and the citizens entertained strangers and their slaves at dinner, which consisted of barley cake, wheat loaf, meat, uncooked greens, broth, figs, nuts and lupines. At the Feast of the Cleaver sausages were nailed up on the walls of the public lounges for the older men to gnaw at.

The *syssition* was looked upon as a school of manners and deportment, boys being admitted to listen to the grave conversation of their elders. They were also trained to endure jokes at their own expense, these being 'without scurrility' as Plutarch[1] hastens to add. He also is careful to say that if this 'ragging' went too far at the mess table, the victim had only to say so and his tormentor ceased.

It was also the custom at meals, Xenophon[2] says, that whatever honourable deed had been performed by anyone should be related 'so that insolence, or disorder from intoxication, or any indecency of conduct or language, has there no opportunity of showing itself'. When the meal and the edifying discussions that followed were over, the company dispersed to their own dwellings. Only the older men were allowed to carry lanterns to guide them through the dark streets; the younger men had to go unaided to accustom them to walking in the dark. Xenophon[3] adds that this had the advantage of obliging them to find their way at night 'and to be careful not to stagger from the effects of wine, knowing they will not remain where they dined and that they must conduct themselves in the night as in the day; for it is not allowable for anyone still liable to military service to walk with a torch'.

As the austerity of the Spartan way of life weakened and luxury took the place of the old-fashioned simplicity, the *syssitia* became degenerate. From being a regular daily

---

[1] *Lyc.* XII. It was all in 'innocent fun' he says in another place, *De recta rat. audi.* 46C, D.   [2] *Resp. Lac.* V, 5.   [3] *Ibid.* V, 7.

practice to dine together in simple fashion, the gatherings took the form of elaborate feasts at the religious festivals. They reclined on luxurious couches with 'a display of many cups and the service of food dressed in every variety, rare unguents, wines and desserts'.[1] The comfort of these couches, however, does not seem to have impressed Cicero, who pronounces them hard.[2] It might be urged in extenuation that with the decline and final disbandment of the Spartan army the practice of messing together lost all significance and value.

As would be expected the reformers Agis IV and Cleomenes III both included in their proposals for a return to the 'Lycurgan' discipline the restoration of the *syssitia*. In the case of Agis, we are confronted with an insuperable difficulty in the account given by Plutarch,[3] who says that he divided the new order of Spartan peers into fifteen *phiditia*, some of four hundred and some of two, with a diet and discipline agreeable to the laws of Lycurgus. σύνταξιν δὲ τούτων εἰς πεντεκαίδεκα γενέσθαι φιδίτια κατὰ τετρακοσίους καὶ διακοσίους καὶ δίαιταν, ἣν εἶχον οἱ πρόγονοι, διαιτᾶσθαι. We are therefore led to believe that messes of as many as 400 members were set up. But this seems to be incredible. In the first place, we know that the 'Lycurgan' *syssition* consisted of about fifteen members. For Agis to institute such huge gatherings would be violently 'un-Lycurgan'. And secondly, we may reasonably ask whether these throngs of diners could be accommodated under one roof? Either the passage is corrupt, or Plutarch has misunderstood what Agis tried to do. Bielschowsky,[4] who discusses the problem at considerable length, suggests the emendation σύνταξιν δὲ τούτων εἰς

[1] Antiphanes ap. Athen. xv, 681c. Cf. also Phylarchus ap. Athen. iv, 142–3. Bielschowsky's surmise (*Spart. Syss.* p. 20) that the Spartans sat at their meals as the Cretans did (Athen. iv, 138f) is impossible to substantiate. It is quite unsafe to draw close parallels between Cretan and Spartan customs.
[2] *pro Murena*, xxxv.   [3] *Agis*, viii.
[4] *Spart. Syss.* pp. 29f. Ringnalda, *De Exerc. Lac.* p. 6, accepts this emendation.

τριακόσια γενέσθαι φιδίτια κατὰ πεντεκαίδεκα, i.e. he set up 300 *phiditia* of fifteen members each. This he defends on the ground that since 4500 was the number of his new citizens, 300 *syssitia* of fifteen members apiece would exactly accommodate that number. Attractive as this emendation may appear, it is altogether too violent. We cannot rewrite Plutarch to fit our own ideas. We are, therefore, left with the problem unsolved and no satisfactory explanation of it can be given. The intriguing passage in Plutarch's *Life of Agis*, in which he says that the ephor Agesilaus collected the taxes payable in the month he added to the year, does suggest that Agis had actually got his *syssitia* going and the contributions of the members were being collected. Perhaps Agesilaus, who was entirely unscrupulous, may have plausibly ordained that in view of their inauguration in the near future it was necessary to collect funds and provisions in preparation for the event. In any case the downfall of Agesilaus and the murder of Agis put an end to it.

CONCLUSION

Aristotle[1] puts his finger on the bad aspect of the system of common meals.

The first introducer of the common meals called phiditia did not regulate them well. The entertainment ought to have been provided at the public cost, as in Crete. But among the Lacedaemonians everyone is expected to contribute and some of them are too poor to afford the expense; thus the intention of the legislator is frustrated. The common meals were meant to be a popular institution, but the existing manner of regulating them is the reverse of popular. For the very poor can scarcely take part in them and, according to ancient custom, those who cannot contribute are not allowed to retain their rights of citizenship.

The degeneration of an institution, begun for a specific purpose, into something quite different is a well-known

[1] *Pol.* 1271 A.

phenomenon visible everywhere. Actually the corruption of the *syssition* may be attributed to more than one cause, of which that named by Aristotle was not the principal. The *syssition* was essentially military in its composition, it was a permanent regimental mess. With the decline of Spartan military power after the disaster of Leuctra, the old system began to degenerate. The outward forms were more or less retained, but their essential features deteriorated. What had been a simple messing together of soldiers on garrison duty changed to social clubs of an exclusive character. The reason for their existence had gone with the extinction of Sparta as a military power.

CHAPTER X

MONEY AND PUBLIC FINANCE

1. MONEY

Along with their system of education, what has always excited the greatest interest in the peculiar practices of the Spartans is their iron money. The generally accepted idea of Spartan discipline, both in ancient and modern times, is that they were forbidden by Lycurgus to use gold and silver as money, only iron being allowed them and that in the most inconvenient forms. Careful examination of all the evidence will show that, while there may have been some form of iron 'money', never, at least in historic times, was it used exclusively as the only legal medium of exchange. Spartans used gold and silver coins just as freely as any other nation, although there was no mint at Sparta until quite late. Nor is it correct to think of the Spartans as living a life of ascetic penury in which money matters were beneath them. There always were rich men in Sparta, and we know the names of some of them. Herodotus tells us of Sparthias and Beulis, men of great wealth who nobly gave themselves up to Xerxes.[1] Lichas won the chariot race at Olympia in 420[2] and chariot-racing was a very expensive amusement. We also know that the kings were reputed to be the richest men in Greece.

The first reference we have to a monetary transaction among the Spartans is the account given by Pausanias[3] of the purchase by them of the house of King Polydorus from his widow, paying the price in oxen.

[1] Herod. VII, 134.

[2] Thuc. v. 50; Xen. *Memor.* I, 2, 61. Mr Toynbee's assertion, *op. cit.* III, p. 67, that the Spartans were forbidden to take part in the great Pan-Hellenic contests cannot be sustained. We know that winners were made members of the king's bodyguard, and as shown above they certainly entered teams in the chariot-races.

[3] III, 12, 3.

For at that time there was as yet neither gold nor silver coinage, but they still bartered in the old way with oxen, slaves, and uncoined silver and gold.

This is perfectly recognisable and takes us back to the Homeric Age when what we may, perhaps somewhat fancifully, call the 'ox standard' was in use, supplemented by silver and gold counted by weight, that is by the talent[1] still 'uncoined', as Pausanias quite correctly says.

But, from the close of the Homeric era to the opening of the historic, there intervenes a 'dark age' of which we have no record. The 'Dorians' have come and swept away the former Mycenaean-Achaean economy and the next thing we find is a tradition that some form of iron 'money' is being used. Why iron? It is not too hard to give an answer to that question. It must be remembered that iron in Homeric times was distinctly one of the precious metals. It was very scarce and highly valued. Since we may suppose with justification that most, if not all, of the iron available was of meteoric origin which evidently fell from the skies, it was referred to as 'heavenly' and no doubt had a certain amount of mystery and sacredness attached to it.[2] Iron was very useful and valuable; it could be made into weapons and implements, and articles made of metal, gold or bronze tripods and bowls, in the absence of coins, were used in Homeric times as a medium of exchange. Laum has amassed a good deal of evidence to show that those curious iron 'sickles', of which several examples have been unearthed in Sparta, were used as a form of money there.[3] These may not only have been 'useful' as

---

[1] Art. 'Talentum' by Lécrivain in D.S.

[2] Cf. F. B. Jevons, 'Iron in Homer', *J.H.S.* (1892), p. 25.

[3] *Das Eisengeld der Spartaner.* Laum's long and detailed argument connecting this 'sickle money' with the cult of Artemis Orthia need not be enlarged upon here. That they were cult instruments is certain, but whether they were used as 'money' is more than doubtful. Cf. *Artemis Orthia*, (Dawkins *et al.*), pp. 312, 406. Also Laum, *Heiliges Gold*, p. 155. For a severe criticism of Laum cf. Blinkenberg's review in *Gnomon*, 11 (1926), pp. 102 ff.

implements in cutting grain, if indeed we suppose them to be sickles.[1] but they also had a religious significance, we may suppose as sacrificial implements, cult instruments which had been brought to Sparta from Crete. Of the same nature were the iron spits or *obeloi*, used to skewer the meat of the victims, if that was actually their use.[2] Perhaps a bundle of six such spits formed a handful or 'drax', from which the Greek word drachma may be derived.[3] Discovery of these in the Heraeum at Argos and the shrine of Artemis Orthia at Sparta seems to confirm this.

At some undetermined date, probably between the eighth and sixth centuries,[4] Pheidon is supposed to have introduced regular silver coins and the primitive and unhandy *obeloi* were superseded by the more convenient forms of currency made from the precious metals.[5] Greece, outside of Lacedaemon, definitely abandoned the 'iron standard', if we may use that term, and from that time onwards the precious metals became the materials of currency. But this was not so in Sparta, which clung to the old iron standard. This seemed so remarkable to ancient writers that they sought, in characteristic fashion, to find an explanation for its use. Since attributing any Spartan peculiarity to the legislation of Lycurgus was the easiest way to explain it, Plutarch does so in the following passage:

[Lycurgus] withdrew all gold and silver money from currency and ordained the use of iron money only. Then to a great weight and mass of this he gave a trifling value, so that ten minas' worth required a large store-room in the house, and a yoke of cattle to transport it. When this money obtained currency, many sorts of iniquity went into exile from Lacedaemon. For who would steal or receive as a bribe, or rob, or plunder that which could neither be

---

[1] Very doubtful, they look more like boomerangs.

[2] Pollux, IX, 77; *Etym. Mag. s.v.* Seltman, *Greek Coins*, p. 33. The Greeks were wretched etymologists.

[3] Cf. H. Berve, *Griechische Geschichte*, I, p. 160; Glotz, *Histoire Grecque*, I, pp. 305 f. Th. Reinach, *L'Histoire par les Monnaies*, p. 28.

[4] The whole historical identity of Pheidon is highly obscure. Hasebroek asserts that he is mythical, *Griech. Wirt.- u. Gesell.-gesch.* p. 285.

[5] *Lyc.* IX. Cf. *Lys.* XVII; Xen. *Resp. Lac.* VII, 5; *Apoph. Lac.* 226; Pollux, VII, 105; IX, 79. Ps.-Platonic *Eryxias*, 400 B.

concealed, nor possessed with satisfaction, nay, nor cut to pieces with any profit? For vinegar was used, as we are told, to quench the red-hot iron, robbing it of its temper and making it worthless for any other purpose, when once it had become brittle and hard to work.

It may be remarked that tempering iron by plunging it while red hot into liquid, usually water but later oil was widely practised. To say that immersion in vinegar had any particular effect is nonsense. Acetic acid was the only one known to the ancients, and all sorts of marvellous properties were, quite erroneously, attributed to it. As a matter of fact, tempering in this way only gives a thin surface hardness and the iron beneath is unaffected. The whole account is absurd and may be disregarded. In any case it is pertinent to remember that the Peloponnese was rich in iron, especially in Laconia where it is mined to this day. Such slabs of iron presumably, but far from certainly, were called 'pelanors',* since they resembled a loaf of bread in shape.[1] There is some doubt as to the existence of these extraordinary 'coins', but several lumps of iron which may possibly be identified as such have been discovered.[2] Strange as they may appear, it is relevant to remark that mere size is not an insuperable objection. Precisely similar lumps of metal—but of bronze (aes rude) not iron—were used in Rome and elsewhere in Italy until after 300 B.C. before silver coins were struck, and the people were obliged to carry any considerable sum in a waggon.[3] The heavy copper slabs that were in use in Sweden in the seventeenth century are evidences of modern usage of the same kind. The Swedish two-dollar piece weighed 3 lb. and, we are told, had to be taken to market in a wheelbarrow.

Any attempt to equate these Spartan pelanors with silver is so vague and unsatisfactory as to be quite useless. Plutarch[4] says that one pelanor weighed an Aeginetan mina, and was

[1] Very uncertain. Hesychius, s.v., alone gives this name. Cf. art. 'Lateres' by Babelon in D.S. and U. Koehler in *Ath. Mitt.* VII (1882), pp. 1, 377.

[2] *A.B.S.A.* XIII, p. 173. But doubtful.

[3] Pliny, *Hist. Nat.* XXXIII, 43; cf. art. in *Oxford Class. Dict.*, 'Coinage, Roman', by Mattingly.   [4] *Apoph. Lac.* III, 278.

worth four *chalkoi* or half an obol. If we accept Hültsch's[1] equation, which is at least arguable, the Aeginetan mina weighed 605 gr. or 1lb. 8 oz. troy weight. According to Plutarch and Hesychius, these iron lumps were worth half an obol of silver, which would give a ratio of 1:1200. This is by no means certain, and Hültsch is of the opinion that the original value of these iron lumps was an obol, which would obviously make the ratio 1:600.[2]

There seems to be no way out of this confusion and, as a matter of fact, to talk of 'mint' ratios is impossible. Neither Xenophon[3] nor Plutarch[4] gives us any assistance. Seneca[5] speaks of leather money used by the Spartans. This may be disregarded; probably Seneca was confused over the so-called primitive 'ox standard'.

The only explanation of these discrepancies is that the Spartans had no mint of their own and the only genuine 'native' money was iron. For ordinary purposes they used whatever foreign currency had come into the country. No coins were struck in Sparta until 280, when King Areus established a mint from which he issued Alexander tetradrachms of Attic weight inscribed with his own name. Nor do we hear of its being in operation again until another fifty years had passed, when Cleomenes III struck silver tetradrachms in 228. The coins both of Cleomenes and Nabis imitated Seleucid models.[6]

[1] Hultsch, *Griech. u. röm. Metrologie*, pp. 502, 535. But cf. Viedebantt in *Hermes*, XLVII (1912), pp. 586ff., who reckons the Aeginetan mina at 636·7 gr. The problem is of the utmost complexity. Cf. also art. 'Gewichte', by Lehmann-Haupt in P.W., Suppl. III.   [2] *Ut supra*, p. 535, n. 6.

[3] *Resp. Lac.* VII, 5.   [4] *Lyc.* IX.

[5] *De Benefic.* V, 14, 4. Seneca's statement certainly did not come from the Ps.-Platonic *Eryxias*, 400 D, but it was handed on to Nicol. Damas. *F.H.G.* III, p. 458, 114, 8. Cf. Trieber, *Quaest. Lacon.* p. 41; Boeckh, *Die Staatshaushaltung d. Athener* (ed. Fränkel), p. 693.

[6] Seltman, *Greek Coins*, p. 256. *C.A.H.* (Plates), III, p. 10, There seems to be no explanation of the θιβρώνειον νόμισμα of Photius other than that Thibron during his campaign in Asia 399 struck coins for local use. Perhaps this was one of the charges against him, other than incompetence during the campaign, that led to his recall and banishment. Xen. *Hell.* III, 1, 8.

That Lycurgus ever forbade the use of any money other than the iron pelanors is a pure fairy tale invented, as we shall see later, to combat corruption among the officials and generals. All through their history the Spartans were plagued with official corruption. After the close of the Persian wars, Themistocles was banished for attempting to corrupt the whole Spartan State with the spoils he had won. If it is true that he bribed Eurybiades with five talents, the sum was enormous for those days.[1] King Leotychidas in 476 was convicted of accepting bribes.[2] In 446 Pleistoanax was fined fifteen talents, an impossibly large sum if the record is true.[3] His accuser Cleandrides was afterwards convicted of bribery and corruption.[4] The victor in Sicily, Gylippus, was condemned for stealing.[5] In 404, when Lysander brought back the booty he had won after the downfall of Athens, the plague of corruption in Sparta seems to have reached a climax, and in order to put some curb upon it a law was passed forbidding the private ownership of the precious metals.[6]

The wisest of the Spartans, dreading the influence of money as being what had corrupted the greatest citizens, exclaimed against Lysander's conduct, and declared to the ephors that all the silver and gold should be sent away as alien mischiefs. These consulted about it and Theopompus says it was Sciraphidas, but Ephorus that it was Phlogidas, who declared they ought not to receive any gold or silver into the city, but to use their own country's coin which was iron.... But Lysander's friends being against it and endeavouring to keep the money in the city, it was resolved to bring in this sort of [iron] money to be used publicly, enacting at the same time that, if anyone was found in possession of any privately, he should be put to death, as if Lycurgus had feared the coin and not the covetousness resulting from it, which they did not repress by letting no private man possess any, so much as they encouraged it, by allowing the state to possess it, attaching thereby a sort of dignity to it over and above its ordinary utility.

---

[1] Herod. VIII, 5.   [2] *Idem*, VI, 72; Paus. III, 7, 10.
[3] Ephorus, in Schol. Aristoph. *Nubes*, 859; Thuc. II, 21; V, 16.
[4] Diod. XIII, 106; Plut. *Pericles*, XXII; *Nicias*, XXVIII.
[5] Plut. *Lys.* XVII.   [6] *Ibid.* XVI, XVII.

This law is of considerable historical importance for two reasons. First, 'the party of strict observance' of the Spartan discipline was appealing to the Lycurgan tradition in the face of wholesale departure from the austerity of former times. As we shall see later, these appeals to the so-called laws of Lycurgus were made again in the subsequent history of Sparta. And secondly, we must suppose that the passing of this law explains two statements which otherwise are obscure. Xenophon[1] says that private persons were forbidden to possess gold or silver. This is a very curious statement to make after he had lived there for some time and must have known that money was used as freely there as anywhere else in Greece. This is one of the passages in *The Government of the Lacedaemonians* which provide so many puzzles for commentators. Poseidonius[2] says that rich Spartans kept their money in Arcadia. It is pertinent to ask why they did not keep it with trusted *perioeci*? Plutarch[3] tells us that Lysander deposited a talent and fifty-two minas, as well as eleven staters in the treasury of the Acantians at Delphi, and dryly remarks that this is hard to reconcile with his supposed poverty.

Like everything else that had to do with this very mysterious people, the wealth of the Spartans sorely puzzled the other Greeks. Plato, in his famous talk with the young Alcibiades,[4] is on firm ground when he talks of 'the temperance and orderliness, the facility and placidity, the magnanimity and

---

[1] *Resp. Lac.* VII, 6.   [2] ap. Athen. VI, 233 F.

[3] *Lys.* XVIII. Cf. Busolt-Swoboda, *Griech. Staatsk.* I, p. 247, n. 6; II, p. 662; also Meier, *Klio*, Beih. XLII, p. 61, n. 5. The inscription in Dittenberger, *Sylloge*, III, 1213; Michel, *Recueil d'Inscriptions Grecques*, 1343, in which a certain Xuthias deposits a sum of money in Tegea in Arcadia to be paid out to his children after his death is doubtfully Laconian. Kirchhoff, in *Monatsberichte der preussischen Akademie der Wissenschaft zu Berlin* (1870), p. 58, on the strength of the above reference in Athenaeus, supposes that Xuthias must be a Spartan. Meister, in *Berichte über der Verhandlungen der sächsischen Akademie der Wissenschaften zu Leipzig*, XXIV, 3 (1904), pp. 266ff., hesitates to accept this and on etymological grounds prefers to identify Xuthias as an Achaean from one of the Lacedaemonian towns of the *perioeci*. The point is incapable of final solution.   [4] *Alcib.* I, 122 C.

discipline, the courage and endurance and the toil-loving, success-loving, honour-loving spirit of the Spartans'. But when he speaks of their wealth in land and slaves, horses, flocks and herds and all their gold and silver treasures, he does not know what to say.

For there is more gold and silver privately held in Lacedaemon than in the whole of Greece; for during many generations treasure has been passing into them from every part of Greece and often from the barbarians also, but not passing out to anyone. And just as in the fable of Aesop, when the fox remarked to the lion on the direction of the footmarks, the traces of the money going into Lacedaemon are clear enough, nowhere are any to be seen of it coming out, so that one can be pretty sure that these people are the richest of the Greeks in gold and silver.

The reasoning is, of course, faulty since we know that Sparta actually was no richer but a good deal poorer than any other Greek state; at least until the end of the Peloponnesian war and Socrates was speaking at its start. A legend had been started of the wealth of the Spartans and Socrates was merely echoing the old and worthless story.

'Love of money will be the ruin of Sparta, that and nothing else' was the old saying.[1] But we may take issue with it and deny that the greed of riches had anything very much to do with the decline and fall of the Spartan State. Polybius[2] has put his finger on the trouble with rare insight:

As long as they aspired to rule over their neighbours or over the Peloponnesians alone, they found the supplies and resources furnished by Laconia itself adequate, as they had all they required ready to hand and quickly returned home whether by land or by sea. But once they began to undertake naval expeditions and to make military campaigns outside the Peloponnese it was evident that neither their iron currency nor the exchange of their crops for commodities which they lacked, as permitted by the laws of Lycurgus, would suffice for their needs. These enterprises demanded a currency in universal circulation and supplies drawn from abroad,

[1] Diod. Sic. VII, 14. [2] VI, 49.

and so they were compelled to beg from the Persians, to impose tribute on the islanders and exact taxes from all the Greeks. For they recognised that under the legislation of Lycurgus it was impossible to aspire, I will not say to supremacy in Greece, but to any position of influence.

One last suggestion merits at least passing consideration. Is it possible that these slabs of iron were in fact 'pigs' or billets which the perioecic smelters exchanged for imported foreign wares? We know that iron entered largely into trade and that the ore deposits in Laconia were rich and must have afforded a valuable source of wealth for barter with other countries. It is not by any means impossible that merchants, taking these slabs or pigs of iron in exchange for their own wares, thought that they constituted the money of the Spartans; or if they knew better themselves, others got that idea and the whole legend of iron money grew up. The suggestion need not be insisted upon; but it may at least partially explain the persistence of the legend. Everything connected with Sparta was mysterious and it was quite in character to suppose that they should use these queer things as money.

Polybius was right. So long as Sparta was a little land-locked state which had little or nothing to do with the outside world, so long could it exist in the primitive state of economy. If the Spartan peers chose to say that their iron slabs were their only money they could get on very well indeed, so long as the helots obediently supported them. As Polybius rightly says, 'the exchange of their crops for commodities which they lacked as permitted by the laws of Lycurgus sufficed for their needs'. But as the precious metals began to seep in and make their influence felt, the old system broke down and, at least in historical times, the Spartan iron money had become no more than a legend. Probably most of the pelanors that remained had been melted down to make weapons and armour or more useful things of iron. The statement of Plutarch[1] that when

[1] *Fabius*, XXVII. In a note in *J.H.S.* L (1930), p. 299, it is remarked that a previous statement in *Artemis Orthia* (Dawkins *et al.*), p. 391, that no iron

Epaminondas died only one small iron spit was found in his house can hardly be regarded as proving that their use had survived up to his time. It is more likely it was a curiosity that he had brought from Sparta.

Any idea that to borrow or lend money in Sparta was illegal must be dismissed at once.[1] The ephors judged all cases that dealt with contracts and, since most contracts involve money, it was impossible that such cases should not come before them. A passage of Dioscorides quoted in Photius[2] gives an interesting picture of the use of 'tally sticks' or *scytalae*. 'Dioscorides, in his treaty on customs Περὶ νομίμων, says that at Sparta lenders used to divide a stick in the presence of two witnesses, writing the agreement upon each piece. They gave one piece to one of the witnesses and kept the other themselves.'

Plato[3] highly disapproved of the Spartan attitude towards money and put it down to faulty educational standards.

Men of this stamp will be covetous of money like those who live in oligarchies; they will have a fierce and secret longing after gold and silver, which they will hoard in dark places, having magazines and treasuries of their own for the deposit and concealment of them; also castles which are just nests for their eggs, and in which they will spend large sums on their wives, or on any others whom they please. They are miserly because they have no means of openly acquiring money which they prize; they will spend that which is another man's on the gratification of their desires, stealing their pleasure, and running away like children from the law, their father; they have been schooled not by gentle influences but by force, for they have neglected her who is the true Muse, the companion of reason and philosophy, and have honoured gymnastic more than music.

spits had been found in strata excavated dating after 635, must be corrected. Later some were found in the strata of the first half of the fourth century. Perhaps they had some ceremonial significance.

[1] As does Fustel de Coulanges, *Études sur la propriété foncière à Sparte*, pp. 76f.

[2] *S.v.* σκύταλη, *F.H.G.* II, p. 193.   [3] *Rep.* 548.

2. Public Finance

'None of Sparta's champions has thought of defending her public finance', remarks Andreades.[1] Indeed, he might have gone much further and said that Aristotle[2] roundly condemns it in no uncertain fashion:

The public revenue is not well managed in Sparta, for their treasury is empty while they are obliged to carry on great wars. The taxes are paid badly, since the Spartans own most of the land themselves, and they do not inquire too closely as to what each pays in, and thus the exact contrary to what the legislator intended has taken place, for the state is poor but the citizens are avaricious.

There is a very familiar ring to all this, the world has seen it only too often. The rich and privileged aristocracy entrenches itself and refuses to do its share in the upkeep of the State. Among themselves there is a 'gentleman's agreement' not to be too curious in other people's affairs. Every revolution in history has had its origins in the breakdown in government through bankruptcy.

To say that there was no system of public finance or taxation in Sparta would be too easy a way out of the difficulties that beset us. All we can say is that there must have been some system whereby the State carried on whatever public services there were, more especially in time of war which with the Spartans was practically continuous. There must have been heavy expenses in the upkeep of fortifications, harbours (for instance the dockyard at Gythium) and frontier defences which would have to be paid out of the public treasury. But it is certain that no direct taxes, other than the monthly dues to the *syssitia*, were paid by the Spartan peers up to the outbreak of the Peloponnesian war. The public treasury was empty and King Archidamus warns his fellow-countrymen against fighting so rich an empire as that of Athens, which can call upon its allies for assistance and its

---

[1] *Hist. Grk. Pub. Fin.* p. 76.   [2] *Pol.* 1271 B.

tributaries for money to carry on with. 'But the Spartans neither have a reserve in the treasury nor will they willingly contribute money from their own private funds.'[1] In ordinary fairness to the Spartans, it must be said that unwillingness to pay taxes was not peculiar to them. All Greeks hated 'direct' taxes, and the only way to get money out of the citizen was through an *eisphora* or capital levy, as is seen so often in Athens. To every Greek to be a citizen meant to receive, not to pay for, benefits—a simple and, within limits, an effective theory of citizenship.

But if the Spartans paid no taxes at the outbreak of the Peloponnesian war, it seems fairly certain that they did when Aristotle wrote, since he says that the father of four sons was exempt from paying any taxes at all.[2] What these were, how they were levied or anything whatever about them we do not know, nor can any surmise be profitably made thereon. As everywhere else the tax-gatherer was despised and his calling ranked with that of keeping a brothel.[3]

The nature of the tribute paid by the *perioeci* to the kings is not certainly known. That some form of tax was paid seems certain. Strabo,[4] in a none too clear passage, says that when King Agis had conquered the lands adjoining Sparta he enslaved some of their inhabitants, i.e. the helots, and others he allowed to remain free but imposed a tribute on them. These latter are obviously *perioeci*, who purchased their freedom by paying heavily for it, as many have done since. Plato[5] speaks of a tax paid to the kings 'of no small amount'.

What was its nature? Was it a capitation tax paid in money, or was it rent paid by tenants of the farms which composed the royal *temenos* or demesne? And lastly, was it paid in cash or in kind? Unfortunately, no certain answer can be given to any of these unsettled points and the differences of opinion among the commentators are extreme. Busolt[6] thought this

---

[1] Thuc, I, 80. Cf. *Idem*, I, 141.　　[2] *Pol.* 1270B.
[3] Plut. *Apoph. Lac.* 236B.　　[4] VIII, 5, 4 (C. 365).
[5] *Alcib.* I, 18.　　[6] *Griech. Gesch.* p. 524, n. 3.

must refer to rents paid by tenants. Guiraud[1] takes the view that the royal demesne must have been so small that the rents received were inconsiderable; but Kahrstedt,[2] while accepting the fact that the kings did receive an income from the *perioeci*, supposes that in this instance it refers merely to royal perquisites. Andreades[3] is quite undecided, but concludes that Plato's statement is a gross exaggeration and that if a tribute was paid, it must have been small enough.

One or two points remain to be noted. The first unfortunately admits of no positive answer. Were the richer citizens of Sparta subject to 'liturgies'? By 'liturgy' was meant, at least in other Greek states, contributions of a special kind for the service of the State. For instance, a rich man might be required to pay for the upkeep of a man-of-war, a trireme, for a certain period, usually a year; or he might pay for a chorus at a festival, or the expenses of athletes at the games. Originally a free-will offering by a patriotic citizen, it came at length to be a regular exaction and often bore very heavily on those unfortunate enough to be saddled with it. A passage in Xenophon[4] might very well suggest that at least one liturgy, that of supplying a horse or horses for the cavalry in time of war, and perhaps of procuring a rider and his equipment, was imposed on rich men in Sparta. Unfortunately, Xenophon's phrase 'the richest men maintained the horses' is not very illuminating; but it is by no means improbable that this was a duty imposed on them by the Sate and that they fitted out the cavalry at their own expense. It is also permissible to surmise that the utter ineffectiveness of the Spartan cavalry may be attributed to this system. It seems pretty certain that the admirable system of liturgies was to the liking of the Romans. Apparently the office of *diabetes*, by which we may suppose is meant *gymnasiarch* or *magister ludorum* was imposed on rich men. The word 'voluntary' (αὐτεπάγγελτος) in the inscriptions in

---

[1] *La Propriété foncière en Grèce jusqu'à la Conquête romaine*, p. 164.
[2] *Griech. Staatsr.* pp. 15, 35, 332.   [3] *Hist. Grk. Pub. Fin.* p. 60.
[4] *Hell.* VI, 4, 11.

commendation of particular holders of the office, shows clearly that it was forced on others who most unwillingly defrayed the heavy expenses involved.[1]

A curious incident, of which it is hardly possible to make very much, was the alleged self-denial of the Spartans when they wanted to make a loan to the Samians. In order to raise the money they and their households fasted for an entire day and sent the proceeds to Samos.[2] This is a queer story, and it is made none the easier to understand when we find a variant of it in Plutarch,[3] who says the gift was made not in money but in grain to the people of Smyrna. The second version seems the more reasonable. It is easier to think of their sending the food they had not consumed than a sum of money.

A loan of 100 talents by the Spartan government to the Thirty Tyrants of Athens is well attested.[4] The desire on the part of the Spartans to see the Thirty remain in power is highly understandable. The honourable decision of the Athenian people to repay this loan after the civil war was over was evidently a source of great satisfaction to everyone, and is frequently referred to as a peculiar evidence of high-mindedness and honesty; of neither of which the Athenians had ever been suspected before.[5]

WAR FINANCE

For a people whose whole existence was circumstanced by never-ceasing readiness for war, the Spartans were singularly inept in any conception of finance necessary for carrying on a campaign. This, obviously, arose from their studied avoidance of any entanglements outside of Greece. If a campaign was undertaken, the warriors joined up with their own weapons and commissariat. The army marched out to battle, and when

---

[1] Tod, *A.B.S.A.* x (1903), p. 75. [2] Ps.-Arist. *Oecon.* 1347B.
[3] *Quomodo Adul.* 64B. [4] Xen. *Hell.* II, 4, 28.
[5] Isocr. *Aréop.* XXVIII; Demosth. *in Lept.* X; Lysias, *in Eratosth.* LIX; Arist. *Resp. Ath.* XL, 3.

the fighting was over disbanded once more. This was obviously a simple and, within its limits, a highly effective method but, equally obviously, it was one that was apt to break down badly when confronted with an unusual situation. For instance, it never seems to have occurred to the Spartans, until the period of the Persian wars, to follow the example of Athens[1] and to put their allies under contribution. When they did so under the stress of necessity, they were so inexperienced, says Plutarch,[2] that they had to ask the advice of the Athenian Aristides how they should do it and how the assessments should be made on an equitable basis. Aristides gave them good advice; but they do not seem to have profited therefrom, since their system of public finance remained primitive and singularly ineffective.

The outbreak of the Peloponnesian war found the Spartans in a serious quandary. The treasury was empty; they had no navy and they were to fight a foe whose wealth was enormous and navy highly efficient. They had no doubt whatever that if they could bring the Athenians to a decisive land battle they could defeat them. But that was exactly what Pericles the Athenian would never do. It was the policy of the Athenians to play a waiting game and wear out the Spartans. But that was a very costly game to play, as old King Archidamus of Sparta warned his people. 'Money not men wins wars', he said, and if Sparta's treasury was empty and her citizens obstinately determined not to tax themselves, the financial problem of the war was going to be a serious one.

All this the Athenians knew very well indeed, and Pericles,[3] in his speech to the Athenian Assembly, makes a good deal of it. He points out that the Spartans are landowners with all their wealth locked up in their estates and little or no ready cash available. They are inexperienced in long overseas wars, and are only used to fighting short campaigns, which cost nothing and may safely be expected to pay for themselves out of the booty taken from the vanquished.

[1] Thuc. I, 19.   [2] Plut. *Arist.* XXIV.   [3] Thuc. I, 140.

Men of this description can neither man fleets nor often send out land armaments. It is abundant resources that support war, rather than compulsory contributions. Men who till the land are more ready to wage war with their persons than with their money.

All of which was perfectly true. But what was also true was that if the Spartans could hang on long enough, the great reserve stored up by the Athenians would be spent, and the forced tribute exacted from her unwilling allies more and more difficult to obtain. If it was to be a quick decision everything was on the side of the Athenians; if a long-drawn out struggle, probably the Spartans would win.

As it turned out, that is precisely what happened. The Spartans were totally unable to finance their allies and so that task was turned over to the allies themselves on a voluntary basis. Each was to finance itself; a system notably different from that of the Athenians who insisted upon contributions to a central fund in Athens, entirely under their own control. The Spartans 'decentralised' their war finance to a very marked degree and probably their system was the better. It did not arouse the violent resentments that the Athenian tribute invariably gave rise to. If such and such an ally wished to fight on the Spartan side it must not look to Sparta for financial aid, it must pay for itself. Naturally some system of contribution must be worked out through consultation, and the trouble was that it was difficult, or rather it was sheerly impossible, to fix a definite scale of payments. We are told that when Sparta's allies in the course of the war were trying to find what sum of money would be sufficient and were demanding that the tax be made definite, Archidamus, the son of Agesilaus replied 'War does not feed on fixed rations'.[1]

This system, or perhaps we might better say lack of system, has been characterised as 'absolutely primitive and a caricature of economic organisation'.[2] Perhaps it was; but it worked all right. It is notable to observe that, when Sparta adopted the

---

[1] Plut. *Apoph. Lac.* 219 A. [2] Kahrstedt, *Griech. Staatsr.* p. 358.

much more scientific 'centralised' policy of Athens in 387–386 and imposed a fixed quota of men on each ally or equivalent money payments,[1] the resentments stirred up were very formidable. The Spartans were hated abroad for their arrogance and greed and their defeat at Leuctra delighted their former allies.

While the Peloponnesian war was at its height all the expenses of building and manning the fleets were turned over to the allies.[2] When, after the defeat of Athens in Sicily, they wanted to put a fleet of a hundred ships into commission the Spartans themselves could only provide twenty-five. Sparta never pretended to be a naval power and if Athens was to be beaten on the sea help was necessary. As the war neared its close Sparta turned shamelessly to Persia for money and ships. Isocrates[3] says the Persians gave them 5000 talents and this is probably not an exaggeration. All the fleets that fought the last battles in the Hellespont came from Persian shipyards.

The end of the Peloponnesian war left Sparta completely victorious, and for the first time wealthy with all the spoils of victory. She was not in the mood for temporising or making concessions. The settlement of 387–386, to which reference has already been made, was a pretty stiff one. Exemption from supplying men to the Lacedaemonian army could be purchased at the rate of three obols a day for a foot-soldier and two drachmas for a mounted man. If any of the allies failed in their allotted contributions, the Lacedaemonians could fine them at the rate of a stater per man per diem.[4] The proceeds were absolutely at the disposal of their Spartan leaders, who were under no obligation to render accounts. In 371 a new allotment according to a revised quota was proposed, the money to be kept in the temple of Apollo.[5] But the disaster of Leuctra put a stop to that.

---

[1] Diod. Sic. xv, 31.   [2] *Idem*, xiv, 17.
[3] *De pace*, xcvii.   [4] Xen. *Hell*. v, 2, 21.
[5] *Hell*. vi, 4, 2. It is uncertain whether this refers to the temple of Apollo at Delos or Delphi.

CHAPTER XI

AGIS—CLEOMENES—NABIS

THE DECLINE OF SPARTA

The story of the decline of the Spartan State after the defeat at Leuctra in 371 is a melancholy and surprising one. It was as if the disaster at Leuctra had, if the expression may be allowed, 'knocked all the stuffing out of them'. Within the next ten years Sparta had been invaded three times. Messenia was lost and along with it the estates of the peers: an economic loss which was never recovered and led to serious social consequences. In 370 Megalopolis was founded as the capital of Arcadia to overawe and keep the Spartans in subjection. In 362 the Spartans were again defeated at Second Mantinea. It is true that with the death of Epaminondas the hegemony of Thebes was destroyed; but all the same the invincibility of the Spartan hoplite was gone for ever. In 338 Philip of Macedon devastated the country and a forlorn rebellion against the Macedonians instigated by King Agis III was ruthlessly crushed by Antipater five years later. A second revolt in 294 was crushed by Demetrius Poliorcetes. The only bright spot in the whole melancholy story was the invasion and defeat of Pyrrhus in 272, when a spirited defence of the town of Sparta was made by the whole population, the one occasion it seems when the women behaved well. In 244 the Aetolians overran Laconia and carried off, we are told, 50,000 captives.[1] This

---

[1] Plut. *Cleom.* XVIII; Polyb. IV, 34, 9. Date uncertain, perhaps 240–239. Cf. Beloch, *Griech. Gesch.* IV, pt. 1, p. 629. The expression πέντε μυριάδας ἀνδραπόδων raises a problem as to who these ἀνδράποδες were. Fustel de Coulanges, in *Nouvelles recherches sur quelques probl. d'hist.* pp. 3 ff., supposes them to have been privately owned slaves of the Spartans. Ehrenberg, *Hermes,* LIX, p. 41, n. 4, thinks they were helots. It is more probable that what Plutarch meant to say was that 50,000 were taken away into slavery. The Aetolians were unlikely to inquire what was the social status of their captives.

number is certainly exaggerated; but whatever it was the event was a grievous disaster to the already impoverished and well-nigh helpless State.

KING AGIS[1]

In the same year as the Aetolian invasion Agis IV of the Eurypontid house, a youth not yet twenty years of age, succeeded to the joint kingship. From his life by Plutarch we can see well enough the generous and impulsive nature of the young man, totally inexperienced in the ways of men and unable, when the crisis came, to cope with a situation that rapidly got out of hand. We are told that, although he had been reared in luxury by his mother and grandmother, who were the richest people in Sparta, being naturally of a serious turn of mind, he set it all aside, prided himself on his short Spartan cloak, observed carefully the old Spartan discipline in his meals, in the taking of none but cold baths and in the general mode of life.

Sparta was in a ruinous state, there was no doubt of that. What was in very considerable doubt was the reason for this woeful condition and whether there was any way of bettering it. Agis had excellent answers for both of these questions. Sparta had become decadent because it had departed from the way of life laid down by Lycurgus. To restore it to its former fame and power it must return to the Lycurgan system and all would be well. The appeal to the Lycurgan tradition was a potent one and in the distress of the times likely to succeed. But the question was, what exactly had been the Lycurgan system? Agis had an answer to that. He said that it meant dividing up the land into lots, or *cleroi*, according to the supposedly ancient pattern whereby the landless men should

[1] E. Bux, 'Zwei sozialistische Novellen bei Plutarch', *Klio*, XIX (1923), pp. 413 ff. Plutarch got his material for his lives of Agis and Cleomenes from Phylarchus who may, or may not, have been a reliable source. Bux points out the romantic character of Plutarch's *Lives* and the similarities in the two narratives. However suspect Plutarch's evidence may be, it is all we have and the events described are not intrinsically impossible.

be endowed with sufficient to support them. Four thousand
five hundred of the *cleroi* should go to the Spartans and fifteen
thousand to the *perioeci*. If there were not enough genuine
Spartans, their numbers should be brought up to the required
level by inclusion of provincials and foreigners 'who had
received the rearing of freemen and were vigorous of body
and in the prime of life'. He also proposed that the old system
of public messes should be revived,[1] and all should practise
the mode of life of the old Spartans. But there was a very
practical difficulty in the way of the division of the land, which
we may surmise Agis had not foreseen. Much of the land was
heavily encumbered with debts, and before it was divided
into lots and given to the people, these debts must be extinguished. It would have been an impossible state of affairs,
a mockery, if a poor Spartan were presented with a *cleros*
upon which was a mortgage. Like many another reformer,
Agis soon found that he was committed to far more than he
had originally intended. To talk about a return to the glorious
days and the simplicity of life of the Lycurgan era was easy
enough; to attain to it was very difficult and dangerous.[2]

Agis then began to sound the people about his ideas and
found that the poor and many of the young men were for
them; but that the old men 'who were far gone in corruption
feared and shuddered at the name of Lycurgus'. The landowners were divided. Those whose lands were heavily
mortgaged saw a good chance of ridding themselves of their
debts and were willing enough to go along with Agis up to
that point. But they were utterly hostile to any division of
land. The other wealthy men were opposed to him on any
count, as they stood to lose everything, both their capital
invested in mortgages and their land. Sparta, unlike Attica,
offered only one outlet for investment of capital—in mortgages

---

[1] The problem involved in the number of the *syssitia* is discussed elsewhere,
cf. p. 295.
[2] Mr Toynbee draws an apposite parallel between the appeal of Agis and
Cleomenes to an ancient tradition and that of the Gracchi in Rome. *Op. cit.*
v, p. 219.

on land. The Athenian capitalist could invest profitably in
loans on overseas commerce but this, we must suppose, was
difficult or impossible for the Spartan.

To help him in his scheme Agis enlisted three men of
standing, Lysander, Mandrocleidas and Agesilaus, the last his
uncle, who joined because he was a landowner overburdened
by debts and thought he saw a chance of getting rid of them.
As we shall see later, this Agesilaus, according to Plutarch's
account, was the evil genius of the whole movement and
through him it came to ruin. Agis also persuaded his mother
and grandmother to consent to throwing all their possessions
into the common lot. He also tried through them to influence
the other women of wealth. But here he suffered his first
reverse, 'for the women were opposed to it, not only because
they would be stripped of the luxury which, in the general
lack of higher culture, made their lives seem happy, but also
because they saw that the honour and influence which they
enjoyed through their wealth would be cut off'.

The women therefore turned to the other king, Leonidas,
to lead the opposition to Agis. Leonidas was afraid to come
out openly against him, and so betook himself to slander,
saying that Agis was trying to make himself a tyrant by
bribing the people with a redistribution of land. Agis acted
with a good deal of vigour and by his influence got Lysander
made ephor, who thereupon introduced into the *Gerousia*
a bill embodying the proposals for annulment of debts and
redivision of the land. The *Gerousia* came to no conclusion
on it, so Lysander appealed to the *Ecclesia* or General
Assembly. When this was convened, Agis came forward and
announced that he was ready to put his entire fortune in land
and 600 talents in money into the common fund, and that his
mother and grandmother were ready to do the same. While
the common people sided with Agis, the rich rallied behind
Leonidas. Lysander indicted Leonidas on the ground that he
had married a foreign woman, had him deposed and put
Cleombrotus on the throne. Leonidas fled and remained in

exile until Lysander's term of office as ephor had expired. Then he returned and indicted Lysander and Mandrocleidas for violating the law in proposing abolition of debts and partition of the land. By this time the situation was constitutionally and legally completely out of hand. Agis, acting with Cleombrotus, dismissed the ephors from office and put in his own nominees, among whom unfortunately was his uncle Agesilaus.

If we are to believe Plutarch, it was the villainy of Agesilaus that wrecked what would otherwise have been a successful and bloodless revolution. Agesilaus may have been a villain; but he could not have been powerful enough single-handed to impose his ideas. He had behind him a body of impoverished landowners, who eagerly grasped at the idea of getting rid of their debts and to accomplish that were ready so far to support Agis. Agesilaus persuaded Agis that if all the evidences of debt were burned publicly the landowners, who were the principal debtors, would come over to his side. This was accordingly done. In so far as no division of land was possible until the mortgages upon it had been extinguished, Agesilaus was right. But as his subsequent actions showed, his motives were far from being inspired by any high-falutin ideas of reform. And unfortunately for Agis the people went on clamouring for a division of land, the last thing that Agesilaus and his party wanted; indeed, they were only able with difficulty on various pretexts to postpone it. Clearly Agis must be got rid of; so he was sent off with the army to meet a threatened invasion of the Aetolians. It was an adroit move, for Agis took with him the young men 'who, being just released from their debts and set at liberty and hoping on their return to receive each man his lot of land, followed their king with wonderful alacrity'.

The behaviour of the army under Agis while on the march was exemplary. 'The cities through which they passed were in admiration to see how they marched from one end of the Peloponnesus to another without the least disorder.' The common people were delighted with the modest and unostentatious behaviour of the young king. 'But rich men viewed the innovation with dislike and alarm, lest haply the example might spread and work changes to their prejudice in their own countries as well.' There was a revolutionary spirit abroad and affairs at Sparta were being carefully watched. If Agis and his party were strong enough to carry their programme of reforms through successfully, the example might be followed elsewhere with disastrous consequences to the capitalists.

The military expedition came to nothing and Agis marched back to Sparta without any fighting. Arrived at home, he found that things had taken a very sinister turn. Agesilaus had been acting in an insolent and overbearing manner. He had intercalated a month in the calendar although (if Plutarch is right) it was not due, thereby prolonging his year of office, and had collected the taxes for it, no doubt to his own enrichment.[1] Furthermore, an unheard of and grossly unconstitutional thing, he had proclaimed that he was going to occupy the office of ephor for another year. He had managed to alienate both parties, for the rich were violently opposed to him and the poor 'were highly incensed for having been defrauded in the promised division of lands'. Leonidas, the exiled king, was brought back, Agesilaus fled and Agis and his mother and grandmother were murdered. So ended the first attempt at reforms in Sparta.

There is a good deal more in the story than the mere impulsive action of an inexperienced youth who was betrayed by designing and unworthy friends. The wonder is not that Agis had tried to bring about reform; but rather that he went as far as he did before meeting disaster. The cancelling of debts was easy—Greek citizens were always ready for that. What was more difficult was the redivision of the land, which was never carried out owing to the opposition of the land-

[1] For previous comment on this incident *vide supra*, p. 129. If Agesilaus was eponymous ephor, as seems likely, his bid for another year in office was even more unconstitutional.

owners. This fact has prompted the supposition by Beloch[1] that, beneath the desire of the idealist Agis for a return to the noble tradition of Lycurgus, was a struggle between the agrarians and the capitalists. Many of the landholders were 'landpoor' who owed large debts to capitalists in Sparta, secured by mortgages on their land. It suited them perfectly that the mortgages should be extinguished; but they had no intention whatever of taking the further step and dividing up the land. No doubt this was true in the case of Agesilaus; but as Kazarow has pointed out[2] it is hard to distinguish between property in land and in capital. If the whole of Laconia was owned by 100 families, they must all have been rich both in land and in capital, just as Agis himself and his female relations were the wealthiest in Sparta. Essentially it was a conflict between rich and poor. The burning of the mortgages meant little to the poor, because they had nothing to borrow on and debt-slavery did not exist in Laconia. They regarded such an action as merely a gesture, a start in the right direction. When they found that Agis could not take the next step and redivide the land, they lost all interest in him and allowed Leonidas and his party to overthrow the reformers, drive out Agesilaus and murder Agis. If Agis had been bold enough to take the next step, they would have supported him and possibly he might have succeeded. But revolutionaries have to be made of sterner stuff than Agis was.

KING CLEOMENES III

Leonidas resumed his interrupted reign and the reactionaries were in full power. We are not explicitly told so, but we are left to infer that the debts were reimposed. The revolution had been a complete failure and the dangerous elements in the country had been effectively silenced. His son, Cleomenes, had been forcibly married to Agiatis, the widow of the

---

[1] *Griech. Gesch.* III, Pt. 1, pp. 328, 646 ff.
[2] 'Zur Gesch. d. sozialen Revolution in Sparta', *Klio*, VII (1907), pp. 45 ff.

murdered Agis, a move which may have been politic at the moment, but was to have unexpected consequences later on.

On his accession to the throne in 237,[1] Cleomenes showed qualities of spirit that foreboded a stormy reign.

He was aspiring and magnanimous, and no less prone by nature than Agis to self-restraint and simplicity. He had not, however, the gentle and scrupulous nature for which Agis was remarkable and his natural courage was always goading him on and impelling him to what appeared to him an honourable course. He thought it excellent to rule over willing subjects; but a good thing also to subdue such subjects as were disobedient and force them towards the better goal.[2]

To this rash and fiery young man the state of his native land was highly distasteful. The citizens had been lulled to sleep by idleness and pleasure; the kings were neglectful of public business and lived only for luxury; every man was intent only on his own private gain. 'And as for practice in arms, self-restraint in the young, hardiness and equality, it was even dangerous to speak of them now that Agis was dead and gone.' 'The rich neglected the common interests for their own private pleasure; the common people, because of their wretched state at home, had lost all readiness for war and all ambition to maintain the ancient Spartan discipline, and Cleomenes himself was king only in name, the whole power was in the hands of the ephors.' The last remark is highly significant. The ephors had wielded supreme power for centuries and the kings, save on the battlefield, had no influence whatever. The troublous times had evidently led to a demand for a resurgence of royal power to supplant the venial ephorate. Cleomenes' *coup d'état* was the natural outcome of such a sentiment.

SPHAERUS AND STOIC PHILOSOPHY

Cleomenes had early come under two influences, that of his wife, who told him of the virtues and ideals of the martyred

---

[1] This seems the most probable date. Cf. Tarn, *C.A.H.* VII, p. 752.
[2] Plut. *Cleom.* 1.

Agis, and his teacher of philosophy Sphaerus of Borysthenes.[1] Actually our knowledge of Sphaerus is very limited, and none of his works has survived.[2] We are told by Diogenes Laertius[3] that he studied under Zeno of Citium and Cleanthes of the Stoic school of philosophy, and at one time was invited to Alexandria by Ptolemy Philadelphus. Evidently also he was for some time in Sparta, although what took him there and how long he stayed we do not know. We are left to infer that his visit was prompted by curiosity, as the Stoics had always admired the Spartan spirit and way of life. He also probably went there to gather materials for his books, *Laconian Polity* and *Lycurgus and Socrates*.[4] Cicero[5] tells us that he was renowned among the Stoics for his accuracy of definition. Plutarch,[6] evidently quoting from his *Laconian Polity*, cites his evidence with regard to the composition of the *Gerousia*.

Ollier surmises that Sphaerus was twice at Sparta, first when Agis made his abortive experiment. It is true that Plutarch says nothing of this visit, but it is not improbable that Agis owed his ideas to him. If he was at Sparta at that time he must have fled at the downfall of Agis. It is easy to imagine that his presence would be highly distasteful to Leonidas and his supporters. This, however, is purely conjectural, and all we do know for certain is that he was at Sparta when Cleomenes III was on the throne. He was consulted by the king with regard to the restoration of the traditional Spartan discipline and education.[7] As an expert who had written a treatise on the subject, he was naturally the one to whom the reformers would turn for guidance when the tradition of the so-called Lycurgan system had grown dim.

---

[1] Plut. *Cleom.* 11.

[2] Art. in P.W. III, A. 1683, by Hobun. F. Ollier, 'Le philosophe stoicien Sphairos et l'œuvre réformatrice des rois de Sparte, Agis IV et Cléomène III'. *Rev. ét. gr.* XLIX (1936), p. 536. M. Hadas, 'The social revolution in third-century Sparta', *Class. Weekly*, XXVI (1932), pp. 65, 73.

[3] VII, 177.

[4] Athen. IV, 141 B; VIII, 334 E. *F.H.G.* III, p. 20.

[5] *Tusc. Disp.* IV, 24, 53.   [6] *Lyc.* V.   [7] Plut. *Cleom.* 11.

More than that we do not know, and we are left to speculate as to the extent of the influence exerted by the Stoic philosopher upon the impetuous and inexperienced young king and his followers. Like all the Stoics, Sphaerus was an enthusiastic admirer of the Spartan State in its idealised form. His teacher Zeno had modelled his own form of polity upon it,[1] and it is natural that the pupil should follow his master, and find in the crisis then confronting the Lacedaemonians a unique opportunity to put his theories into practice.

The times were everywhere disordered and men in their distress, as ever, turned to dreams of better days and ideal states. It is interesting to remember that a number of 'Utopian' romances had appeared, like the *Panchaea* of Euhemerus and the wonderful Sun State of Iambulus, in which men lived in peace and happiness, in equality and brotherly love.[2] Sphaerus must have known these books and, coupled with his reverence for the ideal Spartan discipline, he must have had the strongest motives to put an experiment into operation which might be fruitful of great benefits not only to Sparta but to mankind at large. The impulse must come from above, for, as Mr Tarn[3] has pointed out, 'the poor in Greece had little chance of making a change constitutionally and were badly off for weapons; they rather depended on a lead from some individual who was not one of themselves and possessed some force, for instance mercenaries'.

All the reforms attempted by Agis and Cleomenes were conformable with Stoic philosophy—abolition of debts; division of land to ensure equality among the citizens; augmentation of the citizenry by the inclusion of the worthy; restoration of the former austerity of life; and lastly, a point that must not be overlooked, increase of the royal power to

---

[1] Plut. *Lyc.* XXXI.

[2] Tarn, 'Alexander the Great and the unity of mankind', *Proceedings of the British Academy*, XIX (1933). J. Bidez, 'La cité du monde et la cité du soleil chez les Stoiciens', *Bulletin de l'Académie royale de Belgique*, XVIII (1932), p. 275. Iambulus, Diod. Sic. II, 55.

[3] *The Hellenistic Age*, p. 132.

ensure the effective carrying out of reforms, since without the exercise of *force majeure* such a programme could not be consummated.

CERCIDAS OF MEGALOPOLIS

Some strange little poems, the Meliambs of Cercidas of Megalopolis,[1] to which Mr Tarn has drawn attention, remain for brief mention. It seems fairly certain that the author was the Cercidas mentioned by Polybius[2] as an ambassador from his city to Antigonus Doson in 224 and commander of a contingent of a thousand Megalopolitans in the army that invaded Laconia in 222.[3] The allusion to Sphaerus in Meliamb VI makes it impossible to identify him with Cercidas the Arcadian denounced by Demosthenes.[4] He was, according to Diogenes Laertius,[5] a disciple of Diogenes and, therefore, one of the Cynic school of philosophy. Athenaeus[6] and Stobaeus[7] both speak of him, and Aelian mentions his name.[8] His historicity is therefore undoubted; what is far more uncertain is the nature of his philosophic ideas. The second Meliamb is a fierce denunciation of the grasping rich, 'greedy cormorants' who waste on profitless uses 'rivers of silver', which should have been 'given unto us who deserve it'; usurers who are 'ready to perish for gold.' Are the gods blind or careless that they should go unpunished? But a sudden tempest will overwhelm them, puffed up with wealth and over-proud of their fortunes.

These are strong words and would seem a direct incitement to the despoiling of the rich, an outcome of the social unrest of the time. But in Meliamb VI another note is struck. Evidently the author is frightened. It was all very well to denounce the usurers; but denunciation can go too far, as if a driver of a four-horse team should use an ox-goad to gall them. The

---

[1] *Herodas, Cercidas and the Choliambic Poets*, trans. by A. D. Knox (Loeb ed.).   [2] II, 48–50, 65.

[3] Art. 'Kerkidas' by Gerhard in P.W.

[4] *de Corona*, CCCXXIV, Polyb. XVII, 14.

[5] VI, 76.   [6] VIII, 347E; XII, 554D.

[7] *Flor.* IV, 43; LVIII 10.   [8] *V.H.* XIII, 20.

Stoics in their demands for what they think is social justice have enticed the good and just into the path of villains trodden by the base and wicked. Whoever gives up to Sphaerus anything that is dear to him will find thereby 'no guide unto calm or virtuous life but one that will lead to madness'.

There are several puzzles here which are hard to solve. In the first place, if Cercidas is a Cynic and a faithful follower of Diogenes, while denouncing the wealthy usurer he will also despise wealth himself. It is violently out of character for him to say that the 'rivers of silver' should go 'to us who deserve them'. Cercidas at this stage may have been a social reformer, indignant at the evils of his age; but he is certainly no true Cynic. And secondly, what has happened to him between the writing of Meliambs II and VI? In the first he was demanding the confiscation of wealth and in the sixth he is denouncing Sphaerus for having done that exact thing in Sparta through his influence on Cleomenes. It seems as if his good intentions had been rudely shattered when he saw his native city of Megalopolis threatened by Cleomenes. If so, it is not the only time that the philosophic reformer has been frightened out of his theories when they are violently put into practice by others. The poems of Cercidas provide an amusing little problem.

THE REFORMS OF CLEOMENES

'Stoic doctrines', as Plutarch remarks, 'for great and impetuous natures are a trifle misleading and dangerous.' And so they proved to Cleomenes. No sooner had he ascended the throne than an opportunity presented itself for military glory. Aratus, the leader of the Achaeans, wanted to bring the entire Peloponnesus into one confederation; but the Spartans, Arcadians and Eleians held out. In order to test out Cleomenes, Aratus began to harry the Arcadians, whereupon Cleomenes stood up to him with considerable spirit and gave a good account of himself. His clash with Aratus had made Cleomenes very popular in Sparta, and he soon concluded that he was strong enough to challenge the ephors.

This he proceeded to do with complete effectiveness by murdering four of them and 'above ten more that came to their assistance', banishing a fifth ephor that managed to escape death, and setting himself up as sole dictator or 'tyrant'. Eighty citizens were proscribed and sent into exile.

To justify these harsh actions he made a speech before the General Assembly tracing the encroachment of the college of ephors upon the royal power and prerogatives until they had become supreme rulers. The ephors whom he had caused to be murdered, he said, were reactionaries opposed to the salvation of Sparta. In their place he appointed a board of magistrates named *patronomoi*.[1] He then promised that the whole land should be common property, all debts should be extinguished and all foreigners examined, so that those best fitted should be admitted to citizenship. His own fortune and those of his relations and supporters were thrown into the common fund. Whereupon, we are told, all the rest of the citizens did the same and the land was parcelled out into 4000 *cleroi*,[2] lots even being assigned to those who had been banished. The body of citizens was filled up from the best of the *perioeci*, whereby he was able to raise a force of 4000 hoplites.

Next he devoted himself to the training of the young men and to the so-called ancient discipline, most of the details of which Sphaerus, who was then in Sparta, helped him in arranging. The proper system of bodily training and public messes was quickly resumed, a few obeyed out of necessity, but most with a willing spirit subjecting themselves to the old Spartan regime in all its simplicity.[3]

The success of Cleomenes had been sensational but he was too impetuous to be content with his *coup d'état* in Laconia. He could now put a respectably sized army into the field,

---

[1] For discussion of the functions of these magistrates cf. p. 131.

[2] It is pertinent to note that Agis had originally proposed 4500. Evidently now that Messenia was lost that was too many.

[3] Plut. *Cleom.* 11.

perhaps as many as 15,000 men, and dreams of conquest possessed him. In his plans for reviving the military glory of ancient Sparta there were elements which, if things had turned out otherwise than they did, might have obtained him success. There was a spirit of revolution abroad throughout Greece and the common people would gladly have turned to him had he posed as their champion. His success in Laconia had made a profound impression in the rest of Greece and a revolutionary fever was over all the Peloponnese, almost shattering the Achaean League which was based on the rule of the bourgeois class in the cities.[1] Aratus, head of the league, was caught in a serious dilemma. Was he to join with Cleomenes or turn to their common enemy, Macedonia? He chose the latter, as the lesser of two evils, and Antigonus Doson came to his help. At the battle of Sellasia in 222 Cleomenes was defeated. He fled to Egypt where shortly afterwards he committed suicide. All his reforms were swept away when Antigonus occupied Sparta. Such a revolutionary spirit was entirely distasteful to the Macedonian, who promptly restored the former constitution and many of the supporters of Cleomenes who had obtained land lost it again.

With the fall of Cleomenes Sparta fell a prey to the party of reaction. The ephors had regained their power—we hear nothing of the *patronomoi* who had probably been deposed from office. The ephors, if we are to believe Polybius,[2] 'belonging to the faction of disorder' chose as their tool one Lycurgus who was not of the royal line but who 'by giving a talent to each of the ephors became a descendant of Heracles and king of Sparta'. To give some semblance of legality to their actions, Agesipolis of the Agiad family was raised to the throne as the second king. The choosing of Lycurgus was quite outrageous, as Archidamus of the Eurypontid line had left two sons and 'other members of the house more distant' were living.[3] Lycurgus soon disposed of Agesipolis, and the

---

[1] Rostovtseff, *Social and Economic History of the Hellenistic World*, p. 209.
[2] IV, 35, 10.   [3] Polyb. IV, 35, 14.

famous dyarchy of Sparta, that had existed for eight centuries, came to an inglorious end. Lycurgus died in 211 and for the next five years a Tarentine mercenary, Machanidas, ruled the Lacedaemonians in tyrannical fashion.[1] On his death in battle at Third Mantinea in 206, Nabis[2] seized the power and held it until 192, when he was murdered.

NABIS

With regard to the antecedents of Nabis there is considerable doubt. Homolle ventures the opinion that he may have been a descendant of a side line of the Eurypontids and so of royal blood. The evidence for this is, however, very uncertain.[3] There are extant coins struck by him[4] which bear the title 'Basileus', but this may have been an assumption of his own and does not prove anything. It is unfortunate that the accounts we have of him all come from his enemies, who lose no opportunity to paint him and his actions in the worst possible light. Plutarch, Polybius, Pausanias, Diodorus and Livy[5] all represent him as a cruel and utterly unscrupulous scoundrel, guilty of every villainy and crime to maintain his tyranny.

Polybius is uncompromising in his condemnation:

He utterly exterminated those of the royal houses who survived in Sparta, and banishing those citizens who were distinguished for their wealth and illustrious ancestry, gave their property and wives to the chief of his own supporters and to his mercenaries, who were for the most part murderers, rippers, highwaymen and burglars.

[1] Art. 'Machanidas' in P.W. by Ehrenberg; Plut. *Philop.* x; Pausan. VIII, 50, 2.

[2] Homolle, 'Le roi Nabis', *Bulletin de correspondence hellénique*, xx (1896), p. 502; Mundt, *Nabis König von Sparta* (1903); Wölters, 'König Nabis', *Ath. Mitt.* XXII (1897), p. 139; art. 'Nabis' in P.W. by Ehrenberg; Aymard, *Les premiers rapports de Rome et de la confédération achaienne*, pp. 33 ff.

[3] Cf. also Holleaux in *C.A.H.* VIII, pp. 146, 189 n.

[4] *C.A.H.* (Plates), III, p. 10.

[5] Polyb. XIII, 6; XVI, 13; XVIII, 17; Livy XXXIV, 31; Diod. Sic. XXVII, 1; Paus. VIII, 50, 7, 10; Plut. *Philop.* XII ff.

For such kind of people flocked sedulously to his court from all over the world, people who dared not set foot in their own countries owing to their crimes against God and man. As he constituted himself their protector and employed these men as satellites and members of his bodyguard, it was evident that his rule would long be memorable for its wickedness.

It is entirely possible that Nabis has been maligned and that he was not quite as bad as he has been represented.[1] The opinions of Polybius are certainly suspect. When six years old his native city of Megalopolis was besieged by Nabis and the terrors of that experience no doubt left an ineradicable impression on the child's mind.[2] His father Lycortas was one of Philopoemen's most ardent supporters. It is hardly to be wondered at that Polybius could see only baseness and villainy in Nabis.

But Nabis was certainly no mercenary interloper after the fashion of Machanidas. Mr Tarn[3] has pointed out that he may have been as cruel as Polybius makes out and his mercenaries the scum of the earth, but he did at least accomplish some remarkable things. He abolished debts, redistributed the land, confiscated the money of the rich and freed the slaves. He claimed the money he took was for the expenses of the State, and possibly the State paid for the common meals, which apparently had been resuscitated.[4] 'Certainly in getting rid of the class-state, as he claimed to have done, and substituting one in which all were equal, he for the last time restored Sparta's strength in an extraordinary manner.' He raised large and highly effective armies. 'One can see they must have fought for *some* sort of an idea.' When Nabis was murdered the people avenged him, and when Philopoemen forcibly attached Sparta to the Achaean League, recalled the exiles and abolished the Spartan training and institutions,[5] three thousand

---

[1] Hadas, *loc. cit.* p. 75.   [2] Plut. *Philop.* XIII.

[3] *The Hellenistic Age*, p. 139.

[4] Uncertain. Perhaps the payments were for the upkeep of his mercenaries and the citizens did not share in them.   [5] Livy, XXXVIII, 34.

of the new citizens preferred enslavement to submitting to the new order.

The statement that Philopoemen abolished the Spartan discipline 'being convinced that while they were under the laws of Lycurgus they would never be humble'[1] seems to be borne out by two inscriptions[2] which chronicle the granting of honours and the *proxenia* to certain individuals. What is remarkable is that officials entirely unknown up till then, the *synarchiai*, and others called *epidamiorgos* and *ecdoter* (συν-αρχίαι, ἐπιδαμιοργός, ἐκδοτήρ), are named and there is no mention whatever of ephors or *gerontes*. Swoboda[3] has argued, and carries conviction, that these inscriptions must be dated at some time between 188–183 during which time the Spartans were forced to abandon their 'Lycurgan' consti-tution and adopt that imposed upon them by the Achaean League. We know that the *synarchiai* were officials in other cities of the League.

Sparta is supposed to have stayed in the League for only a short time—barely five years—and we can assume that thereafter she was allowed to revert to her earlier form of constitution. Cicero[4] said that the Spartans had lived under the same laws for 700 years, longer than any other country in the world. When in 146 Sparta passed finally under Roman rule the ancient discipline was evidently more or less in operation, or as much of it as the Romans thought good for them. We may be sure that training for war was not part of it, and we may shrewdly guess that the *syssitia* were not allowed to be revived. The Romans were suspicious of any such clubs among the peoples they conquered. It is significant that a regular rural police force, the *pedianomoi*, was instituted in

---

[1] Plut. *Philop.* XVI.   [2] *I.G.* v. 1, 4, 5.

[3] *Griech. Volksbeschlüsse*, pp. 108, 136–42; cf. H. J. W. Tillyard, *A.B.S.A.* XII (1905), p. 441. The release of Sparta from the Achaean League by favour of the Romans, if we follow Swoboda, was in 184–183. But Niese, *Geschichte d. griech. u. makedon. Staaten*, III, p. 60, prefers the date 178 for the restoration of the 'Lycurgan' constitution and the rebuilding of the walls.

[4] *pro Flacco*, XXVI, 63.

place of the notorious *crypteia*, which certainly would not have met with their approval. How far the 'Lycurgan' system of education was kept intact it is impossible to say; but some of it must have survived. Indeed, we know that as a spectacle the floggings at the altar of Artemis Orthia were very popular in Roman times. Certainly the Romans had no objection to floggings, fighting and ball-playing. It is surprising that Nero refused to visit Sparta when on his tour in Greece.[1] Such strenuous sports should have presented spectacles worthy of his attention.

Later in Roman times in the latter part of the second century A.D. we find a curious practice of naming 'the divine Lycurgus' as *patronomus eponymus*. This is shown by the inscription to have been the custom on at least eleven occasions, if not oftener. Apparently a mortal vicar or vice-gerent was necessary to carry on in the name of the divine Lycurgus. Why this should have been is difficult to say, except on the ground that Lycurgus was a romantic name and sounded well. Woodward[2] suggests that an appeal to the authority of the lawgiver was made by the old conservatives, who saw the gradual decay of the old faith and practices and, like all their predecessors, appealed to the tradition of Lycurgus to preserve the old ways. How far this vice-gerent was the 'expounder of the laws of Lycurgus'[3] (διδάσκαλος or ἐξηγητὴς τῶν Λυκουργείων) is hard to say. Evidently this official must have been an important one, if he was to be the authority of last appeal on what was or was not according to the laws of Lycurgus since, so far as we know, there had never been any written compilation of the legends and traditions clustering round the revered name. The interpreter of the *Lycurgia* could safely put any meaning he thought expedient upon any tradition extant.

[1] Dio. Cass. LXIII, 14.
[2] A. M. Woodward, in *A.B.S.A.* XIV (1907–8), pp. 112 ff.
[3] *Ibid.*

THE END

Sparta declined and fell into impotence and decay. When we seek for the reasons for this it will be well to remember that they arose from two sources. In the first place, all Greece decayed and Sparta merely shared the downfall of the whole country within and without the Peloponnesus. Old Greece decayed because Alexander had flung Egypt and the East open to exploitation by every ambitious Greek who chose to leave his native land to seek fortune under one or other of the successors. Great ports and emporia like Alexandria and the various Antiochs and Seleuceias took the commerce of the Aegean from Old Greece and gradually prosperity waned. It was a slow deterioration, not at once perceptible, but all the same persistent; and when Rome at last subdued the unruly Greeks the process was complete and all Greece lay prostrate. In this decline Sparta was involved and shared in it fully. It is even true to say that Sparta had more than her share of gradual ruination, since she had no commerce nor manufactures to keep her going as had Athens and Corinth. Athens was mildly prosperous long after Laconia had fallen to the status of a little land-locked valley of no importance whatever. To Athens was given custody of the great slave emporium of Delos by the Romans, and Attic olive oil and *objets d'art* were always valuable exports. Laconia had nothing, with the possible exception of iron, of which she had considerable ore beds. But our knowledge of its working and export is practically non-existent.[1]

And secondly, Sparta declined for reasons peculiar to its own particular circumstances. The unique and remarkable characteristics that distinguished the Spartans at the height of their glory and excited the admiration, not unmixed with bewilderment, of their contemporaries of other nations, were the

[1] Mr Tarn, *Hellenistic Civilisation*, p. 220, assumes that the working of the ore deposits lapsed entirely. There is no evidence on the point, and it is more reasonable to suppose that such valuable mines continued in production. They are worked to this day.

very qualities that led to their downfall. It is to be observed that Spartan governors sent abroad were all failures.[1] Removed from the framework of their own rigid discipline, they were utterly unable to adapt themselves to their new conditions and they made a mess of things. They lacked the resilience that made the Athenian in the long run the better man.

It is a strange commentary upon the supposed system of 'equality' that the division between the 'haves' and the 'have-nots' was deeper and more dangerous in Sparta than almost anywhere else. The land system was fundamentally a bad one. The agrarian problem in Attica was solved, or at least a tolerable compromise was reached thereon, through the legislation attributed to Solon. It was never solved in Sparta. The aggregation of large estates into a few hands that was typical of the fourth and third centuries was bad from any point of view. The attempts of Agis and Cleomenes to rectify the abuse came too late.

A vicious accompaniment of this was the concentration of land and wealth in the hands of women and the inevitable dowry-hunting by impoverished suitors. This seems to have been a late appearance; but when it did come it assumed the proportions of a 'virulent disease' and a scandal of the first magnitude. There is a grim humour in the story told by Plutarch[2] of the disappointment of the suitors of the daughters of Lysander who, finding at his death that he had been a poor man, made haste to jilt their prospective brides. We are told, however, that they were fined for this, or rather for not marrying at all.

The monetary and financial system, or perhaps it would be better to say lack of system, was primitive and absurd. The fiscal methods of all the Greek states were faulty and ill-conceived, those of Sparta were impossible. If the Spartans

---

[1] Many references to the harshness and unpopularity of Spartan governors; e.g. Thuc. I, 77, 95; III, 93; V, 52. The only one who ever exhibited any tact and wisdom in dealing with foreigners was Brasidas. Thuc. IV, 81.

[2] *Lys.* XXX.

had been content to shut themselves up in their own lands and not meddle with the surrounding states, or, in fairness to them let it be expressed, if other states had left them alone and not meddled with their affairs, there was no reason why they should not have got along with their primitive economy. But contact with other peoples brought its own problems that the Spartan economic system was unable to grapple with and before which it broke down helplessly. The wisest of them knew that; the saying of Chilon that it would have been better if Cythera had been sunk to the bottom of the sea[1] shows how early was the Spartans' realisation of their difficulties when dealing with affairs outside their own borders. The speech of King Archidamus, or at least the words put into his mouth by Thucydides, is a long and reasoned plea for non-interference with a power whose financial resources were much greater than their own.[2]

It is by no means correct to regard the Spartans as stupid. Their minds were powerful but slow-moving, and their carefully studied taciturnity exasperated the more nimble-witted Athenian. Actually the roster of highly capable Spartans is a long one, a dozen names occur to the mind of men who displayed quite notable powers, as great or even greater than those of any other Greek. They produced few artists and poets, no playwrights or philosophers, simply because their minds were occupied with other things. Their military leaders were generally competent; some of them were in the first rank. We have but to recall the names of Brasidas, Lysander and Agesilaus to realise that Sparta was entirely capable of producing generals of ability.

With all Greece Sparta in due time fell under Roman domination. The Romans treated the Greeks well; better perhaps than they deserved. They looked down upon them as quick-witted, amusing and rather contemptible inferiors, whose glorious past in art and literature had earned for them tolerance and not unkindly treatment. Perhaps in the more

[1] Herod. VII, 235   [2] Thuc. I, 83.

slow-witted Spartans the Romans recognised kindred spirits
and treated them especially well. In Roman times Sparta
became a kind of show-place to which people would go out of
curiosity at their queer ways and long history. No doubt the
Spartans found it paid them well to play up to these ideas, and
in the second century A.D. there was quite an impressive
revival, particularly of the Lycurgan legend and, we may
suppose, of the discipline, or at least of enough of its more
picturesque details as were not too irksome to carry out and
were interesting and amusing to foreigners. We can imagine,
if we are cynical enough, parties of tourists being conducted
about, very interested in the *syssitia*, or in those that were
preserved for show purposes; tasting the black broth;
wondering respectfully at tales of the antiquity of the ephors
and the *patronomoi* and behaving like all tourists down the
ages. The athletic contests were, of course, the great attraction
and the best one was the flogging of the youths. The sadistic
pleasure to be got out of this miserable spectacle was so great
that a theatre was built round the altar for the comfort of the
spectators.[1] No doubt by this time the actual flogging had
been faked sufficiently to give a good show without inflicting
serious injuries on the participants. Unfortunately they had
not two kings to exhibit; they would have been a wonderful
draw. But the Romans did not like kings very much and
would not allow a revival of the dyarchy, which was regret-
table. When Apollonius of Tyana[2] visited Sparta in the time of
the Emperor Nero he found much that interested him and of
which he approved. Evidently the ephors were in full control,
because he begged off a young man who had run away to sea
and whom they wanted to punish for neglecting his duties in
Sparta. There is a pathetic note in the letter[3] that the younger
Pliny writes to his friend Maximus, who has just been appointed

---

[1] Mr Toynbee remarks that the ceremony had been revived 'with a patho-
logical exaggeration which is one of the characteristic robes of archaism in
all its manifestations', *op. cit.* VI, p. 50.

[2] Philostratus, *Vita Apoll.* IV, 31–3.   [3] *Ep.* VIII, 24.

governor of Achaea. He bids him be merciful and kindly to the Athenians and Spartans who now have only 'a shadow still left to them and the relics of their liberty'.

And so in the little land-locked valley of the Eurotas the later Spartans cultivated their fields in peace and strove to remember their ancient fame; forgetting a little more as years passed, until Plutarch 'wrote them up' in the lives of various famous men of Sparta. And how much of what Plutarch tells us is fact and how much legend it is difficult to tell.

ADDITIONAL NOTES

PAGE 11, line 22:

Castor hounds. Cf. Vergil, *Georg.* III, 342, 402. The Molossian breed from Amyclae: 'Fierce, tawny watchdogs, who will protect the flock if the shepherd slumbers'.

PAGE 40, line 16:

Mothaces. Chrimes, *Ancient Sparta* (p. 235 n. 2) suggests that μόθαξ is derived from μόθος, 'a battle', and that the *mothaces* were squires or shield-bearers to the Spartans in campaigns.

PAGE 98, line 6:

komes. A. J. Beattie, 'An Early Laconian Lex Sacra', *Class. Quart.* XLV (1951), p. 46, referring to *S.E.G.* XI, 475 *a*, has added another oba, the ὠβά Ἀρκάλων, thus making seven: Limnai, Mesoa, Pitane, Konosoura, Amyclae, Neapolis and Arkaloi, all wards of the city of Sparta. The number seven is tempting in suggesting four *gerontes* from each ward. But the original four of Pausanias is equally tempting as returning seven from each.

PAGE 106, line 25:

Dioscuri. There is no evidence that the two kings were thought to be lineal descendants of the Dioscuri. All legends pointed to their descent from the Heracleidai, twin sons of Aristodemus.

PAGE 135, line 11:

Gerochia. This may be a joke of Aristophanes on the guttural Spartan pronunciation.

PAGE 155, line 15:

exceptio rei judicatae. A case involving this rule is given by Planudes in a scholia on the Techne of Hermogenes (C. Walz, *Rhetores graeci*, vol. V, p. 269).

A Spartan when on a visit to Athens raped a maiden. He was tried and received the penalty laid down by Athenian law, a fine of 1000 drachmas. On his return to Sparta he was re-arrested and tried for the offence, which carried with it, according to Spartan law, a sentence of death. He pleaded that his crime had not been committed in Sparta, and that he had already received punishment in Athens. We do not know the result of the trial, but it seems likely that he was condemned for bringing disrepute upon the Spartan people, and also because the rule of *exceptio rei judicatae* was not valid in Spartan law.

PAGE 165, line 15:

Lesche. Apparently the headquarters of the tribe. It is not clear if each tribe had a separate Lesche, but we may assume it had. Or it may have been like the Tholos at Athens where the Prytanes met.

PAGE 172, line 20:

σφαιρεῖς. Chrimes (*Ancient Sparta*, p. 131), suggests that these Sphaireis were not ball-players, but youths who went about with boxing gloves (σφαῖραι) on their hands, ready to engage in boxing contests at any moment. In view of the prohibition of fist fights this seems improbable. Woodward (*A.B.S.A.* 46, p. 191) rejects this and accepts the usual view that they were ball-players.

PAGE 251, line 9:

neodamodeis. R. F. Willetts in 'Neodamodeis', *Class. Philol.* 49. 1 (1954) pp. 27 ff., suggests that these were Helots, who owned, or occupied by sufferance, land belonging to the state, and paid rent for it by military service, providing their own panoply and upkeep while in the field.

PAGE 259, para 2:

It was the Theban cavalry that routed the Athenians.

PAGE 270, lines 4–5:

the dyer's art. It seems certain that the purple-fisheries off the coast of Laconia were discovered at an early date by the Phoenicians, who made Cythera, 'the purple isle', the headquarters of their fishing fleet. Later the *perioeci* took over the industry and Laconian purple became famous. Amyclae, apparently, was the chief centre of the dyeing industry. The scarlet shoes, or perhaps the dyed leather from which they were made, were famous. It is not certain whether the battle-dress of the Spartans was dyed with *kermes*, or was given its reddish-purple tinge with *murex*, the mollusc that yielded the famous purple of antiquity.

PAGE 301, line 16:

pelanors. These slabs of iron may have been 'pigs' which were exported from Sparta, and so gave rise to the idea that they were Spartan 'money'. The discovery of several of these slabs is no proof that they were used as currency within the country.

SELECT BIBLIOGRAPHY

ANDREADES, A. M. *A History of Greek Public Finance*, I. Cambridge, Mass., 1933.

ANDREWES, A. 'Eunomia', *Class. Quart.* XXXII (1938), p. 89.

BELOCH, J. 'Die Nauarchie in Sparta', *Rhein. Mus.* XXXIV (1879), pp. 117f.

BERVE, H. 'Sparta', *Hist. Vierteljahrschrift*, XXV (1929), p. 1.

BERVE, H. *Sparta*. Leipzig, 1937.

BUSOLT, G.-SWOBODA, H. 'Griechische Staatskunde', I, II, in I. Müller's *Handb. der klass. Altert.* IV, I, I. Munich, 1920–1926.

BUSOLT, GEORG. 'Spartas Heer und Leuktra', *Hermes*, XL (1905), p. 387.

BUX, E. 'Zwei sozialistische Novellen bei Plutarch', *Klio*, XIX (1925), p. 413.

CARY, M. 'Notes on the History of the Fourth Century', *Class. Quart.* XX (1926), pp. 186f. 'The Spartan Forces at Leuctra', *J.H.S.* XLII (1922), p. 184.

CAVAIGNAC, E. 'De la population du Peloponnèse aux Ve et IVe siècles', *Klio*, XII (1912), pp. 261f.

CHRIMES, K. M. T. *Ancient Sparta*. Manchester, 1949.

CLOCHE, P. 'Isocrate et la politique lacédémonienne', *Revue des études anciennes*, XXXV (1933), p. 129.

COLEMAN-NORTON, P. *Socialism at Sparta in Greek Political Experience*. Princeton, 1941.

COSTANZI, V. *Le Costituzione di Atene e di Sparta*. Bari, 1927.

DE COULANGES, FUSTEL, N. D. *Études sur la propriété foncière à Sparte*. Paris, 1881. Reprinted in *Nouvelles recherches sur quelques problèmes d'histoire*, p. 52. Paris, 1891.

DAUBLER, TH. *Sparta. Ein Versuch*. Leipzig, 1923.

DAVISON, J. A. 'Alcman's Partheneion', *Hermes*, LXXIII (1938), p. 440.

DAWKINS, R. M. (and others). *The Sanctuary of Artemis Orthia at Sparta*. London, 1929.

DE DECKER, J. 'La genèse de l'organisation civique des Spartiates', *Archives sociologiques* (1913), pp. 306f.

DEN BOER, WILLEM. *Laconian Studies*. Amsterdam, 1954.

DICKINS, G. 'The Growth of Spartan Policy', *J.H.S.* XXXII (1912), pp. 1f., 111f.

DILLER, AUBREY. 'A New Source on the Spartan *Ephebia*', *Amer. Journ. Phil.* LXII (1941), pp. 494f.

EHRENBERG, V. 'Der Damos im archaischen Sparta', *Hermes*, LXVIII (1933), p. 288.

EHRENBERG, V. 'Spartiaten und Lakedaimonier', *Hermes*, LIX (1924), p. 23.

EHRENBERG, V. 'Asteropos', *Phil. Woch.* XLVII (1927), p. 27.

EHRENBERG, V. *Neugründer des Staates. Ein Beitrag zur Geschichte Spartas und Athens im VIten Jahrhundert.* Munich, 1925.

EHRENBERG, V. 'Der Gesetzgeber von Sparta', *Epitymbion für Swoboda* (1927), p. 19.

GELZER, H. 'Lykurgos und die delphische Priesterschaft', *Rhein. Mus.* XXVIII (1873), pp. 1 ff.

GERCKE, A. 'Der neue Tyrtaios', *Hermes*, LVI (1921), p. 346.

GILBERT, G. *Handbuch des griechischen Staatsaltertums.* Leipzig, 1881. (Engl. trans.) *The Constitutional Antiquities of Sparta and Athens*, by E. J. Brooks and T. Nicklin. London, 1895.

GINSBERG, M. S. 'Sparta and Judaea', *Class. Phil.* XXIX (1934), p. 117.

GIRARD, P. 'Un texte inédit sur la cryptie des Lacédémoniens', *Rev. ét. gr.* XI (1898), p. 31.

GRUNDY, G. B. 'The Policy of Sparta', *J.H.S.* XXXII (1912), p. 261.

GRUNDY, G. B. 'Population and Policy of Sparta in the Fifth Century', *J.H.S.* XXVIII (1908), p. 77.

HAMPL, F. 'Die lakedaemonischen Perioeken', *Hermes*, LXXII (1937), p. 1.

HOUSSAYE, H. 'La loi agraire à Sparte', *Annuaire des études grecques*, Paris (1884), pp. 161 f.

HUXLEY, G. L. *Ancient Sparta.* London, 1962.

JAEGER, W. 'Tyrtaios über wahre Arete', *Sitz.-Ber. preuss. Akad., Phil.-Hist. Klasse* (1932), p. 537.

JEANMAIRE, A. 'La cryptie lacédémonienne', *Rev. ét gr.* XXVI (1913), p. 121.

KAHRSTEDT, U. 'Sparta und seine Symmachie', *Griechisches Staatsrecht*, I. Göttingen, 1922.

KAHRSTEDT, U. 'Die spartanische Agrarwirtschaft', *Hermes*, LIV (1919), p. 279.

KAZAROW, G. 'Zur Geschichte der sozialen Revolution in Sparta', *Klio*, VII (1907), p. 45.

KESSLER, E. 'Plutarch's Leben des Lykurgos', *Quellen und Forschungen zur alten Geschichte*, XXIII. Berlin, 1910.

KROMAYER, JOH. 'Die Wehrkraft Lakoniens und seine Wehrverfassung', *Klio*, II (1903), pp. 173 f.

KROYMANN, J. 'Sparta und Messenien', *Neue Philol. Untersuch.* XI (1937).

KÜCHTNER, K. *Die Entstehung und ursprungliche Bedeutung des spartanischen Ephorats.* Munich, 1897.

LARSEN, J. A. O. 'Perioeci in Crete', *Class. Phil.* XXXI (1936), p. 11.

LEAKE, W. M. *Travels in the Morea.* London, 1830.

LENSCHAU, T. 'König Kleomenes I von Sparta', *Klio*, XXXI (1938), p. 412.

LURIA, S. 'Asteropos', *Phil. Woch.* XLVI (1926), p. 701.

LURIA, S. 'Zum politischen Kampf in Sparta gegen Ende des 5. Jahrhunderts', *Klio*, XXI (1927), p. 404.

MEIER, THEODOR. 'Das Wesen der spartanischen Staatsordnung', *Klio*, Beiheft 42, Leipzig, 1939.

MEYER, EDUARD. 'Die Entwickelung der Überlieferung über die Lykurgische Verfassung', *Forschungen zur alten Geschichte*, I, pp. 211 ff.

MEYER, EDUARD. 'Tyrtaeos', *Forschungen zur alten Geschichte*, II, p. 544.

MILTNER, F. 'Die dorische Wanderung', *Klio*, XXVII (1934).

MOMIGLIANO, A. 'Sparta e Lacedemone e una ipotesi sull'origine della diarchia spartana', *Atene e Roma*, XIII (1932), pp. 2f.

MÜLLER, K. O. *Die Dorier*. Breslau, 1824. 2nd ed. 1844. (Engl. trans.) *History and Antiquities of the Doric Race*, by H. Tufnell and Cornewall-Lewis. London, 1830, 2 vols.

NICCOLINI, G. 'Per la storia di Sparta. Il sinecismo', *Riv. di stor. ant.* IX (1904), pp. 94f.

NICCOLINI, G. 'Per la storia di Sparta. Elementi del periodo epico nella costituzione di Sparta', *Riv. di stor. ant.* IX (1904), p. 211.

NIESE, B. 'Zur Verfassungsgeschichte Lakedaemons', *Hist. Ztschr.* LXII (1889), p. 58.

NIESE, B. 'Herodot-studien, besonders zur spartanischen Geschichte', *Hermes*, XLII (1907), pp. 419f.

NILSSON, M. P. 'Die Gründlagen des spartanischen Lebens', *Klio*, XII (1912), pp. 308f.

OLLIER, F. *Xenophon, la république des Lacédémoniens*. Texte, trad. et comm. Lyons, 1934.

OLLIER, F. *Le mirage spartiate. Étude sur l'idéalisation de Sparte dans l'antiquité grecque de l'origine jusqu'aux cyniques*. Paris, 1933.

OLLIER, F. 'Le philosophe stoicien Sphairos et l'œuvre réformatrice des rois de Sparte, Agis IV et Cléomène II', *Rev. ét gr.* XLIX (1936), pp. 537f.

PARETI, LUIGI. 'Storia di Sparta arcaica', *Contribuzione alla scienza dell' antichita*, II. Florence, 1917.

PORTER, W. H. 'Antecedents of the Spartan Revolution of 243 B.C.' *Hermathena*, XLIV (1935), p. 1.

ROUSSEL, P. *Sparte*. Paris, 1939.

RUTHERFORD, H. T. 'The Public School of Sparta', *Greece and Rome*, III (1934), p. 129.

SCHACHERMEYR, F. 'Tyrtaios', *Rhein. Mus.* LXXXI (1932), p. 129.

SOLARI, ARTURO. *Ricerche spartane*. Leghorn, 1907.

SOLMSEN, F. 'Vordorisches in Lakonien', *Rhein. Mus.* XLII (1907), p. 329.

TOYNBEE, A. 'The Growth of Sparta', *J.H.S.* XXXIII (1913), p. 249.

TRIEBER, C. 'Zum Kriegswesen der Spartaner', *Neue Jahrbücher für Philologie*, CIII (1871), pp. 443 f.

WIDE, S. *Lakonische Kulte.* Leipzig, 1893.

WILAMOWITZ-MOELLENDORF, F. U. VON. 'Lykurgos', *Philol. Untersuch.* VII (1884), p. 267.

WITKOWSKI, S. 'Die spartanische Heeresgliederung und der Ursprung des Ephorats', *Eos*, XXXV (1934), p. 73.

WOODHOUSE, W. J. *King Agis of Sparta and his Campaign in Arkadia in 418.* Oxford, 1933.

ZIEHEN, L. 'Das spartanische Bevölkerungsproblem', *Hermes*, LXVIII (1933), p. 218.

DAREMBERG-SAGLIO, *Dict. des Ant.*, arts. Gerousia, Homoioi, Hypomeiones (Caillemer), Ephoroi, Helotae (Lécrivain), Karneios (Couve), Krypteia (P. Girard), Lacedaemoniorum Respublica (Fustel de Coulanges), Perioikoi (Glotz).

PAULY-WISSOWA-KROLL, *Real-Encyclopädie*, arts. Ephoroi, Gerontes, Heloten, Homoioi, Kome, Kleomenes, Krypteia, Lykurg, Mothakes, Nabis, Obai, Perioikoi, Rhetrai, Sparta, Tresantes.

INDEX

Acetic acid, 301
Achaean league, 328, 330
Acrotatus, 59
adespotoi, 90
ἀδόκιμος, 41
Aegeidai, 85 n. 2, 100, 103 n. 3
Aegimius, King, 20
Aegospotami, battle, 277
aes rude, 301
Aetolians, invasion by, 315
agathoergi, 98
age groups, 166 ff., 246 f.
Agesilaus, King, 42, 110, 127, 157, 167, 259, 271
Agesilaus, uncle of Agis IV, 129, 296, 318
Agiatis, widow of Agis IV, 321
Agis II, King, 154
Agis IV, King, reforms of, 52, 113, 147, 225, 295, 316 ff.; murder of, 110, 156
ἄγημα, 245
ἀγχιστεία, ἀγχιστεύς, 58
ἄκριτος, 158
ἀκράτισμα, 284
Alcibiades, at Sparta, 15, 157, 286, 291; and Socrates, 304
Alcman, 11, 55, 198, 290
amphora, liquid measure, 16
Amyclae, 98 ff.
Amyclaeans, 238
Anapale, dance, 187
andreion, 282
Antalcidas, 167, 279
Antigonus Doson, 132
Antipater, 315
Apellai, 136, 140 n. 2
aphetai, 90
Apollonius of Tyana, 176, 336
Apothetae, 165
arbitration of disputes, 154
ἀρχαγέτης, 104
ἀρχεῖα, 146

ἀρχεῖα μοῖρα, 220
archers, in army, 257
Archidamus, 312
Archidamus II, King, 32, 106, 308
Archidamus III, King, 257
Archidamus V, 111
Archilochus, banned from Sparta, 51
ἄρχων τῶν σκευοφόρων, 261
Areus I, King, claim to throne, 158
Areus II, King, coins of, 302
ἀριστίνδην, 43 n. 2
Ariston, sculptor, 13
ἄριστον, lunch, 284
arms and equipment, 269
army, Spartan, evolution of, 234 ff.; command, 265; rations of, 288
Artemisium, battle, 275
Artemis Orthia, shrine, 13, 175
assembly, place of, 146
Asteropus, 123
atimia, 44, 160, 214

Babyca, a bridge, 141
baggage train, army, 261
βαγός, 104
ball game, annual, 192
ball-players, σφαιρεῖς, 172
βάφα, black broth, 291
Bathycles of Magnesia, 13
bibasis, dance, 197
bidaioi, 150, 193
Boeotia, tenure in fee-tail, 214
Boeotian musical mode, 184
boonetai, 150
βούαγος, 174
βωμονίκης, 175
boxing, forbidden, 192
Brasidas, 80, 335
Brasideioi, 40, 91, 240
bread, contributed to *syssition*, 293
Bryallicha, dance, 188